Bloom's Modern Critical Views

Bloom's Modern Critical Views

Bloom's Modern Critical Views

DANTE ALIGHIERI

Edited and with an introduction by
Harold Bloom
Sterling Professor of the Humanities
Yale University

CHELSEA HOUSE
P U B L I S H E R S
A Haights Cross Communications Company

Philadelphia

Printed and bound in the United States of America.
10 9 8 7 6 5 4 3 2 1

Library of Congress Cataloging-in-Publication Data
Applied.
ISBN: 0-7910-7658-X

Chelsea House Publishers
1974 Sproul Road, Suite 400
Broomall, PA 19008-0914

http://www.chelseahouse.com

Contributing Editor: Grace Kim

Cover designed by Terry Mallon

Cover: © Stefano Bianchetti/CORBIS

Layout by EJB Publishing Services

Contents

Editor's Note

My "Introduction" presents an overview of Dante, culminating in the vision of Matilda gathering flowers in the Earthly Paradise of *Purgatorio* XXVIII.

Charles S. Singleton begins the sequence of essays with his argument that Dante follows the allegory of the theologians, and not of the poets, while Erich Auerbach rehearses his celebrated thesis on the Christian trope of *figura*, and Dante's supposed relation to it.

The thematizing of *Inferno*, Canto IX, by epic tradition, is analyzed by David Quint, after which John Freccero expounds the poetics of the *Purgatorio* as a process of Dante's liberation from his precursor Virgil's influence.

In the first of her two essays here, Teodolinda Barolini also illuminates Dante's poetic maturation, while Kenneth Gross meditates upon the dialectic of pain and punishment.

Guiseppe Mazzotta, in the first of his two essays, brilliantly tracks the *Vita Nuova* into Inferno XXVII and shows the fate of the rhetoric of love in Dante.

Jaroslav Pelikan, the most learned historian of theology, guides us into the *Paradiso*, which he views as essentially Augustinian rather than Thomistic, after which María Rosa Menocal sagely comments upon Dante's cult of Beatrice.

In reappearances, Barolini finds in Purgatory something like the literal truth, while Mazzotta praises Dante the Pilgrim's intuitive cognition of an imaginative knowledge that surpasses rational processes.

I myself return in a disquisition upon Dante's uncanny *strangeness* in his imaginings both of Ulysses and Beatrice, after which John Kleiner juxtaposes audacity and error in Dante, and William Franke sees the supreme poet as an interpreter in search of truth founded upon belief.

HAROLD BLOOM

Introduction

DANTE ALIGHIERI (1265–1321)

The life of Dante Alighieri itself can seem a turbulent poem, closer to his *Inferno* than to his *Purgatorio*, quite aside from his *Paradiso*. Biographies so far are mostly inadequate to Dante's genius, with the major exception of the very first, Giovanni Boccaccio's, aptly described by Giuseppe Mazzotta as a "self-conscious fictional work akin to Dante's own *Vita Nuova* (*The New Life*) which responds imaginatively to Dante's steady self-dramatization in his works." This need not surprise anyone; Dante, like Shakespeare, is so large a form of thought and imagination that individual biographers, scholars, and critics tend to see only aspects of an extraordinary panoply. I always recommend to my students, in preference to all biographies of Shakespeare, the late Anthony Burgess's *Nothing Like the Sun*, a rather Joycean novel narrated by Shakespeare in the first person.

The exalted Dante regarded himself as a prophet, at least the equal of Isaiah or Jeremiah. Shakespeare, we can assume, had no such self-estimate; the creator of Hamlet, Falstaff, and Lear has much in common with Geoffrey Chaucer, the maker of the Pardoner and the Wife of Bath, and Chaucer subtly mocks Dante. One has to be of Chaucer's eminence, if Dante is to be treated ironically, and even Chaucer clearly admires far more intensely than he dissents.

One cannot discuss genius in all the world's history without centering upon Dante, since only Shakespeare, of all geniuses of language, is richer. Shakespeare to a considerable extent remade English: about eighteen hundred words of the twenty-one thousand he employed were his own coinage, and I cannot pick up a newspaper without finding Shakespearean turns of phrase scattered through it, frequently without intention. Yet Shakespeare's English was inherited by him, from Chaucer and from William Tyndale, the principal translator of the Protestant Bible. Had Shakespeare written nothing, the English language, pretty much as we know it, would have prevailed, but Dante's Tuscan dialect became the Italian language largely because of Dante. He is the national

From: *Genius: A Mosaic of One Hundred Exemplary Creative Minds.* © 2002 by Harold Bloom.

poet, as Shakespeare is wherever English is spoken, and Goethe wherever German dominates. No single French poet, not even Racine or Victor Hugo, is so unchallenged in eminence, and no Spanish-language poet is so central s Cervantes. And yet Dante, though he essentially founded literary Italian, hardly thought of himself as Tuscan, let alone Italian. He was a Florentine, obsessively so, exiled from his city in the last nineteen of his fifty-six years.

A few dates are crucial for the reader of Dante, starting with the death of Beatrice, his beloved ideal or idealized beloved, on June 8, 1290, when the poet was twenty-five. By his own account, Dante's devotion to Beatrice was what we call platonic, though nothing concerning Dante ever can be termed anything but Dantesque, including his Catholicism. He set Easter 1300 as the fictive date of the journey he undertakes in the *Divine Comedy*, and he completed the *Inferno*, its first and most notorious part, in 1314. In the seven years remaining to him, he had the sublime fortune of composing both the *Purgatorio* and the *Paradiso*, so that his magnificent poem was fully composed by almost a year before his death.

Shakespeare died as he turned fifty-two, but we lost nothing by it, because he had stopped writing some three years before. Dante, one feels, would have gone on to other literary achievements, had he lived the quarter-century more that he expected in order to reach the "perfect" age of eighty-one, nine nines in a numerological vision of his own, which cannot altogether be deciphered.

Here is Dante in the *Convivio* (book 4, 24) telling us that age ends at the seventieth year, but that there can be sublimity, if we live on:

> Whence we have it of Plato—whom (both in the strength of his own nature, and because of the physiognomiscope which Socrates cast for him when first he saw him) we may believe to have had the most excellent nature—that he lives eighty-one years, as testifies Tully in that *Of Old Age*. And I believe that if Christ had not been crucified and had lived out the space which his life had power to cover according to its nature, he would have been changed at the eighty-first year from mortal body to eternal.

What change did Dante expect at the eighty-first year? Would Beatrice, the Lady Nine, have appeared to him again, in this life? George Santayana found in Beatrice a Platonizing of Christianity; E. R. Curtius saw her as the center of Dante's personal and poetic gnosis. She has some crucial relation to the transfiguration that Christ would have undergone at eighty-one, since her own death, according to her lover's *Vita Nuova*, is dated by him through a process in which the perfect number nine is completed nine times. At twenty-five she changed from mortal to eternal body. Dante, implicitly and explicitly, tells us throughout the *Comedy* that he, Dante, is the truth. The Sufi martyr Hallaj died for proclaiming that he was the truth, though in the American Religion (in its various forms) such an affirmation is almost commonplace. I talk to dissident Mormons, Baptist sectaries, and many Pentecostals who candidly assure me that they are the truth. Neither Augustine nor Aquinas would have said that he was the truth. The *Commedia* would not work if Beatrice were not the truth, and yet, without Dante, none of us would have heard of Beatrice. I think that too much cannot be made of this, and I never quite understand why Dante, who now defines Catholicism for so many intellectuals, overcame the possibility that his personal myth of Beatrice was as much a heresy as the Gnostic myths of a Sophia, or female principle, in the Godhead. Simon Magus found his Helena in a whorehouse in Tyre, and proclaimed her to be both Helen of Troy and the fallen Sophia, or Wisdom of God. The Samaritan Simon, always denounced by Christians, was the first Faustus, audacious and imaginative, but now is universally regarded as a charlatan. Dante found his unfallen Wisdom of God in a Florentine young woman, and raised her to the heavenly hierarchy. Simon the magician, like Jesus the magician, belongs to oral tradition, while Dante—except for Shakespeare—is the supreme poet of all Western history and culture. And yet Dante was not less arbitrary than Simon, as we ought not to forget. Though he says otherwise, Dante usurps poetic authority and establishes himself as central to Western culture.

How different Dante's centrality is from Shakespeare's! Dante imposes his personality upon us; Shakespeare, even in the Sonnets, evades us, because of his uncanny detachment. In the *Vita Nuova*, Dante immerses us in the story of his extraordinary love for a young woman whom he scarcely knew. They first meet as nine-year-olds, though that "nine" is a warning against any literalization of this story. Nine years after the poet first saw Beatrice, she spoke to him, a formal greeting in the street. Another greeting or two, a snub after he poetically professed love for another lady as a "screen" defense, and one gathering where Beatrice may have joined in a gentle mockery of her smitten admirer: this seems to have been their entire relationship. The best commentary on this mere actuality is that of the Argentine fabulist Jorge Luis Borges, who speaks of "our certainty of an unhappy and superstitious love," unreciprocated by Beatrice.

We can speak of Shakespeare's "unhappy and superstitious love" for the fair young nobleman of the Sonnets, but some other phrase would have to be found for Shakespeare's descent into the Hell of the Dark Lady of the same sequence. To call Dante's love for Beatrice Neoplatonic would be insufficient, but how can we define that love? A passion for one's own genius, for a muse of one's own creation, could seem a dark idolatry of self in almost anyone else, but not in the central man. The myth or figure of Beatrice is fused with Dante's lifework; in a crucial sense she is the *Commedia*, and cannot be understood if you stand outside the poem. And yet Dante presents her as the truth, though not to be mistaken for the Christ, who is the way, the truth, the light.

Dante scholarship, vastly useful for mastering the complexities of the *Commedia*, nevertheless does not much help me in apprehending Beatrice. She is more Christological in the *Vita Nuova* than in the *Commedia*, though sometimes there she reminds me of what the Gnostics called "the Angel Christ," since she breaks down the distinction between the human and the angelic. A fusion between the divine and the mortal may or may not be heretical, depending upon how it is presented. Dante's vision does not impress me as Augustinian or Thomistic, but though hermetic, it is not Hermetist, as it were. Rather than identifying with theology, Dante strives to identify it with himself. The presence of the human in the divine is not the same as God's presence in a person, and in Beatrice in particular.

That sounds perhaps odd, since Dante was not William Blake, who urged us to worship only what he called the Human Form Divine. Yet Dante early on wrote that Beatrice was a miracle. This miracle was for all Florence, and not for Dante alone, though he was its sole celebrant. His best friend and poetic mentor, Guido Cavalcanti, is later condemned by Dante for not joining the celebration, but Dante has the same relation to Cavalcanti that the young Shakespeare had to Christopher Marlowe, a shadow of influence-anxiety. Are we to believe Dante when he implies that Cavalcanti would have been saved if he had acknowledged Beatrice? Is a shared originality still original?

As readers, we can abandon Dante's supposed theology to his exegetes, but you cannot read Dante without coming to terms with his Beatrice. For Dante, she is certainly an Incarnation, which he declines to see as a being in competition with the Incarnation. She is, he insists, whatever happiness he has had, and without her he would not have found his way to salvation. But Dante is not a Faust, to be damned or saved, or a Hamlet, who dies of the truth. Dante is bent upon triumph, total vindication, a prophecy fulfilled. His "fathers," Brunetto Latini and Vergil, are transcended, with love, but still firmly set aside. His poetic "brothers" are acknowledged (rather darkly, in Cavalcanti's case) but are not his companions on the way. Does he persuade us, in the *Commedia*, that Beatrice is something more than his individual genius? He is both inside and outside his poem, as Beatrice was in the *Vita Nuova*. Has she a reality that might enable her to be invoked by others?

Shakespeare's grandest characters can walk out of their plays and live in our consciousness of them. Can Beatrice? Dante's personality is so large that it allows room for no one else; the Pilgrim of Eternity takes up all the space. This is hardly a poetic fault, as it would be in any other poet whatsoever. In Dante it is poetic strength, energized by absolute originality, a newness that cannot be staled by endless rereadings, and that cannot be assimilated to its sources, literary or theological.

Augustine, opposing the great Neoplatonists, Plotinus and Porphyry, insisted that self-confidence and pride were not sufficient for the ascent to God.

Guidance and assistance were necessary, and could come only from God. Is there a fiercer pride or a more resolute self-confidence than Dante's? He portrays himself as a pilgrim, reliant upon guidance, comfort, and assistance, but as a poet he is more a prophet being called than he is a Christian undergoing conversion. Does he bother truly to persuade us of his humility? His heroism—spiritual, metaphysical, imaginative—makes Dante the poet pragmatically as much a miracle as was his Beatrice.

Fortunately, he presents himself as a personality, not as a miracle. We know him so well, in essence rather than in outline, that we can accept his hard-won changes as he develops, throughout the *Commedia*. Indeed, only he can change in the *Commedia*, as everyone else has reached finality, though there is a process of refining that dwellers in the *Purgatorio* must undergo. Outrageously vivid as everyone is in the *Commedia*, they are past altering, in kind. They will not change because of what Dante has them say or do. This makes total revelation possible: Dante gives us the last word upon them, beyond dispute, and always provoking wonder. Whether you can have personality after a last judgment has been passed upon you, is a very pretty question.

Beatrice, as Dante's creation, possesses little enough personality, because she clearly has had an angelic preexistence before her birth into Florence. Dante shows us, in the *Vita Nuova*, only that she is of unearthly beauty, and is capable of severity, a stance towards him that augments in the *Commedia*, though it is merely rhetorical. There is rather a leap from her relative unawareness of her idealizing lover, in life, and her cosmological concern for his salvation, after her death. So clearly is she Dante's good genius or better angel that the transmutation is easily acceptable. Laertes rather wistfully says that the rejected Ophelia will be a ministering angel after her death, presumably one of those flights of angels that Horatio invokes at the close, to one's surprise, when we brood about it. Dante, long preparing his own apotheosis, has had his Beatrice in training for quite some time.

No other writer ever is nearly as formidable as Dante, not even John Milton or Leo Tolstoy. Shakespeare, a miracle of elusiveness, is everyone and no one, as Borges said. Dante is Dante. No one is going to explain Dante away by historicizing him, or by emulating his own audacious self-theologizing: Cavalcanti, had he lived, would doubtless have written even more powerful lyrics than earlier, but he is not likely to have composed a Third Testament which is precisely what the *Divine Comedy* appears to be. The question of Shakespeare's genius is forever beyond us, yet Dante's genius is an answer not a question. With the exception of Shakespeare, who came three centuries later, the strongest poet of the Western world completed its single greatest work of literary art by the close of the second decade of the fourteenth century. To equal the *Commedia*, and in some ways surpass it, you would have to regard the two dozen most remarkable of Shakespeare's thirty-nine plays as somehow a single entity. But Dante and Shakespeare are very difficult to take in sequence: try to read *King Lear* after the *Purgatorio*, or *Macbeth* after the *Inferno*: a curious disturbance is felt. These two most central of poets are violently incompatible, at least in my experience: Dante would have wanted his reader to judge that Beatrice was Christ in Dante's soul; many of us may be uncomfortable with that, for various reasons, but how startled we would be if Shakespeare, in the Sonnets, were to intimate that the fair young lord (Southampton or whomever) was a type of Christ for the poet who would go on to compose *Hamlet* and *King Lear*.

To the common reader who can absorb the *Commedia* in the original, Beatrice is scarcely a puzzle, since Italian critics are very unlike Anglo-American scholars in their approach to Dante, and their more worldly sense of him has filtered down. I treasure the observation of Giambattista Vico that even Homer would have yielded to Dante had the Tuscan been less erudite in theology. Dante, like Freud (and the mystics), thought that erotic sublimation was possible, differing in this from his friend Cavalcanti, who regarded love as an illness that had to be lived through. Dante, who has Francesca and her Paolo down in Hell for adultery, was widely noted for his venery, in regard to women very different (in his view) from the sacred Beatrice. About the only place where Dante and Shakespeare meet is in their mutual supremacy at rendering erotic suffering, of others and their own:

> Yet shall the streams turn back and climb the hills
> Before Love's flame in this damp wood and green
> Burns, as it burns within a youthful lady,
> For my sake, who would sleep away in stone
> My life, or feed like beasts upon the grass,
> Only to see her garments cast a shade.

That is from Dante Gabriel Rossetti's version of the "stony" sestina "To the dim Light," one of the "stony rhymes" passionately addressed by Dante to one Pietra. Beatrice is not very Shakespearean; Pietra is, and would have done well as the Dark Lady of the Sonnets:

> Th'expense of spirit in a waste of shame
> Is lust in action; and, till action, lust
> Is perjured, murd'rous, bloody, full of blame,
> Savage, extreme, rude, cruel, not to trust;
> Enjoyed no sooner but despised straight ...

Pious reactions to Dante are not so clearly useless as attempts to Christianize the tragedies of Hamlet and of Lear, but they do the *Commedia* more harm than feminist resentment, which tends to mistrust the idealization of

Beatrice. Dante's praise of Beatrice is immensely poignant; his exaltation of an unrequited love is more problematic, unless we think back to the profound visions of early childhood, when we fell in love with someone we scarcely knew, and perhaps never saw again. T. S. Eliot shrewdly surmised that Dante's experience of first loving Beatrice must have come before he was nine, and the numerological paradigm indeed could have induced Dante to set the experience two or three years later than it took place. Not being Dante, most of us can do little with so early an epiphany, and part of Dante's achievement is that he could found greatness upon it.

If Beatrice is universal in her origins, she becomes in the *Commedia* an esoteric figure, the center of Dante's own gnosis, since it is by and through her that Dante asserts knowledge rather less traditional than most of his exegetes will grant. The permanent notoriety of the *Inferno* has not obscured the dramatic eloquence of the Purgatorio, which retains a reasonably wide leadership. It is the *Paradiso* which is immensely difficult, and yet that difficulty represents Dante's genius at its most indisputable, breaking beyond the limits of imaginative literature. There is nothing else that resembles the *Paradiso*, unless it be certain sequences in the *Meccan Revelations* of the Andalusian Sufi Ibn Arabi (1165–1240), who had encountered *his* Beatrice in Mecca. Nizam, the Sophia of Mecca, like Beatrice of Florence, was the center of a theophany and converted Ibn Arabi to an idealized, sublimated love.

At seventy-one, I am perhaps not yet ready for the *Paradiso* (where, being of the Jewish persuasion, I am not going to end anyway), and I have begun to recoil from the *Inferno*, an authentically terrifying if sublime work. I do keep going back to the *Purgatorio*, for reasons wonderfully phrased by W. S. Merwin in the foreword to his admirable translation of the middle canticle of the *Commedia*.

> Of the three sections of the poem, only *Purgatorio* happens *on* the earth, as our lives do, with our feet on the ground, crossing a beach, climbing a mountain ... To the very top of the mountain hope is mixed with pain, which brings it still closer to the living present. (xiii).

My friends all differ upon which canto of the *Purgatorio* is their personal favorite; I choose the vision of Matilda gathering flowers, in the Earthly Paradise of canto 28. The first fifty-one lines, beautifully rendered by Merwin, I give here in Percy Bysshe Shelley's ecstatic version, his only extended translation from the *Commedia*:

> And earnest to explore within—around—
> The divine wood, whose thick green living woof
> Tempered the young day to the sight—I wound

Up the green slope, beneath the forest's roof,
With slow, soft steps leaving the mountain's steep,
And sought those inmost labyrinths, motion-proof

Against the air, that in that stillness deep
And solemn, struck upon my forehead bare,
The slow, soft, stroke of a continuous ...

In which the leaves tremblingly were
All bent towards that part where earliest
The sacred hill obscures the morning air.

Yet were they not so shaken from the rest,
But that the birds, perched on the utmost spray,
Incessantly renewing their blithe quest,

With perfect joy received the early day,
Singing within the glancing leaves, whose sound
Kept a low burden to their roundelay,

Such as from bough to bough gathers around
The pine forest on bleak Chiassi's shore,
When Aeolus Sirocco has unbound.

My slow steps had already borne me o'er
Such space within the antique wood, that I
Perceived not where I entered any more,—

When, lo! A stream whose little waves went by,
Bending towards the left through grass that grew
Upon its bank, impeded suddenly

My going on. Water of purest hue
On earth, would appear turbid and impure
Compared with this, whose unconcealing dew,

Dark, dark, yet clear, moved under the obscure
Eternal shades, whose interwoven looms
The rays of moon or sunlight ne'er endure.

I moved not with my feet, but mid the glooms
Pierced with my charmed eye, contemplating
The mighty multitude of fresh May blooms

Which starred that night, when, even as a thing
That suddenly, for blank astonishment,
Charms every sense, and makes all thought take wing,—

A solitary woman! and she went
Singing and gathering flower after flower,
With which her way was painted and besprent.

"Bright lady, who, if looks had ever power
To bear true witness of the heart within,
Dost bask under the beams of love, come lower

"Towards this bank. I prithee let me win
This much of thee, to come, that I may hear
Thy song: like Proserpine, in Enna's glen,

"Thou seemest to my fancy, singing here
And gathering flowers, as that fair maiden when
She lost the Spring, and Ceres her, more dear."

Shelley keeps the *terza rima* (which Dante had invented) at some expense to the original's literal meaning, but he catches the surprises and splendor of the advent of Matilda, who has reversed the fall of Proserpine and of Eve, and who presages the imminent return of the vision of Beatrice to Dante. Shakespeare, in act 4, scene 4 of *The Winter's Tale*, may also hover in Shelley's memory, since Perdita is Shakespeare's equivalent of Matilda.

O Proserpina,
For the flowers now that frighted, thou let'st fall
From Dis's waggon! daffodils,
That come before the swallow dares, and take
The winds of March with beauty ...

Why Dante named this singing girl of a restored Eden Matilda (Matelda) is something of a puzzle, explained away differently by various scholars. Dante's Matilda makes only a brief appearance, but I perversely prefer her to Beatrice, who scolds and preaches, and is endlessly too good for Dante. Like Shakespeare's Perdita, Matilda charms us. Who but the ferocious Dante could fall in love again with the heavenly Beatrice? Who would not fall in love with Matilda, as translated here by William Merwin?

"and it tastes sweeter than any other,
and although your thirst might be completely
satisfied if I revealed no more.

"I will add a corollary, as a favor,
And I do not think my words will be less dear
To you because they go beyond my promise.

"Those who sang in ancient times of the age
Of gold and of its happy state saw this place,
Perhaps, in their dreams on Parnassus.

"Here the root of humankind was innocent.
Here Spring and every fruit lasted forever;
When they told of nectar this is what each meant."

Gracious and beautiful, the mysterious epitome of a young woman in love, Matilda walks with Dante through the meadows as though the Golden Age had returned. Matilda moves like a dancer, and we need not slow her pace by piling allegories upon her, or by relating her to historical noblewomen or blessed contemplatives. Dante, notoriously susceptible to the beauty of women, clearly would fall in love with Matilda, if the transmogrified Beatrice, as much chiding mother as image of desire, were not waiting for him in the next canto.

William Hazlitt, superb literary critic of British Romanticism, had a far more ambivalent reaction to Dante than Shelley and Byron did, yet Hazlitt caught at the truth of Dante's originality, the effect of Dante's genius:

he interests only by his exciting our sympathy with the emotion by which he is himself possessed. He does not place before us the objects by which that emotion has been excited; but he seizes on the attention, by showing us the effect they produce on his feelings; and his poetry accordingly frequently gives us the thrilling and overwhelming sensation which is caught by gazing on the face of a person who has seen some object of horror.

Hazlitt was thinking of the *Inferno*, and not of Matilda in the *Purgatorio*, where the sensation is that of gazing upon a face who has seen an ultimate object of delight.

CHARLES S. SINGLETON

The Two Kinds of Allegory

In his *Convivio* Dante recognizes two kinds of allegory: an "allegory of poets" and an "allegory of theologians." And in the interpretation of his own poems in that work he declares that he intends to follow the allegory of poets, for the reason that the poems were composed after that manner of allegory.

It is well to recall that there is an unfortunate lacuna in the text of the *Convivio* at just this most interesting point, with the result that those words which defined the literal sense, as distinguished from the allegorical, are missing. But no one who knows the general argument of the whole work will, I think, make serious objection to the way the editors of the accepted critical text have filled the lacuna.

The passage in question, patched by them, reads as follows:

> Dico che, sì come nel primo capitolo è narrato, questa sposizione conviene essere literale e allegorica. E a ciò dare a intendere, si vuol sapere che le scritture si possono intendere e deonsi esponere massimamente per quattro sensi. L'uno si chiama litterale [e questo è quello che non si stende più oltre la lettera de le parole fittizie, sì come sono le favole de li poeti. L'altro si chiama allegorico] e questo è quello che si nasconde sotto'l manto di queste favole, ed è una veritade ascosa sotto bella menzogna: sì come quando dice Ovidio che Orfeo facea con la cetera mansuete le fiere, e li arbori e le pietre

From *Dante's Commedia: Elements of Structure.* © 1954 by Charles S. Singleton.

11

a sè muovere; che vuol dire che lo savio uomo con lo strumento de
la sua voce fa[r]ia mansuescere e umiliare li crudeli cuori, e fa[r]ia
muovere a la sua volontade coloro che non hanno vita di scienza e
d'arte: e coloro che non hanno vita ragionevole alcuna sono quasi
come pietre. E perchè questo nascondimento fosse trovato per li savi,
nel penultimo trattato si mosterrà. Veramente li teologi questo senso
prendono altrimenti che li poeti; ma però che mia intenzione è qui
lo modo de li poeti seguitare, prendo lo senso allegorico secondo che
per li poeti è usato.[1]

I say that, as is narrated in the first chapter, this exposition is to be
both literal and allegorical. And to make this clear, one should know
that writing can be understood and must be explained mainly in four
senses. One is called the literal [and this is the sense that does not go
beyond the letter of the fictive words, as are the fables of the poets.
The other is called allegorical], and this is the sense that is hidden
under the cloak of these fables, and it is a truth hidden under the
beautiful lie; as when Ovid says that Orpheus tamed the wild beasts
with his zither and caused the trees and the stones to come to him;
which signifies that the wise man with the instrument of his voice
would make cruel hearts gentle and humble, and would make those
who do not live in science and art do his will; and those who have no
kind of life of reason in them are as stones. And the reason why this
concealment was devised by wise men will be shown in the next to
the last treatise. It is true that theologians understand this sense
otherwise than do the poets; but since it is my intention here to
follow after the manner of the poets, I take the allegorical sense as
the poets are wont to take it.

Dante goes on here to distinguish the customary third and fourth senses,
the moral and the anagogical. However, in illustration of these no example from
"the poets" is given. For both senses, the example in illustration is taken from
Holy Scripture. It is, however, evident from the closing words of the chapter that
in the exposition of the poems of the *Convivio*, the third and fourth senses will
have only an incidental interest and that the poet is to concern himself mainly
with the first two.[2]

It was no doubt inevitable that the conception of allegory which Dante
here calls the allegory of poets should come to be identified with the allegory of
the *Divine Comedy*. This, after all, is a formulation of the matter of allegory by
Dante himself. It distinguishes an allegory of poets from an allegory of
theologians. Now poets create and theologians only interpret. And, if we must
choose between Dante as theologian and Dante as poet, then, I suppose, we take
the poet.[3] For the *Divine Comedy*, all are agreed, is the work of a poet, is a poem.

Why, then, would its allegory not be allegory as the poets understood it—that is, as Dante, in the *Convivio*, says the poets understood it? Surely the allegory of the *Comedy* is the allegory of poets in which the first and literal sense is a fiction and the second or allegorical sense is the true one.[4]

Indeed, with some Dante scholars, so strong has the persuasion been that such a view of the allegory of the *Divine Comedy* is the correct one that it has brought them to question the authorship of the famous letter to Can Grande.[5] This, in all consistency, was bound to occur. For the Letter, in pointing out the allegory of the *Commedia*, speaks in its turn of the usual four senses. But the example of allegory which it gives is not taken from Ovid nor indeed from the work of any poet. Let us consider this famous and familiar passage:

> Ad evidentiam itaque dicendorum sciendum est quod istius operis non est simplex sensus, ymo dici potest polisemos, hoc est plurium sensuum; nam primus sensus est qui habetur per litteram, alius est qui habetur per significata per litteram. Et primus dicitur litteralis, secundus vero allegoricus sive moralis sive anagogicus. Qui modus tractandi, ut melius pateat, potest considerari in hiis versibus: "In exitu Israel de Egypto, domus Jacob ed populo barbaro, facts est Iudea sanctificatio eius, Israel potestas eius." Nam si ad litteram solam inspiciamus, significatur nobis exitus filiorum Israel de Egypto, tempore Moysis; si ad allegoriam, nobis significatur nostra redemptio facta per Christum; si ad moralem sensum significatur nobis conversio anime de luctu et miseria peccati ad statum gratie: si ad anagogicum, significatur exitus anime sancte ab huius corruptionis servitute ad eterne glorie libertatem. Et quanquam isti sensus mistici variis appellentur nominibus, generaliter omnes dici possunt allegorici, cum sint a litterali sive historiali diversi. Nam allegoria dicitur ab "alleon" grece, quod in latinum dicitur "alienum," sive "diversum."[6]

> To elucidate, then, what we have to say, be it known that the sense of this work is not simple, but on the contrary it may be called polysemous, that is to say, "of more senses than one"; for it is one sense that we get through the letter, and another which we get through the thing the letter signifies; and the first is called literal, but the second allegorical or mystic. And this mode of treatment, for its better manifestation, may be considered in this verse: "When Israel came out of Egypt, and the house of Jacob from a people of strange speech, Judaea became his sanctification, Israel his power." For if we inspect the letter alone, the departure of the children of Israel from Egypt in the time of Moses is presented to us; if the allegory, our redemption wrought by Christ; if the moral sense, the conversion of

the soul from the grief and misery of sin to the state of grace is presented to us; if the anagogical, the departure of the holy soul from the slavery of this corruption to the liberty of eternal glory is presented to us. And although these mystic senses have each their special denominations, they may all in general be called allegorical, since they differ from the literal and historical. Now allegory is so called from "alleon" in Greek, which means in Latin "alieum" or "diversum."

and the Letter continues directly as follows:

Hiis visis, manifestum est quod duplex oportet esse subiectum, circa quod currant alterni sensus. Et ideo videndum est de subiecto huius operis, prout ad litteram accipitur; deinde de subiecto, prout allegorice sententiatur. Est ergo subiectum totius operis, litteraliter tantum accepti, status animarum post mortem simpliciter sumptus; nam de illo et circa illum totius operis versatur processus. Si vero accipiatur opus allegorice, subiectum est homo prout merendo et demerendo per arbitrii libertatem iustitie premiandi et puniendi obnoxius est.

When we understand this we see clearly that the subject round which the alternative senses play must be twofold. And we must therefore consider the subject of this work as literally understood, and then its subject as allegorically intended. The subject of the whole work, then, taken in the literal sense only is "the state of souls after death" without qualification, for the whole progress of the work hinges on it and about it. Whereas if the work be taken allegorically, the subject is "man as by good or ill deserts, in the exercise of the freedom of his choice, he becomes liable to rewarding or punishing justice."

Now this, to return to the distinction made in the *Convivio*, is beyond the shadow of a doubt, the "allegory of theologians." It is their kind of allegory not only because Holy Scripture is cited to illustrate it, but because since Scripture is cited, the first or literal sense cannot be fictive but must be true and, in this instance, historical. The effects of Orpheus' music on beasts and stones may be a poet's invention, setting forth under a veil of fiction some hidden truth, but the Exodus is no poet's invention.

All medievalists are familiar with the classical statement of the "allegory of theologians" as given by St. Thomas Aquinas toward the beginning of the *Summa Theologica*:

Auctor Sacrae Scripturae est Deus, in cuius potestate est ut non solum voces ad significandum accommodet, quod etiam homo facere potest, sed etiam res ipsas. Et ideo cum in omnibus scientiis voces significant, hoc habet proprium ista scientia, quod ipsae res significatae per voces, etiam significant aliquid. Illa ergo prima significatio, qua voces significant res, pertinet ad primum sensum, qui est sensus historicus vel litteralis. Illa vero significatio qua res significatae per voces, iterum res alias significant, dicitur sensus spiritualis, qui super litteralem fundatur et eum supponit.[7]

The author of Holy Scripture is God, in whose power it is to signify His meaning, not by words only (as man also can do) but also by things themselves. So, whereas in every other science things are signified by words, this science has the property that the things signified by the words have themselves also a signification. Therefore that first signification whereby words signify things belongs to the first sense, the historical or literal. That signification whereby things signified by words have themselves also a signification is called the spiritual sense, which is based on the literal and presupposes it.

St. Thomas goes on to subdivide the second or spiritual sense into the usual three: the allegorical, the moral, and the anagogical. But in his first division into two he has made the fundamental distinction, which St. Augustine expressed in terms of one meaning which is *in verbis* and another meaning which is *in facto*.[8] And, in reading his words, one may surely recall Dante's in the Letter: "nam primes sensus est qui habetur per litteram, alius est qui habetur per significata per litteram."

An allegory of poets and an allegory of theologians: the Letter to Can Grande does not make the distinction. The Letter is speaking of the way in which a poem is to be understood. And in choosing its example of allegory from Holy Scripture, the Letter is clearly looking to the kind of allegory which is the allegory of theologians; and is thus pointing to a poem in which the first and literal sense is to be taken as the first and literal sense of Holy Scripture is taken, namely as an historical sense.[9] The well-known jingle on the four senses began, one recalls, "Littera *gesta* docet ..."

But, before going further, let us ask if this matter can have more than antiquarian interest. When we read the *Divine Comedy* today, does it matter, really, whether we take its first meaning to be historical or fictive, since in either case we must enter into that willing suspension of disbelief required in the reading of any poem?

Indeed, it happens to matter very much, because with this poem it is not a question of one meaning but of two meanings; and the nature of the first meaning will necessarily determine the nature of the second—will say how we shall look for the second. In the case of a fictive first meaning, as in the "allegory of poets," interpretation will invariably speak in terms of an outer and an inner meaning, of a second meaning which is conveyed but also, in some way, deliberately concealed under the "shell" or the "bark" or the "veil" of an outer fictive meaning. This allegory of the poets, as Dante presents it in the *Convivio*, is essentially an allegory of "this for that," of "this figuration in order to give (and also to conceal) that meaning." Orpheus and the effects of his music yield the meaning that a wise man can tame cruel hearts. It should be noted that here we are not concerned with allegory as expressed in a personification, but of an allegory of action, of event.

But the kind of allegory to which the example from Scriptures given in the Letter to Can Grande points is not an allegory of "this for that," but an allegory of "this *and* that," of this sense plus that sense. The verse in Scripture which says "When Israel went out of Egypt," has its first meaning in denoting a real historical event; and it has its second meaning because that historical event itself, having the Author that it had, can signify yet another event: our Redemption through Christ. Its first meaning is a meaning *in verbis*; its other meaning is a meaning *in facto*, in the event itself. The words have a real meaning in pointing to a real event; the event, in its turn, has meaning because events wrought by God are themselves as words yielding a meaning, a higher and spiritual sense.

But there was a further point about this kind of allegory of Scriptures: it was generally agreed that while the first literal meaning would always be there, *in verbis*,[10] the second or spiritual meaning was not always to be found in all the things and events that the words pointed to. Some events yielded the second meaning, some did not. And it is this fact which best shows that the literal historical meaning of Scriptures was not necessarily a sense in the service of another sense, not therefore a matter of "this for that." It is this that matters most in the interpretation of the *Divine Comedy*.

The crux of the matter, then, is this: If we take the allegory of the *Divine Comedy* to be the allegory of poets (as Dante understood that allegory in the *Convivio*) then we shall be taking it as a construction in which the literal sense ought always to be expected to yield another sense because the literal is only a fiction devised to express a second meaning. In this view the first meaning, if it does not give another, true meaning, has no excuse for being. Whereas, if we take the allegory of the *Divine Comedy* to be the allegory of theologians, we shall expect to find in the poem a first literal meaning presented as a meaning which is not fictive but true, because the words which give that meaning point to events which are seen as historically true. And we shall see these events themselves reflecting a second meaning because their author, who is God, can use events as men use words. *But*, we shall not demand at every moment that the event signified by the words be in its turn as a word, because this is not the case in Holy Scripture.[11]

One should have no difficulty in making the choice. The allegory of the *Divine Comedy* is so clearly the "allegory of theologians" (as the Letter to Can Grande by its example says it is) that one may only wonder at the continuing efforts made to see it as the "allegory of poets." What indeed increases the wonder at this effort is that every attempt to treat the first meaning of the poem as a fiction devised to convey a true but hidden meaning has been such a clear demonstration of how a poem may be forced to meanings that it cannot possibly bear as a poem.[12]

It seems necessary to illustrate the matter briefly with a single and obvious example. All readers of the *Comedy*, whatever their allegorical credo, must recognize that Virgil, for instance, if he be taken statically, in isolation from the action of the poem, had and has, as the poem would see him, a real historical existence. He was a living man and he is now a soul dwelling in Limbo. Standing alone, he would have no other, no second meaning, at all. It is by having a role in the action of the poem that Virgil takes on a second meaning. And it is at this point that the view one holds of the nature of the first meaning begins to matter. For if this is the allegory of poets, then what Virgil does, like what Orpheus does, is a fiction devised to convey a hidden meaning which it ought to convey all the time, since only by conveying that other meaning is what he does justified at all. Instead, if this action is allegory as theologians take it, then this action must always have a literal sense which is historical and no fiction; and thus Virgil's deeds as part of the whole action may, in their turn, be as words signifying other things; but they do not have to do this all the time, because, being historical, those deeds exist simply in their own right.

But can we hesitate in such a choice? Is it not clear that Virgil can not and does not always speak and act as Reason, with a capital initial, and that to try to make him do this is to try to rewrite the poem according to a conception of allegory which the poem does not bear within itself?

If, then, the allegory of the *Divine Comedy* is the allegory of theologians, if it is an allegory of "this and that," if its allegory may be seen in terms of a first meaning which is *in verbis* and of another meaning which is *in facto*, what is the main outline of its allegorical structure?

In the simplest and briefest possible statement it is this: the journey to God of a man through three realms of the world beyond this life is what is given by the literal meaning. It points to the event. The event is that journey to God through the world beyond. "Littera *gesta* docet." The words of the poem have their first meaning in signifying that event, just as the verse of Psalms had its first meaning in signifying the historical event of the Exodus.

And then just as the event of the Exodus, being wrought by God, can give in turn a meaning, namely, our Redemption through Christ; so, in the event of this journey through the world beyond (an event which, as the poem sees it, is also wrought by God) we see the reflection of other meanings. These, in the poem, are the various reflections of man's journey to his proper end, not in the life after death, but here in this life, as that journey was conceived possible in

Dante's day—and not only in Dante's day. The main allegory of the *Divine Comedy* is thus an allegory of action, of event, an event given by words which in its turn reflects, (*in facto*), another event. Both are journeys to God.[13]

What, then, of the *Convivio*? Does not its "allegory of poets" contradict thus "allegory of theologians" in the later work? It does, if a poet must always use one kind of allegory and may not try one in one work and one in another. But shall we not simply face this fact? And shall we not recognize that in this sense the *Convivio* contradicts not only the *Divine Comedy* in its allegory, but also the *Vita Nuova* where there is no allegory.[14] The *Convivio* is Dante's attempt to use the "allegory of poets." And to have that kind of allegory and the kind of figure that could have a role in it—to have a Lady Philosophy who was an allegory of poets—he was obliged to rob the "donna pietosa" of the *Vita Nuova* of all real existence. And in doing this he contradicted the *Vita Nuova*.

The *Convivio* is a fragment. We do not know why Dante gave up the work before it was hardly under way. We do not know. We are, therefore, free to speculate. I venture to do so, and suggest that Dante abandoned the *Convivio* because he came to see that in choosing to build this work according to the allegory of poets, he had ventured down a false way; that he came to realize that a poet could not be a poet of rectitude and work with an allegory whose first meaning was a disembodied fiction.

St. Gregory, in the Proem to his Exposition of the Song of Songs, says: "Allegoria enim animae longe a Deo positae quasi quamdam machinam facit ut per illam levetur ad Deum"[15] and the Letter to Can Grande declares that the end of the whole *Comedy* is "to remove those living in this life from the state of misery and lead them to the state of felicity." A poet of rectitude is one who is interested in directing the will of men to God. But a disembodied Lady Philosophy is not a *machina* which can bear the weight of lifting man to God because, in her, man finds no part of his own weight. Lady Philosophy did not, does not, will not, exist in the flesh. As she is constructed in the *Convivio* she comes to stand for Sapientia, for created Sapientia standing in analogy to uncreated Sapientia Which is the Word.[16] Even so, she is word without flesh. And only the word made flesh can lift man to God. If the allegory of a Christian poet of rectitude is to support any weight, it will be grounded in the flesh, which means grounded in history—and will lift up from there. In short, the trouble with Lady Philosophy was the trouble which Augustine found with the Platonists: "But that the Word was made flesh and dwelt among us I did not read there."[17]

Dante, then, abandons Lady Philosophy and returns to Beatrice. But now the way to God must be made open to all men: he constructs an allegory, a *machina*, that is, in which an historical Virgil, an historical Beatrice, and an historical Bernard replace that Lady in an action which is given, in its first sense, not as a beautiful fiction but as a real, historical event, an event remembered by one who was, as a verse of the poem says, the scribe of it.[18] Historical and, by a Christian standard, beautiful[19] as an allegory because bearing within it the reflection of the true way to God in this life—a way given and supported by the Word made flesh. With its first meaning as an historical meaning, the allegory of the *Divine Comedy* is grounded in the mystery of the Incarnation.[20]

In his commentary on the poem written some half century after the poet's death, Benvenuto da Imola would seem to understand the allegory of the *Divine Comedy* to be the "allegory of theologians." To make clear to some doubting reader the concept by which Beatrice has a second meaning, he points to Rachel in Holy Scripture:

> Nec videatur tibi indignum, lector, quod Beatrix mulier carnea accipiatur a Dante pro sacra theologia. Nonne Rachel secundum historicam veritatem fuit pulcra uxor Jacob summe amata ab eo, pro qua habenda custodivit oves per XIIII annos, et tamen anagogice figurat vitam contemplativam, quam Jacob mirabilirer amavit? Et si dicis: non credo quod Beatrix vel Rachel sumantur unquam spiritualiter, dicam quod contra negantes principia non est amplius disputandum. Si enim vis intelligere opus istius autoris, oportet concedere quod ipse loquatur catholice tamquam perfectus christianus, et qui semper et ubique conatur ostendere se christianum.[21]

> Let it not seem improper to you, reader, that Beatrice, a woman of flesh, should be taken by Dante as sacred Theology. Was not Rachel, according to historical truth, the beautiful wife of Jacob, loved exceedingly by him, to win whom he tended the sheep for fourteen years, and yet she figures the contemplative life which Jacob loved marvelously well? And if you say, I do not believe that Beatrice or Rachel ever had such spiritual meanings, then I say that against those who deny first principles there is no further disputing. For if you wish to understand the work of this writer, it is necessary to concede that he speaks in a catholic way as a perfect Christian and who always and everywhere strives to show himself a Christian.

Dr. Edward Moore once pointed, in a footnote, to these remarks by the early commentator and smiled at them as words that throw "a curious light on the logical processes of Benvenuto's mind."[22] But Benvenuto's words have, I think, a way of smiling back. And to make their smile more apparent to a modern reader one might transpose them so:

> Let it not seem improper to you, reader, that this journey of a living man into the world beyond is presented to you in its first sense as

literally and historically true. And if you say: "I do not believe that
Dante ever went to the other world," then I say that with those who
deny what a poem asks be granted, there is no further disputing.

NOTES

1. *Convivio*, II, i, 2–4, in the standard edition with commentary by G.
Busnelli and G. Vandelli (Florence, 1934). Concerning the lacuna and the
reasons for filling it as this has been done (words in brackets in the passage above)
see their notes to the passage, Vol. 1, pp. 96–97 and 200–242. The "penultimo
trattato" where Dante promises to explain the reason for the "allegory of poets"
was, alas, never written.

2. *Convivio*, II, i, 15: "Io adunque, per queste ragioni, tuttavia sopra ciascuna
canzone ragionerò prima la litterale sentenza, e appresso di quella ragionerò la
sua allegoria, cioè la nascosa veritade; e talvolta de li altri sensi toccherò
incidentemente, come a luogo e tempo si converrà."

3. One recalls, of course, that Boccaccio and many others have preferred the
theologian. On Dante as theologian one may now see E. R. Curtius, *Europäische
Literatur und lateinische Mittelalter* (Bern, 1948), pp. 219 ff. To see the poet as
"theologian" is to see him essentially as one who constructs an "allegory of
poets," hiding under a veil the truths of theology—a view which has a long
history in Dante interpretation.

4. By no means all commentators of the poem who discuss this matter have
faced the necessity of making a choice between the two kinds of allegory
distinguished by Dante. More often than not, even in a discussion of the two
kinds, they have preferred to leave the matter vague as regards the *Divine
Comedy*. *See*, for example, C. H. Grandgent's remarks on Dante's allegory in his
edition of the poem (revised, 1933), pp. xxxii–xxxiii, where the choice is not made
and where allegory and symbolism are lumped together.

5. This, to be sure, is only one of the several arguments that have been
adduced in contesting the authenticity of the Letter; but whenever it has been
used, it has been taken to bear considerable weight. The most violent attack on
the authenticity of the Letter was made by D'Ovidio in an essay entitled
"L'Epistola a Cangrande," first published in the *Rivista d'Italia* in 1899 and
reprinted in his *Studi sulla Divina Commedia* (1901), in which his remarks on the
particular point in question may be taken as typical (*Studi*, pp. 462–463): "Il vero
guaio è che l'Epistola soffoca la distinzione tra il senso letterale meramente
fittizio, poetico vero d'un concetto allegorico e il senso letterale vero in sè,
storico, da cui però o scaturisce una moralità o è raffigurato un fatto
soprannaturale. Dei tre efficacissimi esempi danteschi ne dimentica due (Orfeo e
i tre Apostoli), e s'attacca al solo terzo, stiracchiandolo per farlo servire anche al

senso morale e all'allegorico; nè riuscendo in effetto se non a modulare in tre diverse gradazioni un unico senso niente altro che anagogico. Non è ne palinodia nè plagio; è una parodia. La quale deriva da ciò che, oltre la precisa distinzione tomistica e dantesca del senso allegorico dal morale e dall'anagogico, era in corso la dottrina agostiniana che riduceva tutto alla sola allegoria. Dante ne fa cenno, dove, terminata la definizione del senso allegorico, prosegue: 'Veramente li teologi questo senso prendono altrimenti che li poeti; ma perocché mia intenzione e qui lo modo delli poeti seguitare, prenderò il senso allegorico secondo che per li poeti e usato.' Ne, si badi, avrebbe avuto motivo di mutar intenzione, se si fosse posto a chiosar il Paradiso, che, se Dio vuole, *è poesia anch'esso*." [Italics mine]

It is worth noting in this respect that Dr. Edward Moore, in an essay entitled "The Genuineness of the Dedicatory Epistle to Can Grande" (*Studies in Dante*, third series, pp. 284–369) in which he undertook a very careful refutation, point by point, of D'Ovidio's arguments, either did not attribute any importance to the particular objection quoted above or did not see how it was to be met. For a review of the whole dispute, *see* G. Boffito, *L'Epistola di Dante Aligheri a Cangrande della Scala* in *Memorie della R. Acad. delle scienze di Torino*, Series II, vol. 57, of the *Classe di scienze morali*, etc., pp. 5–10.

6. *Opere di Dante* (ed. Società Dantesca Italiana, Florence, 1921), Epistola XIII, 20–25, pp. 438–439.

7. *Summa Theologica*, I, 1, 10. Resp.

8. *De Trinitate*, XV, ix, 15 (PL 43, 1068) : "non in verbis sed in facto." On the distinction of the two kinds of allegory in Holy Scripture see *Dictionnaire de théologie catholique* (Vacant, Mangenot, Amann), vol. 1 (1923), col. 833 ff. s.v. *Allégories bibliques*. On St. Thomas' distinction in particular, consult R. P. P. Synave, "La Doctrine de S. Thomas d'Aquin cur le sens littéral des Écritures" in *Revue Biblique* XXXV (1926), 40–65.

9. "Literal" and "historical" as synonymous terms for the first sense are bound to be puzzling to modern minds. In the discussion of allegory by St. Thomas and others we meet it at every turn. Perhaps no passage can better help us focus our eyes on this concept as they understood it than one in Hugh of St. Victor (cited by Synave, op. cit., p. 43, from Chapter 3 of Hugh's *De scriptoris et scripturibus sacris*): "*Historia* dicitur a verbo graeco ιστορέω historeo, quod est video et narro; propterea quod spud veteres nulli licebat scribere res gestas, nisi a se visas, ne falsitas admisceretur veritati peccato scriptoris, plus aut minus, aut aliter dicentis. Secundum hoc proprie et districte dicitur historia; sed solet largius accipi ut dicatur historia census qui primo loco ex significatione verborum habetur ad res."

10. It may be well to recall on this point that, in St. Thomas' view and that of others, a parable told by Christ has only one sense, namely that *in verbis*. This

is true of the Song of Songs, also, and of other parts of Scripture. But in such passages there is no "allegory," because there is no other meaning *in facto*.

11. *Cf.* Thomas Aquinas, *Opuscula selecta* (Paris, 1881) vol. II, pp. 399–401: "Ad quintum dicendum quod quatuor isti sensus non attribuntur sacrae Scripturae, ut in qualibet eius parte sit in istis quatuor sensibus exponenda, sed quandoque istis quatuor, quandoque tribus, quandoque duobus, quandoque unum tantum."

12. Michele Barbi sounded a warning on this matter some years ago, but in so doing appealed to a solution (the poem as "vision," as "apocalypse") which needs I think, further clarification: "Io ho un giorno, durante il positivismo che sera insinuato nella critica dantesca, richiamato gli studiosi a non trascurare una ricerca così importante come quella del simbolismo nella Divina Commedia: oggi sento il dovere di correre alla difesa del senso letterale, svilito come azione fittizia, come bella menzogna, quasi che nell'intendimento di Dante l'importanza del suo poema non consists già in quello che egli ha rappresentato nella lettera di esso, ma debba andarsi a cercare in concetti e intendimenti nascosti sotto quella rappresentazione. Non snaturiamo per carita l'opera di Dante; è una rivelazione, non già un'allegoria da capo a fondo. La lettera non è in funzione soltanto di riposti intendimenti, non è bella menzogna: quel viaggio ch'essa descrive è un viaggio voluto da Dio perchè Dante riveli in salute degli uomini quello che ode e vede nel fatale andare." (*Studi danteschi*, I, 12–13.) This is all very well and very much to the point. But the problem which Barbi does not deal with here and which calls for solution is how, on what conceptual basis, is an *allegory* given in a poem in which the first meaning is not a "bella menzogna"?

13. It is essential to remember that I am here concerned with the main allegory of the *Divine Comedy*; otherwise this can appear an oversimplification to any reader familiar with the concrete detail of the poem, and certainly many questions concerning that detail will arise which are not dealt with here. How, for example, are we to explain those passages where the poet urges the reader to look "beneath the veil" for a hidden meaning (*Inferno*, IX, 62; *Purgatorio*, VIII, 19–21)? Do these not point to an "allegory of poets"? I believe that the correct answer can be given in the negative. But, however that may be, we do not meet the main allegory of the poem in such passages.

Likewise, finer distinctions in the allegory of the poem will recognize that the allegory of the opening situation (*Inferno*, I, II) must be distinguished from the main allegory of the poem, and of necessity, since at the beginning the protagonist is still in this life and has not yet begun to move through the world beyond. For some considerations on this point beyond those above in Chapter I, *see* the author's article in *RR* XXXIX (1948), 269–277: "Sulla fiumana ove'l mar non ha vanto: *Inferno*, II, 108."

14. For a discussion of the absence of allegory in the *Vita Nuova*, *see* the author's *Essay on the Vita Nuova* (Cambridge, Mass., 1948), pp. 110 ff. and *passim*.

15. PL 79, 473. In interpreting the Song of Songs, St. Gregory is not speaking of the kind of allegory which has an historical meaning as its first meaning (*see* note 10 above)—which fact does not make his view of the use of allegory any less interesting or suggestive with respect to Dante's use of it.

16. On created wisdom and the distinction here *see* Augustine, *Confessions*, XII, 15.

17. *Confessions*, VII, 9.

18. *Paradiso*, X, 22–27:

> Or ti riman, lettor, sovra 'l tuo banco,
>   dietro pensando a ciò che si preliba,
>   s'esser vuoi lieto assai prima che stanco.
> Messo t'ho innanzi: omai per lo ti ciba;
>   chè a sè torce tutta la mia cura
>   quella materia ond'io son fatto scriba.

As every reader of the *Commedia* knows, a poet's voice speaks out frequently in the poem, and most effectively, in various contexts. But these verses may remind us that when the poet does come into the poem, he speaks as scribe, as one remembering and trying to give an adequate account of the event which is now past.

19. Cf. Menendez y Pelayo, *Historia de las ideas estéticas en España*, chapter X, Introduction: "No vino a enseñar estética ni otra ciencia humana el Verbo Encarnado; pero presentò en su persona y en la union de sus dos naturalezas el protótipo más alto de la hermosura, y el objeto más adecuado del amor ..."

20. Those who refuse to recognize this "mystery" in the allegory of the *Divine Comedy*, who view it instead as the usual "allegory of poets" in which the first meaning is a fiction, are guilty of a reader's error comparable in some way to the error of the Manicheans concerning the Incarnation, as set forth by St. Thomas in the *Summa contra Gentiles*, IV, xxix: "They pretended that whatever He did as man—for instance, that He was born, that He ate, drank, walked, suffered, and was buried—was all unreal, though having some semblance of reality. Consequently they reduced the whole mystery of the Incarnation to a work of fiction."

21. *Contentum* (Florence, 1887), I, 89–90.

22. *Studies in Dante* (second series, 1889), p. 86, n. 1.

ERICH AUERBACH

Figural Art in the Middle Ages

The figural interpretation, or to put it more completely, the figural view of history was widespread and deeply influential up to the Middle Ages, and beyond. This has not escaped the attention of scholars. Not only theological works on the history of hermeneutics but also studies on the history of art and literature have met with figural conceptions on their way, and dealt with them. This is particularly true of the history of art in connection with medieval iconography, and of the history of literature in connection with the religious theater of the Middle Ages. But the special nature of the problem does not seem to have been recognized; the figural or theological or phenomenal structure is not sharply distinguished from other, allegorical or symbolical, forms. A beginning is to be found in T. C. Goode's instructive dissertation on Gonzalo de Berceo's *El Sacrificio de la Misa* (Washington, 1953); although he does not go into fundamental questions, H. Pflaum shows a clear understanding of the situation in his *Die religiose Disputation in der europäischen Dichtung des Mittelalters* (Geneva-Florence, 1935). Recently (in *Romania*, LXIII) his sound understanding of the word *figura* enabled him to give a correct interpretation of some Old French verses that had been misunderstood by the editor and to restore the text. Perhaps other examples have escaped me,[41] but I do not think that there is any systematic treatment of the subject. Yet such an investigation strikes me as indispensable for an understanding of the mixture of spirituality and sense of reality which characterizes the European Middle Ages and which seems so baffling to us.[42] In

---

From *Scenes from the Drama of European Literature*. © 1959 by Meridian Books.

25

most European countries figural interpretation was active up to the eighteenth century; we find traces of it not only in Bossuet as might be expected, but many years later in the religious authors whom Groethuysen quotes in *Les Origines de la France bourgeoise*.[43] A clear knowledge of its character and how it differed from related but differently structured forms would generally sharpen and deepen our understanding of the documents of late antiquity and the Middle Ages, and solve a good many puzzles. Might the themes that recur so frequently on early Christian sarcophagi and in the catacombs not be figures of the Resurrection? Or to cite an example from Mâle's great work, might not the legend of Maria Aegyptiaca, the representations of which in the Toulouse Museum he describes (op. cit., p. 240 ff.), be a figure of the people of Israel going out of Egypt, hence to be interpreted exactly as the Psalm *In exitu Israel de Aegypto* was generally interpreted in the Middle Ages?

But individual interpretations do not exhaust the importance of the figural method. No student of the Middle Ages can fail to see how it provides the medieval interpretation of history with its general foundation and often enters into the medieval view of everyday reality. The analogism that reaches into every sphere of medieval thought is closely bound up with the figural structure; in the interpretation of the Trinity that extends roughly from Augustine's *De Trinitate* to St. Thomas, I, q. 45, art. 7, man himself, as the image of God, takes on the character of a *figura Trinitatis*. It is not quite clear to me how far aesthetic ideas were determined by figural conceptions—to what extent the work of art was viewed as the *figura* of a still unattainable fulfillment in reality. The question of the imitation of nature in art aroused little theoretical interest in the Middle Ages; but all the more attention was accorded to the notion that the artist, as a kind of figure for God the Creator, realized an archetype that was alive in his spirit.[44] These, as we see, are ideas of Neoplatonic origin. But the question remains: to what extent were this archetype and the work of art produced from it regarded as figures for a reality and truth fulfilled in God? I have found no conclusive answer in the texts available to me here and the most important works of the specialized literature are lacking. But I should like to quote a few passages which happen to be at hand, and which point somewhat in the direction I have in mind. In an article on the representation of musical tones in the capitals of the Abbey of Cluny (*Deutsche Vierteljahrsschrift*, 7, p. 264) L. Schrade quotes an explanation of the word *imitari* by Remigius of Auxerre: *scilicet persequi, quia veram musicam non potest humana musica imitari* ("that is, to follow after, for the music of man cannot imitate the true music"). This is probably based on the notion that the artist's work is an imitation or at least a shadowy figuration of a true and likewise sensuous reality (the music of the heavenly choirs). In the *Purgatorio* Dante praises the works of art created by God himself, representing examples of virtues and vices, for their perfectly fulfilled sensuous truth, beside which human art and even nature pales (*Purg.*, 10 and 12); his invocation to Apollo (*Par.*, 1) includes the lines:

O divina virtù, se mi ti presti
  tanto che l'ombra del beato regno,
  segnata nel mio capo io manifesti

(O divine Virtue, if thou dost so far lend thyself to me, that I make
manifest the shadow of the blessed realm imprinted on my brain.)
(Temple Classics ed., p. 5.)

Here his poetry is characterized as an *umbra* of truth, engraved in his mind, and
his theory of inspiration is sometimes expressed in statements. that may be
explained along the same lines. But these are only suggestions; an investigation
purporting to explain the relation between Neoplatonic and figural elements in
medieval aesthetics would require broader foundations. Still, the present remarks
suffice, I believe, to show the need for distinguishing the figural structure from
the other forms of imagery. We may say roughly that the figural method in
Europe goes back to Christian influences, while the allegorical method derives
from ancient pagan sources, and also that the one is applied primarily to
Christian, the other to ancient material. Nor shall we be going too far afield in
terming the figural view the predominantly Christian-medieval one, while the
allegorical view, modeled on pagan or not inwardly Christianized authors of late
antiquity, tends to appear where ancient, pagan, or strongly secular influences are
dominant. But such observations are too general and imprecise, for the many
phenomena that reflect an intermingling of different cultures over a thousand
years do not admit of such simple classifications. At a very early date profane and
pagan material was also interpreted figurally; Gregory of Tours, for example, uses
the legend of the Seven Sleepers as a figure for the Resurrection; the waking of
Lazarus from the dead and Jonah's rescue from the belly of the whale were also
commonly interpreted in this sense. In the high Middle Ages, the Sybils, Virgil,
the characters of the Aeneid, and even those of the Breton legend cycle (e.g.,
Galahad in the quest for the Holy Grail) were drawn into the figural
interpretation, and moreover there were all sorts of mixtures between figural,
allegoric, and symbolic forms. All these forms, applied to classical as well as
Christian material, occur in the work which concludes and sums up the culture
of the Middle Ages: the *Divine Comedy*. But I shall now attempt to show that
basically it is the figural forms which predominate and determine the whole
structure of the poem.

At the foot of the mountain of Purgatory, Dante and Virgil meet a man of
venerable mien, whose countenance is illumined by four stars signifying the four
cardinal virtues. He inquires sternly into the legitimacy of their journey and from
Virgil's respectful reply—after he has told Dante to kneel before this man—we
learn that it is Cato of Utica. For after explaining his divine mission, Virgil
continues as follows (*Purg.*, 1, 70–5):

Or ti piaccia gradir la sua venuta.
     libertà va cercando, che è si cara,
     come sa chi per lei vita rifiuta.
Tu il sai, chè non ti fu per lei amara
     in Utica la morte, ove lasciasti
     la vesta che al gran di sarà sì chiara.

(Now may it please thee to be gracious unto his coming: he seeketh freedom, which is so precious, as he knows who giveth up life for her.

    Thou knowest it; since for her sake death was not bitter to thee in Utica, where thou leftest the raiment which at the great day shall be so bright.)

(Temple Classics ed., p. 7)

Virgil goes on, asking Cato to favor him for the sake of the memory of Marcia, his former wife. This plea Cato rejects with undiminished severity; but if such is the desire of the *donna del ciel* (Beatrice), that suffices; and he orders that before his ascent Dante's face be cleansed of the stains of Hell and that he be girded with reeds. Cato appears again at the end of the second canto, where he sternly rebukes the souls just arrived at the foot of the mountain, who are listening in self-forgetfulness to Casella's song, and reminds them to get on with their journey.

It is Cato of Utica whom God has here appointed guardian at the foot of Purgatory: a pagan, an enemy of Caesar, and a suicide. This is startling, and the very first commentators, such as Benvenuto of Imola, expressed their bewilderment. Dante mentions only a very few pagans who were freed from Hell by Christ; and among them we find an enemy of Caesar, whose associates, Caesar's murderers, are with Judas in the jaws of Lucifer, who as a suicide seems no less guilty than those others "who have done themselves violence" and who for the same sin are suffering the most frightful torments in the seventh circle of Hell. The riddle is solved by the words of Virgil, who says that Dante is seeking freedom, which is so precious as you yourself know who have despised life for its sake. The story of Cato is removed from its earthly and political context, just as the stories of Isaac, Jacob, etc., were removed from theirs by the patristic exegetes of the Old Testament, and made into a *figura futurorum*. Cato is a *figura*, or rather the earthly Cato, who renounced his life for freedom, was a *figura*, and the Cato who appears here in the *Purgatorio* is the revealed or fulfilled figure, the truth of that figural event. The political and earthly freedom for which he died was only an *umbra futurorum*: a prefiguration of the Christian freedom whose guardian he is here appointed, and for the sake of which he here again opposes all earthly temptation; the Christian freedom from all evil impulses, which leads to true domination of self, the freedom for the acquisition of which Dante is girded with the rushes of humility, until, on the summit of the mountain, he actually achieves it and is crowned by Virgil as lord over himself. Cato's voluntary choice of death rather than political servitude is here introduced as a *figura* for the eternal freedom of the children of God, in behalf of which all earthly things are to be despised, for the liberation of the soul from the servitude of sin. Dante's choice of Cato for this role is explained by the position "above the parties" that Cato occupies according to the Roman authors, who held him up as a model of virtue, justice, piety, and love of freedom. Dante found him praised equally in Cicero, Virgil, Lucan, Seneca, and Valerius Maximus; particularly Virgil's *secretosque pios his dantem iura Catonem* (*Aeneid*, 8, 670) ("the righteous in a place apart, with Cato their lawgiver"), coming as it did from a poet of the Empire, must have made a great impression on him. His admiration for Cato may be judged from several passages in the *Convivio*, and in his *De Monarchia* (2, 5) he has a quotation from Cicero[45] saying that Cato's voluntary death should be judged in a special light and connecting it with the examples of Roman political virtue to which Dante attached so much importance; in this passage Dante tries to show that Roman rule was legitimized by Roman virtue; that it fostered the justice and freedom of all mankind. The chapter contains this sentence: *Romanum imperium de forte nascitur pietatis* ("the Roman Empire springs from the fount of justice").[46]

Dante believed in a predetermined concordance between the Christian story of salvation and the Roman secular monarchy; thus it is not surprising that he should apply the figural interpretation to a pagan Roman—in general he draws his symbols, allegories, and figures from both worlds without distinction. Beyond any doubt Cato is a *figura*; not an allegory like the characters from the *Roman de la Rose*, but a figure that has become the truth. The *Comedy* is a vision which regards and proclaims the figural truth as already fulfilled, and what constitutes its distinctive character is precisely that, fully in the spirit of figural interpretation, it attaches the truth perceived in the vision to historical, earthly events. The character of Cato as a severe, righteous, and pious man, who in a significant moment in his own destiny and in the providential history of the world sets freedom above life, is preserved in its full historical and personal force; it does not become an allegory for freedom; no, Cato of Utica stands there as a unique individual, just as Dante saw him; but he is lifted out of the tentative earthly state in which he regarded political freedom as the highest good (just as the Jews singled out strict observance of the Law), and transposed into a state of definitive fulfillment, concerned no longer with the earthly works of civic virtue or the law, but with the *ben dell'intelletto*, the highest good, the freedom of the immortal soul in the sight of God.

Let us attempt the same demonstration in a somewhat more difficult case. Virgil has been taken by almost all commentators as an allegory for reason—the human, natural reason which leads to the right earthly order, that is, in Dante's view, the secular monarchy. The older commentators had no objection to a purely allegorical interpretation, for they did not, as we do today, feel that

allegory was incompatible with authentic poetry. Many modern critics have
argued against this idea, stressing the poetic, human, personal quality of Dante's
Virgil; still, they have been unable either to deny that he "means something" or
to find a satisfactory relation between this meaning and the human reality.
Recently (and not only in connection with Virgil) a number of writers (L. Valli
and Mandonnet, for example) have gone back to the purely allegorical or
symbolic aspect and attempted to reject the historical reality as "positivistic" or
"romantic." But actually there is no choice between historical and hidden
meaning; both are present. The figural structure preserves the historical: event
while interpreting it as revelation; and must preserve it in order to interpret it.

In Dante's eyes the historical Virgil is both poet and guide. He is a poet and
a guide because in the righteous Aeneas' journey to the underworld he
prophesies and glorifies universal peace under the Roman Empire, the political
order which Dante regards as exemplary, as the *terrena Jerusalem*;[47] and because
in his poem the founding of Rome, predestined seat of the secular and spiritual
power, is celebrated in the light of its future mission. Above all he is poet and
guide because all the great poets who came after him have been inflamed and
inspired by his work, Dante not only states this for himself, but brings in a
second poet, Statius, to proclaim the same thing most emphatically: in the
meeting with Sordello and perhaps also in the highly controversial verse about
Guido Cavalcanti (*Inf.*, 10, 63) the same theme is sounded. In addition, Virgil is
a guide because, beyond his temporal prophecy, he also—in the Fourth
Eclogue—proclaimed the eternal transcendent order, the appearance of Christ
which would usher in the renewal of the temporal world without, to be sure,
suspecting the significance of his own words, but nevertheless in such a way that
posterity might derive inspiration from his light. Virgil the poet was a guide
because he had described the realm of the dead—thus he knew the way thither.
But also as a Roman and a man, he was destined to be a guide, for not only was
he a master of eloquent discourse and lofty wisdom but also possessed the
qualities that fit a man for guidance and leadership, the qualities that characterize
his hero Aeneas and Rome in general: *iustitia* and *pietas*. For Dante the historical
Virgil embodied this fullness of earthly perfection and was therefore capable of
guiding him to the very threshold of insight into the divine and eternal
perfection; the historic Virgil was for him a *figura* of the poet-prophet-guide,
now fulfilled in the other world. The historical Virgil is "fulfilled" by the dweller
in limbo, the companion of the great poets of antiquity, who at the wish of
Beatrice undertakes to guide Dante. As a Roman and poet Virgil had sent Aeneas
down to the underworld in search of divine counsel to learn the destiny of the
Roman world; and now Virgil is summoned by the heavenly powers to exercise a
no less important guidance; for there is no doubt that Dante saw himself in a
mission no less important than that of Aeneas: elected to divulge to a world out
of joint the right order, which is revealed to him upon his way. Virgil is elected
to point out and interpret for him the true earthly order, whose laws are carried

out and whose essence is fulfilled in the other world, and at the same time to direct him toward its goal, the heavenly community of the blessed, which he has presaged in his poetry—yet not into the heart of the kingdom of God, for the meaning of his presage was not revealed to him during his earthly lifetime, and without such illumination he has died an unbeliever. Thus God does not wish Dante to enter His kingdom with Virgil's help; Virgil can lead him only to the threshold of the kingdom; only as far as the limit which his noble and righteous poetry was able to discern. "Thou first," says Statius to Virgil, "didst send me towards Parnassus to drink in its caves, and then didst light me on to God. Thou didst like one who goes by night, and carries the light behind him, and profits not himself, but maketh persons wise that follow him.... Through thee I was a poet, through thee a Christian."[48] And just as the earthly Virgil led Statius to salvation, so now, as a fulfilled figure, he leads Dante: for Dante too has received from him the lofty style of poetry, through him he is saved from eternal damnation and set on the way of salvation; and just as he once illumined Statius, without himself seeing the light that he bore and proclaimed, so now he leads Dante to the threshold of the light, which he knows of but may not himself behold.

Thus Virgil is not an allegory of an attribute, virtue, capacity, power, or historical institution. He is neither reason nor poetry nor the Empire. He is Virgil himself. Yet he is not himself in the same way as the historical characters whom later poets have set out to portray in all their historical involvement, as for example, Shakespeare's Caesar or Schiller's Wallenstein. These poets disclose their historical characters in the thick of their earthly existence; they bring an important epoch to life before our eyes, and look for the meaning of the epoch itself. For Dante the meaning of every life has its place in the providential history of the world, the general lines of which are laid down in the Revelation which has been given to every Christian, and which is interpreted for him in the vision of the *Comedy*. Thus Virgil in the *Divine Comedy* is the historical Virgil himself, but then again he is not; for the historical Virgil is only a *figura* of the fulfilled truth that the poem reveals, and this fulfillment is more real, more significant than the *figura*. With Dante, unlike modern poets, the more fully the figure is interpreted and the more closely it is integrated with the eternal plan of salvation, the more real it becomes. And for him, unlike the ancient poets of the underworld, who represented earthly life as real and the life after death as shadow, for him the other world is the true reality, while this world is only *umbra futurorum*—though indeed the *umbra* is the prefiguration of the transcendent reality and must recur fully in it.

For what has been said here of Cato and Virgil applies to the *Comedy* as a whole. It is wholly based on a figural conception. In my study of Dante as a poet of the earthly world (1929) I attempted to show that in the *Comedy* Dante undertook "to conceive the whole earthly historical world ... as already subjected to God's final judgment and thus put in its proper place as decreed by the divine judgment, to represent it as a world already judged ... in so doing, he does not destroy or weaken the earthly nature of his characters, but captures the fullest intensity of their individual earthly-historical being and identifies it with the ultimate state of things" (p. 108). At that time I lacked a solid historical grounding for this view, which is already to be found in Hegel and which is the basis of my interpretation of the *Divine Comedy*; it is suggested rather than formulated in the introductory chapters of the book. I believe that I have now found this historical grounding; it is precisely the figural interpretation of reality which, though in constant conflict with purely spiritualist and Neoplatonic tendencies, was the dominant view in the European Middle Ages: the idea that earthly life is thoroughly real, with the reality of the flesh into which the Logos entered, but that with all its reality it is only *umbra* and *figura* of the authentic, future, ultimate truth, the real reality that will unveil and preserve the *figura*. In this way the individual earthly event is not regarded as a definitive self-sufficient reality, nor as a link in a chain of development in which single events or combinations of events perpetually give rise to new events, but viewed primarily in immediate vertical connection with a divine order which encompasses it, which on some future day will itself be concrete reality; so that the earthly event is a prophecy or *figura* of a part of a wholly divine reality that will be enacted in the future. But this reality is not only future; it is always present in the eye of God and in the other world, which is to say that in transcendence the revealed and trite reality is present at all times, or timelessly. Dante's work is an attempt to give a poetic and at the same time systematic picture of the world in this light. Divine grace comes to the help of a man menaced by earthly confusion and ruin—this is the framework of the vision. From early youth he had been favored by special grace, because he was destined for a special task; at an early age he had been privileged to see revelation incarnated in a living being, Beatrice—and here as so often figural structure and Neoplatonism are intertwined. In her lifetime she had, though covertly, favored him with a salutation of her eyes and mouth; and in dying she had distinguished him in an unspoken mysterious way.[49] When he strays from the right path, the departed Beatrice, who for him was revelation incarnate, finds the only possible salvation for him; indirectly she is his guide and in Paradise directly; it is she who shows him the unveiled order, the truth of the earthly figures. What he sees and learns in the three realms is true, concrete reality, in which the earthly *figura* is contained and interpreted; by seeing the fulfilled truth while still alive, he himself is saved, while at the same time he is enabled to tell the world what he has seen and guide it to the right path.

    Insight into the figural character of the *Comedy* does not offer a universal method by which to interpret every controversial passage; but we can derive certain principles of interpretation from it. We may be certain that every historical or mythical character occurring in the poem can only mean something closely connected with what Dante knew of his historical or mythical existence, and that the relation is one of fulfillment and figure; we must always be careful

not to deny their earthly historical existence altogether, not to confine ourselves
to an abstract, allegorical interpretation. This applies particularly to Beatrice.
The romantic realism of the nineteenth century overemphasized the human
Beatrice, tending to make the *Vita Nova* a kind of sentimental novel. Since then
a reaction has set in; the new tendency is to do away with her entirely, to dissolve
her in an assortment of increasingly subtle theological concepts. But actually
there is no reality in such a choice. For Dante the literal meaning or historical
reality of a figure stands in no contradiction to its profounder meaning, but
precisely "figures" it; the historical reality is not annulled, but confirmed and
fulfilled by the deeper meaning. The Beatrice of the *Vita Nova* is an earthly
person; she really appeared to Dante, she really saluted him, really withheld her
salutation later on, mocked him, mourned for a dead friend and for her father,
and really died. Of course this reality can only be the reality of Dante's
experience—for a poet forms and transforms the events of his life in his
consciousness, and we can take account only of what lived in his consciousness
and not of the outward reality. It should also be borne in mind that from the first
day of her appearance the earthly Beatrice was for Dante a miracle sent from
Heaven, an incarnation of divine truth. Thus the reality of her earthly person is
not, as in the case of Virgil or Cato, derived from the facts of a historic tradition,
but from Dante's own experience: this experience showed him the earthly
Beatrice as a miracle.[50] But an incarnation, a miracle are real happenings;
miracles happen on earth, and incarnation is flesh. The strangeness of the
medieval view of reality has prevented modern scholars from distinguishing
between figuration and allegory and led them for the most part to perceive only
the latter.[51] Even so acute a theological critic as Mandonnet (op. cit., pp. 218–19)
considers only two possibilities: either Beatrice is a mere allegory (and this is his
opinion) or she is *la petite Bice Portinari*, a notion that he ridicules. Quite aside
from the misunderstanding of poetic reality that such a judgment shows, it is
surprising to find so deep a chasm between reality and meaning. Is the *terrena
Jerusalem* without historical reality because it is a *figura aeternae Jerusalem*?

In the *Vita Nova*, then, Beatrice is a living woman from the reality of
Dante's experience—and in the *Comedy* she is no *intellectus separatus*, no angel, but
a blessed human being who will rise again in the flesh at the Last Judgment.
Actually there is no dogmatic concept that would wholly describe her; certain
events in the *Vita Nova* would not fit into any allegory, and in regard to the
Comedy there is the additional problem of drawing an exact distinction between
her and various other persons of the *Paradiso*, such as the Apostle-Examiners and
St. Bernard. Nor can the special character of her relation to Dante be fully
understood in this way. Most of the older commentators interpreted Beatrice as
theology; more recent ones have sought subtler formulations; but this has led to
exaggeration and mistakes: even Mandonnet, who applies to Beatrice the
extremely broad notion of *ordre surnaturel*, derived from the contrast with Virgil,
comes up with hairsplitting subdivisions, makes mistakes,[52] and forces his

concepts. The role that Dante attributes to her is perfectly clear from her actions and the epithets attached to her. She is a figuration or incarnation of revelation (*Inf.*, 2, 76): *sola per cui l'umana spezie eccede ogni contento da quel ciel, che ha minor li cerchi sui* ("through whom alone mankind excels all that is contained within the heaven which has the smallest circles"); (*Purg.*, 6, 45): *che lume fia tra il vero e l'intelletto* ("who shall be a light between truth and intellect") which, out of love (*Inf.*, 2, 72), divine grace sends to man for his salvation, and which guides him to the *visio Dei*. Mandonnet forgets to say that she is precisely an incarnation of divine revelation and not revelation pure and simple, although he quotes the pertinent passages from the *Vita Nova* and from St. Thomas, and the above-mentioned invocation, *O Donna di virtù, sola per cui, etc.* One cannot address the "supernatural order" as such, one can only address its incarnate revelation, that part of the divine plan of salvation which precisely is the miracle whereby men are raised above other earthly creatures. Beatrice is incarnation, she is *figura* or *idolo Christi* (her eyes reflect her twofold nature, *Purg.*, 31, 126) and thus she is not exhausted by such explanations; her relation to Dante cannot fully be explained by dogmatic considerations. Our remarks are intended only to show that theological interpretation, while always useful and even indispensable, does not compel us to abandon the historical reality of Beatrice—on the contrary.

With this we close for the present our study of *figura*. Our purpose was to show how on the basis of its semantic development a word may grow into a historical situation and give rise to structures that will be effective for many centuries. The historical situation that drove St. Paul to preach among the Gentiles developed figural interpretation and prepared it for the influence it was to exert in late antiquity anti the Middle Ages.

NOTES

41. Many allusions may be found in Gilson, *Les idées et les lettres*, esp. pp. 68 ff. and 155 ff. In his article, "Le moyen âge et l'histoire" (in *L'Esprit de la philosophie médiévale*, Paris, 1932) he refers to the figural element in the medieval philosophy of history, but with no great emphasis, since his main concern was to uncover the medieval roots of modern conceptions. Cf. also, for the German religious drama, T. Weber, *Die Praefigurationen in geistlichen Drama Deutschlands*, Marburg Dissertation 1909, and L. Wolff, "*Die Verschmelzung des Dargestellten mit der Gegenwartswirklichkeit im deutschen geistlichen Drama des Mittelalters*," *Deutsche Vierteljahrsschrift für Literaturwissenschaft und Geistesgeschichte*, 7, p. 267 ff. On figural elements in the portrayal of Charlemagne in the *Chanson de Roland*, cf. A. Pauphilet's well-known article in *Romania*, LIX, esp. pp. 183 ff.

42. Of course there are numerous analyses of the fourfold meaning of Scripture, but they do not bring out what strikes me as indispensable. It is natural that medieval theology, while distinctly differentiating the various forms of

allegory (e.g., Petrus Comestor in the prologue to his *Historic scholastics*), should attribute no fundamental importance, but only a kind of technical interest to these distinctions. But even so outstanding a modern theologian as the Dominican Père Mandonnet, who gives an outline of the history of symbolism in his *Dante le Théologien* (Paris, 1935, pp. 163 ff), regards the knowledge of these differentiations as a mere technical instrument for the understanding of texts, and takes no account of the different conceptions of reality involved.

43. By that time of course the foundations of figural interpretation had already been destroyed; even many ecclesiastics no longer understood it. As Emile Mâle tells us (*L'Art religieux du 12ème siècle en France*, 3d ed., 1928, p. 391) Montfaucon interpreted the rows of Old Testament figures at the sides of certain church porches as Merovingian kings. In a letter from Leibniz to Burnett (1696, Gerhardt edition, III, 306) we find the following—"M. Mercurius van Helmont believed that the soul of Jesus Christ was that of Adam and that the new Adam repairing what the first had ruined was the same personage paying his old debt. I think one does well to spare oneself the trouble of refuting such ideas."

44. In speaking of the architect, St. Thomas says *quasi idea* (*Quodlibetales*, IV, 1, 1). Cf. Panofsky, *Idea* (Leipzig, 1924), p. 20 ff. and note, p. 85; cf. also the quotation from Seneca in our note 15.

45. See Zingarelli, *Dante*, 3d ed., 1931, pp. 1029 ff., and the literature cited in the note.

46. Cf. J. Balogh in *Deutsches Dante-Jahrbuch*, 10, 1928, p. 202.

47. Accordingly Dante, *Purg.*, 32, 102. describes *quelle Roma onde Cristo è Romano* ("that Rome whereof Christ is a Roman") as the fulfilled kingdom of God.

48. *Purg.*, 22, 69–73, Temple Classics ed. The fact that in the Middle Ages Virgil often appears among the prophets of Christ has been several times discussed in detail since Comparetti. A certain amount of new material is to be found in the festival volume, *Virgilio nel medio evo*, of the *Studi medievali* (N.S.V., 1932). I should like to make special mention of R. Strecker's *Iam nova progenies caelo dimittitur alto*, p. 167, where a bibliography and some material on figural structure in general may be found; further E. Mâle, *Virgile dans l'art du moyen âge*, p. 325, particularly plate 1; and Luigi Suttina, *L'effigie di Virgilio nella Cattedrale di Zamorra*, p. 342.

49. The words *mi converrebbe essere laudatore di me medesimo* ("it would behove and to be a praiser of myself"), *Vita Nova*, (Temple Classics ed., p. 109) 29, are an allusion to II Cor. 12:1. Cf. Grandgent in *Romania*, 31, 14, and Scherillo's commentary.

50. This is indicated by the title of the book, by his first designation of her as *la gloriosa donna de la mia mente* ("the glorious lady of my mind"), by the name-mysticism, the trinitarian significance of the number nine, by the effects

emanating from her. etc., etc. Sometimes she appears as a *figura Christi*; one need only consider the interpretation of her appearance behind Monna Vanna (24); the events accompanying the vision of her death (23): eclipse, earthquake, the hosannas of the angels; and the effect of her appearance in Purg, 30. Cf. Galahad in the "*Queste del Saint Graal*," Gilson, *Les idées et les lettres*, p. 71.

51. To avoid misunderstandings it should be mentioned here that Dante and his contemporaries termed the figural meaning "allegory," while they referred to what is here called allegory as "ethical" or "tropological" meaning. The reader will surely understand why in this historical study we have stuck to the terminology created and favored by the Church Fathers.

52. He denies that she ever smiles in spite of *Purg.*, 31, 133 ff., and 32, beginning. His remarks on Beatrice may be found in op. cit.. pp. 212 ff.

DAVID QUINT

Epic Tradition and Inferno *IX*

When Dante's itinerary stalls before the gates of Dis, he and Virgil stand at a crossroads where two epic traditions of underworld descent diverge in opposite directions. The Furies misapply the typology of Theseus to the pilgrim; but Dante has not come to deprive the infernal kingdom of one of its denizens, nor will he, as the guardians of Dis demand, retrace his steps back to earth by the way he came. Passing through and beyond the underworld, Dante's journey rather imitates the descent of Aeneas. For both protagonists the endpoint of death turns into a point on a continuum: Aeneas moves on to his divinely ordained mission in Roman history, Dante to salvation and the vision of God. But in Canto ix the appropriation and parodistic inversion of the classical texts of Lucan and Statius point towards a second Stygian literary topos: the raising up of dead souls.

Virgil informs Dante of a prior descent from Limbo to lower Hell.

> Ver è ch'altra fïata qua giù fui,
> congiurato da quella Eritón cruda
> che richiamava l'ombre a' corpi sui.
>   Di poco era di me la carna nuda,
> ch'ella mi fece intrar dentr'a quel muro,
>   per trarne un spirto del cerchio di Giuda.
>   Quell'e 'l più basso loco e 'l più oscuro
> e 'l più lontan dal ciel che tutto gira:

From *Dante Studies* 153. © 1975 by the Dante Society of America.

ben so 'l cammin; però ti fa sicuro.

$$(22–30)^1$$

Shortly after his death but before the Crucifixion, Virgil had been conjured by Erichtho, the Thessalian sorceress of Lucan's *Pharsalia*, with instructions to draw forth a spirit from the circle of traitors. His statement, accounting for his knowledge of infernal geography, recalls the moment in *Aeneid* vi, 564–565, when the Sibyl claims a similar expertise. But if the passage reasserts the Dante–Aeneas analogy, it simultaneously suggests its inversion. Erichtho is a structural opposite to Beatrice. Beatrice summons Virgil up to earth to lead Dante down through Hell. Erichtho sends Virgil to the bottom of Hell to bring a spirit up to earth. This double movement, coming and going, is repeated at v. 82 where the heavenly messenger brushes aside the heavy air of the Stygian swamp; his action imitates Mercury at the opening of Book ii of the *Thebaid* (1–6). But while Dante's messenger descends to Dis, Statius's Mercury is ascending, bringing the soul of Laius beside him to earth; the souls in Hades speculate whether Laius has been called to earth by a witch of Thessaly (ii, 21–22). Dante quotes Statius precisely where Statius alludes to Erichtho, both here and in the description of Tisiphone (*Theb.* i, 103) echoed at v. 41; the glow in Tisiphone's eyes resembles the moon under the witch's spell (*Theb.* i, 104–106). Statius clearly admired the Erichtho episode, for he made it the model for Tiresias's conjuration and prophecy in *Thebaid* iv.

During their demonic invocations, both Erichtho and Tiresias run into temporary opposition from the infernal spirits. The conjurors threaten the recalcitrant shades with higher authority. Erichtho cries out:

> Paretis? an ille
> Compellandus erit, quo numquam terra vocato
> Non concussa tremit, *qui Gorgona cernit apertam*,
> Verberibusque suis trepidam castigat Erinyn
> Indespecta tenet vobis qui Tartara, cuius
> Vos estis superi, Stygias qui peierat undas?[2]
>
> (*Phars.* vi, 744–749, my italics)

and Tiresias:

> novimus et quidquid dici noscique timetis,
> et turbare Hecaten, ni te, Thymbraee, vererer
> et triplicis mundi summum, quem scire nefastum.[3]
>
> (*Theb.* iv, 514–516)

These two texts, cited in the first chapter of the *Genealogia Deorum*, occupy an important place in the history of the literary imagination. Together they form the textual authority for Boccaccio's figure of Demogorgon, the all-powerful creator and master of the gods.

The tradition of Demogorgon, however, predates Boccaccio. The fourth or fifth century *Thebaid* scholiast Placidus Lactantius found in Tiresias's menacing words an allusion to the *demiourgos* of Plato's *Timaeus*.

> iuxta picturam illam veterem, in qua tormenta descripta sunt et ascensio ad deum. dicit autem deum δημιουργός, cuis scire nomen non licet.[4]

Carlo Landi notes the distortions that take place in the Latin translations of δημιουργός in the manuscript tradition of Lactantius's commentary. Citing instances of *demogorgon* and *demogorgona*, Landi plausibly argues for a fusion or confusion of *demiourgos* with the analogous passage in Lucan: "qui Gorgona cernit apertam."[5] Indeed, I have found a reference to a recognizable predecessor of Boccaccio's Demogorgon in the gloss to Erichtho's speech in the twelfth-century commentary on the *Pharsalia* of Arnulfus of Orleans.

> Ille Demogorgon, qui fuit pater Omagionis, Omagion Celii, Celius Saturni, Saturnus Iovis. QUI GORGONA CERNIT APERTAM id est aperte, nec mutatur in lapidem, sed non aperte dicit pro Perseo qui eam vidit nec mutatus fuit, sed non aperte vidit immo per egidem.[6]

This is Demogorgon the divine progenitor as Boccaccio would later describe him. Dante appears to have been aware of this interpretative tradition behind the conjuration passages of Lucan and Statius, particularly of the Demogorgon's ability to withstand the gorgon's glance, from which one half of his composite name derived. The gorgon in question, as Arnulfus makes clear, is Medusa, the supreme barrier halting the pilgrim in Canto ix. The heavenly messenger who arrives to let Dante *into* Dis thus parodies "Demogorgon," invoked to free the conjured shades out of Hades. The messenger descends from above while Lucan's chthonic deity would rise from the primeval depths beneath the underworld. The up and down trajectories converge at the walls of Dis.

By now the pattern of literary allusion in the canto is clear. The two alternatives which the uncertain pilgrim faces outside Dis—to continue his descent or to return to earth—both have precedents in the epic tradition. Dante makes the first correspond to the journey of Aeneas, the second to the conjuration of Erichtho. The heavenly messenger breaks the impasse and decisively reaffirms the Virgilian model. Yet the messenger himself, by his allusive associations with Statius's Mercury and with "Demogorgon," draws attention to the road not taken.

*　*　*

When Dante represents the rejection of one epic model that is implicit in his choice of another, he reverses the history of late Latin epic, where conjuration is, in fact, a conscious poetic substitution for the Virgilian topoi of the underworld descent and the intervention of the divine messenger. These latter episodes in the *Aeneid* provide moments for the poem to interpret itself, to assert the ideology of Roman destiny which gives meaning to the violence of the epic agon. These interpretative moments lie *outside* the human world of the poem and dramatize its claim to an extratextual significance: Anchises predicts the future greatness of his race from the timeless perspective of death, Mercury brings down the pronouncements of the gods.[7] When Lucan and Statius invert Virgil's fictions, they are attacking not only his political ideology but also the authority of such privileged moments: they are attacking ideology itself.

The Erichtho episode, which takes place in the sixth book of what was to be a twelve-book epic, occupies the same position as Aeneas's underworld journey in the *Aeneid*. The reanimated Pompeian soldier evokes the same catalogue of distinguished Roman souls whom Anchises had pointed out in their embryonic state to his son: the Decii, the Gracchi, Scipio, Camillus, Cato the Censor, etc. But there is no joy in their vision of the future: they are weeping for the carnage of the civil wars and the demise of the republic. Moreover, the soldier's prophecy is vague, aside from its threat of punishment to Caesar and promise of reward to Pompey in their respective afterlives. It is tinged with Stoic renunciation: death is the only certainty.[8] The attempt to contact superhuman authority not only fails to arrive at an interpretative statement, but is in itself an act of horrible and most un-Virgilian impiety. Lucan dwells lovingly upon the stomach-turning details of the witch's rite in order to emphasize the monstrosity of the *literary* incarnation of a "divine" voice in the human poetic text. Paradoxically, the *Pharsalia* makes history its subject matter in order to demonstrate the inauthenticity of poetic interpretations of history. The poetic text remains either "disembodied" or "inanimate," its authority self-contained.

In Book II of the *Thebaid*, we have seen that Statius makes explicit the obverse relationship between the descent of the heavenly messenger and the demonic conjuration by conflating the two conventions. Recalling still a third epic topos, the journey to the realm of Sleep, Statius's Mercury descends not to earth but to the underworld in order to raise up the soul of Laius. His mission is not the revelation of meaning but the instigation of further violence.[9] The episode illustrates emblematically the *Thebaid*'s adaptation of the epic machinery of the *Aeneid* to the *Pharsalia*'s climate of demystification. The interrelationship of the three epics derives in large part from their common inspiration in the Roman civil wars.

Civil conflict, with its reciprocal violence and interchangeable victims, poses what René Girard has recently characterized as a crisis of undifferentiation. According to Girard, each contending faction claims divine sanction for its violence in order to distinguish itself from its opposition. Suppressing their human sameness, the sacred becomes the sign of the conqueror over the vanquished and oscillates according to the vicissitudes of battle.[10] With its Aeneas–Augustus analogy, Virgil's mythological poem proposes an ideological interpretation to recent history. The victorious imperial party has the last word: its poet-propagandist discovers in the ascendancy of Augustus the fulfillment of a divine historical plan.[11] When Lucan dramatizes those same events as the spokesman for the lost republican cause, he cannot, of course, change their outcome, but he can at least remove the divine machinery which masks their undifferentiated structure. The Olympic gods of the *Aeneid* recede into the background of the *Pharsalia* and leave the wars to the play of Fortune. Statius's recourse to myth is a return to Virgilian form that only reiterates the insights of the *Pharsalia*. Beginning and ending in fratricide, the Theban cycle is *the* archetypal myth of civil warfare. The gods of the *Thebaid* become figures for that very Violence which indiscriminately consumes the rival factions and refuses to explain its own origin.

*   *   *

The confrontation of epic traditions in *Inferno* IX pits the Virgilian underworld descent and heavenly messenger against the conjuration scenes of Lucan and Statius. The former are conventions by which divine significance enters the poetic universe, while the latter renounce the possibility of such extratextual authority. It is not hard to see why the Christian poet Dante chooses the Virgilian model, for he is assured of the spirit beyond the letter.

Looking at the classical environment of Canto ix, Benvenuto da Imola identifies the heavenly messenger as Mercury.

> nam Mercurius poetice loquendo est nuncius et interpretes Deorum, qui mittitur a superis ad infernos ad executionem omnis divinae voluntatis, sicut patet apud Homerum, Virgilium, Statium, Martianum, et alios multos.[12]

Both Benvenuto and Pietro di Dante assimilate the *verghetta* of verse 89 with the caduceus of the god. The two commentators follow the allegory of the *De Nuptiis Mercurii et Philologiae* and identify Mercury with Eloquence. But they also understand him in his traditional epic role as the angel of mediation. Pietro cites St. Augustine's etymology.

> Et Augustinus 7° de civitate Dei dicit Mercurius *portitorem sermornis Dei*. Et ideo dicitur Mercurium quasi sermo *medius currens*.[13]

The descent of this Christian Mercury is analogous to the "condescension" of Scripture which Beatrice describes in *Paradiso* iv. The revelation of the Word sanctions the *Commedia*'s converse poetic ascent towards reunion with the Word; in the dramatic representation, the heavenly messenger opens the gates of Dis and allows the resumption of the pilgrim's journey. During the frightening impasse which halts the Virgilian descent outside the walls of the infernal city, the "other" tradition of Lucan and Statius is recognized as an inversion of Dante's poetics, a literary alternative which must be confronted and discarded before the pilgrim-poet may proceed.

NOTES

1. I am quoting from the critical text of the Società Dantesca Italiana, *La Commedia secondo l'antica vulgata*, a cura di Giorgio Petrocchi (4 vols.; Milano: Mondadori, 1966–1967).

2. Lucan, *The Civil War* (Loeb Classical Library; Cambridge, Mass.: Harvard University Press and London: William Heinemann Ltd., 1962), p. 358.

3. Statius, *Works* (Loeb Classical Library; Cambridge, Mass.: Harvard University Press and London: William Heinemann Ltd., 1961), Vol. 1, p. 544.

4. Lactantius Placidus, *Commentarios in Statii Thebaida et Commentarium in Achilleida*, ed. R. Jahnke (Leipzig: B.B. Teubner, 1898), p. 288.

5. Landi, *Demogorgone* (Palermo: Casa Editrice Remo Sandron, 1930), p. 17. Boccaccio's Demogorgon had already been deconstructed by Lillius Gregorius Gyraldius in the *Historia de deis gentium* (1548). See the dedicatory letter to Ercole d'Este immediately preceding the table of contents in the *Opera Omnia* (Leyden, 1696), Vol. 1.

6. Arnulfus of Orleans, *Glosule super Lucanum*, ed. Berthe M. Marti, Papers and Monographs of the American Academy in Rome, Vol. 18 (American Academy in Rome, 1958), p. 350.

7. In his admirable study, *The Descent from Heaven* (New Haven, Yale University Press, 1963), Professor Thomas M. Greene has traced the topos of the heavenly messenger through the history of epic. I have built upon Professor Greene's insights when I suggest that Mercury's chthonic function in the *Thebaid* reflects the mediating presence of the conjuration scene in the *Pharsalia*. Professor Greene notes but does not examine the messenger's descent in *Inferno* IX.

8. Cf. vv. 810–811:

Quem tumulum Nili, quem Thybridis adluat unda,
Quaeritur, et ducibus tantum de funere pugna est

In the same vein is Cato's refusal to consult the oracle of Ammon in Book IX, 544–586. On Lucan as an anti-Virgilian poet see A. Guillemin, "L'Inspiration Virgilienne dans la Pharsale," *Revue des études latines*, XXIX (1951), pp. 214–227, esp. 222–223.

9. Greene, *Op. cit.*, pp. 100–103.

10. René Girard, *La Violence et le sacré* (Paris: Bernard Grasset, 1972). See especially chapter VI, "Du désir mimétique au double monstrueux," pp. 201–234.

11. On the relationship of the fictions of the *Aeneid* to the events of Roman history, see W. A. Camps, *An Introduction to Virgil's Aeneid* (London: Oxford University Press, 1969), pp. 95–104, 137–143.

12. Benvenuto Rambaldi da Imola, *Commentum super Dantis Aldigherij Comoediam*, ed. J. P. Lacaita (Firenze: G. Barbèra, 1887), Vol. I, p. 321.

13. Pietro di Dante, ... *Commentarium*, ed. V. Nannucci (Firenze: Guglielmo Piatti, 1845), p. 126.

JOHN FRECCERO

Manfred's Wounds and the Poetics of the 'Purgatorio'

In the third canto of the *Purgatorio*, one of the excommunicants calls to Dante to ask if the pilgrim recognizes him:

> biondo era e bello e di gentile aspetto
> ma l'un de' cigli un colpo avea diviso.

> (Fair was he and beautiful and of gentle aspect, but one of his brows had been cleft by a blow.)

The mark is not enough to identify him, so that the spirit names himself:

> ... 'Or vedi';
> e mostrommi una piaga a sommo 'l petto.
> Poi sorridendo disse, 'Io son Manfredi,
> nepote di Costanza imperadrice ...'

> ('Look here.' and he showed me a wound at the top of his chest. Then smiling he said, 'I am Manfred, the grandson of the Empress Constance ...')

The episode marks one of the most famous moments of the *Purgatorio*: a generic description of masculine beauty, slightly skewed by rhetorical distortion, is

From *Center and Labyrinth: Essays in Honour of Northrop Frye*. © 1983 by the University of Toronto Press.

interrupted by the adversative 'but' that suffices to mar the ideal with what appears to be an accident of history. That cleft brow helped to make Manfred a romantic hero in the nineteenth century and serves as testimony today of Dante's prodigious power of representation.

At first glance, the representation might appear to be an example of what Erich Auerbach referred to as mimesis, especially since his classic work on the subject began with a chapter entitled 'Odysseus' Scar.' Manfred's wounds are equally unforgettable and perhaps for some of the same reasons, but they serve a deeper purpose than Dante's desire to hold up a mirror to reality. In fact, the wounds are an anomaly in the representation, a flaw that seems to undermine the bases of Dante's fiction: we learn, later on in the *Purgatorio*, that the souls wending their way up the mountain have aerial bodies, fictive replicas of their real bodies and exact reflections of the soul itself. Wounds are inexplicable on such bodies, because they seem to be accidental intrusions into the ideal corporeity of the afterlife. If Manfred's wounds are reminiscent of Odysseus' scar, it cannot be at the level of descriptive detail. Odysseus' scar, Auerbach tells us, is an example of Homeric realism, described by the poet because it is *there*; Manfred's wounds, on the other hand, demand an interpretation. They are *there*, on a body made of thin air, and ought not to be.

The basis for associating the two texts is mythic, rather than mimetic, and becomes clear when we challenge Auerbach's reading of Odysseus' scar. The thesis of Auerbach's essay seems undermined by its title. The purpose of the essay was to reveal 'the need of the Homeric style to leave nothing which it mentions half in darkness and unexternalized.'[1] In the style that 'knows only a foreground, only a uniformly illuminative, uniformly objective present, ... never is there a form left fragmentary or half-illuminated, never a lacuna, never a gap, never a glimpse of unplumbed depths.'[2] Yet Odysseus' scar is itself precisely all of those things: an indelible mark of the past within the present, an opaque sign healed over a hidden depth. The scar is the mark of Odysseus' identity and manhood, or there could be no recognition. In a passage whose significance Auerbach does not discuss, Homer tells us that the hero, when hunting as a boy, was gored in the thigh by a wild boar which he then killed with his lance. Almost seventy lines are devoted to describing the nobility of his lineage and his youthful courage, so that the scar remaining from the hunting accident takes upon itself a meaning never hinted at by Auerbach: it is a sign of Odysseus' coming-of-age, almost a ritual scar, and it identifies him in the eyes of his former nurse, not fortuitously, but rather as the sign at once relating him to his ancestors and distinguishing him from them. In the succession of fathers and sons, Odysseus' scar marks his place precisely, bracketing him between his ancestors and Telemachus, his son, who is about to undergo his own baptism of blood.

At some level, of course, Auerbach knew that the primordial drama of male identity was hidden beneath the apparently innocuous and realistic detail. When he turned for contrast in the same essay to an equally ancient epic in a totally different tradition, he chose the story of Abraham and Isaac, the foundation story for Israel and a foreshadowing of the circumcision. Odysseus' scar is also a kind of circumcision. It bears the same relationship to Adonis' fatal wound (in Northrop Frye's masterful reading of the myth)[3] that circumcision bears to castration. For all of the irreducible differences between the two epics, they are united by a common theme: the rites of violence that have traditionally been used by males to mark their identity and manhood.

Manfred's wounds hide a similar story, for they signify his relationship to his father, yet, by an ironic reversal of earthly values that is one of the functions of Dante's other-worldly perspective, they mark his passage away from patrilinear succession toward the mother. Critics have noticed that Manfred identifies himself only as the grandson of the Empress Constance; in fact, he was the son of Frederick ii Hohenstaufen, known in Dante's day as *Stupor Mundi*.[4] This pointed reticence has been explained in various ways: psychologizing critics have suggested that Manfred, although Frederick's favourite, was a natural son and not the legitimate heir of the mighty emperor. It is indelicate, according to this line of reasoning, for a bastard to name his father. A slightly more sophisticated view, the thematic interpretation, insists that Frederick is in Hell, with the rest of the Epicureans, and thus is erased from the memory of his son. The contrast between Manfred's radiant smile and his ghastly wound serves as a contrast between the vicissitudes of history and the power of grace for the late repentant.

A more interesting thematic reading of the passage involves Dante's own political ideals. Frederick was the founder of the Ghibelline imperial dream, but was by Dante's time totally discredited as a heretic and an excommunicant. The fictive salvation of his son, mortally wounded at the battle of Benevento, might then represent a survival of the Ghibelline ideal, to which Dante clung against all the evidence of his senses. On this reading, Manfred's insistence on Grace, 'mentre che la speranza ha fior del verde,' might then mask a much more specific hope for Dante's own political dream. In the *Purgatorio*, Manfred remembers his daughter, 'la mia buona Costanza,' the honour of Sicily and Aragon, and asks the pilgrim to tell her that he has been saved, in spite of his excommunication. Manfred is therefore bracketed between the two Constances, his grandmother in Paradise and his daughter on earth. The ideal of Empire lives on, but in matrilinear succession, outside the city of man, and reconciled at last to *Mater Ecclesia*. Manfred's message to his daughter repeats, yet transforms, the popular oracle that was said to have kept Germany dreaming imperial ideals for centuries after the death of Frederick ii: 'He lives not; yet he lives.'[5] The body of the father is entombed in porphyry, the monument to imperial aspirations in Palermo or, for that matter, in Paris, but Manfred's bones are scattered to the four winds:

> Or le bagna la pioggia e move il vento
>   di fuor dal regno, quasi lungo 'l Verde,
>   dov' e' le trasmutò a lume spento.

(Now they are drenched by the rain and the wind shifts them *outside of the realm*, along the course of the river Verde, to which the Bishop brought them, with extinguished candles).

The dispersion of Manfred's corpse suggests that, in so far as he is still a hero of a realm, the kingdom is not of this world.

Manfred's wounds are the scars of history, but his smile is a revisionist smile, belying the official versions of his fate. In spite of the fact that he was excommunicated by the Church, Dante places him among the late repentant, who will ultimately reach Paradise. Manfred tells us that the Bishop who had his body disinterred had misread that page in God's book; the implication seems to be that the poet, unlike the Church, has read God's book correctly. Manfred's salvation therefore represents an interpretation of the brute details of history, an allegorical reading of those wounds that belies the horror that they literally imply. As Manfred survived extinction, so Dante's political ideal survives historical contradiction by assimilation into the unity of his vision.

If Manfred's real body is dispersed, then it is clear that his fictive body is a representation, bearing symbolic wounds, diacritical marks slashed across the face of his father. Frederick's beauty won for him the title of *Sol invictus*: the adjectives *biondo, bello e di gentile aspetto* might have been taken from contemporary chronicles describing the Emperor.[6] At the same time, Frederick's *persona* is the mystical body of Empire, the head of state, as we still say, whose heart is the law. The dazzling incongruity of Manfred's smile serves to affirm the triumph of the ideal in spite of the apparently mortal wounds to both the head and heart. Like the scar of Odysseus, the adversative 'ma' serves to affirm sameness with a profound difference—that is to say, the syntax performs the function of ritual scarring. The wounds incurred in his father's name win for him his own: 'Io son Manfredi'—so that the mortal wounds are in fact a baptism, a rebirth into a new order, with what Saint Paul called 'a circumcision of the heart' (Romans 2:2).

For all of the apparently mimetic power of Dante's verses, there can be no doubt that corporeal representation in the poem is self-consciously symbolic. In this respect the *Purgatorio* does not differ greatly from the *Inferno*. The recognition of Manfred has its infernal counterpart in Mohammed among the schismatics, who bares his cloven chest as an emblem of theological schism and is introduced by similar syntax—'vedi com'io mi dilacco.' In the same canto (xxviii), Bertrand de Born's decapitated body suggests the schism in the political order. The clinical horror—Bertrand carrying his head like a lantern—lends horror to the more abstract political enormity. Bertrand is said to have set father against son:

> Perch'io parti' così giunte persone,
>   partito porto il mio cerebro, lasso!

dal suo principio ch'è in questo troncone.
Così s'osserva in me to contrapasso—

(Because I divided persons who were so conjoined I carry my brain
separated from its source in this trunk. Thus is observed in me the
counterpass—).

Applying the same figure, we may say that the marks on Manfred's fictive body
also stand for his relationship to a wounded theological and political order which
he has survived and, in a sense, redeemed.

The representation of Manfred is meant to bear witness of this redemption
within the fiction of Dante's purgatorial journey. His wounds, apparently
accidental, are in fact signs of his identity and distinction. They are like the
marks of *history*, which cannot be accommodated by the abstract mimetic claim
of a one-to-one correspondence between the aerial bodies of the Purgatory and
the souls which produce them. At some level, the disfiguring marks of history
mark the soul as well. Like writing itself, they deface in the name of significance.
Their presence in the *Purgatorio* is at the same time the poet's mark, his
intervention in the fiction that otherwise purports to be an unmediated
representation of the other world. As wounds are inexplicable on an aerial body,
so writing is inexplicable on what is claimed to be an exact representation of an
other-worldly vision. Paradoxically, the text 'mirrors' the other world only by
virtue of its cracks.

Lest the parallel between Manfred's wounds and the text itself seem too
ingenious for a medieval text, it should be pointed out that such an analogy is
implied in what is probably the most famous and most solemn of recognition
scenes. The newly risen Christ shows his wounds to Thomas so that he may
believe what he has *seen*: 'Thomas, because thou hast seen me, thou hast believed:
blessed are they that have not seen, and yet have believed.' Christ's wounds, made
manifest to Thomas, bear witness to the Resurrection. The solemnity of that
moment lends to the representation of Manfred a theological force that serves to
underscore the strength of Dante's Imperial faith.

It is, however, the passage immediately following Thomas' recognition in
the gospel of John that I wish especially to recall in this context. The narrative of
Jesus' works ends with his remark to Thomas and, almost as if to end his work,
John adds these words: 'And many other signs truly did Jesus in the presence of
his disciples, which are not written in this book, but these are written, that ye
might believe that Jesus is the Christ, the Son of God, and that believing, ye
might have life through his name.' The writer of the gospel thereby establishes
a parallel between the wounds of Christ's body and his own text, filled with signs
that demand of the reader the same assent that is demanded of the doubting
Thomas. As Christ's scarred body is *seen* by the disciples, so John's text is *read* by
the faithful. That analogy is operative in Dante's poem. Manfred's wounds,

slashed across a body made of thin air, stand for Dante's own intrusion into the course of history. They are, as it were, writing itself, Dante's own markings introduced across the page of history as testimony of a truth which otherwise might not be perceived. It is this parallelism between the text and the aerial body of the Purgatorio that establishes the fiction of the *Purgatorio*, the vision of the pilgrim translated by the writing of the poet, scars of history erased and assimilated into God's Book, where the Truth is finally conveyed, according to Saint Augustine, without letters and without words.

The analogy between the aerial body and the poem itself is consistently developed throughout the *Purgatorio*. It underlies the apparently gratuitous account that Dante gives us in canto xxv of the formation of the body in the afterlife. The question is how the souls in this circle can speak of nourishment or grow thinner in their askesis when there is no need of food. Virgil answers with generic theories of mimesis and poetic representation: the bodies of the *Purgatorio* are related to real bodies as the torch was related to the life span of Meleager in the eighth book of the *Metamorphoses* or as an image in a mirror is related to what it reflects. This statement of the relation of the aerial bodies to nature-like a mirror or like a lamp—establishes the context as unmistakably aesthetic, with ancient figures for doctrines of poetic inspiration that have become particularly familiar to us since they were studied by M.H. Abrams.[7] If the bodies of the Purgatory are related to nature as either mirror or lamp, then the poem itself is either a mimetic or metaphoric representation of nature. This is as far as Virgil will go in his explanation, asserting that a complete understanding of the process transcends human understanding. He then defers to Statius for a fuller explanation than he can provide.

At this point, Dante enters upon a digression that has been something of a scandal in the history of Dante criticism, not only because of its apparent irrelevance, but also because of its reputed technical aridity. In the midst of six cantos of the Purgatorio that deal more or less explicitly with poetry, Dante now embarks upon what amounts to a lesson in medieval embryology. This occurs when Statius chooses to answer the question about the fictive bodies of the Purgatory with a discussion of the general relationship of body and soul, on earth as well as in the afterlife. As we shall see, the lesson has at least as much to do with poetics as it has with embryology. Like an analogously technical discussion in the Paradiso on the nature of moon spots, this scientific disquisition can be skipped over by the general reader only at the risk of missing something essential about the nature of Dante's poetic theory.

To anticipate somewhat, I should like to suggest that Statius' discussion about conception and reproduction in canto xxv also serves as a gloss on canto xxiv, where the subject is literary creation and conception. More than that, it seems to suggest strongly an analogy between the act of writing and the act of procreation. Dante begins with the clinically obvious and proceeds to explain its metaphysical significance. Sexuality is, for Dante, nature's expression of creativity, rather than the repressed subject matter of literary expression. This is one important sense in which it may be said that art imitates nature. As the soul is inspired in the foetus, so the inspiration of the poet comes from God. The body, however, is the work of parenthood. In the same way, the poetic corpus is sired by the poet, who provides the vehicle for God's message.

Statius begins by telling us how the seed is formed. A small portion of blood is stored and purified in the heart of the male and is eventually transformed into the male seed, which contains within it an informing power, *virtute informativa*, that will gradually mould the blood of the female into a human body, with all of its organs. When this power is released into the female, the two bloods unite and the foetus is formed. The foetus then naturally grows into a vegetative and then into a sensitive soul. As yet, there is no human life at all, strictly speaking; it is not until the brain is completely formed, in about the sixth month of pregnancy, that God directly inspires the intellective soul into the embryo:

> ... sì tosto come al feto
> l'articular del cerebro è perfetto,
> lo motor primo a lui si volge lieto
> *sovra tant' arte di natura, e spira*
> *spirito novo, di vertù repleto,*
> che ciò che-trova attivo quivi, tira
> in sua sustanzia, e fassi un'alma sola,
> che vive e sente e se in sé rigira.

(... as soon as the brain of the foetus is perfectly formed, the prime mover turns joyfully to such a work of nature's art and inspires in it a new spirit, filled with power, so that what it finds active there it draws into its substance and makes of itself a single soul, that grows and feels and reflects upon itself.)

Statius then moves directly to a discussion of the formation of the fictive body in the afterlife. At the moment of death, the soul falls to the shore to which it is destined and there the informing virtue which it possesses irradiates the surrounding air, as a ray of light irradiates moist air to form a rainbow, in order to form its aerial body. The soul imprints, 'suggella,' the surrounding air with its own form and so creates the ghostly body that the pilgrim sees.

Except for a passing reference in Hugh of Saint Victor, there does not seem to be a precedent in specifically Christian thought of the Middle Ages for the belief that the soul could unite with the air in order to form an aerial body, although that demons had such power was a commonplace of popular and learned belief. Neo-Platonic thought might well admit such a possibility, but the Christian emphasis on the indissoluble unity of the human composite and the Aristotelian theory of hylomorphism to which Dante subscribed rule out the possibility that Dante means us to take the fiction seriously as metaphysics.[8] It does not require a great deal of the reader's imagination to see in this fiction a disguised poetic claim. The seal of reality is stamped upon the dreamlike medium of the Purgatory as the seal of the soul is affixed to the wax of the body. Dante's poem seems to make a claim for a kind of mimetic essentialism—realism in the medieval sense of the word.

The 'realistic' quality of the *Purgatorio* is the central theme of this portion of the poem. It has often been remarked that the second realm of the poem is the most lifelike, the most modern part of the vision. Here souls are on the move, on pilgrimage as they were on earth, possessed of a temporality that is measured by the imagination of the pilgrim. His subjectivity is the stage of the action here. Unlike the claim of objective presence in the *Inferno* or the ethereal non-representation of the *Paradiso*, the surrounding world is here filtered through the pilgrim's fantasia, which is itself the power that creates images in the form of dreams, out of thin air. The action of fantasia is exactly analogous to the process of the afterlife as Dante imagines it. The bodies of the Purgatorio are of the same order of reality as the bodies of the imagination, quite literally the 'stuff that dreams are made on.' The pilgrim's initial question about the mode of existence of the bodies here amounts to a question about the relationship of his poem to the real world.

With this hypothesis in mind, Statius' discussion of conception takes upon itself a new dimension of meaning. There are echoes, in Statius' speech, of Dante's doctrine of poetic inspiration contained in the canto immediately preceding this. In canto xxiv, Bonagiunta da Lucca asks the pilgrim if he is the man who drew forth, 'trasse fore,' the new rhymes of the sweet new style. The verb unmistakably suggests childbirth and the adjective *new*, repeated several times, prepares the way for the discussion of the infusion of the intellective soul by God: 'spirito novo, di vertu repleto.' Most interesting, however, is the pilgrim's reply, which for centuries has been taken as Dante's definition of his own art:

> I' mi son un che, quando
> Amor mi spira, noto, e a quel modo
> ch'e' ditta dentro vo significando ...

(As for me, I am one who, when love inspires me, take note, and in the manner that it is written within, I go signifying ...)

The moment of poetic inspiration exactly matches the moment of inspiration of the new soul: 'sovra tant' arte di natura ... spira spirito 'novo.' The work of art is not nature's art but that of the poet, although the source of inspiration, *spirito novo*, is the same. The forcefulness and syntactic isolation of the verb 'noto,' etymologically, 'I mark,' seems to highlight the moment of inscription; given the analogy with procreation, it would seem to correspond with the moment of conception, recalling Jean de Meung's playful references to 'nature's stylus' in the sexual act.[9] Dante's emphasis is however on the unitary source of spiritual inspiration, the soul of the foetus or the spirit of the text. At the same time, the gerund 'vo significando' suggests that literary creation is not a moment but a process, a constant approximation approaching but never quite reaching God's text within as its limit. The construction used in that sense has since been hallowed by literary tradition. When the Romantic Leopardi wrote his own lyric on the subject of literary inspiration, invoking the wind rather than God's spirit, he used a similar construction to describe his own effort: in 'L'Infinito,' the act of writing is rendered 'vo comparando'—'I am comparing'—presumably the present text with Nature's own. For Dante, the gerund depicts the *process* of writing, the askesis that will bring the 'body' of the text closer and closer to the spirit which informs it. The words suggest that the poem, like the pilgrim, is still en route in the *Purgatorio*.

Manfred's wounds constitute the marks that must be expunged in order for history to be brought into conformity with God's will, just as sin must be purged in order for the soul to be made 'puro e disposto a salire alle stelle.' At the same time, the wounds have served a providential purpose, in much the same way that sin can prepare the way for conversion. In this respect, both history and sin are analogues for writing itself. As history *disfigures* the face of Manfred with apparently accidental marks that in fact give him his significance under the aspect of eternity, so writing progressively disfigures the page ('vo significando') in order paradoxically to make it clear. The process of interpretation, like the process of purgation, is an assimilation and a gradual *effacement* of the marks, like melting footprints in the snow: 'così la neve al sol si disigilla.' The phrase from the *Paradiso* signals the ending of the poet's work and the vision of God's Book, 'legato con Amore in un volume, ciò che per il mondo si squaderna.'

Readers of the *Purgatorio* will remember that its central action, for the pilgrim, is the *erasing* of his sins, sins that are at once *wounds* and *letters*. The instrument is not nature's stylus, nor that of the poet, but history's pen. The angel guardian of the Purgatory draws seven letter P's on the forehead of the pilgrim with his sword, as a representation of his history:

> Sette P ne la fronte mi descrisse
>   col punton della spada e 'Fa' che lavi
>   quando se' dentro, queste piaghe' disse.

(He drew seven P's on my forehead with the point of his sword and 'see that when you are within, you wash these wounds,' he said.)

The penitential process for the pilgrim consists in the eradication of wounds inflicted by a sword. We may imagine this also to be the case with Manfred's wound, eternally there in the space of canto iii, but effaced in the process of refinement toward the resurrected body. Later on, Statius describes the whole penitential process in this way: 'Con tal cura conviene e con tai pasti, / che la piaga da sezzo si ricucia.' (With such care and with such a cure will the wound be completely healed.) Underlying these images is the affirmation that the poem we read has its counterpart in Manfred's face.

In God's Book, Manfred's brow is clear. This is implied by a verse that has always presented a certain difficulty for commentators. Speaking of the Bishop who had his body disinterred and thrown into the river, Manfred says that had the pastor realized that Manfred was saved, he would have spared his body. The difficult sentence reads: 'Se 'l pastor di Cosenza ... avesse in Dio ben letta questa faccia,' and the difficulty resides in the translation of the word 'faccia,' which means either 'face' or, as Charles Singleton has translated it, 'page.' 'Had the pastor of Cosenze well *read* that page of God.' Our discussion thus far suggests, however, that one might equally well have translated the word 'faccia' as 'face,' thereby giving more force to the Bishop's misreading and more concreteness to the demonstrative adjective 'questa': 'Had the pastor of Cosenza well read *this face* in God.' God's Book has no marks that are subject to misinterpretation; Manfred's wounds, however, might have been taken as signs of his damnation when read from a purely human perspective, without benefit of that radiant smile.

Finally an additional nuance of meaning can be derived from comparing this passage with what is undoubtedly its source. There is a culminating moment at the end of Book VI of the *Aeneid* when Anchises points out to his son the shadow of a soul who might have been a hero of Rome equal to Marcellus had he not died prematurely. Scholars tell us that he was the adopted son of the Emperor and Octavia is said to have fainted with grief when Virgil first recited his lines. They describe the handsome boy in terms that recall, if only by contrast, the description of Manfred, even to the adversative *sed*, which serves to indicate not a wound, but an enveloping darkness suggestive of premature death:

> A man young, very handsome and clad in shining armour, *but* with face and eyes down cast and little joy on his brow ... What a noble presence he has, *but* the night flits black about his head and shadows him with gloom ... Alas his goodness, alas his ancient honour and right hand invincible in war! ... Ah poor boy! If thou mayest break the grim bar of fate, thou shall be Marcellus. Give me lilies in full hands ...   (*Aeneid* vi.860–85)

The foreboding darkness contrasts with the smile of Manfred in the same way that Virgilian pathos contrasts with the hope of the *Purgatorio*; even the eternity of Rome must bow before the death of this beautiful young man. He too is an emperor's son, but the success of Empire cannot mitigate individual grief. We are left with Anchises' futile funereal gesture.

From Dante's standpoint, of course, this is the Virgilian misreading of death; Manfred's smile, with an imperial dream in shambles, is in a sense a smile at Virgil's expense. It happens that this passage contains the only verse from the *Aeneid* literally quoted, in the original Latin, in the *Divine Comedy*: 'Manibus O date lilia plenis!' It occurs in a very different context, toward the end of the *cantica*, as Beatrice approaches for the first time. The angels sing out for the lilies of the Resurrection and Anchises' funereal gesture is turned into a note of triumph.

This deliberate misreading of Virgil brings me to the final point I want to make concerning the effacement of heterogeneity in Dante's text. I have said that Dante's doctrine of poetic inspiration cannot account for what may be called the 'body' of his text as opposed to its spirit. If the inspiration is claimed to be God-given, the poetic *corpus* is very much Dante's own. To extend the procreative image that Dante has established, we may say that the claim of inspiration does not account for the ancestry of the text, especially for the influence of Virgil, whom Dante refers to as his 'dolcissimo patre' at precisely the moment when he quotes the *Aeneid* verbatim, thereby acknowledging Virgil's part in the genesis of his own poem. Once more, heterogeneity is assimilated by an effacement before our eyes. The foreignness of the Virgilian sentiment here at the top of the mountain, underscored by the foreignness of the original language, is neutralized by the otherwise seamless context; death is transformed into resurrection, leaving behind the distinctive mark of the disappearing father, his text in Latin like a foreign element. Like Manfred's wound, the sign of the father is most in evidence at the moment of the son's triumph and, again like Manfred's wound, it is about to be effaced.

After that quotation from Virgil's text, the pilgrim trembles at the approach of Beatrice and turns to tell Virgil, 'Conosco i segni dell'antica fiamma,'—'I recognize the signs of the ancient flame'—which is, not a direct quotation this time, but a literal translation of Dido's words of foreboding when she first sees Aeneas and recalls her passion for her dead husband while she anticipates the funeral pyre on which she will die: 'Agnosco veteris flammae vestigia' (*Aeneid* IV.23). Dante transforms those words as well, for he uses them to celebrate the return of his beloved and a love stronger than death. He turns to Virgil for support and finds him gone. Calling to him three times, the text evokes the merest allusion to a Virgilian text, the disappearance of Eurydice in the Fourth Georgic: 'Eurydice, Eurydice, Eurydice':

> Ma Virgilio n'avea lasciati scemi
>   di sé, Virgilio dolcissimo patre,
>   Virgilio a cui per mia salute die'mi.

(But Virgil had left us bereft of himself, Virgil sweetest father, Virgil to whom I gave myself for my salvation.)

The calling out to Eurydice is the culmination of Virgilian pathos, lamenting death that is stronger than poetry, as it is stronger than love and even than Rome. Dante's adversative *ma* records the loss, yet transcends it with an affirmation. The progression from direct quotation to direct translation to merest allusion is an effacement, further and further away from the letter of Virgil's text, as Virgil fades away in the dramatic representation to make way for Beatrice. It is at that point, for the first time, that the poet is called by name: 'Dante!' The intrusion of Virgil's words into Dante's text is at that point the mark of poetic maturity.

NOTES

1. Erich Auerbach, *Mimesis*, trans. Willard Trask (Princeton, 1953), 3.

2. Ibid., 4–5.

3. Northrop Frye, *Anatomy of Criticism* (Princeton, 1957), 189.

4. On Frederick, see Ernst Kantorowicz, *Frederick the Second*, trans. W. Trask (Princeton, 1948).

5. Ibid., 421.

6. Ibid., 75.

7. Meyer H. Abrams, *The Mirror and the Lamp* (Cambridge, Mass., 1958).

8. Robert Klein, 'L'Enfers de Marsile Ficin,' in *L'umanesimo e esoterismo*, ed. E. Castelli (Roma, 1955), 264.

9. *Roman de la Rose*, xxxiv.72.

TEODOLINDA BAROLINI

Autocitation and Autobiography

PRELUDE: THE *INFERNO*

In a text that functions largely through a dialectical process of revision and appropriation, the moments in which the poet looks to his own poetic past, through autocitation, acquire a peculiar significance; indeed, in a study of the *Comedy*'s poets, one must begin by examining Dante's retrospective treatment of his poetic self. Nowhere can this palinodic self-analysis that permeates the *Comedy* be more tellingly isolated than in the episodes in which Dante quotes from his earlier literary achievements. In this chapter I propose to approach these episodes as a unified and continuous autobiographical meditation purposely inscribed by the poet into the text of his poem.[1]

There are three autocitations in the *Comedy*: two in the *Purgatorio* and one in the *Paradiso*. All are incipits of *canzoni*, all from love poems. The fact that none occurs in the *Inferno* is relevant to this discussion, representing as it does a deliberate omission. Autocitations appear in the *Comedy* as integral parts of larger deliberations on textuality; the very nature of Dante's infernal commentary on this issue precludes the possibility of quotation, since the mimesis of the first canticle is dedicated to reproducing instances of textual distortion. Textually, the governing principle of the *Inferno* is misuse, which is objectified into a series of misquotations operating at all levels of textual activity, from the religious hymn, in the case of "*Vexilla regis prodeunt itifemi*" (*Inf.* XXXIV, 1), to the secular lyric.

The most explicit evocation of love poetry in the *Inferno* occurs in canto V, where the dense fabric of literary reminiscences, ranging from Vergil and Augustine to Boethius and the vernacular traditions, is intended to sustain an investigation into the status of authoritative texts.[2] The material for Dante's inquiry is provided by Francesca, whose monologue can be conveniently divided into two parts: the first (88–107) contains her celebrated anaphoric invocation of Love; the second (121–138) responds to the pilgrim's question regarding the specifics of her fall. In this latter, more representational phase of her discourse Francesca relies on the authority of the *Lancelot du Lac*; in the first preparatory phase she draws on the tenets of the established amatory code, explaining that love flourishes in the noble heart and that reciprocity in love is obligatory. Here commentators uniformly point not only to the presence of Andreas Capellanus, but also to that of the Italian, specifically stilnovist, lyric.[3]

The first of Francesca's precepts regarding the gird of Love, "Amor, ch'al cor gentil ratio s'apprende" ("Love, which is quickly kindled in the noble heart" [100]), is far from original; Contini points out that it is in fact a conflation of two verses from Guinizzelli's programmatic canzone "Al cor gentil," considered a manifesto for the poets of the *dolce stil novo*.[4] Onto the canzone's incipit, "Al cor gentil rempaira sempre amore" ("Love always returns to dwell in the noble heart"), which formulates a necessary and causal relationship between love and inborn—rather than conferred—nobility, is grafted the first verse of the second stanza, "Foco d'amore in gentil cor s'aprende" ("The fire of love is kindled in the noble heart"), which introduces the element of love as a kindling fire. But for the addition of the adverb "ratto," an intensifier characteristic of Francesca's speech patterns, the result is pure—albeit misquoted—Guinizzelli.

The density of line 100 is further augmented by the fact that it also echoes the first verse of a sonnet from the *Vita Nuova* in which Dante is openly imitating his precursor Guinizzelli. The young poet formulates the relation between love and the gentle heart in terms of identity (they are "one thing"), and ascribes his beliefs to his Bolognese predecessor, the *saggio* of the sonnet's second verse: "Amore e 'l cor gentil sono una cosa, / si come it saggio in suo dittare pone" ("Love and the noble heart are one thing, as the wise man claims in his verse" [*Vita Nuova*, XX]). The love poetry of Dante's early years, as inherited from poets like Guinizzelli, would therefore seem to be implicated in the condemnation of literature that critics have discerned as a primary theme of *Inferno* V. But although Dante is undoubtedly alerting readers of the *Comedy* to the perils inherent in the lyric tradition, *Inferno* V cannot be seen as positing a final damnation of the genre; its practitioners—including Guinizzelli and the poet of the *Vita Nuova*—are firmly lodged in the *Purgatorio*, where they figure in the review of contemporary poetry that runs through the second canticle.

Moreover, Dante is careful to draw immediate attention to the positive as well as negative dimensions of the lyric. To this end he devises the stilnovistic discourse between Vergil and Beatrice in *Inferno* II, a canto imbued with the kind of morally unambiguous lyric atmosphere that characterizes the final cantos of the *Purgatorio*. Indeed, canto II anticipates not only the *Purgatorio's* later positive treatment of the lyric, but also—by contrast—the negative treatment of *Inferno* V. There are a number of intriguing correspondences between the two cantos, correspondences intended, I believe, to proleptically defuse and unmask the values underlying Francesca's discourse. Both cantos are, for instance, unusually verbal. Canto II consists almost entirely of referred speech, from the pilgrim's to that of the heavenly intercessors. Beatrice's speech is mediated through Vergil, who repeats it to Dante, using his "parola ornata" (67) and "parlare onesto" (113).[5] Like Francesca (whose word is as ornate but less honest), Vergil draws on both the lyric and romance registers in his account, thus anticipating her discourse and establishing the stylistic complementarity of the cantos.

Vergil's use of the lyric register is especially apparent in his initial description of Beatrice's arrival, a passage whose stilnovist flavor has been remarked:

> Io era tra color the son sospesi,
>   e donna mi chiamò beata e bella,
>   tal che di comandare io la richiesi.
> Lucevan li occhi suoi più che la stella;
>   e cominciommi a dir soave e piana,
>   con angelica voce, in sua favella

> I was among those who are suspended, and a lady called me, so blessed and so beautiful that I requested her to command me. Her eyes shone more than the stars, and she smoothly and softly began to speak, with angelic voice, in her tongue
>
> (*Inf.* II, 52–57)

The paired adjectives "beata e bella" and "soave e piana" remind us of the synonymic reduplication typical of the early lyric.[6] Her angelic voice and the likening of her eyes to stars are reminiscent of stilnovist developments in the lyric; we think for instance, of Guinizzelli's comparison of his lady to the *stella diana* or morning star.[7] The tone of the passage matches the description of Beatrice; it is "smooth and soft," like the praise sonnets of Dante's high *stil novo* phase, in which he aimed precisely at creating a *stilus planus*.

The presence of the romance register is less explicit in canto II than in canto V, if only because canto II does not contain a protagonist—text like the *Lancelot du Lac*. Instead, the canto's words and actions are superimposed onto a backdrop of romance conventions: Vergil is the chivalrous knight, begging Beatrice to command him; she is the anxious romance heroine, concerned for her lost friend. Indeed, the context of romance relations, with their prerequisite courtly network, helps to explain Beatrice's promise to praise Vergil to her lord, a remark that has puzzled critics because it seems so gratuitous: is Beatrice suggesting that she can alter Vergil's fate?[8] Her words, "Quando sarò dinanzi al segnor mio, / di lo mi loderò sovente a lui" ("When I am before my lord, I will praise you frequently to him" [73–74]), suggest a secular context, in which *il segnor mio* takes on the connotations of a secular lord. Like the repeated commands and "recommendations" that run through the canto, they belong to the courtly register to which we are introduced in line 17, where the description of God as *cortese* implicitly likens Him to a beneficent king. This adjective, etymologically connected to "court," will reoccur twice: in Beatrice's opening words to Vergil ("O anima cortese mantoana" [58]), and again in the pilgrim's words of gratitude to his guide ("e to cortese ch'ubidisti tosto" [134]). *Inferno* II is the only canto in the poem where *cortese* appears more than once, as part of a calculated stress on courtliness; in the *Convivio* Dante explicitly links the word *cortesia* to the notion of the court, saying "Si tolse quello vocabulo da le corti, e fu tanto a dire cortesia quanta use di torte" ("that word was taken from the courts, for to say courtesy was as much as to say the practice of the court" [II, x, 8]). The canto's insistence on courtliness reaches its metaphoric peak when Vergil, toward the end, refers to the domain of the assisting luminaries as the "court of heaven": "tre donne benedette ... ne la torte del cielo" (124–125).

Dante, then, goes to great lengths to create the ambience of a court in *Inferno* II. Whereas the canto's lyric echoes may be accounted for by the poet's desire to introduce Beatrice to the *Comedy* in a stylistic environment consonant with the last text in which she figures prominently, the *Vita Nuova*, the creation of the "court of heaven" is less easily explained. I would suggest that it belongs to an associative network designed with an express purpose: Dante intends us to recall this evocation of a courtly scenario when, a few cantos later, we encounter a similar figurative construct. Francesca too invokes an imagined court in which God is king, also in order to offer her protection to the pilgrim: "se fosse emico il re de l'universo, / noi pregheremmo lui de la tua pace" ("if the king of the universe were a friend, we would pray to him for your peace" [*Inf.* V, 91–92]). This remark is curiously analogous to Beatrice's offer to Vergil, with the difference that Francesca—an exile from the court of heaven—uses a conditional mode that contrasts sharply with Beatrice's self-assured use of the future tense: "di te mi loderò sovente a lui" (*Inf.* II, 74).

Similarly, much of the diction of *Inferno* V can be seen as an inverse reflection of that of *Inferno* II. *Talento* in *Inferno* II refers to Beatrice's desire to save the pilgrim (81); in *Inferno* V it occurs in the definition of the carnal sinners, "che la ragion sommettono al talento" ("who submit reason to desire" [39]). *Disio* and its derivatives in *Inferno* II refer to Beatrice's desire to return to heaven (71), or to the pilgrim's desire to move forward on his journey (136), whereas in *Inferno* V they occur four times and always in the context of physical passion (82, 113, 120, 133). "Eyes" in the second canto are either Beatrice's shining eyes or Beatrice's tearful eyes (55, 116); in the fifth canto they are the medium through which passion is first expressed (130). A lady in *Inferno* II is a "donna di virtù" (76;

cf. also 94, 124); in *Inferno* V she is immediately coupled and—more dangerously—romanticized (in the most literal sense of the word: she becomes a heroine of romance): "le donne antiche e' cavalieri" (71). *Amor*, so over-invoked in canto V (in various forms, we find 13 occurrences), is used in canto II with a deliberately chaste infrequency (only twice). And finally, the first words spoken by Beatrice and Francesca offer an interesting contrast. Francesca's "O animal grazïoso e benigno" (*Inf.* V, 88) syntactically parallels Beatrice's "O anima cortese mantoana" (*Inf.* II, 58); both statements are direct addresses consisting of a vocative preceded by "O," followed by a noun and two adjectives. The similarity underlines the shift from *anima* in one case to *animal* in the other. In a context where the poet has already indicated the difference that changing one letter can make, in reference to Semiramis' legalization of lust ("che *li*bito fé *li*cito in sua legge" "she made lust licit in her law" [*Inf.* V, 56]), the contrast is suggestive of the larger difference between these two ladies and their two "courts."

Dante's analogous treatment of cantos II and V, his drawing in both cantos on the same genres in order to create a similar textual environment, points to an implied comparison; the two "courts" of these cantos illustrate in fact the two possible outcomes for courtly literature. Dante's statement regards especially the lyric, the courtly genre in which he conducted his own early poetic experiments and whose development he traces throughout the *Comedy*. In *Inferno* V the lyric is criticized for its tendency to conceptual banality; its philosophical underpinnings are susceptible to being reduced to the level of Andreas Capellanus' maxims. The same lack of sufficient critical self-awareness that afflicts the genre also afflicts the youthful Dante, whose willingness to defer to a *saggio* finds its precise echo in Francesca's deference to authorities (and, even verbally, in her naming of "'l tuo dottore" in line 123). If misquotation in a broad sense is the issue of this episode, there is nonetheless also a strong implication that these particular texts are unusually capable of misrepresenting themselves, of creating traps for the inattentive reader, and of generating the occasions for their own misquotation and misuse.

Inferno V represents one possible outcome for the love lyric; *Inferno* II points ahead to the other. The general rebirth of the *Purgatorio* does not leave poetry unaffected: "Ma qui la morta poesì resurga" ("But here let dead poetry rise up again" [*Purg.* I, 7]), from the poet's invocation to the Muses at the beginning of the canticle, is emblematic of the renewal that the *Purgatorio* works at all levels of textuality. The redemption of the love lyric, in particular, is signified in the second canto by the verbatim citation of a verse of love poetry, no longer misquoted but faithfully transcribed. The lyric surfaces on the shores of the mountain in much the same condition as the pilgrim, functioning in fact like all other newcomers to this realm: in need of purgation, refinement, but definitely saved.

The love lyric is a major theme of *Purgatorio* II as it is of *Inferno* V; indeed, one could say that *Purgatorio* II stands as a corrective to *Inferno* V, and that

Casella is in this sense a new version of Francesca. "Amorous song," as the lyric is dubbed in *Purgatorio* II, is a key component of both episodes; its reception is in both cases a paradigm for the relation to textuality obtaining in each canticle. Whereas in the *Inferno* tension is generated from the interplay between the "subjective" sinners who view themselves as victims and the "objective" structure (mirrored by the "objective" text) that views them as recipients of justice, in the *Purgatorio* tension results from the dialectic between the souls' conflicting desires, rendered in the purgatorial topos of voyagers who are not sure whether they are more drawn to what lies ahead or to what they leave behind. The dialectic of the *Purgatorio* derives its power from the fact that the sentiments that must be put aside are not, from an earthly perspective, wrong per se; rather, we are dealing here with the highest of earthly loves: love of friends, love of family, love of one's native city and country, love of poetry and poetic masters.

Art, as mankind's supreme collective accomplishment, pervades the *Purgatorio*. Like the worsen who are insistently invoked throughout this canticle, art is the emblem of the *Purgatorio's* fundamental problematic: the transcending of an object of desire that is intrinsically worthy but earthbound and subject to time. All aspects of artistic endeavor are represented and find expression in the Purgatorio: music, the pictorial and plastic arts, poetry. Of these, however, poetry is the most thoroughly explored; this one canticle contains the episodes of Casella, Sordello, Statius, Forese Donati, Bonagiunta da Lucca, Guido Guinizzelli, and Arnaut Daniel, to mention only those episodes that may be categorized by name. Poetry has a central role in the *Purgatorio* because this is the canticle where even poets must rearrange their priorities; by the same token, this is the only one of the three realms where poetry can truly come into its own as a theme. In the *Inferno* it is only valuable in so far as it is exploitable; in the *Paradiso* it is out of place, surpassed.

In the first two cantos of the *Purgatorio* Dante rehearses the canticle's theme of detachment with respect to a woman (Cato's wife, Marcia), a friend (Casella), and the *amoroso canto* that Casella sings. All three inspire a love that is in need of being redirected upward, away from the earthly catalyst. Of particular interest is Casella, the first of many "old friends" in this canticle, and his song, "Amor che ne la mente mi ragiona," which, as the *Comedy's* first autocitation, also establishes Dante as the first lyric poet of the *Purgatorio*. If we look at the three episodes that contain autocitations in the *Comedy*, we notice that they are all linked to encounters with friends: in *Purgatorio* II Casella sings "Amor che ne la mente"; in *Purgatorio* XXIV the recital of "Donne ch'avete intelletto d'amore," although executed by Bonagiunta, is part of the larger episode of Forese Donati; in *Paradiso* VIII "Voi che 'ntendendo il terzo ciel movete" is quoted by Charles Martel. Autocitations, or poetic reminiscences, are thus linked to personal encounters, or biographic reminiscences, so that the literary and literal moments of the poet's life are fused together in a highly suggestive pattern.

In the same way that the personal encounters of the *Comedy* have furnished clues to Dante's actual biography—for instance, by allowing its to date the canzone "Voi che 'ntendendo" with respect to the year in which Charles Martel visited Florence—so the *Comedy*'s autocitations may furnish clues to a more internal poetic biography.[9] The linking of all three self-quotations to episodes that relate to Dante's previous life is a signpost; as those meetings reflect an experiential history, so the autocitations reflect a poetic history. In that they are depositories of a poetic past, deliberately inscribed into a poetic present, the autocitations are markers of a space in the text, a space defined as the relation between their previous existence outside the poem and their new existence within it. Why did Dante choose these specific poems for inclusion in the Comedy? Why did he place them where he did? Such questions face its with authorial decisions whose unraveling yields a definitive autobiography of the poet's lyric past, Dante's final statement regarding the way he wants us to perceive his poetic development, from its origins to the engendering of the great poem.

Textual History

The complexity of the issues raised by the choice of these particular incipits becomes apparent when we consider their provenance: one from the *Vita Nuova* and two from the *Convivio*. Thus, each of the major stages in Dante's poetic development before the *Comedy* is involved. The *Vita Nuova* and the *Convivio* are both texts in which Dante overtly reassesses his previous performance and seeks to revise his audience's perception of his poetic production. Indeed, these texts are both primary examples of Dante's tendencies toward autoexegesis, for the genesis of each can be located in an act of revision.

Dante's quintessential authorial persona first manifests itself in the reflexivity that generates the *Vita Nuova*: circa 1292 to 1294 the poet looks over the lyrics he has already composed, which run the gamut from those in his earliest Guittonian mode of a decade earlier to more recent poems of the most rigorous stilnovist purity, and he chooses some of them to be set in a prose frame. The lyrics thus chosen undergo not only a passive revision in the process of being selected for inclusion, but also an active revision at the hands of the prose narrative, which bends them into a new significance consonant with the poet's "new life." The violations of original intention that occur result in certain narrative reversals; poems written for other ladies in other contexts are now perceived as written for Beatrice. The prose is the chief witness to the author's revised intentions, since through its agency poems composed as isolated love lyrics are forced into a temporal sequence that places them in a predetermined and significant relation to each other. In such a context, "Donne ch'avete intelletto d'amore," for example, is no longer a beautiful canzone that develops the themes of its precursors in some striking ways, but is emblematic of a moment described in the prose: the moment in which the poet finds his own voice and creates the "new style."

This line of reasoning is even more applicable to the Convivio, for whereas the *Vita Nuova* is the result of an implicit revaluation of the *rime*, the *Convivio* finds its pretext in an explicit revaluation of the *donna gentile* sequence of the *Vita Nuova*. In chapter XXXV of the *libello*, after the anniversary of Beatrice's death, Dante sees in a window a "gentile donna giovane e bella molto" who looks pityingly at him. He writes the next two sonnets to her (chaps. XXXV and XXXVI): in both she is characterized by her "pietate," and in the prose of XXXVI he comments that her appearance is reminiscent of Beatrice's, thus linking her to the *gentilissima*. Subsequently, the pendulum begins to swing back to his first love: in chapter XXXVII he rebukes his eyes for taking pleasure in the *donna gentile* in chapter XXXVIII his heart, defending the newcomer, is in litigation with his soul, which represents Beatrice. Beatrice herself then appears to Dante in a "forte imaginazione" in chapter XXXIX, prompting him to regret his temporary inconstancy and to return his thoughts entirely to her. The *donna gentile* episode thus extends from chapter XXXV, when he first sees the new lady, to chapter XXXIX, where he reconverts to Beatrice.

This brief sequence from the *Vita Nuova* has become the subject of much critical speculation because Dante, true to his pattern of autoexegesis, returns to it in the *Convivio*. At the treatise's outset, in the first chapter of Book I, Dante places his new work in relation to its predecessor, explaining that where the *Vita Nuova* was "fervida e passionata," the Convivio will be "temperata e virile" (I, i, 16). He further explains that the treatise will consist of fourteen previously written canzoni which will be expounded according to both their literal and allegorical senses. The first of these canzoni, commented on in Book II, is "Voi che 'ntendendo il terzo ciel movete"; it describes the same struggle between the new love for the *donna gentile* and the old love for Beatrice previously described in the sonnets of the *Vita Nuova*. Indeed, the canzone is essentially an expansion" of the sonnet "Gentil pensero che parla di vui," from *Vita Nuova* XXXVIII, in which the heart defends its new attraction to the disapproving soul. The key difference between the sonnet and the canzone is, of course, that the sonnet is followed by a return to Beatrice, while in the canzone the new love triumphs.

In his commentary to the canzoni of the *Convivio*, Dante begins with the exposition of the literal meaning. Regarding "Voi che 'ntendendo," therefore, he begins with the identity of the new love, who is specifically introduced as the *donna gentile* of the *Vita Nuova*. She is presented, moreover, not in a temporal vacuum but in strict chronological relation to Beatrice, whom she will supplant; we learn that Venus had completed two revolutions after the death of Beatrice when the *donna gentile* first appeared to him: "... quando quella gentile donna, cui feci menzione ne la fine de la *Vita Nuova*, parve primamente, accompagnata d'Amore, a li occhi miei e prese luogo alcuno ne la mia mente" ("when that gentle lady whom I mentioned at the end of the *Vita Nuova* first appeared to my eyes, accompanied by Love, and occupied a place in my mind" [II, i, 1]). Continuing, Dante describes the psychomachia waged within him between the thoughts supporting the *donna gentile* and those supporting Beatrice. This image of mental combat, deriving from *Vita Nuova XXXVIII* where "la battaglia de' pensieri" was the subject of the sonnet "Gentil pensero," is dramatized and escalated in "Voi che 'ntendendo."

The three central stanzas of the canzone take the form of an internalized *tenzone* in which the Beatrician thought is the first to state its case, only to be overcome by the thoughts of the *donna gentile*. Before being vanquished, Beatrice is memorialized in precisely the terms in which she last appears in the *Vita Nuova*. In the *libello*'s final sonnet, "Oltre la spera che più larga gira" (chap. XLI), Dante's thoughts (specifically, his sighs) follow Beatrice beyond the farthest of the circling heavens to the presence of God. The fortunate *sospiro* witnesses Beatrice in splendor:

> Quand'elli è giunto là dove disira,
> vede una donna, che riceve onore,
> e luce sì, che per lo suo splendore
> lo peregrino spirito la mira.

> When he arrives there where he desires, he sees a lady who receives honor, and gives off such light that for her splendor the pilgrim spirit gazes at her.

> (5–8)

In "Voi che 'ntendendo" the Beatrician thought is described as undertaking just such a journey:

> Suol esser vita de lo cor dolente
> un soave penser, che se ne gìa
> molte fiate a' piè del nostro Sire,
>   ove una donna glorïar vedia,
> di cui parlava me sì dolcemente
> che l'anima dicea: 'lo men vo' gire.'

> The life of my sorrowing heart used to he a sweet thought, who would go many times to the feet of our Lord, where he would see a lady in glory of whom he would speak to me so sweetly that my soul would say: "I wish to go to her..."

> (14–19)

Here the celestial vistas are described in better detail; where the *Vita Nuova*'s pilgrim-sigh simply saw the lady in glory, the canzone specifies that the location achieved by the poet's envoy, the "soave penser" of line 15, is "a' piè del nostro Sire" (16). However, this recapitulation and expansion of the *Vita Nuova*'s last sonnet is not the canzone's final statement; "Voi che 'ntendendo" ends not with the pursuit of Beatrice "oltre la spera" but with her defeat, and with an injunction to accept the newcomer as his lady: "e pensa di chiamarla donna, omai!" ("and resolve to call her your lady from now on!" [48]). The narrative overlap between the *Convivio*'s beginning and the *Vita Nuova*'s ending makes the later text's reversal of the former all the more striking.

The transfer of allegiance from Beatrice to the *donna gentile* is complete in the *Convivio*'s next canzone, "Amor che ne la mente mi ragiona," expounded in Book III. This is a song of praise dedicated to the triumphant new lady, not a debate like "Voi che 'ntendendo" but an unqualified celebration. It is interesting that Dante removes Beatrice from his treatise in the course of the prose commentary of Book II, before achieving the victorious stasis of "Amor che ne la mente." In chapter viii of Book II Dante suggests that he deliberately inserts his last mention of Beatrice into a digression on the immortality of the soul, because this lofty topic is an appropriate one with which to commemorate her final appearance: "perchè, di quella [la immortalità de l'anima] ragionando, sarà bello terminare lo parlare di quella viva Beatrice beata" ("it will be beautiful to terminate our speaking; of that living, blessed Beatrice while discussing the immortality of the soul" [II, viii, 71). Although tactfully accomplished, the implication nonetheless remains that there is no place for Beatrice in a text dedicated to another lady: "... quella viva Beatrice beata, de la quale più parlare in questo libro non intendo per proponimento" ("that living blessed Beatrice, of whom I do not propose to speak further in this book" [II, viii, 7]). Shortly after this dismissal Dante completes the literal exposition of "Voi che 'ntendendo" and begins, in chapter xii, to explain the poem's allegorical significance; it is here that we first learn that the *donna gentile* is to be identified with Lady Philosophy.

When, in chapter xii of Book II, Dante finally reveals the true identity of the *donna gentile*, the context is overtly Boethian. He recounts that, finding himself inconsolable after the death of Beatrice, he turned to philosophy as a form of comfort that had revived others in similar straits. Thus, he begins to read Boethius ("e misimi a leggere quello non conosciuto da molti libro di Boezio" "and I began to read that book by Boethius not known to many" [II, xii, 2]) and Cicero's *De Amicitia* ("E udendo ancora che Tullio scritto avea un altro libro ... trattando de l'Amistade" "and hearing further that Tully had written another book ... touching on Friendship" [II, xii, 3]). Although both texts are of great importance to the *Convivio*, Dante's treatise is more explicitly modeled on the *Consolatio Philosophiae*; in fact, in Book I he justifies his first-person confessional narrative by invoking Boethius and Augustine (I, ii, 13–14).[10] If the *Consolatio Philosophiae* influenced Dante's adoption of alternating; prose and verse in the *Vita Nuova*, we should remember that the *Convivio* too is a modified form of *prosimetrum*. Most significantly, Boethius offers Dante, in the topos of the consoling lady, the way out of his impasse with the *donna gentile*.

The critical controversy surrounding the *donna gentile* may be reduced to essentially the following question: are we to believe Dante when he claims that she is Philosophy? Scholars are to be found at all points of the critical spectrum: the realists believe that the *donna gentile* is real (or conceived as real) in the *Vita Nuova* and that all the poems written about her, including "Voi che 'ntendendo" and "Amor che ne la mente," were originally composed with a real woman in mind; the allegorists believe that the *donna gentile* was always a symbol of philosophy, even in the *Vita Nuova*, and that all poems about her, including "Voi che 'ntendendo" and "Amor che ne la mente," were originally composed with allegorical intentions.[11] Perhaps the single most authoritative position on this issue has been Barbi's, endorsed by Pernicone in his commentary to the *Rime* as well as by Foster and Boyde in theirs; Barbi argues for a middle course, claiming that the original *donna gentile* of the *Vita Nuova* was indeed conceived as flesh and blood, but that, by the time Dante came to write the later poems in the sequence devoted to her, he had already come under the sway of Lady Philosophy.[12] With regard to "Voi che 'ntendendo" and "Amor che ne la mente," therefore, he suggests that we accept the statements of the *Convivio*, reading them as allegorical lyrics composed for philosophy.

Barbi's thesis is doubtless correct at least with regard to the *Vita Nuova*; an impartial reader of that text would be hard pressed to make a case for the *donna gentile* as Lady Philosophy.[13] The *Vita Nuova* does not admit the type of personification allegory employed by Dante in the *Convivio*, where he refers to it as the allegorical mode used by the poets (II, i, 4); instead the *libello* adumbrates, perhaps unwittingly, the figural allegory of the *Comedy*, in which a literal reality is revealed to be miraculous.[14] The historical level—i.e. Beatrice exists in the *Vita Nuova*; the poet's task is to discover that she is a signifier, that she has come "from heaven to earth to show forth a miracle," that she is the number nine. Once he has discerned her significance, he must hold fast to his knowledge without the assistance of her presence, a presence from which he is weaned gradually through the revoking of her greeting. Like Christ, whose analogue she is, she makes the invisible visible; after her death the poet assumes this responsibility for himself. It is in this context, as a lapse into an opaque nonsignifying but visible and literal reality, that the *donna gentile* episode fits into the *Vita Nuova*. As an alternative to Beatrice, the *donna gentile* must possess an equally historical identity.

Dante's concern regarding the public repercussions of his inconstancy is already evident in the *Vita Nuova*, where he worries that the *donna gentile* episode may continue to reflect negatively on him even after his return to Beatrice, and says that the sonnet of chapter XXXIX is intended to lay the matter to rest once and for all.[15] In the *Convivio* this concern for his reputation and the impulse to present the *donna gentile* episode in a less derogatory light are recurrent: from the start of the treatise, Dante treats the *Vita Nuova* as a product of his youth whose evidence, it may he inferred, is suspect; moreover, his insistence that he does not

wish to detract from the *Vita Nuova*, but only to promote the *Convivio*, does little
to enhance the credibility of the earlier work. He openly states his fear that the
content of the canzoni will brand him as one who passes lightly from one passion
to the next: "Temo la infamia di tanta passione avere seguita, quanta concepe chi
legge le sopra nominate canzoni in me avere segnoreggiata" ("I fear the infamy
of having yielded to and having been conquered by such passion, as will be
conceived by him who reads the above mentioned canzoni" [l, ii, 16]); he believes
that the treatise will restore his integrity by revealing that the motive force
behind the canzoni is "non passione ma vertù" ("not passion but virtue" [1, ii,
16]). It seems noteworthy that such sentiments are consistently followed, in the
Convivio, by an appeal to allegory; to show that the canzoni deal not with passion
but with virtue he must uncover their true—allegorical—significance: "Intendo
anche mostrare la vera sentenza di quelle, che per alcuno vedere non si può s'io
non la conto, perchè è nascosa sotto figura d'allegoria ..." ("I intend also to show
their true meaning, which no one will see if I do not explain it, since it is hidden
under the figure of allegory" [1, ii, 17]).

The *Convivio* owes its existence to a convergence of new interests,
concentrated primarily in the areas of classical culture and philosophy. The
countless citations from philosophical and religious authors, the opening
sentence under the sign of Aristotle, the new prominence of classical poets—all
testify to the extent of Dante's development away from the primarily vernacular
and courtly world of his earlier texts. To this philosophical inclination, we may
add an interest in the formal properties of allegory which overtakes Dante at this
stage in his career; it is not fortuitous that *Convivio* II, i contains Dante's only
discussion of the four modes of allegory outside of the Epistle to Cangrande, not
that he should use the treatise to formulate his distinction between the allegory
of poets and the allegory of theologians. Dante is, moreover, consistent in his
application of the allegory of poets throughout the *Convivio*, from his Fulgentian
reading of the *Aeneid* to his interpretation of his own poems. Indeed, "Voi che
'ntendendo," whether or not originally written as allegory, stands as Dante's first
non-imitative allegorical work.[16] Finally, a third factor to be considered in the
genesis of the *Convivio* is the urge, demonstrated by Dante throughout his career,
to reconcile his narratives. These three factors—an interest in philosophy and in
allegory combined with a pattern of self-correction—add up to the solution of
the *Convivio*: the *donna gentile* as Lady Philosophy.

The *Convivio*'s position along the itinerary of Dante's development is an
ambivalent one. In its essential historicity, its insistence on a sign-bearing reality,
the *Vita Nuova* is the *Comedy*'s truer precursor. The promise of a new text for a
new lady with which the *Vita Nuova* ends ("io spero di dicer di lei quello che mai
non fue detto d'alcuna" "I hope to say of her that which has never been said of
another" [XLII, 2]) is a promise fulfilled only by the *Comedy*. On the other hand,
although the *Convivio* cannot claim newness (both personification allegory and
Lady Philosophy have long and venerable histories), the fact remains that the

Beatrice of the *Comedy* is in many ways a synthesis of the *Vita Nuova*'s heroine with the *Convivio*'s. Thus, certain descriptions of Lady Philosophy, "la sposa de lo Imperadore del cielo" ("the bride of the Emperor of heaven" [III, xii, 14]), prepare us for the Beatrice of Paradise, "O amanza del primo amante, o diva" ("O beloved of the first lover, o divine one" [*Par.* IV, 118]). In fact, the *Comedy* as a whole cannot be imagined without the prior existence of the *Convivio*; not only does the treatise rehearse the poem's philosophical, linguistic, and political ideas, but it is also the first text to articulate fully the *Comedy*'s indispensable supporting metaphors of pilgrimage and voyage.[17]

Even in its dependence on the allegory of poets, the *Convivio* represents a detour that is simultaneously an essential forward step in Dante's poetic journey. From the love poems of the *Vita Nuova*, Dante passes to the allegorized love poems of *Convivio* II and III; here the allegory permits him to add a moral dimension he considers lacking in love poetry, to show that the canzoni treat "non passione ma vertù." This progression toward an overt moral content continues; the fourth and last book of the *Convivio* glosses a canzone, "Le dolci rime d'amor ch'i solia," which no longer acquires an allegorical commentary because it is a straightforward moral discussion of the nature of true nobility. Because the canzone's ethical concerns are not hidden under a "beautiful" (i.e. amorous) exterior, allegory is not required to decipher its "vera sentenza." Book IV is an indication of the direction in which Dante was moving: "Le dolci rime" is but one of a number of moral poems that cap Dante's lyric career, poems like "Poscia ch'Amor" on the chivalric virtue *leggiadria* and "Doglia mi reca" on avarice. By mirroring the social and ethical concerns of the contemporaneous prose treatises, these late lyrics are an important part of Dante's preparation for the *Comedy*.

The essential fact, then, regarding the *Convivio*'s first two canzoni, is that they eventually receive an allegorical dress. Although this fact is finally more significant than the question of Dante's original intentions, the basic arguments on either side of the debate should be noted. There are cogent reasons for questioning Dante's retroactive assertions regarding the two canzoni: first, they belong stylistically, like the *Vita Nuova* sonnets to which they are thematic sequels, to the climax of Dante's *stil novo* period, i.e. they are written in a style appropriate for love poetry. Second, they repeat the same erotic hyperbole that had heretofore been addressed to Beatrice and they function admirably as love poems, an assertion that Dante himself corroborates by dedicating lengthy glosses to their literal senses and expressing concern lest they tarnish his reputation. Dante's very preoccupation with disjoining the *Convivio* from the *Vita Nuova* strengthens one's impression that he was casting about for a way to change his image, and that he found it in allegory.[18]

On the other hand, true cannot categorically discount the allegorical potential harbored by the texts of the canzoni themselves. In the case of "Voi che 'ntendendo," allegorists point especially to the *congedo*, where the poet alludes to the difficulty of his poets and distinguishes between its abstruse content and beautiful form. Also interesting is the characterization of the new lady as "saggia e cortese ne la sua grandezza" ("wise and courteous in her greatness" [47]); it has been noted that Beatrice is never called *grande*, and that *grandezza* does not belong to the lexicon of the conventional love lyric." Regarding "Amor che ne la mente," the pro-allegory arguments are based on the contention that certain verses go beyond the domain of erotic hyperbole and cannot designate a real woman, no matter how miraculous. The verses most often singled out are those in which the poet paraphrases or translates passages from Scripture referring to Sapientia: for instance, "però fu tal da etterno ordinata" ("for this she was established from eternity" [54]) echoes Sapientia's words about herself, "ab aeterno ordinata sum," from Proverbs viii, 23.[20]

"Voi che 'ntendendo" and "Amor che ne la mente" are also noteworthy for their textual situation prior to the *Convivio*. They belong to an interlocking sequence of lyrics, which consists, besides the two canzoni, of a *ballata*, "Voi che savete ragionar d'Amore," and two sonnets: "Parole mie che per lo mondo siete" and "O dolci rime che parlando andate." "Voi che 'ntendendo" initiates the series by announcing the sovereignty of a new lady, whom, in the *ballata* "Voi che savete," the poet renounces because of her cruelty. This renunciation is then retracted in the *congedo* of "Amor che ne la mente," where the poet asserts that the *ballata* (referred to as the "sorella" of the canzone) is mistaken in its harsh judgment:

> Canzone, e' par che tu parli contraro
> al dir d'una sorella che tu hai;
> chè questa donna, che tanto umil fai,
> ella la chiama fera e disdegnosa.

> Canzone, it appears that you speak contrary to the words of one of your sisters, because this lady, whom you consider so humble, she calls harsh and disdainful.

(73–76)

This first cycle of contradiction and resolution is then followed by a second; in the sonnet "Parole mie" Dante again repudiates the new lady. The opening quatrain of this sonnet is interesting because it specifically names "Voi che 'ntendendo" as the starting point of this spasmodic textual love affair:

> Parole mie che per lo mondo siete,
> voi che nasceste poi ch'io cominciai
> a dir per quella donna in cui errai:
> 'Voi che 'ntendendo il terzo ciel movete',

> andatevene a lei ...

Words of mine who are throughout the world, you who were born when I began to write for that lady in whom I erred "Voi che 'ntendendo il terzo ciel movete," go to her ...

(1–5)

This sonnet is in turn retracted in the following sonnet, "O dolci rime," where the poet denies "Parole mie" and recommits himself to the service of his new love.

The two complete cycles of renunciation and recommitment described by these poems are ultimately resolved in the first stanza of the canzone "Le dolci rime," which effectively brings this series to a close. Here too the poet refers to the hardness of the lady, not as a motive for renouncing her but as an explanation for his shift to explicit didacticism; her coldness has prompted him to temporarily put aside love poetry for the brisker pleasures of polemical verse. In the *Convivio* gloss, Dante explains this statement in terms of the allegory of Lady Philosophy, saying that he had not been able to penetrate certain metaphysical problems and had therefore turned to the more accessible ethical issue of *gentilezza*. The opening of "Le dolci rime" is thus the final scene in a drama that extends from the episode of the *Vita Nuova* to Book IV of the *Convivio*, from the pale and pitying countenance of the *libello* to the social concerns of the treatise. This series of poems, linked by a complex system of palinodic recalls and further related by the adoption of genetic terminology ("sorella" in "Amor che ne la mente" [741; "vostre antiche sore" in "Parole mie" [11]; "nostro frate" in "O dolci rime" 141), testifies to the textual importance of the *donna gentile* and to her resilience as an imaginative construct.

Due to the circumstantial nature of most of the evidence, the debate over the canzoni of the *Convivio* is not likely to be resolved. For our purposes, however, the issue of Dante's original intentions vis-à-vis the canzoni is not crucial. From the perspective of the *Comedy* and Dante's overall development, the significant fact is that he did, at a certain point in his career, choose to read (or write) selected love poems allegorically. In so doing, he effects a transition from one stage of his career to the next, moving from poems that function only as love poems to poems that function only as doctrine. The allegorized lyrics of the *Convivio* mark a precise moment in Dante's development in that they mediate between the exclusively erotic and the exclusively moral, thereby pointing to the eventual fusion of the affective with the intellective that will characterize the *Comedy*.

Dante's poetic career achieves such absolute retrospective coherence—a coherence whose emblem is the proleptic ending of the *Vita Nuova*—that we are perhaps tempted to endow his early poetic shifts with too much teleological significance. Nonetheless, if the *Comedy* returns to Beatrice and to the *Vita Nuova* for its point of departure, resuming in fact where the final sonnet of the *libello* leaves off, the departure itself would not be conceivable without the mediating experience of the *Convivio* and the poems to Lady Philosophy. Thus, although retrospectively all the texts written before the *Comedy* and after the *Vita Nuova* could be similarly classified as mistaken but necessary, the *Convivio* is in this respect first among equals: it is the most necessary of the erring prerequisites for the *Comedy*. For, unlike the *De Vulgari Eloquentia* and the *Monarchia*, which address themselves (albeit sweepingly) to single issues, the *Convivio* knows no limits; it sets itself the *Comedy*'s task, and fails.

In one of the sonnets in which he temporarily renounces the *donna gentile*, Dante calls her "quella donna in cui errai." Although "errai" is variously translated as "I erred," "I suffered," "I was deceived," *errare* conserves its primary meaning of "to wander," hence "to stray."[21] This use of *errare* with respect to a poetic mistake reinforces our sense of a textual *selva oscura*, a poetic wandering which only from the providential perspective of the *Comedy* could be retrospectively arranged as a *diritta via*. From this point of view, the strange shifts and turnabouts of the *donna gentile* poems begin to fall into place as signs of textual stress, external indicators of a profound uneasiness. Indeed, Dante's restlessness during this period is confirmed by his irresolution; the unfinished status of two major works from these middle years, the *Convivio* and the *Dc Vulgari Eloquentia*, indicates his recognition of being textually on the wrong path. And, of course, from the perspective of the *Comedy*, the substitution of another for Beatrice would constitute an unparalleled failure; for the later Dante any lady who is not Beatrice is "quella donna in cui errai," as any poetic path not directed toward her is, by definition, a false one.

The issues raised in the above discussion are all implicit in the *Comedy*'s autocitations. Thus, a problem facing decipherers of *Purgatorio* II is whether Dante intends us to view "Amor che ne la mente" as an allegorical poem. Two points should be borne in mind: (1) the central fact regarding the canzoni of the *Convivio* is that they are not dedicated to Beatrice; (2) the poet who places these incipits in the *Comedy* surely expects us to know that they have a history of being singled out. As "Donne ch'avete" was selected for the *Vita Nuova*, so "Voi che 'ntendendo" and "Amor che ne la mente" were placed in the *Convivio*. We may reasonably believe, therefore, that Dante intends us to read these incipits in the light of their previous histories; indeed, it seems not unlikely that he chose these poems precisely for the archeological resonance they afford.

"AMOR CHE NE LA MENTE MI RAGIONA"

The autocitation of *Purgatorio* II has received considerable attention of the kind we are here concerned with; Casella's song has been studied in the context of the episode and in the light of its past associations.[22] The canto has also generated a great deal of speculation regarding such issues as the reasons for Casella's delay on the banks of the Tiber, his identity, and whether a "doctrinal" song like "Amor che ne la mente" may be sung—this despite the fact that in *Purgatorio* II it is sung. Marti answers this last question by drawing on musicological data which shows that the canzone form was still set to music in Dante's time; he also points out that Casella would in any case have few qualms about singing "Amor che ne la mente," since he would be unlikely to consider it a doctrinal poem.[23] Indeed, the poem makes its appearance in canto II in two guises. Vis-à-vis Casella, a musician who died before the composition of the *Convivio* and whose sphere of interest seems to have been far removed from that work's concern with transforming eros into ethos, the canzone "Amor che ne la mente" functions according to its literal sense in the *Convivio* gloss, as a love poem. Thus Casella, who is unacquainted with the Convivio, sings the canzone in response to a specific request from the pilgrim for an "antoroso canto":

> E io: "Se nuova legge non ti toglie
>   memoria o uso a l'amoroso canto
>   che mi solea quetar tutte mie voglie,
> di ciò ti piaccia consolare alquanto
>   l'anima mia, che, con la sua persona
>   venendo qui, è affannata tanto!"
> '*Amor che ne la mente mi ragiona*'
>   cominciò elli allor sì dolcemente,
>   che la dolcezza ancor dentro mi suona.[24]

> And I: "If a new law does not take from you memory or practice of the amorous soul; which used to quiet all of my desires, with this let it please you to console my soul somewhat, which coming here with its body is so wearied!" "Amor che ne la mente mi ragiona" he began then so sweetly, that the sweetness still rings inside of me.
>
> (*Purg.* II, 106–114)

The emphatic presence of "dolcemente" and "dolcezza" in lines 113–114 further underscores the status of "Amor che ne la mente" as a love lyric, since, from the canzone "Le dolci rime d'amor" to the discourses of *Purgatorio* XXIV and XXVI, "sweetness" is considered by Dante to be the external sign and stylistic prerequisite of love poetry as a genre. The inclusion of the code word *dolce* thus confirms that Casella has complied with the pilgrim's request; he sings what he presumes to be nothing more than a love song.

   This stress on the love lyric serves to place *Purgatorio* II in direct contrast to *Inferno* V, opposing the present verbatim citation of the *amoroso canto* to its former misquotation. A number of textual correspondences—the simile of the doves with which *Purgatorio* II ends, the use of expressions that echo *Inferno* V ("persona" for "body" in line 110 is a Francescaism; "affannata" in line 111 recalls "O anime affannate"), and especially the reference to the love lyric as "that which used to quiet all my desires" (108)—evoke the lovers of *Inferno* V and put them into purgatorial perspective. As—erotically—fulfillment of desire at the level of canto V is a narcissistic illusion ("lust") that leads to the *bufera infernal*, so—textually—love poetry at the level of canto V lacks the upward momentum that will redeem its physical point of departure. With respect to Dante's poetic autobiography, *Inferno* V represents a stage in which the poet operates entirely within the confines of a tradition and its authorities, a stage of nonexploratory stasis in which desire is prematurely satisfied.

If desire in the *Inferno* is eternally misplaced, in the *Purgatorio* it functions dialectically as both the goad that keeps the souls moving upward and the source of the nostalgia that temporarily slows them down. *Purgatorio* II is a paradigm for the rest of the canticle in this respect, dramatizing both these aspects of purgatorial desire in the lull created by the song and Cato's subsequent rebuke. Whereas formerly scholars tended to understand the idyllic qualities of the interlude with Casella, effectively ending their readings with the poet's strong endorsement in line 114 (where he says that the song's sweetness still reverberates within him), recently they have stressed Cato's rebuke as a correction—and indeed condemnation—of previous events. Thus, Hollander judges Casella's song severely, as a secular poison in contrast to the canto's other song, the Psalm "In exitu Isräel de Aegypto."[25] Freccero, on the other hand, views the episode in a more positive light, claiming that "The 'Amore' celebrated here marks an advance over the 'Amore' of Francesca's verses in the same treasure that the *Convivio* marks an advance over the *Vita Nuova*."[26] These views should be integrated as two facets of the same problematic within the dialectical structure of the canto: the quotation of "Amor che ne la mente" does indeed mark an advance over the misquotation of *Inferno* V; Cato's rebuke simultaneously suggests that it too is in need of correction.

The target of the criticism that Dante levels at an earlier self in *Inferno* V, and that he to some extent revokes or palliates in *Purgatorio* II, cannot be simply the *Vita Nuova*; rather, we must remember that the *Vita Nuova* encompasses both the experiments of a poet overly subjected to his models and the moment in which he frees himself from them. "Amor che ne la mente mi ragiona" marks an advance over "Amor, ch'al cor gentil ratto s'apprende" in the same way that submission to Lady Philosophy implies forsaking the physical eros of the tradition ("ch'al cor s'apprende") for the rationally propelled eros of the *Comedy* ("che ne la mente mi ragiona"). Moreover, the textual misuse that characterizes *Inferno* V is no longer present in *Purgatorio* II, where it is deflected not only by Cato but by the pilgrim himself; line 108, "che mi *solea* quetar tutte mie voglie," indicates—both in its use of the past tense and in its echo of another distancing verse, "Le dolci rime d'amor ch'i' *solia* / cercar" (italics mine)—that he recognizes the limits of love poetry.

On the other hand, there is no doubt that a correction of "Amor che ne la mente" is implied by Cato's rebuke. On the literal level—Casella's level—the rebuke addresses the episode as a whole, and includes the vain attempt to re-create the ties of friendship in the same form in which they existed on earth (emblematized in the thrice-failed attempt to embrace), as well as the temporary succumbing to the blandishments of love poetry. Appearances by Cato frame the meeting with Casella, offering proleptic as well as retrospective corrections. Indeed, Casella's beautifully nostalgic projection of his love for Dante from the earthly past to the purgatorial present—"Così com' io t'amai / nel mortal corpo, così t'amo sciolta" ("As I loved you in the mortal body, so do I love you freed from it" [88–89])—is undermined by Cato even before it is spoken. In the preceding canto, Cato repudiates Vergil's all too human attempt to win favor by mentioning his wife, "Marzia tua, he 'n vista ancor ti priega, / o santo petto, che per tua la tegni" ("your Marcia, who in her look still prays you, o sainted breast, to hold her for your own" [I, 79–80]). As in his reply to Vergil Cato rejects all earthly ties to his wife, placing her firmly in the past definite ("Marzïa piacque tanto a li occhi miei / mentre ch'i' fu' di là" "Marcia so pleased my eyes while I was over there" [85–86]), so later he reminds Dante and Casella that the earthly ties of friendship are less important than the process of purgation awaiting them.

Although Casella views the canzone he sings as a simple love song, we who have read the *Convivio* are obliged to take its allegorical significance into consideration as well. A textual signpost noticed by critics is the pilgrim's use of the verb *consolare* in his request to Casella: "di ciò ti piaccia consolare alquanto / l'anima mia ..." (109–110).[27] Echoing as it does Boethius' title, *consolare* is a verb that figures prominently in the *Convivio* chapter where Dante announces the true identity of the *donna gentile*. Given its connection to Boethius and Lady Philosophy, it may be profitable to briefly consider the history of this word in the *Vita Nuova* and *Convivio*.

Consolare first occurs in the prose of *Vita Nuova* XXXVIII (and in the accompanying sonnet "Lentil pensero") where it refers negatively to the thought of the *donna gentile*: "Deo, che pensero è questo, che in così vile modo vuole consolare me e non mi lascia quasi altro pensare?" ("God, what thought is this, which in so vile a way wants to console me and almost does not let me think of anything else?" [XXXVIII, 2]). If we were to take *consolare* as the sign of Boethius, its presence here would support the notion that the *donna gentile* is Philosophy as far back as the *Vita Nuova*. But the next appearance of *consolare* demonstrates that originally Dante did not always connect the word with Philosophy; he uses it in "Voi che 'ntendendo" to refer not to the thought of the *donna gentile* as one would expect, but to the consoling thought of Beatrice ("questo piatoso the m'ha consolata" of line 32 is the thought that used to go, as in "Oltre la spera," to view Beatrice in heaven). Thus, at a purely textual level *consolare* does not necessarily signify Philosophy and does not necessarily involve Boethius.[28] It is only in the allegorical gloss to "Voi che 'ntendendo" that Dante for the first time deliberately links the notion of consolation to Philosophy. In *Convivio* II, xii, where *consolare* is repeated in various forms six times ("consolare," "sconsolato," "consolarsi," "consolato," "consolazione," "consolarme"), there is no trace of the negative valence the word bore in *Vita Nuova* XXXVIII. There, in the context of Beatrice's victory, the consoling thought of the *donna gentile* is "vile"; here, in the context of the *donna gentile*'s victory, consolation is ennobled by being presented in Boethian terms.

By the time, then, that we reach "di ciò ti piaccia consolare alquanto / l'anima mia" in *Purgatorio* II, *consolare* has overtly Boethian associations. It also carries with it a history of signifying (with one exception) consolation from an incorrect source, whether the source be labeled the *donna gentile* or Lady Philosophy. As a canzone devoted to the wrong lady, "Amor che ne la mente" is corrected in the *Comedy*: first, in *Purgatorio* II, by Cato's rebuke; then, within the larger context of the autocitations, by being placed below "Donne ch'avete." The canzone from the *Vita Nuova* is located above the canzone from the *Convivio* in order to demonstrate that—chronology notwithstanding—the praise song for Beatrice must be ranked spiritually and poetically above the praise song for Lady Philosophy. In terms of his inner poetic itinerary as reconstructed in the *Comedy*, Dante views the earlier canzone as an advance over the later one.

This point is further conveyed through a consideration of the form and structure of "Amor che ne la mente." It has frequently been noted that "Amor che ne la mente" is closely modeled on "Donne ch'avete." It contains the same number of stanzas (five) and is organized on the same principle: in both an introductory stanza is followed by a graduated series of stanzas dedicated to praising various aspects of the lady (general praise in the second stanza, praise of her soul in the third, and praise of her body in the fourth) followed by a *congedo*. Moreover, the divine scheme of the *fronte* of "Amor che ne la mente" repeats that of "Donne ch'avete." Such precise metrical and structural correspondences draw attention to a more basic resemblance, both belong to the *stilo de la loda* or praise-style, in which the poet eschews any self-involvement in order to elaborate an increasingly hyperbolic discourse regarding his lady. The marked similarities between the two canzoni have led critics to suggest that the later poem was conceived as a deliberate attempt to outdo the former.[29] If Dante once intended that his praise of the new lady should surpass his praise of Beatrice, in confirmation of his changed allegiance, then the hierarchy of the *Comedy*'s autocitations serves as a reversal that reinvests "Donne ch'avete" with its original priority.

In *Purgatorio* II we witness a scene in which newly arrived souls are enchanted by a song to a new love, a song that is the textual emblem of their misdirected newcomers' enthusiasm. The *Convivio*'s misdirected enthusiasm for Lady Philosophy is thus replayed on the beach of purgatory; the singing of "Amor che ne la mente" in *Purgatorio* II signals the re-creation of a moment spiritually akin to the poem's first home, the prose treatise, where indeed philosophy's sweetness is such as to banish all care from the mind: "cominciai tanto a sentire de la sua dolcezza, che lo suo amore cacciava e distruggeva ogni altro pensiero" ("and I began so to feel her sweetness, that her love drove away and destroyed all other thoughts" [II, xii, 7]). To my knowledge, no one has noted that the drama of *Purgatorio* II exactly reproduces the situation of the first stanza of "Amor che ne la mente" in which the lover is overwhelmed by the sweetness of Love's song:

> Amor che ne la mente mi ragiona
> de la ma donna disïosamente,
> move cose di lei meco sovente,
> *che lo 'ntelletto sovr'esse disvia.*
>   *Lo suo parlar sì dolcemente sona,*
> che l'anima ch'ascolta e che lo sente
> dice: 'Oh me lassa, ch'io non son possente
> di dir quel ch'odo de la donna mia!'

> Love which in my mind reasons so desiringly about my lady often tells me things about her *which cause my intellect to go astray. His speech sounds so sweetly* that the soul which listens and hears says: "Alas that I am not able to utter what I hear about my lady!"
>
> (1–8; italics mine)

Here too we are faced with a verbal sweetness—"Lo suo parlar sì dolcemente sona," echoed in the *Comedy* by "che la dolcezza ancor dentro mi suona"—whose effect is debilitating; as in the *Comedy* the rapt pilgrims are unable to proceed up the mountain, so in the poem the listening soul—"l'anima ch'ascolta e che lo sente"—loses its powers of expression. In both passages, beauty causes the intellect to go temporarily astray.

Line 4 of "Amor che ne la mente"—"che lo 'ntelletto sovr'esse disvia"—thus provides the paradigm that synthesizes all the facets of this discussion: the souls go off the path (temporarily) as they succumb to the sweetness of the song in *Purgatorio* II; Dante went off the path (temporarily) when he allowed himself to be overly consoled by the sweetness of Philosophy in the *Convivio*. Lady Philosophy was indeed a mistake. On the other hand, the location guarantees salvation; like the serpent which routinely invades the valley of the princes, the distractions of the *Purgatorio* have lost their bite. For all that they are new arrivals, easily led astray by their impulsive attraction to the new delights—erotic or philosophical—which cross their path, the souls of *Purgatorio* II are incapable of erring profoundly. For them, as for their more advanced companions on the terrace of pride, the last verses of the *Pater noster* no longer apply. As in the case of the *donna gentile* episode of the *Vita Nuova*, the Casella episode functions as a lapse, a backward glance whose redemption is implicit in its occurrence.

"Donne ch'avete intelletto d'amore"

The second autocitation takes us to one of the *Comedy*'s most debated moments, the culminating phase of the encounter between the pilgrim and the poet Bonagiunta da Lucca. If we briefly rehearse the dialogue at this stage of *Purgatorio* XXIV, we note that it is tripartite: Bonagiunta asks if Dante is indeed the inventor of a new form of poetry, which begins with the poem "Donne ch'avete intelletto d'amore" (49–51); Dante replies by apparently minimizing his own role in the poetic process, saying that he composes by following Love's dictation (52–54); Bonagiunta then claims to have finally understood why the poetry practiced by himself, his peers, and his predecessors is inferior to the new poetry, which he dubs—in passing—the "sweet new style" (55–63).

Bonagiunta's remarks, which frame the pilgrim's reply, are grounded in historical specificity: his initial query concerns Dante's personal poetic history, invoked through the naming of a precise canzone; his final remarks concern the history of the Italian lyric, invoked through the names of its chief practitioners, "'l Notaro e Guittone e me" (56). The concreteness of Bonagiunta's statements contrasts with the indeterminate transcendentality of the pilgrim's reply, in which poetic principles are located in an ahistorical vacuum. Not only are the famous *terzina*'s only protagonists the poet and Love ("I' mi son un che, quando / Amor mi spira, noto ..."), but the absence of any external historical referent is emphasized by an insistent subjectivity, articulated in the stress on the first person ("I' mi son un") at the outset.

Structurally, Dante's reply functions as a pivot between Bonagiunta's first question and his later exclamation. The "Amor mi spira" passage thus enables the poet of the *Comedy* to accomplish that shift in subject matter that has so puzzled critics: from the problematic of an individual poet to that of a tradition. Indeed, precisely the neutrality of the pilgrim's reply allows it to serve as a narrative medium conferring significance both on what precedes and what follows; because of its lack of specific content, the pilgrim's statement—"I am one who takes note when Love inspires me—is able to provide a context first for the composition of "Donne ch'avete," and then for the emergence of the "sweet new style" as a poetic school. Both are defined in terms of a privileged relation to Amor.

By the same token, however, that the central *terzina* confers significance, it also generates ambiguity, by obscuring the terms of the very transition that it facilitates and by deliberately failing to clarify the application of the key phrase "dolce stil novo." Reacting against what they consider the reflex canonization of a school on the basis of a misreading of Bonagiunta's remarks, recent critics have insisted that the expression "dolce stil novo," as used in *Purgatorio* XXIV, is intended to apply only to Dante's own poetry. In other words, they refer Bonagiunta's latter comments back to his initial query. From this point of view (one which seeks to disband, at least within Dante's text, the group of poets known as *stilnovisti*), the "new style" begins with "Donne ch'avete," and it encompasses only Dante's subsequent poetry in the same mode.[30]

Whereas the historiographical potential of Bonagiunta's concluding statements has sparked controversy, critics have not been similarly divided in their reaction to his earlier remark on "Donne ch'avete." Perhaps one reason for the general consensus regarding the status of "Donne ch'avete" is the unusual consistency in Dante's own attitudes toward this canzone as displayed throughout his career, from the *Vita Nuova* to the *De Vulgari Eloquentia* to the *Comedy*. As the first of the *Vita Nuova*'s three canzoni, it marks a decisive moment in the *libello*: in narrative terms it signals the protagonist's total emancipation from the Provençal *guerdon*, and in poetic terms it signals his liberation from the so-called tragic, or Cavalcantian, mode. In the *Vita Nuova*, where aesthetic praxis is viewed as a function of ethical commitment, developments in form are strictly coordinated with developments in content; a stylistic triumph can only exist within the context of a conceptual breakthrough. Nowhere is this procedure mole observable than in the chapters describing the genesis of "Donne ch'avete."

The account begins with an impasse in the poet's love for Beatrice. In *Vita Nuova* XIV Dante attends a wedding where he sees the *gentilissima*; his resulting collapse is ridiculed by the ladies present. In the aftermath of this event, Dante writes three sonnets: the first is a direct appeal to Beatrice for pity ("Con l'altre donne mia vista gabbate" [chap. XIV]); the second details his physical disintegration upon seeing her ("Ciò che m'incontra, ne la mente more" [chap. XVI]); the third further chronicles the state to which he has been reduced by the erotic conflict, "questa battaglia d'Amore," waged within him ("Spesse fiate vegnonmi a la mente" [chap. XVI]). All share an insistence on the self (the three incipits all contain the first-person pronoun), a tendency to self-pity ("e venmene pietà" from "Spesse fiate"), and a preoccupation with death.[31] Moreover, they presume the lover's right to air grievances and ask for redress; the first two sonnets are directly addressed by the lover to the lady, who is implicitly viewed as responsible for his suffering.

The last of these sonnets is followed by a strikingly brief chapter consisting of only two sentences, in which the poet quietly announces a major transition; whereas the preceding poems deal obsessively with his own condition, he shall now undertake to write in a new mode, selflessly:

> Poi che dissi questi tre sonetti, ne li quali parlai a questa donna però che fuoro narratori di tutto quasi lo mio stato, credendomi tacere e non dire più però che mi parea di me assai avere manifestato, avvegna che sempre poi tacesse di dire a lei, a me convenne ripigliare matera nuova e più nobile che la passata.

> After I had composed these three sonnets, in which I had spoken to this lady since they were the narrators of nearly all of my

condition, deciding that I should be silent and not say more because it seemed that I had revealed enough about myself, although the result would be that from then on I should cease to write to her, it became necessary for me to take up a new and more noble subject matter than the past one.

(XVII, 1)

We notice that the "matera nuova e più nobile che la passata" is predicated on a double-edged verbal renunciation: he may no longer speak about himself ("credendomi tacere e non dire più"), and he may no longer speak to her ("avvegna che sempre poi tacesse di dire a lei"). The result of blocking both traditional outlets and traditional responses will be a new poetry.

The archaic dialogue imposed by the poet on the lady is thus replaced by a monologue whose morphology is based on a poetics of sublimation, a poetics illuminated for the poet by the Florentine Muse of chapter XVIII. Here the topos of the *gabbo* is replayed, but with positive results; both lover and poet are provoked into defining new goals. Rather than locating his supreme desire ("fine di tutti li miei desiderii" XXVIII, 4]) in an event outside of his control (Beatrice's greeting) whose presence is transformational but whose denial induces narrative lapses into self-pity and poetic lapses into regressive modes, the lover learns to use the lady to generate a happiness ("beatitudine") that cannot fail him ("che non mi puote venire meno" [XVIII, 4]) because it is under his own governance. Such total autonomy from referentiality—true beatitude—translates, in poetic terms, into the praise-style; by placing his poetic happiness "in quelle parole che lodano la donna mia" ("in those words that praise my lady" [XVIII, 6]), the poet foregoes the traditionally dualistic mechanics of love poetry and discovers a new mode.

The privileged status of the first poem written in the new style is immediately apparent. Only on this occasion does Dante chronicle the birth of a poem, a birth that is described as a quasi-miraculous event, a creation *ex nihilo*: "la mia lingua parlò quasi come per sé stessa mossa, e disse: *Donne ch'avete intelletto d'amore*" ("my tongue spoke as though moved by itself, and said: 'Donne ch'avete intelletto d'amore'" [XIX, 2]). The inspirational emphasis of this statement from *Vita Nuova* XIX foreshadows the poetic credo of *Purgatorio* XXIV; both texts present "Donne ch'avete" as deriving from a divinely inspired exclusionary relation existing between the poet and a higher authority. The *De Vulgari Eloquentia* also sanctions, albeit in less mystical terms, the special status of "Donne ch'avete": in a text where Dante uses many of his later poems to serve as exempla of excellence in various stylistic and metrical categories, he nonetheless chooses the youthful "Donne ch'avete" as the incipit to follow the formal definition of the canzone, thus establishing this early lyric as emblematic of the entire genre.[32]

The testimony of the *Vita Nuova* and the *De Vulgari Eloquentia* clarifies the appearance of "Donne ch'avete" in *Purgatorio* XXIV, where Bonagiunta invokes the canzone as a badge of poetic identity:

> Ma dì s'i' veggio qui colui che fore
>   trasse le nove rime, cominciando
>   *'Donne ch'avete intelletto d'amore.'*

> But tell me if I see here him who brought forth the new poems, beginning "Donne ch'avete intelletto d'amore"?
>
>   (*Purg.* XXIV, 49–51)

In fact, Bonagiunta both revives and integrates each of the canzone's previous textual roles: in that "Donne ch'avete" is an inaugural text ("le nove rime") he recapitulates the *Vita Nuova*; in that the canzone sets a standard by which to measure other poetry ("'l Notaro e Guittone e me") he recapitulates the *De Vulgari Eloquentia*. But Dante does not limit himself to recapitulation, in cantos XXIII and XXIV of the *Purgatorio* he constructs a sustained tribute to "Donne ch'avete" that effectively designates this canzone his supreme lyric achievement.

The episode surrounding the citation of "Donne ch'avete" is complicated by the fact that it involves a double set of characters, issues, and retrospective allusions, for the statements of *Purgatorio* XXIV acquire their full significance only when viewed on the backdrop of *Purgatorio* XXIII. The first sign directing us to a contextual reading of canto XXIV is the apparent absence of the requisite autobiographical marker, an absence rectified by the figure of Forese Donati, the friend Dante meets in canto XXIII. As we shall see, the encounter with Forese provides the necessary prelude to the conversation with Bonagiunta. Structural considerations further support reading canto XXIV in tandem with canto XXIII; we do well to bear in mind that the entire Bonagiunta episode: takes place literally within the meeting with Forese.[33]

Purgatorio XXIII begins with a description of the pilgrim peering through the green boughs of the tree he and his guides have discovered on the terrace of gluttony, "like one who wastes his life chasing little birds": "come far suole / chi dietro a li uccellin sua vita perde" (2–3). The emphasis on loss in "sua vita perde" sets the canto's tone; as well as initiating the episode, the verb *perdere* will also bring it to a close, in Forese's final words in canto XXIV:

> Tu ti rimani omai; ché 'l tempo è caro
>   in questo regno, *sì ch'io perdo troppo*
>   venendo teco sì a paro a paro.

> Now you remain behind, for time is dear in this realm, *so that I lose too much* by coming thus with you at equal pace.
>
>   (*Purg.* XXIV, 91–93; italics mine)

The encounter with Forese is precisely about loss, a loss which is recuperated through that redemption of history which is the chief matter of the *Purgatorio*. It is no accident that this of all episodes is used to articulate the fundamental relation of the *Purgatorio* to time. Forese's remark on the importance of time in Purgatory, "ché 'l tempo è care, / in questo regno," echoes the crucial definition of the previous canto, where the pilgrim comments that he had expected to find his friend down below, in Ante-Purgatory, where time is restored for time: "Io ti credea trovar là giù di sotto, / dove tempo per tempo si ristora" (XXIII, 83–84). Although the pilgrim's maxim refers directly to the Ante-Purgatory, with its formulaic insistence on literal time, it in fact glosses the whole of the second realm.

Time is the essential commodity of the *Purgatorio*, the only real eye for an eye that God exacts. The *Purgatorio* exists in time because the earth exists in time; time spent sinning in one hemisphere is paid back in the other.[34] Because earth is where "vassene 'l tempo e l'uom non se n'avvede" ("time passes and man does not notice" [*Purg.* IV, 9]), Purgatory is where "tempo per tempo si ristora." Climbing Purgatory allows the reel of history to be played backward; the historical fall of the race through time, symbolized by the Arno in Guido del Duca's discourse as it was in Hell by the Old Man of Crete, is reversed.[35] The journey up the mountain is the journey back through time to the place of beginnings, which is in turn the new ending; it is a journey whose goal is the undoing of time through time. The fall that occurred in history can only be redeemed in history; time is restored so that with it we may restore ourselves. This reversal of the fall, most explicitly reenacted in the ritual drama of *Purgatorio* VIII, finds its personal and autobiographical expression in the meeting with Forese Donati.

If Purgatory is the place where we are given the chance, desired in vain on earth, to undo what we have done, the Forese episode is chosen by the poet as the vehicle for articulating these basic principles of the canticle because it is emblematic, more than any other episode, of a fall in Dante's own spiritual biography. The episode's thematics of loss rehearse at a personal level what will later be fully orchestrated in the Earthly Paradise, where Matelda reminds Dante of Proserpina in her moment of loss ("Proserpina nel tempo che perdette / la madre lei, ed ella primavera" "Proserpina in the time when her mother lost her, and she lost spring" [*Purg.* XXVIII, 50–51]), and where Eve, signifying loss, is continually insinuated into the discourse. Indeed, the opening simile of *Purgatorio* XXIII may be seen as in anticipation of Beatrice's Edenic rebuke; the vain pursuit of little birds finds its metaphorical equivalent in another distracting diminutive, the *pargoletta* of canto XXXI:

> Non ti dovea gravar le penne in giuso,
>   ad aspettar più colpo, o pargoletta
>   o altra novità con sì breve uso.

No young girl or other novelty of such brief use should have weighed
your wings downward to await further blows.

(*Purg.* XXXI, 58–60)

The fall that Forese Donati marks in Dante's life is redeemed in cantos
XXIII and XXIV of the *Purgatorio,* both biographically and poetically. The
moment of failure is placed before the moment of triumph, the encounter with
Forese before the dialogue with Bonagiunta. Thus, Dante's so-called
traviomento morale, as remembered in canto XXIII, is ultimately seen from the
perspective of an enduring conquest, as formulated in canto XXIV. The poetic
correlative of Dante's spiritual fall is the *tenzone* of scurrilous sonnets exchanged
by him and Forese; the *tenzone* stands in contrast to the *stil novo,* celebrated here
as the pinnacle of Dante's lyric form in the canzone "Donne ch'avete."[36] There
is no further autocitation in the *Purgatorio* because "Donne ch'avete" is the end-
term in the search for the purgatorial mode of pure love poetry; like the Earthly
Paradise, the beginning is revealed to be the end.

As a poetic experience, the *tenzone* is present only obliquely, in Dante's
encounter with his former verbal antagonist. The lexical gains of the
uncompromisingly realistic *tenzone* are registered less in the second canticle than
in the first, where we find, for instance, the exchange between Sinon and Maestro
Adamo.[37] Far from containing a particularly realistic lexicon, *Purgatorio* XXIII is
saturated with lyric elements like the antithesis. As the lyric figure par excellence,
Dante uses antithesis in canto XXIII to chart the lyric's transcendence of itself.
From a traditionally private and rhetorical figure, it stretches to accommodate
the deepest moral significance; in narrative terms, we move from the Petrarchism
avant la lettre that describes the gluttonous souls in the first part of the canto
("piangere e cantar" [10]; "diletto e doglia" [12]; "piangendo canta" [64]) to the
passion of Christ, expressed through an antithesis whose rigor is foreign to the
lyric experience:

E non pur una volta, questo spazzo
   girando, si rinfresca nostra pena:
   io dico pena, e dovria dir sollazzo,
ché quella voglia a li alberi ci mena
   che menò Cristo lieto a dire 'Elì,'
   quando ne liberò con la sua vena.

And not just one time as we circle this space is our pain refreshed—
I say pain, and I ought to say pleasure, for that desire leads us to the
trees which led Christ happy to say "Elì" when He freed us with His
blood.

(*Purg.* XXIII, 70–75; italics mine)

That most banal of amatory expedients—pain that is pleasure—thus renders the sublime.[38] The rhetorical achievement of line 72 is concretized in two further antithetical expressions, again radically new: "buon dolor" in "l'ora / del buon dolor ch'a Dio ne rimarita" ("the hour of the sweet grief that rewds us to God" [80–81]), and "dolce assenzo" in "a ber lo dolce assenzo d'i martìri" ("to drink the sweet wormwood of the torments" [86]). Thus, in the *Purgatorio* "sweet wormwood" describes not the contradictory love of the poet for his lady (as in Petrarch's *Canzoniere*, where his lady's eyes can make honey bitter, or sweeten wormwood: "e 'l mel amaro, et addolcir l'assenzio" [CCXV, 14]), but the soul's paradoxical attachment to the martyrdom of purgation.

Through such textual strategies the poet sets the stage for the elaboration of a new poetic category in *Purgatorio* XXIV, that of the transcendent lyric. Indeed, as though to underscore the importance of canto XXIII for our reading of canto XXIV, Dante introduces the souls of the terrace of gluttony, at the beginning of XXIII, in a *terzina* that proleptically glosses the role of the canzone "Donne ch'avete":

> Ed ecco piangere e cantar s'udie
> '*Labia mëa, Domine*' per modo
> tal, che diletto e doglia parturìe.

> And suddenly in tears and song was heard "Labia mea, Domine" in
> such a way that it gave birth to delight and sorrow.
>
> (*Purg.* XXIII, 10–12)

Embedded within lyric antitheses is a verse with enormous resonance for Dante's conception of the lyric, from the Vulgate's Fiftieth Psalm: "Domine, labia mea aperies; et os meum annuntiabit laudem tuam" ("Lord, open my lips, and my mouth will announce Your praise"). Thus, the gluttons pray to the Lord to open their once closed mouths so that they may sing forth His praises, a fact that illuminates the positioning of Bonagiunta and his poetic discourse on this terrace. As a poet, Bonagiunta also failed to "open his mouth" in praise; he is emblematic of an archaic poetics that stopped short of discovering the praise-style, the "matera nuova e più nobile che la passata" of *Vita Nuova* XVII.[39]

The gluttons of canto XXIII have turned their months from the basest of concerns—"eating," or unrelieved self involvement—to praising God, in the "same way that the discovery of the *stil novo* turns the Italian lyric from the conventional poetics of the "I" to the deflection of the "I" in the poetry of praise. Thus, the gluttons chanting their Psalm are described as souls who are loosening the knot of their obligation, "forse di lor dover solvendo il nodo" (XXIII, 15), in a phrasing that anticipates the loosening of Bonagiunta's "knot" (his uncertainty regarding the reasons for his poetic failure) by the pilgrim. The artifact that symbolizes the conversion that the gluttons have only now achieved—away from the self toward a disinterested focusing on the Other—is "Donne ch'avete," which attains its prominence within the *Comedy* precisely because it marks the moment in which Dante first opens his mouth in a song of praise.

Within the new order imposed by the *Comedy*'s confessional self-reading, in which literal chronology becomes irrelevant, Forese signifies the fall preceding the conversion to Beatrice. Moreover, the pilgrim will specify, in the detailed account of his journey that he offers at the end of canto XXIII, that he proceeded directly from the experience shared with his friend to the meeting with Vergil; thus, we can state that Forese signifies, within the *Comedy*'s ideal scheme, no less than the final fall before the final conversion. That this fall is connected to the displacement of Beatrice is suggested by the fact that Dante's friendship with Forese seems to correspond to the period of depression following Beatrice's death, a period documented by the *Convivio* (and perhaps by Cavalcanti's sonnet rebuking Dante for his *vile vita*), in which Beatrice was replaced by other interests to a degree later judged intolerable.[40]

In the absence of precise indices regarding the years after 1290, the decadence of the *tenzone* (dated by internal evidence to 1293–1296) was originally viewed as symptomatic of a literally dissolute period in Dante's life. The illegitimate biographical status once assumed by these texts has been defused by studies insisting that the low style of the *tenzone* is just as conventional as the high style of the courtly lyric. As a result, Dante's straying after the death of Beatrice is now generally interpreted in a more metaphorical light, as a phase of moral and political secularism, involving a philosophical and/or religious deviation from orthodoxy.[41] To the extent that any strictly personal or erotic failure is involved, it is viewed as part of a larger problematic; the *pargoletta* cited by Beatrice is not only a rival lady (as witnessed by her place in the *Rime*), but is also the central symbolic node of a cluster of transgressions. Among these transgressions are the poems of the *donna gentile*, composed at this time, most likely in 1293–1294. The episode of his life to which Dante later attached the rubric "Forese Donati" is, therefore, a synthesis of the deviations catalogued by Beatrice: the moral ("o pargoletta / o altra novità" [*Purg.* XXXI, 59–60]), and the philosophical ("quella scuola / c'hai seguitata" [*Purg.* XXXIII, 85-86]).[42]

Beatrice forecasts her more specific rebukes with a single compact charge, that of turning away from her to someone else: "questi si tolse a me, e diessi altrui" ("he took himself from me and gave himself to another" [*Purg.* XXX, 126]). Indeed, the hallmark of Beatrice's personal discourse throughout the Earthly Paradise is negative conversion. She concentrates insistently on the illicit presence of the other; "altrui" is echoed by "altra novità," and finally by "altrove" in the verse "colpa ne la tua voglia altrove attenta" ("the fault of your will elsewhere intent" [*Purg.* XXXIII, 99]). To the thematics of negative conversion is opposed the positive conversion of canto XXIII, where the pilgrim registers the forward turn of *Inferno* I:

> Di quella vita mi volse costui
>   che mi va innanzi, l'altri' ier, quando tonda
>   vi si mostrò la suora di colui

From that life he who goes before me turned me the other day, when
the sister of him [the sun] showed herself round to you

(Purg. XXIII, 118–120)

The full moon over the *selva oscura* marks the poet's tryst with the conversion that
will take him, as he explains to his friend, ultimately to Beatrice, "là dove fia
Beatrice" (*Purg.* XXIII, 128).

When Dante says to Forese "Di quella vita mi volse costui," he defines the
new moment with Vergil ("mi volse") in terms of the old moment with Forese
("quella vita"), the conversion in terms of the preceding fall. The words "quella
vita" refer literally to the past life shared by the two friends, a past whose
memories are still burdensome (the flip side of Casella's song, which is still sweet):

> Se tu riduci a mente
>   qual fosti meco, e qual io teco fui,
>   ancor fia grave il memorar presente.
> Di quella vita mi volse costui ...

If you call to mind what you were with me and I with you, the
present memory will still be grievous. From that life he turned the ...

(Purg. XXIII, 115–118)

The life-experience shared by Dante and Forese thus assumes a metaphoric value
in the *Comedy* that bears little relation to anything we know about the two men.
Forese stands in Dante's personal lexicon for his own compromised historical
identity, the past—"qual fosti meco, e qual io teco fui"—brought painfully into
the present—"il memorar presente." Their life together represents everything
the saved soul regrets before being granted forgetfulness: the sum total of
personal falls, little deaths, other paths. For Dante, this is everything he left
behind when he turned to Beatrice.

In directly linking his friendship with Forese to the encounter with Vergil,
in casting the Florentine *traviamento* as the immediate predecessor to the dark
wood, Dante far outstrips the literal content of the tenzone, which (with its
gluttonies, petty thieveries, and untended wives) tells of a more social than
spiritual collapse. Nor is he concerned with strict chronology; Forese, who died
in 1296, had been dead for four years when the pilgrim wanders into the first
canto of the *Inferno*. Such underminings of the factual record, combined with the
evasion of textual echoes from the *tenzone*, underscore the metaphorical
significance of the Forese episode in the *Comedy*.

The paradigmatic value assigned to the episode necessarily extends to the poetic sphere as well. The conversion from "that life" with Forese to "new life" with Beatrice is also the conversion from the fallen style of the *tenzone* to the new style of "Donne ch'avete." In this ideal chronology, the *tenzone* occupies a position antecedent even to Bonagiunta's old style; it is as complacently rooted in fallen reality as the stil novo is free of it. As Dante's personal fall—"quella vita"—is redeemed by the restorative time of Purgatory, so the poetic fall—the *tenzone*—is redeemed by the converted style of the *stil novo*. This poetic conversion takes place in a context of lyric anthitheses so overriding that they embrace even the episode's personnel; in the violent contrast between Forese's chaste wife Nella and the "sfacciate donne fiorentine" ("brazen women of Florence" [XXIII, 101]) one could see a continuation of the canto's antithetical mode, carried from the lexical to the figural level. In fact, the terrace of gluttony is played out on a backdrop of contrasting women, good and bad, courtly and anti-courtly: not only Nella and her Florentine opposites, but Beatrice, Piccarda, Gentucca, Mary (from the exempla at the end of canto XXII), and (mentioned in XXIV, 116) Eve.

An episode that deals with lyric themes is thus sustained by the genre's narrative prerequisites, by women. It is not coincidental that in the course of this episode Dante should ask his friend about the location of his sister, or that Bonagiunta should prophesy the aid of a young woman from Lucca; both Piccarda and Gentucca are historical correlatives of the terrace's true heroines, the "ladies who have understanding of love." Most important is the fact that only here does the pilgrim take the opportunity to name Beatrice as the term of his voyage, thus relinquishing his usual practice of indicating her through a periphrasis. He names her because Forese—unlike the majority of the souls he has encountered—knows her, a simple fact with less simple implications. Precisely Forese's historical identity, his connection to a literal past, makes him valuable to a poet whose metaphors require grounding in reality. The fall must have a name, Forese, as salvation has a name, Beatrice, and as conversion occurs under the aegis of Vergil, specifically five days ago, when the moon was full. The irreducible historicity of this poem—the radical newness of its style— retrospectively guarantees all those other poems, and the newness of their style: "le nove rime, cominciando / 'Donne ch'avete intelletto d'amore.'"

"Voi che 'ntendendo il terzo ciel movete"

The last of the *Comedy*'s autocitations, "Voi che 'ntendendo il terzo ciel movete," belongs to *Paradiso* VIII. In the heaven of Venus Dante meets Charles Martel, who declares his whereabouts by citing his friend's canzone, appropriately addressed to the angelic intelligences of this third heaven:

> Noi ci volgiam coi principi celesti
> 	d'un giro e d'un girare e d'una sete,

ai quali tu del mondo già dicesti:
'*Voi che 'ntendendo il terzo ciel movete*'

With one circle, with one circling and with one thirst we revolve
with the heavenly princes, to whom you of the world once did say:
"Voi che 'ntendendo il terzo ciel movete"

(*Par.* VIII, 34–37)

Although readings of *Paradiso* VIII routinely point to the coincidence between
incipit and geographical location, critical inquiry has on the whole done little
more than confirm the canzone's superficial suitability.[43] But "Voi che
'ntendendo" is, in fact, far from an obvious choice as the autocitation of the
Paradiso, in that it encompasses the defeat and replacement of Beatrice, Dante's
paradisiacal guide. Whereas *Purgatorio* XXIV establishes the *Vita Nuova* as the
bedrock of Dante's poetics, implying that the *Convivio* is a mistaken detour along
the way (an implication confirmed by *Purgatorio* II), the Comedy's final
autocitation—privileged by its position in the *Paradiso*—seems to return to the
Convivio and to Lady Philosophy.[44]

"Voi che 'ntendendo" appears in the context of an episode that
intentionally recalls earlier episodes; the pilgrim's meeting with Charles Martel
is modeled on his previous encounters with Casella and Forese. Despite the
brevity of Charles' stay in Florence (his visit to the city in 1294 seems to have
provided Dante with his only opportunity to meet the Angevin heir), the poet of
the *Comedy* views him as a friend, a celestial version of the comrades who
populate the slopes of Purgatory. A friendship that is prized but somewhat
remote, certainly based on a lesser degree of intimacy, is precisely what the poet
wants for his last canticle; friendship in the *Paradiso* is intended to contrast with
friendship in the *Purgatorio*. Instead of many friends, now there is only one, and
this one is a prince whom the poet respected but barely knew. As emblems of the
will's attachment to things of this world, friends belong to the dialectic of the
second realm, where the soul learns to forego what it most desires for something
it desires even more. In *Paradiso* VIII the pilgrim's meeting with a friend
underscores, by contrast to earlier meetings, the distanced affectivity of Heaven.
Moreover, the meeting is deliberately situated in the sphere of Venus, because
the third heaven is dedicated by Dante to dispelling earthly expectations
regarding love.

Dante conceives the heaven of Venus as an anticlimax, the textual means by
which to disengage the reader (and the pilgrim) from any lingering expectations
for earthly (or purgatorial) sentiment. He chooses the heaven where both reader
and pilgrim most expect to encounter eros—transcendent but still
recognizable—as the stage on which to introduce an eros transformed beyond
recognition. The poet's intent is to defuse the accumulated conventional
significance of "Venus," a significance on which he had capitalized earlier in the

poem, and which he preserves in the psychological inclination ascribed to, the souls of this heaven. But although the souls of Venus (excluding Charles) avow or are known for their venereal tendencies, these tendencies possess a purely formal value that is countered by the pervasive tone and emphasis of cantos VIII and IX. The denial of the third heaven is the more striking because it is not inviolable; after undercutting affectivity where we expect it, in the heaven of Venus, Dante resurrects it in all its dialectical vigor in the Cacciaguida cantos.

The poet signals his awareness of our expectations in the celebrated opening of the eighth canto, whose twelve verses unfold the intricate Dantesque problematic of "folle amore" (2):

> Solea creder lo mondo in suo periclo
>   che la bella Ciprigna il folle amore
>   raggiasse, volta nel terzo epiciclo;
> per che non pur a lei faceano onore
>   di sacrificio e di votivo grido
>   le genti antiche ne l'antico errore;
> ma Dïone onoravano e Cupido,
>   quella per madre stia, questo per figlio,
>   e dicean ch'el sedette in grembo a Dido;
> e da costei ond' io principio piglio
>   pigliavano il vocabol de la stella
>   che 'l sol vagheggia or da coppa or da ciglio.

Once the world believed, to its peril, that the beautiful Cyprian rayed down mad love, turning in the third epicycle; so that the ancient peoples in their ancient error did honor not only to her, with sacrifice and votive cry, but they honored also Dione and Cupid, the former as her mother, the latter as her son, and they recounted that he had sat in Dido's lap; from her whence I take my beginning they took the name of the star which the sun courts now from behind and now from in front.

(Par. VIII, 1–12)

From "the beautiful Cyprian" and her presumed effects, the poet passes, in the next *terzina*, to her cult, practiced by "le genti antiche ne l'antico errore" (6); thence, in lines 7 through 9, to the connection between the "ancient error" and classical culture: line 9, with its reference to Cupid and Dido, implicates no less a text than the *Aeneid*, in whose fourth book the story of Cupid's ruse and Dido's surrender is told. The final *terzina* brings us to the present, and to the issue of the poet's own relation to Venus; whereas the ancients took from this star only a "vocabol," a name or external referent, he—conceiving her differently—takes from her his "principio," his beginning and foundation.[45]

Two key points emerge from this opening passage. First, *folle amore* is recognized, registered, and immediately put into perspective; it is not by chance that the first word of the canto is "Solea." It used to be thus, says the poet, in the time of the "genti antiche ne l'antico errore" (the repetition of the adjective stresses the disjunction from the present), but no longer. The heaven of Venus in this Christian paradise is thus from the start presented in terms of its radical difference: the difference between a *vocabol* and *a principio*, between a superficial and a profound understanding of love. Second, this conceptual difference is immediately related to poetic practice. There is an implied corrective of classical poetry running throughout this heaven: from Vergil whose Dido is compromised at the outset, to Ovid whose volcanic theories are corrected later on. In sharp juxtaposition to these revised ancient poets and texts stand some newer ones; in this heaven we find not only the *Comedy*'s last autocitation but also the *Comedy*'s last lyric poet, the troubadour Folquet de Marselha.

Beginning with the issue of the Cyprian's influence, this heaven presents us with a graduated series of views regarding Venus: from that of the classical poets, represented by Vergil and Ovid, to that of the courtly lyric, represented by Folquet, to that of Dante's own lyrics, represented by "Voi che 'ntendendo," whose rarified perspective is apparent even in its first verse. Within the contest of the third heaven, then, the autocitation serves as part of a general undermining of *folle amore* in all its aspects, both classical and medieval; critics have commented on the canzone's severity, its lack of amorous sweetness, and considered it suitable on these grounds for inclusion into this heaven.[46] In fact, in that "Voi che 'ntendendo" treats love more analytically than passionately, it fits into the general tenor of this heaven's nonerotic treatment of eros. But such a reading, while not incorrect, fails to take into account either the relation of this incipit to the other incipits in the poem, or the actual content of the canzone.

Putting the autocitation of *Paradiso* VIII into diachronic perspective alerts us to the fact that "Voi che 'ntendendo," for all its synchronic aptness, is an apparently inappropriate choice as the canzone to follow and supersede "Donne ch'avete." Such a perspective also encourages us to compare the episode of *Paradiso* VIII with the others that contain quotations from the pilgrim's own poetry. Some commentators have moved in this direction: Bosco establishes a parallel between Charles Martel and Casella, based especially on the reciprocal affection displayed in both episodes and on the presence in both of a canzone; Sapegno, for similar reasons, draws attention to parallels between Charles Martel and Forese.[47] I would carry their observations a step further, suggesting that the meeting with Charles Martel is in fact conceived, both structurally and thematically, as a conflation of the two previous meetings.

The moment of encounter between the pilgrim and the prince, in what is the most personalized section of the canto, is modeled on *Purgatorio* II. The inhabitants of Venus are described, immediately before the appearance of Charles Martel, in terms of a beautiful sound; a "Hosanna" heard from within

the approaching group of souls is such that the pilgrim will never again cease to
desire it:

> e dentro a quei che più innanzi appariro
>   sonava '*Osanna*' sì, che unque poi
>   di rïudir non fui sanza disiro.

> and among those who appeared most in front rang such a "Hosanna"
> that I have never since been without the desire to hear it again.
>
> (*Par*. VIII, 28–30)

The sound at the beginning of this episode corresponds to the sound at the end
of the Casella episode, whose "sweetness still rings inside of me"; both are
characterized by the poet's desire to perpetuate their beauty into the present. In
the following verses Charles begins to speak; like Casella, he initiates the
encounter by revealing that he is Dante's friend. Where Casella attempted to
embrace the pilgrim, Charles cites a verse of Dante's poetry as a sign of
friendship; he concludes with an offer to interrupt their joyful singing: "e sem sì
pien d'amor, che, per piacerti, / non fia men dolce un poco di quïete" ("we are so
full of love that, to please you, a little quiet will not be less sweet" [37–39]).

If the language of this last passage is markedly reminiscent of the pilgrim's
speech to Casella in *Purgatorio* II (especially the use of "dolce" and "quïete"), line
45 of canto VIII, in which the pilgrim's voice is "di grande affetto impressa"
("stamped with great affection"), solely recalls, as Vaturi noticed, the "grande
affetto" with which Casella sought to embrace his friend (*Purg*. II, 77). Most
telling are the verses in which Charles presents himself, not by name (his name
is not used until the beginning of canto IX, when he is about to disappear), but
by evoking the past relation between himself and his visitor:

> Assai m'amasti, e avesti ben onde;
>   che s'io fossi giù stato, io ti mostrava
>   di mio amor più oltre che le fronde.

> Much did you love me, and you had good reason, for had I remained
> down below, I would have shown you of my love more than the leaves.
>
> (*Par*. VIII, 55–57)

"Assai m'amasti" is a celestial variant of Casella's "Così com' io t'amai / nel
mortal corpo, così t'amo sciolta" (*Purg*. II, 88–89), a variant that, by deliberately
recalling the purgatorial verses, gives us a measure of the vast difference between
the two encounters.

Here the souls converse with the pilgrim not for their own enjoyment, but
"per piacerti," for the pilgrim's sake; there they, like the pilgrim, were too ready

to sink into the repose generated by Casella's illicit music. Here the pilgrim is entranced by the *Osanna* of the souls, there by a secular song. Here Charles Martel is an oxymoron—a distant friend who provides the final gloss on Casella's earthbound present tense ("così t'amo") by restricting such affection in heaven for the past absolute ("Assai m'amasti"). Given these facts, we are less surprised by the abrupt transition from the *terzina* quoted above, Charles' most personal and affective statement, to the political discourse which dominates the latter two-thirds of canto VIII, first in relation to Charles' own situation and the house of Anjou, and then in a more theoretical vein, regarding the problem of heredity. As we shall see, politics is used throughout this heaven as the poet's chief means of deflecting the personal, the affective, and the erotic.

The other distancing tool used by the poet in this heaven is rhetoric: the rhetoric of the lengthy geographical periphrases invariably singled out as a feature of these cantos, and employed first by Charles in canto VIII, then by Cunizza and Folquet in canto IX. Charles begins his political discourse in line 58 with a series of periphrases encompassing 18 verses (through line 75), by which he indicates the kingdoms that would have been his to rule had he lived: Provence, Naples, Hungary, and Sicily. The periphrasis for Sicily is particularly complex; he begins by situating the island geographically, continues by overturning classical (mythological) volcanic theory and substituting a more naturalistic account, and finishes with a résumé of the island's social history leading to the Sicilian Vespers. The rebellion was caused by bad government, "mala segnoria" (73), in this case that of his grandfather, Charles I of Anjou, who thus provides Charles Martel with a pretext for attacking another member of his family, namely his brother Robert.

While Charles' initial meeting with the pilgrim imitates the Casella episode, this latter part of Charles' discourse (76–84) constitutes the Forese section; it is, I believe, loosely modeled on Forese's invective against his brother, Corso Donati. In both discourses there is a political emphasis, a concern about bad government, a prophetic element, and—strikingly—a brother impugning a brother. Charles' castigation of his brother (the same King Robert so admired by petrarch and Boccaccio) leads into the didactic sequence on heredity, which corresponds to Forese's didactic diatribe on the lax morals of Florentine women. The most precise parallel between the two episodes is provided by the prophetic element, introduced by the verse "E se mio frate questo antivedesse" ("and were my brother to foresee this" (761), where the verb *antivedere*, used rarely in the *Comedy*, echoes its appearances in both of Forese's cantos, *Purgatorio* XXIII and XXIV.[48] Although Robert's fate is neither as severe nor as specific as Corso Donati's (who is dragged to Hell on the tail of a diabolical beast), both fraternal prophecies invoke a coming disaster.

The patterning of this episode on those of Casella and Forese points through sameness to difference; from the intensely familiar use of Forese's name (repeated three times in *Purgatorio* XXIII–XXIV), we have moved to a situation where Charles' name is not even introduced into the episode until after his encounter with the pilgrim has ended. The poet, in what is another example of this heaven's distancing rhetoric, first calls the prince by name in the apostrophe to Clemence, Charles' wife, at the beginning of canto IX: "Da poi che Carlo tuo, bella Clemenza, / m'ebbe chiarito ..." ("After your Charles, beautiful Clemence, had enlightened me" [1–2]).[49] Eros is evoked—in the possessive "tuo," the adjective "bella"—but simultaneously deflected by two rhetorical strategies: by the apostrophe, which distances itself from the episode it hand through its temporal dislocation into an unspecified future, in which the poet's voice takes the place of the pilgrim's (who had originally asked, in VIII, 44, "Deh, chi siete?"), and by the fact that Carlo and Clemenza both belong to a subordinate clause. The main clause to which they are linked deals with Charles further remarks ("mi narrò li 'nganni / che ricever dovea la sua semenza" "he narrated the treacheries his seed was to receive" [2–3]), remarks that belong once more to the realm of politics.

The thematic concerns of this heaven are intractably political, indeed such as to compel us to revise the purely autobiographical and retrospective value thus (in assigned to Charles Martel, and to reconsider the significance of his identity. In *Purgatorio* II Casella's identity as an enthusiastic but uninformed newcomer is linked to his misdirected singing; of "Amor che ne la mente"; in *Purgatorio* XXIII and XXIV the triumph of the *stil novo* is connected via Forese to a previous fall. In both instances the canzoni are praise songs, one for the wrong lady (Philosophy) and one for the right lady (Beatrice). In *Paradiso* VIII, however, the situation is dramatically different: the pilgrim meets neither a fellow Florentine musician nor versifier, but a prince; and the autocitation is not a praise poets, but a poem of conflict.

"Voi che 'ntendendo," the poem in which the new love for philosophy is privileged over the old love for Beatrice, was written during a period in which Dante experienced these two loves as conflicting; as Foster and Boyde point out, Beatrice's place was "taken by an enormous interest in philosophy and in politics."[50] The incompatibility of these interests is dramatized by the uncompromising stance of the canzone, the exhortation to "resolve to call her your lady henceforth" (48) marks the definitive transfer of allegiance from the first love to the second. Thus, a poem celebrating a lady allegorized as philosophy, written during the decade (following Beatrice's death and the completion of the *Vita Nuova*) in which the poet displays an increasing involvement in philosophy and politics, appears in *Paradiso* VIII in the mouth of a character with a highly political identity—a prince—and in the context of a heaven devoted to political and philosophical concerns.

It is difficult not to see such thematic coincidence as deliberate, especially in the light of the developments of canto IX, where Cunizza and Folquet both inveigh against political corruption, bringing this heaven's quota of politically motivated prophecies to a record high (three in all: Charles predicts disaster for the house of Anjou; Cunizza pits herself against the northern cities of Padova, Treviso, and Feltre; Folquet attacks the Roman curia). Like the canzone "Voi che 'ntendendo," in which the literal content strikes an uneasy balance with the *Convivio*'s allegorical interpretation, the characters of this heaven are all dichotomous. Charles is a political figure with no record of venereal excess; as the first soul in Venus' heaven, he serves antiphrastically to underscore the principle of displacement at work here. As eros is deflected by allegory in the canzone, so the remaining characters of this heaven are deflected from their primary personalities: Cunizza's notoriously erotic life is dismissed in 6 lines (31–36), while 27 lines (25–30 and 43–62) are devoted to condemning "la terra prava / italica" ("the depraved land of Italy" [25–26]); likewise Folquet sums up his amatory and poetic career in 12 lines, concentrating instead on his presentation of Raab and his invective against the papal curia. Raab is, of course, symptomatic of this heaven; a Hebrew prostitute who achieves salvation for her aid to Joshua's men, she is presented in canto IX exclusively as a crusader.

The poetics of displacement that governs the heaven of Venus serves to isolate and represent a particular moment in the process of conversion, a moment *in fieri* in which the dialectical elements of the achieved synthesis are still visible in their component parts. The conversion from eros to *caritas* undertaken in cantos VIII and IX is achieved at the outset of canto X, where—in the heaven of the Sun and no longer under the shadow of earth—love is newly defined in relation to the dynamics of the Trinity: "Guardando nel suor Figlio con l'Amore / che l'uno e l'altro etternalmente spira ..." ("Looking on his Son with the Love which the one and the other eternally breathe forth" [1–2]). The nonachievement of the previous heaven is not a positive lack, but a symptom of the original conflict, which is still obliquely present, like the shallow of earth that is still felt (a shadow which is, significantly, mentioned for the first and last time in the heaven of Venus [IX, 118]); the fact that Cunizza and Folquet are converts from *folle amore* is registered not positively but negatively, by the duality of their discourses and by the compensation that dictates their political diatribes. The textual status thus assigned by the poet to the third heaven, conceived as the representation of a stage in which the elements of a prior conflict and duality are still visible although no longer conflicting, accounts for the presence and choice of this particular autocitation.

"Voi che 'ntendendo" is a poem about conflict, the conflict experienced by the poet between his love for Beatrice—his mystical, spiritual, and poetical interests—and the other chief interests of his life. Everything about the heaven of Venus speaks to the integration of concerns that on earth were viewed as separate and antagonistic; thus, the pilgrim meets a prince who can quote love poetry, a political lady who loved a poet (a political poet at that), and a poet who became a political figure.[51] The point of the resolutely nonamatory treatment of this heaven is that love can be, and must be, integrated with political and philosophical concerns; in terms of Dante's own career, the point is that the poet must transcend his *Vita Nuova* phase, dominated by an all-consuming if sublimated love, in order to arrive at the *Comedy*, in which eros is welded to a complex of other issues. Although the *Convivio* is the text that effects this transition, the *Convivio's* error is that it still posits a conflict: either Lady Philosophy or Beatrice. But the conflict that it posits is also a measure of its critical importance as the text that points the poet away from the lyric and parochial sphere of the *Vita Nuova* toward the universality of the *Comedy*.[52] If, in Heaven, Beatrice tolerates the citation of a canzone whose original purpose was to displace her for "others," she does so to indicate that she and they can now be simultaneously present.

The *Convivio's* error, then, is in not achieving synthesis, and for this it is in Paradise once more pointedly corrected. When Charles Martel greets the pilgrim, he explains that he is turning with the angelic intelligences of the third heaven, the Principalities, "whom you of the world thus addressed: 'Voi che 'ntendendo il terzo ciel movete'" (36–37). While Dante's canzone is, indeed, addressed to the intelligences of the third heaven, he did not, in the *Convivio*, consider these intelligences to be principalities. Thus, by way of Charles' polite adjustment, the heaven of Venus becomes the first locus for Dante's self-correction on the matter of angelic hierarchy, on issue resolved finally by Beatrice in canto XXVIII. There she confirms the order laid out by the pseudo-Dionysius in the *De Coelesti Hierarchio*, explaining that Gregory the Great (whom Dante follows in the *Convivio*) had erred.

The most notable difference between the two schemes is the position of the Thrones, whom Gregory lowers from third place (behind the Seraphim and Cherubim) to seventh (above the Angels and Archangels). In *Paradiso* XXVIII the Thrones are the only angelic order to whom Beatrice dedicates a full *terzina*, stating that they belong to the first and highest angelic triad:

> Quelli altri amori che 'ntorno li vonno,
>   si chiaman Troni del divino aspetto,
>   per che 'l primo ternaro terminonno

> Those other loves who go around them are called Thrones of the divine aspect, because they completed the first triad
> (*Par.* XXVIII, 103–105)

Besides this general statement from canto XXVIII, the specific judicial duties of the Thrones are mentioned by Cunizza, who also emphasizes their elevation ("Sù sono specchi, voi dicete Troni, / onde refulge a neri Dio giudicante" "Above are mirrors whom you call Thrones whence God in judgment shines on us" [IX, 61–62]), and much later by the pilgrim ("Ben so io che, se 'n cielo altro reame / la divina giustizia fa suo specchio" "I know well that although divine justice makes its mirror in another realm of heaven" [XIX, 28–29]). Not only are the

Thrones the most talked about angelic hierarchy in the poem, but a good deal of the interest in there seems to stem from the heaven of Venus, to which they were inappropriately linked in the *Convivio*. Indeed, it seems as though the *terzina* devoted to raising the Thrones at the end of canto XXVIII is matched by the *terzina* devoted to lowering Venus at the canto's beginning; in a context where God is a tiny point, and the heavens nearest to Him are smallest, Venus is singled out for its width, so great that an entire rainbow could not contain it (31–33). The *Comedy* thus redresses the *Convivio*'s imbalance.

In *Paradiso* VIII the emphasis on the Thrones begins indirectly, when Charles Martel locates himself in the third heaven; by specifying that this is the realm of the Principalities, he implies that it is not the realm of the Thrones. The result of his statement is that "Voi che 'ntendendo" is introduced into the text by way of the new order, the Principalities; the sentence structure thus ensures that the canzone is immediately linked to self-correction. In the same way that the third angelic order is made of Principalities, and not of Thrones as the *Convivio* would have it, so the lady now at Dante's side is Beatrice, and not the *donna gentile*. The *Convivio*'s limits are again underscored; as a text it was next able to see with the penetration of the Comedy, but rather, like Gregory the Great at the end of canto XXVIII, it must now laugh at its mistakes.

Unlike Gregory, however, the *Convivio*'s mistakes are not restricted to a single issue; its imaginative failures are far more profound. The correction of the *Convivio* in *Paradiso* VIII therefore goes beyond angelology to invest the major thematic concerns of the prose treatise. In the fifth chapter of Book II the *Convivio*'s author, having just outlined the order of the angels, proceeds to apply this doctrine to the first verses of the canzone he is glossing, "Voi che 'ntendendo"; he stoves in his discussion from the Thrones, governors of the third heaven, to the inclinations and qualities proper to their sphere of influence. As we know, the heaven is Venus, and the disposition is amorous:

> Per che ragionevole è credere che li movitori del cielo de la Luna siano de l'ordine de li Angeli, e quelli di Mercurio siano li Arcangeli, e quelli di Venere siano li Troni, li quali, naturati de l'amore del Santo Spirito, fanno la loro operazione, connaturale ad essi, cioè lo movimento di quello cielo, pieno d'amene, dal quale prende la farina del detto cielo uno ardore virtuoso per lo quale le anime di qua giuso s'accendono ad amore, secondo la loro disposizione.

> So that it is reasonable to believe that the movers of the heaven of the Moon are the order of Angels, and those of Mercury are the Archangels, and those of Venus are Thrones. These last, informed and nourished with the love of the Holy Spirit, effect their operation which is connatural to there, that is the movement of that heaven full of love, from which movement the form of that heaven takes on a

virtuous ardor through which the souls down below are kindled to
love according to their disposition.

(II, v, 13)

Having established the relation between the Thrones, Venus, and love, and
stressing the ability of this heaven to inflame love in souls so disposed, the author
passes to the ancients, and to their views on the effects of this heaven: "E perchè
li antichi s'accorsero che quello cielo era qua giù cagione d'amore, dissero Amore
essere figlio di Venere ..." ("And because the ancients realized that that heaven
was the cause of love down here, they said that Love was the son of Venus" [II,
v, 14]).

This set of relations, first established by Dante in the *Convivio*, is
resurrected in the opening of *Paradiso* VIII, where the poet once more links the
heaven of Venus to classical culture, and where he pursues an identical chain of
reasoning: from Venus ("la belle Ciprigna"), to the ancients ("le genti antiche"),
to Venus' son Cupid ("ma Dione onoravano e Cupido / quella per madre sua,
questo per figlio"), to Vergil ("e dicean ch'el sedette in grembo a Dido"). We now
see that this progression is inherited from the *Convivio*, where the links are much
more explicit, links between Venus and love and the ancients, and—picking up
from where we left off in our quotation of Book II, chapter v—links between
Cupid ("Amore" in the *Convivio*) and Vergil: "... [li antichi] dissero Amore essere
figlio di Venere, sì come testimonia Vergilio nel primo de lo Eneida, ove dice
Venere ad Amore: 'Figlio, vertù mia, figlio del sommo padre, che li dardi di Tifeo
non curi'" ("the ancients said that Love was the son of Venus, as Vergil testifies
in the first book of the *Aeneid*, where Venus says to Love: 'Son, my strength, son
of the highest father, you who fear not the bolts of Typhoeus'" [II, v, 14]). Here,
as again in the *Comedy*, the poet demonstrates the pagan belief that Cupid was
Venus' son by citing the *Aeneid*; whereas in the *Convivio* he cites a passage from
Aeneid I in which Venus addresses her son, in the *Comedy* he much more
powerfully depicts Cupid's role by evoking in one verse the tragedy of Book IV.

Our passage from the *Convivio* concludes by citing not only Vergil on
Cupid, but also Ovid ("e Ovidio, nel quinto di Metamorphoseos, quando dice
che Venere disse ad Amore: 'Figlio, armi mie, potenzia mia'" "and Ovid, in the
fifth book of the *Metamorphoses*, when he says that Venus said to Love: 'Son, my
arms, my power'" [II, v, 14]), thus invoking both classical authorities on love.
And, as we know, both these authorities are present, and in the same order, in
Paradiso VIII, where Vergil's indirect presence in line 9 is followed by Ovid's even
more indirect presence in Charles Martel's periphrasis for Sicily. The Angevin
prince describes Sicily as that island which is darkened by a thick fog between the
capes of "Pachino" to the south (Cape Passero) and "Peloro" to the north (Cape
Faro), a darkness that is caused not—as the ancients believed—by the ashes
spewed forth by the giant Typhoeus imprisoned under Mount Etna, but by
sulfurous gases: "non per Tifeo ma per nascente solfo" ("not by Typhoeus but by

rising sulfur" [VIII, 70]). The Dantesque periphrasis for Sicily, beginning "E la bella Trinacria" in line 67, is inspired by Ovid throughout, specifically by a passage in Book V of the *Metamorphoses* in which the Latin poet ascribes the eruptions of Etna to the spouting of the giant Typhoeus, and in which the island (called "Trinacris") is parceled into the same geographical segments picked up by Dante: "He [Typhoeus] struggles hard, and often fights to rise again, but his right hand is held down by Ausonian Pelorus and his left by you, Pachynus."[53]

Dante relies on Ovid in order to revise him, his point being, of course, that Typhoeus is no more to be taken seriously than the beautiful Cyprian of the canto's opening verses; he is not responsible for volcanic eruptions, and she is not responsible for *folle amore*. Both the giant and the goddess are rendered impotent in *Paradiso* VIII. And, if Dante goes out of his way to introduce Ovid into this canto, he does so as part of his overall correction of the passage from the *Convivio*, a passage that contains all the elements later raised in *Paradiso* VIII: the Thrones, the ancients, Vergil, Ovid. Even Typhoeus is present in the *Convivio*, in the citation from *Aeneid* I, where Venus refers to her son as "contemptuous of the Typhoean bolts," i.e. unafraid even of Jupiter, whose thunderbolt had chastened the giant. The *Convivio* passage, in which Dante translates the Vergilian verse with the phrase "che li dardi di Tifeo non curi," constitutes the only occasion, prior to the *Comedy*, in which the giant figures in one of Dante's texts.[54]

These details serve to confirm the relation between *Convivio* II, v and *Paradiso* VIII.[55] In canto VIII Dante systematically presents and discounts point after point from the passage in the *Convivio*: the Thrones have become Principalities; Venus and Cupid alike are an "antico errore"; the poets who believed in them are dupes. But canto VIII goes beyond these particulars to the larger error behind them, to wit, the privileging of classical culture—philosophy over revelation, the *donna gentile* over Beatrice—which is, from the perspective of the later Dante, the *Convivio's* most serious flaw.[56] The true error of the *Convivio* is the status it accords to ancient beliefs; the critique of canto VIII focuses on one set of ancient beliefs, those regarding Venus. Thus, the *Convivio* passage recounts that, because the ancients realized that the heaven of Venus was the cause of love on earth, they believed that Love or Cupid was her son: "E perchè li antichi s'accorsero che quello cielo era qua giù cagione d'amore, dissero Amore essere figlio di Venere ..." (II, v, 14). Although the *Convivio's* author does not accept the classical conclusions, that there is a goddess Venus whose son is Love, he seems not to argue with the basic premise, i.e. that the heaven of Venus causes love on earth. His choice of words, especially his use of the verb *s'accorso*, seems to indicate his fundamental agreement on this score.

The relation between Venus and causality is precisely what is at issue in the *Comedy*; *Paradiso* VIII is at pains to revoke the notion of celestially induced eros. Outright celestial influence is, of course, denied in general terms throughout the *Comedy*, from Marco Lombardo's discourse on free will to Beatrice's attack on the "poison" in Plato's theory of astral return. But, perhaps because the belief in a necessary inclination toward *folle amore* is particularly widespread and pernicious, the poet uses the heaven of Venus specifically to combat the idea that Venus causes love on earth;[57] the perils inherent in such beliefs are therefore immediately raised in this heaven's first verse—"Solea creder lo mondo in suo periclo"—with its emphasis on the dangers besetting a misguided world. Nor is the classical position criticized only in these verses; Charles Martel later resumes the topic in his discourse on heredity, explaining that the influences of the heavens, which left to themselves would he disastrously mechanistic, are in fact ordered and regulated by divine providence. This concluding emphasis on astral limitation reinforces the admonition regarding excessive credence with which the canto begins.

The world's peril is perhaps also the peril of the *Convivio*'s author; it is interesting that Charles, naming a canzone from the *Convivio*, refers to its author as "del mondo," of the world. At any rate, the correction of the *Convivio* that runs through *Paradiso* VIII ultimately addresses itself for the major issue of the treatise's erroneous trust in classical culture and thought, a trust that is openly condemned by Beatrice in *Purgatorio* XXXIII, where she refers deridingly to the pilgrim's faith in "that school which you have followed" (85–96). This issue is related to the autocitation of *Paradiso* VIII by way of the *donna gentile*, who is allegorized as Lady Philosophy, and whose preeminence in the canzone and in the treatise is part of the *Convivio* error, and part of what the *Comedy* is correcting. If, then, "Voi che 'ntendendo" belongs to a generally corrective framework in *Paradiso* VIII, how do we account for its privileged position among the *Comedy*'s autocitations.

Let us begin by considering the tale of "Voi che 'ntendendo" in the context of Dante's lyric poetry. Editions of the *Rime* place the canzone shortly after the poems of the *Vita Nuova*, establishing the priority of "Voi che 'ntendendo" for Dante's post-*Vita Nuova* production.[58] The use of "Voi che 'ntendendo" as a new starting point is, moreover, justified by Dante's own practice; he uses it as lead canzone and point of reference for the sequence of poems devoted to the *donna gentile*, and he places it first in the *Convivio*. The importance attached to this canzone is also signaled by the fact that "Voi che 'ntendendo" is the only one of his lyrics whose incipit Dante cites twice, not only in the *Comedy* but also in the sonnet "Parole mie."

We recall that "Parole mie" explicitly refers to "Voi che 'ntendendo" as a new poetic beginning. Summoning back all the poems previously sent to this lady, the poet addresses his errant words:

Parole mie che per lo mondo siete,
voi che nasceste *poi ch'io cominciai*
a dir per quella donna in cui errai:
'Voi che 'ntendendo il terzo ciel movete'

> Words of mine who are throughout the world, you who were born
> *when I began* to write for that lady in whom I erred "Voi che
> 'ntendendo il terzo ciel movete"
>
> (1–4; italics mine)

"Voi che 'ntendendo" is thus named as the text in which the poet began ("poi ch'io cominciai") to write about "that lady in whom I erred." The judgment expressed by this last phrase, "quella donna in cui errai," is shared by the *Comedy*; indeed, we have thus far concentrated on the *Paradiso*'s correction of "Voi che 'ntendendo" as a poem that subscribes to that misleading lady. But the sonnet "Parole mie" testifies also to a positive significance possessed by the canzone, a significance whose emblem is the expression "poi ch'io cominciai."[59] "Voi che 'ntendendo" is a song of conflict, but also a song of beginning; in the history of Dante's artistic growth, the canzone initiates those fundamental developments that follow Beatrice's death and the writing of the *Vita Nuova*.

The status of "Voi che 'ntendendo" in the *Comedy* hinges on the fact that the canzone marks a turning point, a crucial watershed, in Dante's career. Its position in Dante's canon is in fact analogous to that of the *Convivio*. From the perspective of the *Comedy*, the *Convivio* is both an erring text that has been eclipsed by the return to Beatrice as a primary source of signification, and also—paradoxically—the text that makes the *Comedy* possible. Although in the later Dante's retrospective scheme the *Vita Nuova* is idealized as the repository of the *Comedy*'s fundamental thematics, there is nonetheless an acknowledgment that these themes could not have matured in scope and complexity without the prior intervention of the *Convivio*. "Voi che 'ntendendo," as the *Convivio*'s first canzone and the text in which the poet first adopts a stance that is decisively not that of the *Vita Nuova*, signifies the moment of turning from "lyric" to "epic" concerns, a turning that is ultimately responsible for the *Comedy*.

As an autocitation, then, "Voi che 'ntendendo" marks the passage from the restricted world of the *Vita Nuova* to the larger world of the *Convivio*. In one sense the canzone marks this turn negatively, by positing a conflict that was in fact unnecessary, and as the harbinger of a phase that would need to be surpassed. In the *Comedy*, however, the *Convivio*'s conflict is resolved through the simultaneous presence of the two terms that in the treatise could not coexist: "politics" (the prince, and the other figures of this heaven who all bear a political significance) on the one hand, and "Beatrice" on the other. In the *Comedy*, in other words, the conflict of the canzone is reviewed and reread; from this final perspective it is seen as not conflict but poetic growth, forward motion after the stasis of the *Vita Nuova*'s completion.

As the *Convivio* stands in dialectical relation to the *Vita Nuova*, so "Voi che 'ntendendo" stands in dialectical relation to "Donne ch'avete." Whereas the latter text is a summa, a fulfillment (and is therefore celebrated in *Purgatorio* XXIV as the pinnacle of Dante's achievement in the lyric mode), the former achieves significance not for what it has done but for what it leaves undone. Whereas "Donne ch'avete" is important for itself, "Voi che 'ntendendo" is important as a sign pointing beyond itself. Whereas "Donne ch'avete" signifies an end (an end that later will be valorized as a repository of all beginnings), "Voi che 'ntendendo" signifies a beginning. Moreover, it draws its value precisely from its relation to its precursor; if "Voi che 'ntendendo" is a new beginning in Dante's career, it is so by virtue of the fact that it is the first of his texts to challenge the assumptions of the *Vita Nuova*.

Not surprisingly, "Voi che 'ntendendo" presents itself as different from its forerunners. The emblem of its difference is the nonlyric word "grandezza," used here in order to praise the new lady, who is "saggia e cortese ne la sua grandezza" (47). Thus, even as a love poem, "Voi che 'ntendendo" bears the signs of its unlikeness; "grandezza" is the lexical representative—along with "transmutata," from line 44, which appears only here in Dante's lyrics—of all the larger and nonlyric themes and concerns that will surface in the *Convivio*. The canzone continues to insist on its special status: its discourse can be proffered only to the angelic intelligences of the third heaven, being too "new" for other ears ("udite il ragionar ch'è nel mio core, / ch'io nol so dire altrui, sì mi par novo" "listen to the speech which is in my heart, for I do not know how to express it to others, it seems so new to me" [2–3]); again in the first stanza the poet draws attention to the novelty of his condition ("Io vi dirò del cor la novitate" "I will tell you of the newness of my heart" [10]). The emphasis on the poem's originality reappears in the *congedo*, where the poet comments that, due to the canzone's difficulty, few will understand it; in the penultimate verse he calls it "diletta mia novella." This sense of literal newness finds its confirmation in the other newness with which this poem is invested; as the first of Dante's love lyrics to carry an allegorical significance. "Voi che 'ntendendo" is a particularly fitting emblem for a turning point.

There is, however, a poem in Dante's canon that might be said to mark a shift more explicitly than "Voi che 'ntendendo," and this is "Le dolci rime," the last poem of the *Convivio*. In the first stanza the poet situates the canzone with respect to its predecessors:

> Le dolci rime d'amor ch'i' solia
> cercar ne' miei pensieri,
> convien ch'io lasci; non perch'io non speri
> ad esse ritornare,
>   ma perché li atti disdegnosi e feci,
> che ne la donna mia
> sono appariti, m han chiusa la via
> de l'usato parlare.
>   E poi che tempo mi par d'aspettare,
> diporrò giù lo mici soave stile,

ch'i' ho tenuto nel trattar d'amore;
e diró del valore,
per lo qual veramente omo è gentile,
con rima aspr'e sottile

I must leave the sweet love poems that I was accustomed to seek out
in my thoughts; not because I do lot hope to return to them, but
because the disdainful and harsh acts which have appeared in my lady
have closed the way of my usual speech. And since it now seems a
time for waiting, I will lay down my sweet style which I have used in
treating love, and I will speak of the quality through which man is
truly noble, with harsh and subtle rhymes

(1–14)

The exordium explains how the poem came to be written: because his lady's
proud behavior has blocked all further discourse with her, the poet is temporarily
putting aside "le dolci rime d'amor"; while waiting for her to soften, he proposes
to write about nobility, the "valore, / per lo qual veramente omo è gentile," not
in his accustomed "soave stile," but with "rima aspr'e sottile."

Like the sonnet "Parole mie," this canzone is introduced as a moment in
which the poet is out of his lady's favor. Unlike the sonnet, however, "Le dolci
rime" finds a radical solution to the problem. Whereas "Parole mie," in that it is
a negative love poem, a renouncing of the beloved, remains within the narrative
structure that links the various poems to the *donna gentile*, "Le dolci rime" breaks
out from this structure altogether. In the canzone her coldness produces not the
lover's quarrel sanctioned by the plot, as in the previous renunciations, but
something more significant, namely a change of genre. Rather than continuing
to write "sweet love poems," the poet undertakes a new kind of poetry, written
in a new register, "with harsh and subtle rhymes." The writing of "Le dolci rime"
thus marks the transition to a later stage in Dante's poetic development, the stage
characterized by his moral and doctrinal verse; the canzone is in fact, as was
noted earlier, the first in a series of moral poems. We see, then, why Foster and
Boyde can claim that in "Le dolci rime" Dante "comes about as near to making
a fresh start as any mature poet can do," for it is here that Dante first becomes a
moral poet.[60] And, because the doctrinal canzoni accommodate a lyric mode to
moral themes, they constitute the indispensable link between Dante's early
poetry and the *Comedy*.

If the last of the *Comedy*'s autocitations is chosen with a view to marking an
internal transition toward the *poema sacro*, we may wonder why "Le dolci rime"
is not recited in the *Paradiso* instead of "Voi che 'ntendendo." The fact that the
three autocitations are stylistically homogeneous, and that all belong stylistically
to the poet's *stil novo* phase, seems not unimportant in this regard. "Le dolci
rime" effects a radical discontinuity with respect to the style of its predecessors;

as its first stanza declares, it is no longer *soave*. Precisely this characteristic, which on the one hand strengthens its connection to the *Comedy* (where the poet will request, when he needs them, "rime aspre e chiocce"), on the other unsuits it for inclusion among the autocitations. Unlike "Le dolci rime," "Voi che 'ntendendo" can mark the transition to larger themes from *within* the lyric mode, a mode that is essentially amatory and "sweet"; in fact, the canzone's stylistic continuity with "Amor che ne la mente" and "Donne ch'avete" is a major part of its point.

"Voi che 'ntendendo" works both ways: as the initiator of the conflict that would eventually lead Dante to devote himself entirely to philosophy, it points forward to his moral and ethical verse, to "Le dolci rime"; as a love poem to the *donna gentile*, it looks back to the *Vita Nuova*, and to "Donne ch'avete." As compared to the later didactic canzoni, "Voi che 'ntendendo" is part of a continuum that begins in the *Vita Nuova*: Beatrice is still present (although about to be displaced); the *Vita Nuova*'s dictum against nonamatory lyric has not yet been explicitly reversed (although the use of allegory would in itself imply that lyrics can now be composed "sopra altra matera che amorosa").[61] The poem's form links it to the past, and even though its meaning may be more difficult to comprehend than that of earlier poems, "tanto la parli faticosa e forte" ("so tiring and hard is your speech" [55]), its last verse exhorts us to remember its beautiful appearance, "Ponete mente almen com'io son bella!" ("Consider least how beautiful I am!").

If the canzone's exterior beauty connects it to the past, its inner difficulty connects it to the future, to Dante's didactic verse and ultimately to the *Comedy*. And it is, finally, this difficulty that accounts for the presence of "Voi che 'ntendendo" in the heaven of Venus, a "difficult" heaven. As it appears in the second book of the *Convivio*, accompanied by its allegorical gloss, "Voi che 'ntendendo" implies the transition that "Le dolci rime" renders explicit; it implies transition through conflict and ambivalence, the same conflict and ambivalence represented in the heaven of Venus. Precisely because it is about conflict, "Voi che 'ntendendo" can best serve as a marker for the stage beyond conflict, a stage in which both terms have not yet been resolved out of existence, but rather coexist, as Beatrice and the canzone coexist in *Paradiso* VIII. At the same time, in that it is ostensibly a love poem, to which a deeper and more public meaning has been added, "Voi che 'ntendendo" can best dramatize Dante's transition, from within the lyric, to a nonlyric and nonprivate mode.

This last duality, the coexistence of a private mode with a public meaning, is mirrored in the episode of the *Paradiso*. It is appropriate that in the heaven of love we should find the *Comedy*'s last lyric love poets as well as its last lyric love poet; yet, in this heaven, both function less as themselves than as signifiers of what lies beyond them. Both "Voi che 'ntendendo" and Folquet de Marselha (of whom more will be said later) are chosen as emblems of transition from the private to the public, a transition that they themselves do not fully achieve but to which they bear a deictic relation. And perhaps, when all is said and done, all of the *Comedy's* autocitations are chosen for their ability to point beyond. The three poems share two common features; they all belong to Dante's *stil novo* register, and their incipits all emphasize the intellect. That is, they all point, from within the *stil novo*, to beyond the *stil novo*, to the radically transformed eros of the *Comedy*. "Amor che ne la *mente* mi *ragiona*," "Donne ch'avete *intelletto* d'amore," "Voi che 'ntendendo il terzo ciel movete"—the intellective stress of these verses unite all these canzoni as redeemed poetry.

The aim of this chapter has been to clarify some of the autobiographical impulses at work in the *Comedy*. If autobiography is a mode in which the urge for order is particularly acute, an urge that is translated into a teleological imperative, the autobiography of the *Comedy* is governed by a dual pressure: the one exerted by the mode, and the other by the providential framework. In the *Comedy*, all characters, all themes, all texts and their makers are inserted into a providential structure that guarantees the nature of the ending. In the autobiographical instance (and all of Dante's texts are profoundly autobiographical), the pressure imposed by providence is supplemented by the pressure implicit in the discourse, a narrative exigency that accounts for the self-consuming revisionism of these texts. This pressure, always present as the deep meaning of Dante's narrative structure, appears on the surface in some more "superficial" forms: the prose and the *divisioni* of the *Vita Nuova*, the gloss of the *Convivio*, the autocitations of the *Comedy*. From this point of view it was a foregone conclusion that the final autocitation would signify not itself but the guaranteed ending; "Voi che 'ntendendo" is yet one more new beginning to be transformed—"transmutata"—into a sign for the *Comedy* itself. And finally, in passing from Dante's treatment of himself to his treatment of his peers, we should note that the teleological imperative structured into his own "life" is, naturally, imposed onto the lives of others.

NOTES

1. Scholars dealing with autobiography or autoexegesis in Dante have adopted a variety of approaches. The critic who has most illuminated the dialectical intersecting of the *Comedy* with its poetic past is Gianfranco Contini, who comments that "la *Commedia* è, dopo tutto, anche la storia, stavo per dire l'autobiografia, di un poeta" ("Dante come personaggio-poeta della *Commedia*," *L'Approdo letterario*, 4 [1958], 19–46, repr. in *Un'idea di Dante* [Turin: Einaudi, 1976], pp. 33–62; the quotation is from *Un'idea di Dante*, p. 40). Giovanni Fallani, *Dante autobiografico* (Naples: Società editrice napoletana, 1975), reconstructs Dante's biography on the basis of his texts. Marziano Guglielminetti, *Memoria e scrittura: l'autobiografia da Dante a Cellini* (Turin: Einaudi, 1977), places the *Vita Nuova* and *Convivio* in a historical framework (see in this context the questions raised by Paul Zumthor, "Autobiography in the Middle Ages?" *Genre*, 6 [1973], 29–48). William C. Spengemann discusses the

Vita Nuova from an autobiographical perspective in *The Forms of Autobiography* (New Haven and London: Yale U. Press, 1980), as does Jerome Mazzaro, *The Figure of Dante: An Essay on the Vita Nuova* (Princeton: Princeton U. Press, 1981). The *Convivio* and Epistle to Cangrande della Scala are situated within the tradition of medieval exegesis by L. Jenaro MacLennan, "Autocomentario en Dante y comentarismo latino," *Vox Romanica*, 19 (1960), 82–123, and Gian Roberto Sarolli, "Autoesegesi dantesca e tradizione esegetica medievale," *Convivium*, 34 (1966), 177–112, repr. in *Prolegomena alla Divina Commedia* (Florence: Olschki, 1971), pp. 1–39. John Freccero has written on the role of the Augustinian model in shaping the Comedy as a confessional narrative; see especially "Dante's Novel of the Self," *Christian Century*, 82 (1965), 1216–1218, "Dante's Prologue Scene," *Dante Studies*, 84 (1966), 1–25, and "Dante's Medusa: Allegory and Autobiography," in *By Things Seen: Reference and Recognition in Medieval Thought*, ed. David L. Jeffrey (Ottawa: U. of Ottawa Press, 1979), pp. 33–46. A recent proposal for reading the *Comedy* in an autoexegetical key is provided by Amilcare A. Iannucci, "Autoesegesi dantesca: la tecnica dell' 'episodio parallelo' nella *Commedia*," *Lettere italiane*, 33 (1981), 305–328.

2. The following studies focus on textuality in *Inferno* V: Paget Toynbee, "Dante and the Lancelot Romance," in *Dante Studies and Researches* (London: Methuen, 1902), pp. 1–37; Gioacchino Paparelli, "*Galeotto fu il libro e chi lo scrisse*" (Naples: Conte, 1954), repr. as "Ethos e pathos nell'episodio di Francesca da Rimini," in *Ideologia e poesia di Dante* (Florence: Olschki, 1975), pp. 171–200; Renato Poggioli, "Tragedy or Romance? A Reading of the Paolo and Francesca Episode in Dante's *Inferno*," *PMLA*, 72 (1957), 313–358, repr. in *Dante: A Collection of Critical Essays*, ed. John Freccero (Englewood Cliffs, N.J.: Prentice-Hall, 1965), pp. 61–77; Gianfranco Contini, "Dante come personaggio-poeta della *Commedia*," esp. pp. 42–48; Roger Dragonetti, "L'Épisode de Francesca dans le Cadre de la Convention courtoise," *Romanica Gandensia*, 9 (1961), 93–116; Daniele Mattalia, "Moralità e dottrina nel canto V dell'*Inferno*," *Filologia e letteratura*, 8 (1962), 41–70; Antonino Pagliaro, "Il canto di Francesca," in *Ulisse: ricerche semantiche sulla Divina Commedia*, 2 vols. (Messina-Florence: D'Anna, 1967), vol. 1, pp. 115–159; Lanfranco Caretti, "Il canto V dell'*Inferno*," *Nuove letture dantesche* (Florence: Le Monnier, 1968), vol. I, pp. 105–131; Anna Hatcher and Mark Musa, "The Kiss: *Inferno* V and the Old French Prose Lancelot," *Comparative Literature*, 20 (1968), 97–109; Robert Hollander, *Allegory in Dante's Commedia* (Princeton: Princeton U. Press, 1969), esp. pp. 106–114; Nicolas J. Perella, *The Kiss Sacred and Profane* (Berkeley-Los Angeles: U. of California Press, 1969), pp. 140–157; D'Arco Silvio Avalle, "... de fole amor," in *Modelli semiologici della Divina Commedia* (Milan: Bompiani, 1975), pp. 97–121; John A. Scott, "Dante's Francesca and the Poet's Attitude towards Courtly Literature," *Reading Medieval Studies*, 5 (1979), 4–20; Giuseppe Mazzotta, *Dante, Poet of the Desert* (Princeton: Princeton U. Press, 1979), esp. pp. 160–170; Stephen Popolizio, "Literary Reminiscences and the Act of Reading in *Inferno*

V," *Dante Studies*, 98 (1980), 19–33; Susan Noakes, "The Double Misreading of Paolo and Francesca," *Philological Quarterly*, 62 (1983), 221–239; Karla Taylor, "A Text and Its Afterlife: Dante and Chaucer," *Comparative Literature*, 35 (1983), 1–20. See also Baldo Curato, *Il canto di Francesca e i suoi interpreti* (Cremona: Editrice Padus, 1963).

3. Contini points out that Francesca's verse, "Amor, ch'a nullo amato amar perdona," draws on two of Andreas' Rules of Love: Rule IX, "Amare nemo potest nisi qui amoris suasione compellitur" ("No one can love unless he is compelled by the persuasion of love"); Rule XXVI, "Amor nil posset amore denegare" ("Love can deny nothing to love") ("Dante come personaggio-poeta della *Commedia*," p. 46). The theme of love and the noble heart in its various transmutations from Andreas to Guittone, Guinizzelli, and Dante is discussed by D'Arco Silvio Avalle, "Due tesi sui limiti di amore," in *Ai luoghi di delizia pieni: saggio sulla lirica italiana del XIII secolo* (Milan-Naples: Ricciardi, 1977), pp. 17–55. On Dante's relation to Andreas, see also Maria Simonelli, "Il terra della nobiltà in Andrea Cappellano e in Dante," *Dante Studies*, 84 (1966), 51–68, and Antonio Viscardi, "Andrea Cappellano," *Enciclopedia Dantesca*, 6 vols. (Rome: Istituto dell'Enciclopedia Italiana, 1970–1978), vol. I, pp. 261–263.

4. "Dante come personaggio-poeta della Commedia," p. 43. For the poetry of Guinizzelli and his peers, the edition used throughout, unless otherwise noted, is Contini, *Poeti del Dueceuto*, 2 vols. (Milan-Naples: Ricciardi, 1960).

5. The high incidence of language relating to speech supports the notion that *Inferno* II is a markedly verbal canto; besides the various forms of *dire* employed to relate what one person said to another, we note the frequent iteration of "parlare" and "parola": "S'i' ho ben la parola tua intesa" (43), "Or movi, e con la tua parola ornata" (67), "amor mi mosse, che mi fa parlare" (72), "com' io, dopo cotai parole fatte" (111), "fidandomi del tuo parlare onesto" (113), "e 'l mio parlar tanto ben ti promette" (126), "a le vere parole che ti porse" (135), "si al venir con le parole tue" (137). The court of heaven seems to rely heavily on words. For more on this issue, see Chapter III, note 100.

6. For examples of synonymic reduplication in the early Dante and the relation of this stylistic feature to the Italian poetic tradition, see Kenelm Foster and Patrick Boyde, *Dante's Lyric Poetry*, vol. II: *Commentary*, p. 35. Regarding the stilnovist resonance of Canto II, Sapegno comments that "L'atmosfera in cui si colloca questa prima presentazione di Beatrice è tipicamente stilnovistica, anche nei particolari, e prima di tutto in questo gesto di 'omaggio' di Virgilio" (Natalino Sapegno, comm., *La Divina Commedia*, 2d ed., 3 vols. [Florence: La Nuova Italia, 1968], vol. I: *Inferno*, p. 22.

7. See the sonnet "Vedut' ho la lucente stella diana," where the poet not only compares his lady to the morning star, but also refers in line 6 to her "occhi lucenti," thus anticipating both terms of Dante's "Lucevan li occhi suoi più che la stella." Other comparisons to the *stella diana* appear in line 3 of Guinizzelli's

"Io voglio del ver la mia donna laudare" ("più che la stella diana splende e pare"), and in the second line of Cavalcanti's "In un boschetto trova' pasturella" ("più che la stella—bella").

8. The sixteenth-century commentator Lodovico Castelvetro sums up the perplexity of the critics in his question "Questo che monta a Virgilio che è dannato?" ("How does this help Vergil, who is damned?"). The quotation is from Guido Biagi, ed., *La Divina Commedia nella figurazione artistica e nel secolare commento*, 3 vols. (Turin: Unione Tipografico-Editrice Torinese, 1924–1929), vol. I, p. 68. The commentators closest to Dante tend to do away with the problem by reading the passage allegorically; for instance, Benvenuto comments: "Hoc autem significat quod theologia saepe utitur servicio rationis naturalis" ("this moreover signifies that theology often makes use of the services of natural reason"). See Benvenuti de Rambaldis de Imola, *Comentum super Dantis Aldigherij Commediam*, ed. J. P. Lacaita, 5 vols. (Florence: Barbèra, 1887), vol. I, p 93. With the exception of Benvenuto, who will be cited according to Lacaita, all quotations from the early commentators will be taken from Biagi's edition.

9. Following the evidence of *Paradiso* VIII, the *terminus ante quem* of this canzone has been placed by most critics as March of 1294, the date given by Villani for Charles Martel's three-week visit to Florence; Foster and Boyde accept Santangelo's suggestion that the canzone could not have been written substantially later than the spring of 1294 (*Commentary*, pp. 345–346). See their Appendix, "The Biographical Problems in 'Voi che 'ntendendo,'" *Commentary*, pp. 341–362, for a lucid exposition of the debate surrounding the dating of this canzone and the other poems to the *donna gentile*.

10. On the importance of the *De Amicitia* and its medieval epigones for Dante, see Domenico De Robertis, *Il libro della Vita Nuova*, 2d ed. rev. (Florence: Sansoni, 1970), pp. 21–24 and 93–115. De Robertis links Cicero's notion of disinterested friendship with the *Vita Nuova*'s elaboration of a disinterested love. See also Alessandro Ronconi, "Cicerone," *Enciclopedia Dantesca*, vol. I, pp. 991–997. Marziano Guglielminetti, in "Dante e il ricupero del 'parlare di se medesimo,'" chap. 2 of *Memoria e scrittura: l'autobiografia da Dante a Cellini*, stresses the role of Boethius as Dante's confessional model in the *Convivio* over that of Augustine, esp. pp. 74–75 and 97–99. For Dante and Boethius, see Rocco Murari, *Dante e Boezio* (Bologna: Zanichelli, 1905); Marie Thérèse D'Alverny, "Notes sur Dante et la Sagesse," *Revue des Études Italiennes*, 11 (1965), 5–24; Francesco Tateo, "Boezio," *Enciclopedia Dantesca*, vol. I, pp. 654–658.

11. Perhaps the most conspicuous among the allegorists is Bruno Nardi, who argues that the *donna gentile* was born allegorical; for an explicit formulation see "Le figurazioni allegoriche e l'allegoria della 'donna gentile,'" in *Nel mondo di Dante* (Rome: Edizioni di Storia e Letteratura, 1944), pp. 23–40. Another strong advocate of this view is James E. Shaw, *The Lady "Philosophy" in the Convivio* (Cambridge: Dante Society, 1938). Among the realists are Fausto Montanari,

L'esperienza poetica di Dante, 2d ed. (Florence: Le Monnier, 1968), esp. chap. III, "Tra la *Vita Nuova* e il *Convivio*"; also Amerindo Camilli, "Le prime due canzoni del *Convivio* di Dante," *Lettere italiane*, 4 (1952), 70–91. De Robertis offers a cogent dismantling of Nardi's position in "Il libro della *Vita Nuova* e il libro del *Convivio*," *Studi urbinati*, 25 (1951), 5–27. For a survey of the critical positions, see Giorgio Petrocchi, "Donna gentile," *Enciclopedia Dantesca*, vol. II, pp. 574–577, repr. in *L'ultima dea* (Rome: Bonacci, 1977), pp. 97–104.

12. Barbi states his position in his Introduction to the *Convivio*, ed. G. Busnelli and G. Vandelli; his insistence that we distinguish the problems inherent in the *Vita Nuova* from those of the *Convivio* ("Bisogna risolverci ... a intendere ciascun'opera di Dante secondo la reale ispirazione del momento" [I, xxiii]) is picked up and endorsed by De Robertis, who stresses the disjunction between the two texts in his title "Il libro della *Vita Nuova* e il libro del *Convivio*." This line of reasoning eventually leads, however, to sundering what Dante deliberately conflated, and thus bypassing the problem altogether; as an example of this tendency, see Maria Simonelli, "'Donna pietosa' e 'donna gentile' fra *Vita Nuova* e *Convivio*," in *Atti del Convegno di studi su aspetti e problemi di critica dantesca* (Rome: De Luca, 1967), pp. 146–159.

13. In order to support his thesis Nardi was forced to defend Pietrobono, who had postulated the existence of a first version of the *Vita Nuova* in which the *donna gentile* was victorious; accordingly, we possess the second version, to which the author returned after the experience of the *Convivio* with the intention of providing a new ending (Beatrice victorious) that would be consonant with the *Comedy*. See "Dalla prima alla seconda *Vita Nuova*," in *Nel mondo di Dante*, pp. 3–20; "Filosofia dell'amore nei rimatori italiani del Duecento e in Dante," in *Dante e la cultura medievale*, 2d ed. rev. (Bari: Laterza, 1949), esp. pp. 49–51; "Sviluppo dell'arte e del pensiero di Dante," *Bibliothéque d'Humanisme et Renaissance*, 14 (1952), 29–47; "Dante e Guido Cavalcanti," in *Saggi e note di critica dantesca* (Milan: Ricciardi, 1961), pp. 190–219. This theory of two redactions of the *Vita Nuova* (which unfortunately runs through all of Nardi's work on the subject) never gained general acceptance and was laid definitively to rest by Mario Marti, "Vita e morte della presunta doppia redazione della *Vita Nuova*," in *Studi in onóre di Alfredo Schiaffini*, 2 vols. (Rome: Edizioni dell'Ateneo, 1965), vol. II, pp. 657–669 (= *Rivista di cultura classica e medioevale*, 7 [1965]).

14. Singleton stresses the analogical rather than allegorical nature of the *Vita Nuova* in *An Essay on the Vita Nuova* (1949; repr. Baltimore: Johns Hopkins U. Press, 1977), esp. pp. 22–24 and 110–114. In "Dante *Theologus-Poeta*," *Dante Studies*, 94 (1976), 91–136, repr. in *Studies in Dante* (Ravenna: Longo, 1980), pp. 31–89, Robert Hollander argues that "Had Dante assigned a designation to the mode of signifying of the *Vita Nuova*, using the same two possibilities he set before us in the *Convivio*, he would not have hesitated to have told us that the *Vita Nuova* was written in the allegory of theologians" (p. 56). At this point I

should like to alert the reader to my fundamental agreement with Singleton as regards Dante's use of the so-called allegory of theologians in the *Comedy*; for bibliography on this subject, see Hollander's *Allegory in Dante's Commedia* and "Dante *Theologus-Poeta*," and Jean Pépin, *Dante et la Tradition de l'Allégorie* (Montréal: Institut d'études médiévales, 1971).

15. "Onde io, volendo che cotale desiderio malvagio e vana tentazione paresse distrutto, si che alcuno dubbio non potessero inducere le rimate parole ch'io avea dette innanzi, propuosi di fare uno sonetto ne lo quale io comprendesse la sentenzia di questa ragione" ("Wherefore I, desiring that such a wicked desire and vain temptation would appear to be destroyed, so that no doubts could be adduced with respect to the rhymed words I had composed heretofore, proposed to write a sonnet which would include the essence of this discourse" [*Vita Nuova*, XXXIX, 61).

16. The qualification is intended to leave room for the *Fiore* as possibly Dante's first allegorical venture, in imitation of the *Roman de la Rose*. The attribution of the *Fiore* to Dante is now widely accepted in the wake of the internal evidence demonstrated by Gianfranco Contini; see his "La questione del *Fiore*," *Cultura e scuola* 4, nos. 13–14 (1965), 768–773, and his article in the *Enciclopedia Dantesca*, vol. II, pp. 895–901. A recent book that takes Dante's authorship of the *Fiore* for granted is that of Luigi Vanossi, *Dante e il Roman de la Rose: Saggio sul Fiore* (Florence: Olschki, 1979). The *Fiore* is not discussed at greater length in this study because it lacks explicit literary references; although the text is a sustained tribute to the *Roman de la Rose*, and although it names philosophers (Socrates in XLIII, Sigier of Brabant in XCII, Ptolemy in CLXX), kings (Solomon in LXV and CIX, Justinian in CX), and literary lovers (Tristan and Isolde in CXLIV, Dido and Aeneus in CLXI, Jason and Medea in CXLI and CXC), it names no precursor poets.

17. One of the most striking features of the *Convivio* is its adumbration of the *Comedy*'s metaphors, in the "pane de li angeli" (I, i, 7), the "selva erronea di questa vita" (IV, xxiv, 12), and especially in the recurrent images of wayfaring, by land and by sea, that run through the treatise. The sustained metaphorization of life as a pilgrimage in *Convivio* IV, xii, 14–19 renders explicit what in the *Vita Nuova* is implied by the pilgrims who pass through the city. On the *Convivio* as the most important source of the *Comedy*, see the article on the treatise by Maria Simonelli, *Enciclopedia Dantesca*, vol. II, pp. 193–204.

18. This view is shared by Montanari, *L'esperienza poetica di Dante*, p. 118, and De Robertis, "Il libro della *Vita Nuova* e il libro del *Convivio*," p. 20. For the stylistic homogeneity of these canzoni with Dante's *stil novo* phase, see De Robertis, p. 11; Foster and Boyde comment as follows on the style of "Voi che 'ntendendo": "There are no describable innovations in style with respect to the preceding sonnets: this and the following poems represent the climax of Dante's *stil novo* period" (*Commentary*, p. 161). Dante himself essentially admits that his

canzoni do not appear allegorical, for instance when he writes "E con ciò sia cosa che la vera intenzione mia fosse altra che quella che di fuori mostrano le canzoni predette. per allegorica esposizione quelle intendo mostrare" ("And since my true intention was other than that revealed by the surface of the aforementioned canzoni, I intend to reveal them through an allegorical exposition" [*Convivio* I, i, 18]).

19. Foster and Boyde, *Commentary*, p. 167. On the other hand, *grandezza* need not have allegorical implications; it could serve merely as a means of distinguishing the new lady from Beatrice.

20. Other verses seized on by the allegorists are "Ogni Intelletto di là su la mira" ("All the Intelligences from above gaze on her" [23]) and "costei pensò chi mosse l'universo" ("He who moved the universe thought of her" [72]). In his gloss to line 72 (*Convivio* III, xv, 16) Dante makes the connection to Sapientia, citing Proverbs viii, 27–30.

21. Numerous possibilities for "errai" are listed in M. Barbi and V. Pernicone, eds., *Rime della maturità e dell'esilio* (Florence: Le Monnier, 1969), p. 461. Contini notes that the verse is usually interpreted as referring to the lady "in whom I erred" ("nella quale presi errore"), but prefers Barbi's suggestion "because of whom I suffered" ("per la quale soffersi"); see his edition of the *Rime* (1946; repr. Turin: Einaudi, 1970), p. 107. Although Foster and Boyde translate the verse with "the lady in whom I was deceived," they note that "the sense could be 'through whom I went astray'" (*Commentary*, p. 184).

22. Two studies meriting particular attention are John Freccero, "Casella's Song (*Purg.* II, 112)," *Dante Studies*, 91 (1973), 73–80; and Robert Hollander, "*Purgatorio* II: Cato's Rebuke and Dante's *scoglio*," *Italica*, 52 (1975), 348–363, now repr. in *Studies in Dante*, pp. 91–105. Gian Roberto Sarolli, "*Purgatorio* II: dal *Convivio* alla *Commedia*," in *Prolegomena alla Divina Commedia*, pp. 55–74, does not deal with "Amor che ne la mente," but with general thematic convergences between the canto and the prose treatise.

23. Mario Marti, "Il canto II del *Purgatorio*," *Lectura Dantis Scaligera* (Florence: Le Monnier, 1963). On the performance value of "Amor che ne la mente" and Dante's other texts, see John Ahearn, "Singing the Book: Orality in the Reception of Dante's *Comedy*," *Annals of Scholarship* 2, no. 4 (1981), 17–40. Also useful on this canto is the reading of Vittorio Russo, "Il canto II del *Purgatorio*," in *Esperienze e/di letture dantesche* (Naples: Liguori, 1971), pp. 53–99.

24. Although Petrocchi replaces the customary "voglie" of line 108 with "doglie," I have followed Singleton in preserving a variant that, in my opinion, is more consonant with the voluntarist emphasis of the episode and of the *cantica* whose paradigm it is; see Charles S. Singleton, trans. and comm., *The Divine Comedy*, 6 vols. (Princeton: Princeton U. Press, 1970–1975), *Purgatorio*, 2: *Commentary*, p. 40.

25. Hollander's position is well represented by his first sentence: "Casella's song is a Siren's song" ("*Purgatorio* II," p. 348). In response, I would point out that the poet deliberately defuses the severity of Cato's charges in the opening of *Purgatorio* III, where he calls Vergil's lapse a "picciol fallo" ("little fault" [9]).

26. Freccero, "Casella's Song," p. 74.

27. Both Freccero and Hollander make much of Boethius in their articles on Casella's song. Freccero draws attention to a Boethian meter describing the feeding of caged birds, who scorn the food given them in their desire to return home to the woods; this same Boethian passage is noted by Vincent Moleta, "'Come l'ausello in selva a la verdura,'" *Studi danteschi*, 52 (1979–1980), 1–67, repr. in *Guinizzelli in Dante* (Rome: Edizioni di Storia e Letteratura, 1980). In this book Moleta provides a reading of the *Comedy*'s incipits in a Guinizzellian key, suggesting that Dante "chooses to recall in his last work precisely those canzoni in which the inspirational force of *Al cor gentil*, and above all his transformation of the last two stanzas of that canzone, are most in evidence" (p. 145).

28. This fact could serve, I believe, as an argument against the original allegorical significance of "Voi che 'ntendendo." If the canzone had been written with the allegory of Lady Philosophy in mind, would Dante not have taken pains to attach the key word *consolare* to her in the text of the poem, rather than to Beatrice? The strenuous attachment of *consolare* to the *donna gentile* in the allegorical gloss of *Convivio* II, xii almost seems, from this point of view, like a cover-up. My tendency to believe that the canzoni were initially composed as love poems is strengthened by *Purgatorio* II: Casella's attitude toward "Amor che ne la mente" might be taken as a sign that it too was originally nonallegorical, especially considering that the verses confirming the poem's *dolcezza*—i.e. its status as a love poem—are delivered not by the pilgrim but by the poet.

29. This view is expressed by Vincenzo Pernicone in the article "Amor che ne la mente mi ragiona," *Enciclopedia Dantesca*, vol. I, pp. 217–219.

30. These verses have given rise to essentially two divergent critical camps: one traditionally sees in Bonagiunta's words an implied reference to a "school" of new poets, and the other maintains that the only *stilnovista* so designated by Bonagiunta is Dante himself. This last position is presented by De Robertis in "Definizione dello stil novo," *L'Approdo*, 3 (1954), 59–64. The matter is complicated by the recent emergence of a third camp which insists not only that there is no school of *stilnovisti* referred to within Dante's text, but further that there is no such school at all. For this point of view, see Guido Favati, *Inchiesta sul Dolce Stil Nuovo* (Florence: Le Monnier, 1975). The historiographical aspects of Bonagiunta's remarks will be discussed in the following chapter, where the critical response will be reviewed as well.

31. Dante's "e venmene pietà" echoes Cavalcanti's incipit, "A me stesso di me

pietate vene." The relation of these sonnets to the Cavalcantian mode will be discussed further in Chapter II.

32. The canzone is defined and "Donne ch'avete" cited for the first time in *De Vulgari Eloquentia* II, viii, 8. Dante also cites the following later canzoni in the treatise "Doglia mi reca ne lo core ardire" (II, ii. 8); "Amor, che movi tua vertù da cielo" (II, v, 4 and II, xi, 7); "Amor che ne la mente mi ragiona" (II, vi, 6); "Al poco giorno e al gran cerchio d'ombra" (II, x, 2 and II, xiii, 2); "Traggemi de la mente amor la stiva" (lost) (II, xi, 5); "Donna pietosa e di novella etate" (II, xi, 8); "Poscia ch'Amor del tutto m'ha lasciato" (II, xii, 8); "Amor, tu vedi ben che questa donna" (II, xiii, 13). "Donne ch'avete" is cited a second time in II, xii, 3.

33. The thematic and structural coherence of these two cantos is noted by Umberto Bosco, who makes a point of treating them as a unit in the commentary of his edition with Giovanni Reggio, *La Divina Commedia*, 3 vols. (Florence: Le Monnier, 1979), *Purgatorio*, pp. 386–394. This same dialectical emphasis pervades the readings of Alberto Del Monte, "Forese," *Cultura e scuola* 4, nos. 13–14 (1965), 572–589; and Vittorio Russa, "*Pg.* XXIII: Forese, o la maschera del discorso," *MLN* 94 (1979), 113–136.

34. This underlying notion of debt translates into the economic images that run through the *Purgatorio* to culminate in the startling metaphor of canto XXVIII, 91–96, whereby Eden was God's downpayment on Paradise, but man defaulted while paying back the loan. The economic motifs of the *Comedy* are treated by Joan M. Ferrante, *The Political Vision of the Divine Comedy*, chap. 6, "Exchange and Communication, Commerce and Language" (Princeton: Princeton U. Press, 1984). On time in the *Comedy*, see Franco Masciandaro, *La problematica del tempo nella Commedia* (Ravenna: Longo, 1976).

35. The Arno's role in personifying the fall of history is succinctly expressed by Guido del Duca's phrase with its emphatic progressive construction: "Vassi caggendo" ("It goes on falling") in *Purg.* XIV, 49. Giuseppe Mazzotta discusses the Old Man of Crete in *Dante, Poet of the Desert*, chap. 1.

36. Bosco, Del Monte, and Russo all point to the contrast between the *tenzone* and the *stil nolo*, referred to by Bosco respectively as the "poison" and the "antidote" (*Purgatorio*, p. 391). Before proceeding, some mention should be made of the doubts that exist regarding the attribution of the *tenzone* to Dante. Domenico Guerri's suggestion that the sonnets are in fact an obscene literary correspondence of the early Quattrocento (*La corrente popolare nel Rinascimento* [Florence: Sansoni, 1931], pp. 104–148) went counter to the expressed opinion of Michele Barbi ("La tenzone di Dante con Forese," orig. 1924, repr. in *Problemi di critica dantesca, Seconda serie* [Florence: Sansoni, 1941], pp. 87–188, and in *Rime della Vita Nuova e della giovinezza*, ed. M. Barbi and F. Maggini [Florence: Le Monnier, 1956], pp. 275–373), by whom it was refuted ("Ancora della tenzone di Dante con Forese," orig. 1932, repr. in *Problemi di critica dantesca, Seconda serie*, pp. 189–214). Guerri's thesis was revived forty years later by Antonio Lanza in an

Appendix to his *Polemiche e berte letterarie nella Firenze del primo Quattrocento* (Rome: Bulzoni, 1971) entitled "Una volgare lite nella Firenze del primo Quattrocento: la cosidetta tenzone di Dante con Forese Donati—nuovi contributi alla tesi di Domenico Guerri," only to be refuted again by Mario Marti, "Rime realistiche (la tenzone e le petrose dantesche)," *Nuove letture dantesche* (Florence: Le Monnier, 1976), vol. VIII, pp. 209–230, who insists on the evidence of the early commentators (some verses of the *tenzone* are cited by the Anonimo Fiorentino) and of the manuscripts (which are assigned with greater probability to the end of the fourteenth than to the beginning of the fifteenth century). Were Dante's authorship of the tenzone to be revoked and my analysis of canto XXIII to lose its textual factor, the biographical/poetic triumph of canto XXIV would still be dialectically preceded by a biographical—if not poetic—fall. On the other hand, precisely the striking parallelism between the two cantos that the existence of the tenzone adds to the episode in the *Comedy* seems to constitute further support of its authenticity.

37. Although Russo points to the presence of "rime realistiche" in *Purgatorio* XXIII ("Forese o la maschera del discorso," p. 126), they seem not extensive enough to constitute a textual echo of the *tenzone* in the canto. Reverse echoes pervade the canto according to Francesco D'Ovidio, who argues that the repetition of Forese's name here makes amends for the use of the nickname "Bicci" in the sonnets, and likewise that the tender insistence on Forese's face (*Purg.* XXIII, 48 and 55) is connected to the "faccia fessa" of the sonnet "Bicci novel, figliuol di non so cui." D'Ovidio's chief claim is that the rhyming of "Cristo" only with itself in the *Comedy* is intended to correct its rhyme with "tristo" and "male acquisto" in the same sonnet; all these points are to be found in "Cristo in rima," *Studii sulla Divina Commedia* (Milan-Palermo: Sandron, 1901), pp. 215–224. More recently, Piero Cudini has returned to the question of the *tenzone* in the *Comedy*, both with respect to its impact on the language of Sinon and Maestro Adamo in *Inferno* XXX, and with respect to the encounter with Forese (in key moments of the latter he finds the use of rhyme schemes from the sonnets); see "La tenzone tra Dante e Forese e la *Commedia* (*Inf.* XXX; *Purg.* XXIII–XXIV)," *Giornale storico della letteratura italiana*, 159 (1982), 1–25.

38. À propos of antithesis in canto XXIII and of line 72 in particular, Sapegno cites the anonymous verse "E sto in sollazzo e vivo in gran pena" ("I exist in joy and in great pain"), where "sollazzo" and "pena" are present in their most hackneyed form (*Purgatorio*, pp. 256–257).

39. In "Dante's Sweet New Style and the *Vita Nuova*," *Italica*, 42 (1965), 98–107, John Scott links these verses of Psalm 50 to the spontaneous speech that generated "Donne ch'avete," so emphasized in the *libello*. For the importance of this Psalm, see Robert Hollander, "Dante's Use of the Fiftieth Psalm," *Dante Studies*, 91 (1973), 145–150, repr. *Studies in Dante*, pp. 107–113. Richard Abrams connects Bonagiunta's gluttony to his inability to achieve the praise-style in

"Inspiration and Gluttony: "The Moral Context of Dante's Poetics of the 'Sweet New Style,'" *MLN*, 91 (1976), 30–59), as does Mark Musa, "The 'Sweet New Style' That I Hear," in *Advent at the Gates: Dante's Comedy* (Bloomington and London: Indiana U. Press, 1974), pp. 111–128.

40. Cavalcanti's famous and enigmatic sonnet, "I' vegno 'l giorno a lo 'nfinite volte," has spawned a variety of interpretations. In answer to D'Ovidio's claim that the sonnet was intended to reprove Dante for his low associations, and in particular for his friendship with Forese ("L'intemerata di Guido," 1896; repr. "La rimenata di Guido," in *Studii sulla Divina Commedia*, pp. 202–214), Barbi asserted that the sonnet enjoins Dante against excessive depression, not decadence ("Una opera sintetica su Dante," 1904; repr. *Problemi di critica dantesca, Prima serie* (Florence: Sansoni, 19341, pp. 40–41). In support of Barbi's thesis is Dante's own use of the expression employed by Cavalcanti in line 9, "la vil tua vita," in the *donna gentile* sequence of the *Vita Nuova*, where "la mia vile vita" refers to the life of tears and suffering he had been leading since Beatrice's death (XXXV, 3). Another current of criticism sees an underlying political motivation; Marti suggests that the resentment of the aristocratic and therefore politically excluded Cavalcanti may have been provoked by Dante's growing political involvement ("Sulla genesi del realismo dantesco," in *Realismo dantesco e altri studi* [Milan: Ricciardi, 1961], pp. 1–32). A convincing reading of the sonnet in a poetic key is that of Marco Santagata, "Lettura cavalcantiana," *Giornale storico della letteratura italiana*, 148 (1971), 295–308, according to whom Guido accuses Dante of leaving the restricted sphere of stilnovist poetics, as in fact he did. The recent contribution of Letterio Cassata, "La paternale di Guido," *Studi danteschi*, 53 (1981), 167–185, is notable mainly for its helpful review of the sonnet's complex hermeneutic history. In conclusion, I would note that there could well be some merit to all the chief interpretations of "I' vegno 'l giorno a te," since all facets of the problematic—depression, Forese, politics, poetic divergence—come together in the critical years following the death of the *gentilissima*.

41. In "Sulla genesi del realismo dantesco," Marti insists on the stylistically conventional aspect of the *tenzone*, which he says should be viewed in the context of anti-courtly poetry in general. In the matter of Dante's potentially more serious deviations, Nardi maintains that although Dante never strayed as far from orthodoxy as his friend Cavalcanti, he was not immune from Averroistic influences ("Dante e Guido Cavalcanti," p. 213); his "Dal *Convivio* alla *Commedia*" (in *Dal Convivio alla Commedia: sei saggi danteschi* [Rome: Istituto Storico Italiano per il Medio Evo, 1960), pp. 37–150) delineates Averroistic tendencies in the *Convivio* and even finds residual Averroism it the *Paradiso*. Another critic who stresses the philosophical component of Dante's error is Joseph Anthony Mazzeo, who suggests that the temptations cited by Beatrice, the "serene" of *Purgatorio* XXXI, 45 as well as the "pargoletta" of line 59, should be read in the context of Cicero's passage on Ulysses and the Sirens in the *De*

Finibus as representing "simultaneously the sins of the flesh and a misuse of knowledge" ("The 'Sirens' of *Purgatorio* XXXI, 45," in *Medieval Cultural Tradition in Dante's Comedy* [Ithaca: Cornell U. Press, 1960], pp. 205–212). In his commentary to the Comedy (which devotes particular attention to the autobiographical aspects of the poem), Bosco stresses the philosophical/religious nature of the *traviamento* (see, for instance, *Purgatorio*, p. 391).

42. Beatrice refers not only to "that school which you followed" but also to "its doctrine"; as Edward Moore points out, the expression "sua dottrina" (*Purg.* XXXIII, 86) Implies a philosophical school of thought (see "The Reproaches of Beatrice," in *Studies in Dante*, Third Series: *Miscellaneous Essays* [1903; repr. New York: Greenwood Press, 19681, p. 234). Etienne Gilson makes the same point, saying that "Since it is here a question of a *school* and a *doctrine*, Beatrice cannot have been speaking of moral transgressions in this passage" (*Dante and Philosophy*, trans. David Moore [1939; repr. Gloucester, Mass.: Peter Smith, 1968], p. 97). Moore argues against an overly literal interpretation of Dante's fall, concluding that "Religion, as I believe, lost its practical hold on him after the death of Beatrice" (p. 249).

43. In this vein are the readings of Vittorio Vaturi, "Il canto VIII del *Paradiso*," *Lettura Dantis* (Florence: Sansoni, 1922); Giovanni Fallani, "Il canto VIII del *Paradiso*," *Lectura Dantis Romana* (Turin: Società Editrice Internazionale, 1964); André Pézard, "Charles Martel au Ciel de Venus," in *Letture del Paradiso*, ed. Vittorio Vettori (Milan: Marzorati, 1970), pp. 71–140; Vincenzo Cioffari, "Interpretazione del canto VIII del *Paradiso*," *Alighieri*, 13 (1972), 3–17; Salvatore Attardo, "Il Canto VIII del *Paradiso*," *Nuove letture dantesche* (Florence: Le Monnier, 1973), vol. VI, pp. 27–44. Discussions of the heaven of Venus tend to involve comparisons with Francesca, of which Pézard's is the most extreme; the French critic decides that Charles' wife Clemente is in fact present in this heaven, a silent partner for her husband as Paolo is for Francesca. For historical information regarding Dante and the house of Anjou, see Luigi Rocca, "Il canto VIII del *Paradiso*," *Lectura Dantis* (Florence: Sansoni, 1903).

44. In "*Purgatorio* II: Cato's Rebuke and Dante's *scoglio*," Hollander states that only "Donne ch'avete" is cited approvingly in the *Comedy*: "Here is a *canzone* that is not only true to Beatrice (and that is precisely what the two Convivial odes are *not*), but, one might argue, true to God (while the Convivial odes are not, at least when they are considered as caring more for philosophy than for Revelation)" (p. 353). While I would agree with these remarks in so far as they refer to the status of the canzoni before they enter the *Comedy*, I believe that Dante's decision to use them in the *Comedy*, i.e. in a context where positioning implies value, constrains us to look at them from a new perspective. This view is shared by Rachel Jacoff, whose article on Dante's palinodic intent in *Paradiso* VIII provides a complementary analysis of the same episode; see "The Post-Palinodic Smile: *Paradiso* VIII and IX," *Dante Studies*, 98 (1980), 111–122. I do not agree with

Carlo Muscetta, "Il canto VIII del *Paradiso*," *Lectura Dantis Scaligera* (Florence: Le Monnier, 1966), who sees "Voi che 'ntendendo" as rising above earthly confusion, nor with Vincent Moleta, who relates the position of the canzone to the fact that it "brings to perfection a notion of spiritual elevation through love" begun by Guinizzelli in "Al cor gentil" (Guinizzelli in *Dante*, p. 129).

45. The importance of this *terzina* is stressed by Pézard, "Charles Martel au Ciel de Venus," pp. 78–83.

46. As a poem dominated by "razionalismo cristiano" (p. 11), Muscetta feels that "Voi che 'ntendendo" is an appropriate choice for this heaven; he is seconded by Accardo and Cioffari.

47. Accardo comments on the resemblances between the meeting with Charles and the meeting with Casella, while Musetta points to tote meeting with Forese as a term of comparison, explaining that Dante suppresses the earlier dialogue in his later encounter because "Siamo in Paradiso e non più in Purgatorio" (p. 30).

48. The verb *antivedere* appears only four times in the *Comedy*: it is used in *Inf.* XXVIII, 78, by the schismatic Pier da Medicina; in *Purg.* XXIII, 109, by Forese in the course of his political invective and prophecy against the Florentine women and their descendants; in *Purg.* XXIV, 46, by Bonagiunta regarding the help to be proffered Dante in his exile by Gentucca; and in *Par.* VIII, 76, by Charles.

49. The commentators have debated as to whether "Clemenza" here refers to Charles' wife or to his homonymous daughter. Those who argue against the wife do so on the grounds that she died in 1295, and that she was therefore dead when Dante apostrophizes her in canto IX. Although the evidence is inconclusive, most modern commentators concur with Del Lungo, cited by Sapegno to the effect that the possessive adjective "tuo" is "essenzialmente coniugale"; in my opinion, the context dictates a wife rather than a daughter.

50. *Commentary*, p. 356. Foster and Boyde comment further that if Dante for a time considered philosophy to be implicitly opposed to Beatrice, this is because he then conceived philosophy "in a decidedly 'temporal' light, as though its chief function were to bring man to happiness in this present world" (pp. 356–357). On Dante's Aristotelian rather than Thomistic bias during the period of the *Convivio*, see Gilson, "The Primacy of Ethics," in *Dante and Philosophy*, esp. pp. 105–112.

51. Cunizza, from a family in political power (she was the sister of the tyrant Ezzelino III da Romano), loved, among others, Sordello, whom this study will show to be—for Dante—a political poet; Folquet became a political figure as Bishop of Toulouse, participating in the Albigensian Crusade. Sordello and Folquet will be discussed in greater detail in Chapter II.

52. On the transition between the *Vita Nuova* and the *Convivio*, see Salvatore

Battaglia, "Il metodo di Dante tra *Vita Nuova* e *Convivio*," in *Esemplarità e antagonismo nel pensiero di Dante* (Naples: Liguori, 1956), pp. 101–120. The importance for the *Comedy* of Dante's political thought as expressed in the last book of the *Convivio* and then in the *Monarchia* is treated by Nardi, "Le rime filosofiche e il *Convivio* nello sviluppo dell'arte e del pensiero di Dante" and "Dal *Convivio* alla *Commedia*," in *Dal Convivio alla Commedia: sei saggi danteschi*, pp. 1–36 and 37–150.

53. The Latin text, taken from the Loeb Classical Library edition, trans. F. J. Miller, 2 vols. (1916; repr. Cambridge: Harvard U. Press and London: William Heinemann, 1971 [vol. I] and 1968 [vol. II]), reads as follows: "nititur ille quidem pugnatque resurgere saepe, / dextra sed Ausonio manus est subiecta Peloro, / laeva, Pachyne, tibi" (*Metamorphoses* V, 349–351).

54. Typhoeus is among the giants in the pit surrounding Cocytus, and is named in *Inf.* XXXI, 124: "Non ci fare ire a Tizio né a Tifo."

55. Another corroborative detail of the relation between the two texts is Dante's use of the word *epiciclo* at the outset of *Paradiso* VIII, where Venus is "volta nel terzo epiciclo" (3). This unique occurrence of *epiciclo* in the *Comedy* reflects the *Convivio* passage, which continues, after the section quoted above, with a discussion of the threefold movements of Venus, listed as follows: "uno, secondo che la stella si muove per lo suo, epiciclo l'altro, secondo che lo epiciclo si muove con tutto il cielo igualmente con quello del Sole; lo terzo, secondo che tutto quello cielo si muove seguendo lo movimento de la stellata spera" ("one, according to which the star moves along its epicycle; next, according to which the epicycle moves with the entire heaven and equally with that of the Sun; third, according to which that entire heaven moves following the movement of the starry sphere" [*Convivio*, II, v, 16]). Like the other sections from *Convivio* II, v we have discussed, this passage was undoubtedly in Dante's mind when he composed *Paradiso* VIII.

56. Mazzeo demonstrates that the *Convivio* is excessively dependent on ancient philosophers in its enthusiastic assessment of nature's role in the formation of human beings, and also shows how in the *Paradiso* Dante returns to a position of "greater Christian rigor" (p. 35); see "*Convivio* IV, xxi and *Paradiso* XIII: Another of Dante's Self-Corrections," *Philological Quarterly*, 38 (1959), 30–36. In "*Panis Angelorum*: A Palinode in the *Paradiso*," *Dante Studies*, 95 (1977), 81–94, Daniel J. Ransom contrasts Dante's use of the phrase "pan de li angeli" in *Paradiso* II, ii with its previous appearance in the *Convivio*, showing how "in the *Paradiso* 'pan de li angeli' reacquires its theological substance" (p. 92).

57. Dante's desire to discredit erotic determinism may have autobiographical and palinodic roots; one thinks, for instance, of the sonnet to Cino in which Dante proclaims the subjugation of free will to Love ("Io sono stato con Amore insieme"), a position he dramatizes in the great canzone *montanina* ("Amor, da che convien pur ch'io mi doglia").

58. Foster and Boyde place one poem, the sonnet on Lisetta, between "Oltre la spera" (the last sonnet of the *Vita Nuova*) and "Voi che 'ntendendo"; they do this because of Barbi's opinion that the Lisetta sonnet ("Per quella via che la bellezza corre") represents a phase in the conflict between Beatrice and her rival of the *Vita Nuova*. In explaining the order of the poems in their edition, Foster and Boyde comment that they take as a "firm starting point for Dante's development after the *Vita Nuova* the canzone 'Voi che 'ntendendo'" (Introduction, *The Poems*, p. xxxix). The Barbi-Maggini edition passes from "Rime del tempo della *Vita Nuova*" to "Tenzone con Forese Donati"; Barbi-Pernicone picks up with "Rime allegoriche e dottrinali," of which the first is "Voi che 'ntendendo." Thus the canzone is separated from the poems of the *Vita Nuova* only by the *tenzone* which, not being love poetry, does not affect the priority of "voi che 'ntendendo." In "Le rime filosofiche e il *Convivio* nello sviluppo dell'arte e del pensiero di Dante," Nardi posits "Voi che 'ntendendo" as the beginning of a new poetic cycle (p. 2).

59. De Robertis notices the authority "Parole mie" confers on "Voi che 'ntendendo," saying that for the sonnet the canzone marks "il vero inizio, il decisivo riconoscimento del *nuovo* fatto" ("Il libro della *Vita Nuova* e il libro del *Convivio*," p. 19).

60. *Commentary*, p. 211.

61. In *Vita Nuova* XXV Dante states that the vernacular lyric should be devoted exclusively to love poetry: "E questo è contra coloro che rimano sopra altra matera che amorosa, con ciò sia cosa che cotale modo di parlare fosse dal principio trovato per dire d'amore" ("and this is against those who write poetry on a subject other than love, since this method of writing was from the beginning discovered in order to write on love" [XXV, 6]).

KENNETH GROSS

Infernal Metamorphoses: An Interpretation of Dante's "Counterpass"

Exilio poenam potius gens inpia pendat
vel nece vel siquid medium est mortisgue fugaeque
idque quid esse potest, nisi versae poena figurae?

Ovid, Metamorphoses

Atque ea nimirum quaecumque Acherunte profundo prodita
stint esse, in vita sunt omnia nobis.

Lucretius, De Rerum Natura

I

This is an essay in the poetics of pain and punishment, in the symbology of sin. I do not have anything new to add, as might otherwise be expected, to scholarly accounts of the philosophical system which informs the horrific, orderly landscape of Dante's *Inferno*, and the machinery of suffering deployed within it—the progression downwards, that is, from sins of Incontinence to those of Violence and Fraud, from Lust to Treachery. Rather, I want to explore a way of describing the conceptual and metaphoric logic underlying Dante's mode of representing such suffering, a logic which must bridge the gap or muddle any easy distinctions between the theological and the poetical. My investigation starts from the realization that the pains of the damned are in truth their own

From *Modern Language Notes* 100, no. 1 (January 1985). © 1985 by the Johns Hopkins University Press.

living sins, but sins converted to torturing images by what Dante would persuade us is the allegorizing eye of eternal Justice. These pains become portions of a total metaphoric vision of human evil, one in which the damned souls' existence is doubly circumscribed, first by the orientation of their affections—which defines the individual nature of their transgression—and second by the fact of their being dead and placed in a realm beyond that of ordinary life. This implies in turn, as I shall argue more fully below, that it is the states or powers of Death and Love which become the progenitors of all allegorical representation in the punishments themselves. Such speculations are grounded not only in the theological background of Dante's ideas about sin (especially in Augustine and Aquinas), but emerge from a study of the more purely literary sources of the poet's fantastic inventions. My arguments about the ways in which Dante transforms such a mixed genealogy may produce some unusual conclusions. Nevertheless, the picture of what I have called Dante's "infernal metamorphoses" fundamentally interprets the familiar dynamics of that mode of ironic judgment known as the counterpass, or *contrapasso*.[1]

Since Dante himself introduces this term into Italian, a preliminary discussion of its context in the *Commedia* is necessary. Indeed, it may be a useful way of defamiliarizing and for a moment putting into question a term which critical tradition has idealized into too neutral a descriptive term. The word's first and only appearance is at the very end of *Inferno*, XXVIII, where it closes the apologia of Bertran de Born, whom Dante and Virgil discover in the circle of the schismatics. Decapitated by a sword-wielding angel, healed as he marches around his circle, and struck again as he repasses that angel, Bertran provides the pilgrims with the following commentary on his situation:

> Perch'io parti' così giunte persone
>   partito porto il mio cerebro, lasso!
>   dal suo principio ch'è in questo troncone.
> Così s'osserva in me lo contrapasso.
>
> (XXVIII, 139–142)[2]

Contrapasso is derived from the Latin *contrapassum*, used in Aquinas's translation of the *Nichomachean Ethics* to render a Greek phrase meaning "he who has suffered something in return"; hence the Latin sense of the word as "retribution" or "retaliation." (An oddity which will become significant for Dante is that the translator chose to join the prefix *contra* with the noun *passum*—"pace" or "step"—rather than with the more likely *passio*, "suffering."[3]) Aristotle, in his discussion of civil justice, asserts that retaliation is a part of commutative but not of distributive justice, and is thus only a portion of the larger scheme by which punishments are to be meted out in a just society. Aquinas, in his *Summa Theologica*, though following Aristotle's lead in severely limiting the scope of retaliation in the workings of justice, does at least claim that "this form of Divine judgment is in accordance with the conditions of commutative justice, insofar as rewards are apportioned to merits, and punishments to sins."[4] He also associates retaliation with the Old Testament *lex talionis*: "I answer that, Retaliation (*contrapassum*) denotes equal passion repaid for previous action; and the expression applied most properly to injurious passions and actions, whereby a man harms the person of his neighbor; for instance, if a man strike, that he be struck back. This kind of justice is laid down in the Law (Exod. xxi:23,4): 'He shall render life for life, eye for eye, etc.'"[5] Despite the first passage cited, there is really no evidence that Aquinas would have found the word fitting for an eschatological scheme like Dante's, where no single, particular action is repaid, and where the "equal passion" is really a highly metaphorical rendering back of suffering for the soul's entire career of sin. Furthermore, the term's direct association with a tenet of the Old Law specifically overturned by Christ (see Matt. 5:38–9) suggests that the idea of punishment by *contrapassum* falls somewhat outside the Christian dispensation of Grace and Love.

That the word is supplied by a damned soul should give pause to those critics who have appropriated the term to refer to Dante's entire theory of punishment. For by Canto XXVIII the reader should have learned that even the most eloquent of the damned have major blind spots in their understanding of religion, philosophy, and language. So if Bertran does invoke the word strictly in Aquinas' sense, one may suppose that he is subtly misreading his situation. Although I will continue to use the word "counterpass" in this essay—both for simplicity and because I do not think that Bertran is completely mistaken—I want at the outset to point to the possible mixture of error and unwitting accuracy in his speech, if only to remind critics of how strange a conceptual trope the word offers up to us. To do this, however, it will be necessary to look briefly over two relevant medieval theories regarding the workings of sin, and to point out their influence on Dante.

The phenomenological totality which one might call the "state" of each of the damned in Dante's Hell—a condition embracing body, mind, language, landscape, and weather—is a complex reflection of and on the sinful disorder of his soul. As Charles Singleton has suggested, Dante's view of the proper order and motion of the soul may derive from Aquinas, in his Christian rereading of Aristotle's central assertion that every organism is bound by an inner drive to fulfill its own generic form.[6] Aristotle himself applied this principle metaphorically in his *Ethics*, where he asserts that the authentic "form" of human life lay in our realizing an inner justice, the "inner rule of the rational part of the soul over the other parts."[7] Aquinas raises this further to a spiritual principle, so that sin would be defined as a state wherein the soul is misdirected or Halted in its movement toward its true form: the justice of subjecting itself to God's will and the reception of sanctifying Grace.[8] The "punishments" of the *Inferno*, then, insofar as they reflect sin, show this deviation of the soul's proper motion. The worm of the human soul, "nato a formar l'angelica farfalla, / che vola alla giustizia sanza schermi" (*Purg.* X, 125–26, slightly altered), is hindered in its spiritual morphosis. It acquires a monstrous, mutated form, "quasi entomata in difetto, / sì come vermo in cui formazion falla" (X, 128–29), instead of realizing itself as a blessed psyche. This half-generated form—which yet retains evidence of the soul's original deviation—is in a sense the shape of the soul's suffering after death.

Augustine provides a related but, for the purposes of this essay, more usefully dialectical model of the workings of sin. As Kenneth Burke has shown in *The Rhetoric of Religion*, *The Confessions* describes the soul's motion in relation to God in terms of a series of "turnings."[9] Thus the sinful soul is one that has wrongly turned itself aside or askew (*perversus*), that has turned away (*aversus*) from God and so has turned against (*adversus*) the true, rational, and divine good. True Christian love, *caritas*, leads the soul toward this good, but is changed into sinful *cupiditas* when the soul turns from God in order to seek a false or limited object. Because Hell is the domain of those who have lost the good of the intellect by subjecting rational love of God to mere desire, the structure of punishment is patterned on that of human appetite.[10]

This aspect of the problem brings us closer to Aquinas, but there is more. Implicit in Dante is also the conviction that sin inverts or parodies two processes that are central to Augustine's theology: the divine act of Grace, symbolized by the Incarnation of Christ, and the human act of conversion. These two acts, which always entail each other in the work of salvation, represent respectively the turning of love from God to man, and the turning or returning of love from man to God. The states of the damned, then, can be read not so much as simple retributive punishments, but instead as various incarnations of false love or as emblems of false, downward, or parodic conversion.[11] For after death the sinful soul loses all chance of real conversion, and so exists "in bondage to an incessant repetition of its own slavery to finite objectives."[12] Thus the perverse love that in life was a result of free will and the cause of the soul's loss of Grace, becomes in Hell an inescapable state of being.[13]

The Augustinian model will become more significant later in this essay. But neither Aquinas nor Augustine will help us finally if we do not see the ways in which Dante's idea of the infernal state transforms theological concepts of sin into central poetic principles, or, perhaps more accurately, exposes the allegorical or figurative logic that is already at work in traditional accounts of the negative, imitative, or grotesque processes of sin. As I have said, the pains of the damned are more revelation than retribution; they compose difficult moral emblems which shadow forth sin's inward nature. The Gluttonous, for example, who neglected their souls to pleasure their bodies, their "muddy vesture of decay," wallow eternally in mud—like the pigs which are also emblems of their crime. Tempestuous lovers are whirled forever in a mad, windy storm. Hypocrites walk weighed down by leaden cloaks with ornate gilded surfaces, symbolizing the sinful, false exteriors which burdened their souls in life. Dante's didactic method becomes less objectionable when one realizes that the fallen reader is to be deterred from sin not by threat of retroactive punishment, but by seeing how horrifying his crimes are in themselves, from the perspective of God or the poet. Dante does not predict a future but says, with prophetic literalness, "this is what you are." More generally, we might suggest that the forms of punishment, whatever their pathos, have the ironic structure of satirical images, reflecting Augustine's notion (as explicated by Burke) that sinful "perversity" equals "parody"—the fatal turning of sin yielding a demonic turn or trope on the authentic forms of Christian virtue.[14] For rather than correcting sin, Dante's symbolic ironies show how the infernal states actually perpetuate the spiritual disorder which constitutes sin.

In this sense, we should observe that the moral function and metaphoric structure of the punishments in the *Inferno* are not strictly commensurable with those of the sufferings meted out in Dante's Purgatory. There, the burdens of the souls eventually blessed are not so much ironic allegories of sin as antithetical, curative conditions: the proud are weighed down with stones, the gluttonous are gaunt and starving, and the envious—the name of whose sin, *invidia*, derives from the Latin for evil or improper looking—have the eyes with which they sinned sewn shut. The Purgatorial states are simpler than those of Hell; they never involve any complex or grotesque reshaping of the human form; and they allow for real spiritual change, as the sufferings of Hell do not. The damned souls are described in corporeal imagery of great vividness, but the forms they inhabit are only like a body which is a dead thing, a torture house, and not something with the potential for future resurrection. If in life the *anima* is the *omnia corporis*, in Hell the body is a corpse which deforms the soul.

This long excursus puts us in a better position to judge the implications of Bertran's speech. If he uses the word *contrapasso* to refer to some sort of retaliatory punishment which he suffers under the hand of the Old Law, then he is clearly wrong. Bertran alone bears responsibility for the shape of his soul. However, his choice of the word would reveal a limitation of vision quite appropriate to a worldly, politically-minded troubadour. Part of his counterpass, in the broad sense, is to use the word *contrapasso*. Furthermore, Dante's idiosyncratic use of a virtual calque of the original Latin, *contrapassum*, especially in the context of Bertran's puns on "parti'" and "partito," makes for an expanded awareness of the word's etymological implications. Thus one is conscious that *contrapasso* literally means something like a "step against," a "reverse step," or even a "step away from." This recalls Augustine's depiction of the sinfully turned soul as *adversus*, *perversus*, and *aversus*. In the context of an allegorical narrative which images the conversion of the soul as a long walk, Bertran's term thus becomes an uncannily accurate description of the motions of sin which the counterpass is supposed to represent.

If nothing else, Bertran retains enough of his poetic insight to see that his punishment makes out of his sensible, corporeal form a symbol of the divisions he had formerly wrought within the body politic. Indeed, he sets up this image of himself with a punning wit that suggests a similar rhetorical or etymological key to many other punishments in the *Inferno*: "I parted then, thus I carry my head parted from its base, my trunk." Still, he seems to consider his condition as the grim joke of a vengeful God, rather than as the inevitable form of his soul—hence his assertion regarding "retaliation." It is also important that his reading of the allegory behind his decapitation does not exhaust the possible meanings of his counterpass. For instance, one recent critic has argued that Bertran is made to stand for his own poetics of strife and division; his being "*due in uno*" embodies among other things his tendentious joining of the unifying poetry of love and the divisive poetry of war.[15]

Bertran's mistakes and incapacities point to one other important aspect of the counterpass. That each damned soul knows only the partial truth about his or her moral and symbolic state is a consistent feature of experience in the *Inferno*. But the *conversio* of the pilgrim and the trial of the reader depend largely on the continual effort to bridge the gap between the remarkable things which the self-limited souls say about themselves, and the ironic qualifications or additional knowledge which arise from a more detached view of their words and sufferings. (That this is the point of view of any self-conscious reader as well as that provided by the higher perspective of Christian truth effectively dramatizes Augustine's assertion that the labor of interpretation is implicitly a labor of divination, a means of recognizing God.) In some sense, then, the damned souls are like those condemned prisoners in Kafka's parable, "In the Penal Colony," criminals who are strapped to an intricate ancient machine (the "harrow") which incises into the back of each an exact account of his transgressions, executed in elaborate, hieroglyphic script. Ideally, the sufferer deciphers the inscription only at the moment of death, and then with a dark rapture of recognition which, says the Warden, "would tempt one beneath the harrow oneself."[16] Likewise, those souls trapped in that machine which is the Inferno have been turned into animated hieroglyphs of sin, pages written on by the hand of God.[17] But in Dante, only the pilgrim and the reader seem to have the potential for real enlightenment; the damned cannot fully decipher themselves, since they have lost true *caritas*, the key to all divine coding. They also lack the free will necessary to pursue fully any restorative act of interpretation. Nor, as in Kafka, will the machinery break down or they die into oblivion, since Hell is eternal and the sinners already dead.

II

Our chief concern in dealing with the counterpass is to locate the inward crossing of image and idea for each of the pains of Hell. Iconographic source-hunting is of some use here, but only if it proceeds within a larger conceptual framework, even a semi-mythic one. One might begin by saying that, while it is the shape of a soul's love which defines the trajectory of its sin, it is the singular event of human death which is responsible for the transformations of appearance by which that sin is represented in the *Inferno*. Only by dying into Eternity does the damned soul discover and become the emblematic form of its inward life; Dante himself gains access to such forms only by entering and moving through the realms of eternal death. Death, the portal of divine vision, the threshold of revelation, is then the mother of trope, if not (as Stevens said) the mother of beauty. Indeed, to say that Death and Love, by dint of an obscure marriage, generate between them the allegorical imagery of Dante's Hell, is not merely to play with personifications, especially in the context of a theology which sees sinful love as death or recognizes a sacrificial death as the great type of love. In any case, it is only by reflecting on such a strange marriage that I can connect some of my remarks on the theology of sin to arguments about a more strictly literary source for Dante's treatment of the counterpass, one in which the powers of death and love are similarly intertwined. This subtext should also illuminate numerous other aspects of infernal suffering: its symbolic ironies, its binding together of life and afterlife, its fatality, repetitiveness, and endlessness. The source I have in mind is no Christian eschatological work, but the *Metamorphoses* of Ovid, or, more precisely, the principle of symbolic change which gives life to that poem.

Let me say now that the influence which I am suggesting does not necessarily depend on any particular body of allegorical exegesis attached to the *Metamorphoses*. Nor need such influence appear only in details specifically drawn from Ovid's own fables. Certainly Dante may have found precedent in works like the *Ovide Moralisé* for reading the various metamorphoses as allegories of conversion or sinful perversion. Such is the case with the story of Io, who is first loved by Jupiter (God the Father), but then turned into a cow (falls into sinful, carnal desires), and kept from her freedom by Argus (Satan). Liberated by Mercury (Christ), she is restored to human form when, through the merciful offices of Juno (the Church), she reaches the waters of the Nile (Scripture).[18] One of the limitations of this basically homiletic mode of exegesis, however, is that it must flatten out and schematize the Ovidian tales, more often than not wholly ignoring their affective power as literary narratives.[19] While the allegorists are able to shift quite serenely between reading the same myth now *in bono*, now *in malo*, they seem incapable of distinguishing when Ovid is being serious and when he actually parodies the high rhetoric of the mythological mode, or in any way manipulates the decorum of pastoral or epic narrative. Even setting aside the oppressively doctrinal thrust of the allegories—the emphasis on salvation through the sacraments of the Church, the work of good and bad preachers, and so forth—there is no sense of dialectic, and no feeling for the real poetic risks of mythological representation. The *Ovide Moralisé* shows no direct interest in Ovidian change as an intricate metaphoric language in its own right; nor does that poem examine, as Dante's does, both the strengths and limits of such a complex, grotesque, and often arbitrary language for symbolizing either false or true forms of conversion.

I will yet be making some reference to the commentary tradition below. If, however, one for the moment takes Ovid's poetic machinery as a relatively self-sufficient, if sometimes ironic and fragmentary grammar of myth, one sees at least three aspects of his treatment of metamorphosis that find precise reflection in Dante's counterpass.[20]

First, the event of transformation usually represents a kind of death, and at the same time a substitution for or evasion of death brought about through the agency of some supernatural power (though often such a power is only implicit in the fantastic turns of the narrative itself). Such a death does not mean total annihilation but rather survival in a new form. The changed individual may eventually rise into a transmundane realm, deified like Hercules or Julius Caesar, but more often he or she falls out of humanity into the cycle of a merely natural growth and decay. The metamorphosis is then not so much a rebirth as a debasement of human life; at least it problematizes the threshold between human life and human death, even (as Harold Skulsky argues) raising an epistemological crisis by straining our habitual ways of relating mind or personality to bodily form.[21] Given the fluidity and arbitrariness of both identity and change in Ovid, the images of "the mind in exile" are as often comic or parodic as they are tragic. But though the pathos of metamorphosis may be minimal, still in those cases where the transformed figure puts on the merely generic or mortal immortality of an animal or plant we have, if not a loss of life, then a loss of self. He or she is reduced to a form which cannot truly develop or transcend its being (pre-Darwinian species did not evolve). As part of nature, the new being only commemorates or repeats the occasion of its original change, like the damned souls who repeat the form of their false conversions of value. Metamorphosis, that is, becomes a perverse form of stasis. Thus in Ovid, the nightingale Philomel exists only to lament (VI. 668f); the daughters of Cadmus are turned to stone, caught in their violent positions of mourning (IV. 564); the flower Narcissus always grows by the banks of streams (III. 510); the violet or heliotrope, originally Phoebus's lover Clytie, always turns its face to the betrayed and betraying sun (IV. 268); and Hyacinth, whose stained petals spell out the Greek *AI AI*, perpetually echoes the wailing of the dead youth's divine lover, Apollo (X. 217).

We have here, then, what Northrop Frye schematizes as the tragic or elegiac side of the mythic world-picture, where the activity of original creation is converted into merely

> a recreation of memory and frustrated desire, where the spectres of
> the dead, in Blake's phrase, who inhabit the memory take on living
> form. The central symbol of the descending side is metamorphosis,
> the fall of gods or other spiritual beings into mankind, of mankind,

through Circean enchantments, into animals, of all living things into dead matter.[22]

Such a tragic structure partly informs the second relevant aspect of Ovidian transformation, one that accounts as well for much of the naive aesthetic and moral interest in metamorphosis. I am referring to the severe, ironic logic and inevitability reflected in many of the changes, something pointed up by the fact that they are often divinely imposed, and function either as reward or punishment. As in Dante, death is the threshold of metaphor, and while Ovidian metamorphosis does entail the loss of a flexible, human self, yet it may also be a grotesque sort of self-realization, since men and women "die" into emblems of their own moral characters. A grim and bloodthirsty man becomes a wolf; a steadfast servant of Jove becomes an adamant; a faithful husband and wife become an intertwining oak and linden; a chattering tattletale becomes a voice which can only repeat what it hears. The randomly allegorical structure of metamorphosis comes out even more directly in the case of the stories of Erysichthon (VIII. 738ff) and Aglauros (II. 740ff), both of whom encounter early in the narrative personifications of the passions—Hunger and Envy respectively—which will later transform them. Many of the changes, of course, show no precise metaphoric or thematic continuity, being little more than supernatural flourishes which close tales of purely dramatic interest. But even here Ovid may provide a kind of conceptual coherence through proleptic or teleological naming: Hyacinthus becomes a hyacinth (X. 217), Myrrha a myrrh tree (X. 489), Lycaon a *lycus* or wolf (I. 237), and Cygnus a *cygnus*, or swan (XII. 14.5). Thus if a human being does not quite become an impersonal symbol, at least an individual name turns, through Ovid's invented etiologies, into a generic one. Dante is more problematic in this respect, no doubt, since the generalizing symbolic structures of punishment, which often tend to level all sinners within a particular circle, are played off against the highly individualized presentation of historical characters, each of which usually retains his or her own name.[23]

Thirdly, and here we approach the more disturbing center of Ovid's metamorphic fictions, the characters' confrontations with literal or symbolic death are linked to the transforming power of love. Daphne's conversion into a laurel evades an unwanted love (I. 525ff); Philomel's pricking thorn and lamenting song speak of love's fierce, corruptive power (VI. 668ff); the fusing of Salmacis and Hermaphroditus becomes a grotesque figure for the sexual union (IV. 373ff); while Pygmalion's miracle, accomplished by Venus (X. 243ff), is both a myth of love's sublimation into art and a reflection on the relation between erotic love and idolatry.[24] Not only are the forms of love, like death, most often a crossing of boundaries—incest, narcissism, hermaphroditism, divine rape, etc.[25]—but it is the encounter with *eros*—human or divine, creative or destructive, ennobling or perverted—which is the direct occasion of most metamorphoses, and Hence the key to their moral and psychological meanings.

Indeed, it is the love-goddess Venus who in Ovid speaks of metamorphosis as a penalty "midway between death and exile."[26] Dante merely replaces Ovid's focus on the multitudinous forms of pagan *eros* with a parallel attention to the perversions of Christian love classifiable under the term cupiditas, which derives from the Roman name for the god of love. For it is *cupiditas*, as the Christian rereading of *eros* and the antithesis of *caritas* or *agape*, which animates the strange shapes of punishment in Hell.

III

In what remains of this essay, I want to support my thesis about the counterpass by an analysis of Cantos XXIV and XXV of the *Inferno*, those which describe the punishment of the thieves in the seventh *malebolgia* of the eighth circle of Hell. Here, though I will comment by turns on the relevance of the Ovidian allusions and metamorphic imagery to the particular sin of theft, I am more interested in using this rich episode to consider questions about the counterpass in general. That is to say, I have used these cantos as a kind of critical synechdoche, in order to show how Dante's fantastic inventions unfold the mythographic logic of all infernal punishment, as it can be viewed in the mirror of Ovid's poem and in relation to the hermeneutic dilemmas discussed at the end of section I.

The account of the sixth *malebolgia* of the eighth circle is worth looking at briefly, since this sets the tone and context for Dante's encounters in the seventh, that of the thieves. The false directions given to Virgil by the devils in Canto XXII, the confrontation with the hypocrites, the *finta imagine* of snow created by the hoarfrost which is described in the simile at the opening of Canto XXIV—all of these turn our attention to problems of representation, the dangers of false appearance and false advice. The rapid passing of Virgil's anger and the subsequent change from fear to joy in the pilgrim, like that of an anxious shepherd joyful at the sudden disappearance of the mimic snow, dramatize not only the flux of human feeling but its shifting relation to natural or artificial appearances. The false may speak true: it is left to the hypocrites to remind the misguided Virgil that the Devil is called a liar in Bologna, even the Father of Lies.

A more acute dilemma of perception arises on the verge of the seventh of the *malebolgie*, where the thieves are punished. From the top of the slope, Dante hears nothing but garbled voices; because of the darkness, he can see no definite fortes at all. "Com'i'odo quinci e non intendo / così giù veggio e neente affiguro" (XXIV, 74–75). He has eyes but does not see, and ears but does not hear, as Christ says of those disciples who fail to get the point of his instructive, elliptical tales. Literal perceptual problems of the sort described above are a constant feature of experience in the smoky, noisy, garishly shadowed Inferno. They are the sensory analogues of the ignorance and inner division of the fallen, sinful soul. Dante's subdued echo of the Gospel, therefore, stands as a crucial reminder to the reader that the physical complexities of the punishments about to be described must be scrutinized by a mind alive to the demands of metaphor and parable, one aware of the unstable correspondence between inner and outer states. It also suggests that the truths concealed may be equivalent to those which Christ himself propounds.

When he has descended somewhat, Dante sees a bare plain, swarming with uncountable numbers of poisonous snakes. Grandgent (perhaps following Benvenuto) argues that such creatures symbolize the peculiarly secret and insinuating nature of thievery, the sin here punished; but the snakes are also the symbols of sin in general.[27] In fact, it is most appropriate that they are associated with theft, since a gratuitous theft is the origin and original type of sin, as set forth in both the Book of Genesis and the *Confessions*. Moreover, we may recall that the first theft was accomplished largely through the agency of Satan, metamorphosed into a beguiling serpent. Dante's snakes entangle and knot together the limbs of the damned, thus becoming literal emblems of the bondage of sin; their venom suggests sin's inner, corruptive power.[28] And so these snakes are logically implicated in the three remarkable episodes of infernal transformation which dominate the narrative of Cantos XXIV and XXV.

Dante witnesses first the metamorphosis of the Pisan robber, Vanni Fucci. A snake attacks him at the base of the neck, "là dove'l collo a le spalle s'annoda" (XXIV, 99), the point where rational head is joined to impulsive body, the subtle knot of the human here undone by the knotting snake of sin. In a process repeated throughout eternity, the wound or venom reduces Vanni to a pile of ashes, which then gather together again, until he stands up amazed in his former shape. "Never was o nor i written so fast as he took fire and burned" (XXIV, 100–01), observes Dante, in a simile which does more than emphasize the demonic speed of the change. For if the shapes of punishment in Hell are indeed divine ciphers, Dante's comparison tells us that this paradoxical form of infernal inscription dissolves rather than defines a form, reducing the self and its bodily expression to a dead heap of particles.[29] The juxtaposition of the circular *o* and the linear *i* may also remind its of dialectical relations between cycle and progress that come into play in the second of Dante's similes:

> E poi che fu a terra sì distrutto,
>   la polver si raccolse per sé stessa
>   e'n quel medesmo ritornò di butto.
> Così per li gran savi si confessa
>   che la fenice more e poi rinasce,
>   quando al cinquecentesimo anno appressa;
> erba né biado in sua vita non pasce,
>   ma sol d'incenso lagrime e d'amomo,
>   e nardo e mirra son l'ultime fasce.
>
> (XXIV, 103–11)[30]

The allusion to the Phoenix illustrates the dislocation of meaning typical of Hell, for Dante's account of the fate of a damned soul sublimely and ironically appropriates a myth which by tradition is read as a symbol of Christ's self-sacrifice and resurrection—and by extension may figure the inward repetition of that act in every Christian soul.[31] In life, Vanni tells us he stole the sacred ornaments of the Church; here the text mocks him by misappropriating an image which is a fit ornament only for the story of a true conversion. The irony is sharpened by the contrast between the lovely elegiac description of the fabled bird and the rapid meanness of Vanni Fucci's change, which is at best a demonic travesty of such rebirth. His is not the destruction of an illusory selfhood, the putting off of the "Old Man" and the putting on of a new spiritual form. Rather, he is reformed into exactly what he was. His physical conversion is emphatically not a Christian *conversio*, but merely a cyclical alteration of form which furthers our sense of his eternal pain and stasis, his perpetual isolation in his distorted soul. The sin that was once a result of free will is now imaged in a process which is beyond his power to control. The Phoenix simile is not only "too good" for him, but it does not quite work; it fails to transform its subject in the way any metaphor ought to. Dante's "misuse" of metaphor emphasizes the fact that Vanni's condition also wears the absurd and deathly aspect of the untranscended literal. (Hell may be the place of failed poetry, as well as of failed conversion.)

As to the matter of *contrapasso* as metamorphosis, the reader may at this point complain that I have failed to maintain a distinction between the cyclical changes of figures like Vanni Fucci and Bertran de Born that occur within the eternity of Hell, and the putative metamorphosis undergone by all of the damned souls in their passage from the world to the underworld, from time to eternity, from life to afterlife. Such a distinction breaks down, however, when one realizes that the changes of the first sort are in themselves metaphors for the second sort, and also for changes that altogether precede physical death. Literal death is itself less significant than the threshold of spiritual life and death which the souls eternally cross and recross.

Throughout these two cantos, the falling off of humanity's power of spiritual regeneration is associated with subtle images of degraded sexual generation. This mode of symbolism is unusual in Dante, but here it is unmistakable. The serpents do not merely bind the limbs of the thieves, but thrust themselves through their loins—"quelle ficcavan per le ren la coda / e'l capo" (XXIV, 95–96)—as if they were demonic phalloi. In Canto XXV, a small fiery serpent attacks another soul at the navel, "quella parte onde prima è preso / nostro alimento" (XXV, 85–86); the trail of smoke that stretches between the snake's jaw and the wound constitutes a demonic umbilical cord. The serpent and the human figure are soon painfully, sacrificially "reborn," each into the shape of the other. Prior to the second of these episodes, and making an intriguing triad of them is the obscene gesture of the "figs," which Vanni aims at God. The crudity of the gesture is important, standing as it does at the opposite extreme of literary refinement from the obscure mythological prophecy which the Pisan robber had uttered moments before. Language and generation are debased simultaneously. Dante, of course, does not in turn transcendentalize human sexuality with the same explicitness as a poet like William Blake; but in corrupted, demonic form, the poet can assimilate such sexual imagery to the other violent physical images through which he figures forth the corruption of the spirit. In this Dante also has the precedent of the Old Testament prophets and the Book of Revelation, where idolatry and false prophecy are figured as harlotry and sexual abomination. It is also worth noting that Isaiah and Ezekiel envision the unfaithful land of Israel, when turned away from God's love and commandments, as the dwelling place of snakes, dragons and basilisks.

Vanni's blasphemous sign and shout open Canto XXV, but he is rapidly silenced by a serpent which knots itself over his mouth. After he disappears, Dante and Virgil catch a glimpse of the monstrous guardian of this *bolgia*, the centaur Cacus.[32] He is separated from his fellow centaurs on the circle of the violent, and placed among the thieves for his fraudulent theft of the Cattle of Hercules. Dante's earlier description of the centaurs—who share their circle with the Minotaur—paid careful attention to their conjunction of human and equine characteristics; the pilgrim had directed his eyes to that point "dove le due nature son consorti" (XII, 84).[33] But as if to distinguish Cacus from these others, Dante, with his usual shrewdness in varying the monsters of classical literature, makes this man-horse into an even more complex double composite. For mounted on Cacus's shoulder and nape, though not physically joined to him, is a fire-breathing, serpent-tailed dragon. This startling form appears only briefly; and, as far as we are told, it addresses neither the pilgrims nor the damned. Nevertheless, by virtue of its compound duplicity or doubleness, this bizarre hybrid provides a symbolic aperçu to the two variations on the theme of metamorphosis which will dominate the rest of Canto XXV.

In the first of these, Dante sees a six-footed serpent fasten himself to the back of Agnolo de' Brunelleschi (one of the Florentines gathered on the plain below), a situation echoing the dragon mounted on the shoulders of Cacus. But after immobilizing Agnolo's limbs and somehow twisting his head so that its jaws are able to puncture both of Agnolo's cheeks, the reptilian figure begins to fuse with the human. Dante compares the inextricable joining of the two beings to that of a tree and the ivy that winds around it, or to the mingling of colors in a mixed lump of wax. These similes—not to mention the literal situation—recall Ovid's description of Hermaphroditus caught in the inescapable embrace of Salmacis (*Metamorphoses* IV, 361–65):

> denique nitentem contra elabique volentem
> inplicat ut serpens, quam regia sustinet ales
> sublimemque rapit: pendens caput illa pedesque

adligat et cauda spatiantes inplicat alas;
utve solent hederae longos intexere truncos.[34]

Finally, in spite of all his efforts to slip from her grasp she twirled
around him, like a serpent when it is being carried off into the air by
the king of birds: for, as it hangs from the eagle's beak, the snake coils
round his head and talons and with its tail hampers his beating wings.
She was like the ivy encircling tall tree trunks.[35]

Even if we know that the Middle Ages could refer to all sin as "fornication," there
is a painful irony in Dante's mapping of such a strongly erotic fable onto what
seems a more purely horrific union of the human and the serpentine. That the
soul-destroying clasp of the serpent should be like the embrace of a lover
dramatizes the real conflict involved in attempting to escape *cupiditas*, the
perverse love only some of whose forms are literally sexual (it being here a
thieving love which, in seeking possession of a neighbor's goods, does violence
against the social aspects of *caritas*).[36] Dante's account of Agnolo's fate also
echoes an Ovidian passage from somewhat later in the same tale, but the strange
simile he substitutes is wholly his own:

... velut, si quis conducat cortice ramos,
crescendo iungi pariterque adolescere cernit,
sic ubi conplexu coierunt membra tenaci,
nec duo sunt et forma duplex, nec femina dici
nec puer ut possit, neutrumque et utrumque videntur.
                                        (*Met.* IV, 375–79)

As when a gardener grafts a branch on to a tree, and sees the two
unite as they grow, and come to maturity together, so when their
limbs met in that clinging embrace the nymph and the boy were no
longer two, but a single form possessed of a dual nature, which could
not be called male or female, but seemed to be at once both and
neither.[37]

Dante gives us:

né l'un né l'altro già parea quel ch'era:
come procede innanzi da l'ardore,
    per lo papiro suso, un color bruno
    che non è nero ancora e'l bianco more.
Li altri due 'l riguardavano, e ciascuno
    gridava: "Omè, Agnel, come ti muti!

Vedi che già non se' né due né uno."

(XXV, 63–69)[38]

The image of the liminal "bruno" of burning paper shows Dante's interest in the most delicate and transient of visual phenomena, as critics trained in the canons of modern poetry love to observe. But the image rises above mere optical notation, however subtle. It presents instead a remarkable metaphor for the paradoxical nature of change in Hell. For the paper described in these lines takes color from an element which destroys it, rather than from the paint or the ink of inscription. Ash-grey and black arise out of the dying of white. These colors are thus ciphers of a spiritual corruption born of the death of purity in a fire which consumes rather than refines.

The condition of being "neither two nor one" will be considered more fully later. For the moment it is sufficient to note that in this case—despite Dante's image of a shifting, burning edge—there remains no real dividing line by which to distinguish the forms of man and snake; both creatures are reduced to an "imagine perversa" composed of "membra non mai viste."

As this composite monster moves off, with all the terrible slowness of Yeats's "rough beast," Dante sees a small viper, "livido e nero come un gran di pepe," attack another Florentine, Buoso Donati, at the navel (as mentioned above). The snake falls away, and the two transfix each other with a prolonged, stunned, and terrifying stare. As the smoke flowing from wound and jaws meet the poet relates how the snake and the man exchange forms. In more than thirty lines of Ovidian description (which I quote only in part), more precise and grotesque than anything the Latin poet ever shows us, the paired limbs of the human figure fuse together, while the linear, serpentine body—which does possess legs of a sort—reshapes itself into a man, the members of either being made to do bizarre service for each other:

Io vidi intrar le braccia per l'ascelle,
  e i due piè de la fiera, ch'eran corti,
  tanto allungar quanto accorciavan quelle.
Poscia li piè di rietro, insieme attorti,
  diventaron lo membro che l'uom cela,
  e 'l misero del suo n'avea due porti.
Mentre che 'l fummo l'uno e l'altro vela
  di color novo, e genera 'l pel suso
  per l'una parte e de l'altra il dipela,
l'un si levò e l'altro cadde giuso,
  non torcendo però le lucerne empie,
  sotto le quai ciascun cambiava muso.

(XXV, 112–23)[39]

Here, as Skulsky has eloquently argued, the thieves can only change by stealing their form from another, both committing and suffering theft at the same time. The rule which governs such transformations is one of

> distortive reflection, in which the vicious image is intelligible only by reference to its [vanishing] paradigm—intelligible, that is, only as a privation. Each partner in crime is condemned to view in the mirror of his counterpart's change the gradual emergence of an aspect of himself: the erstwhile snake, the depravity whose moral essence it can never shed; the erstwhile man, the decency whose moral essence he can never retrieve.[40]

As this critic further points out, Dante gives us a dark parody of that tradition in which the dialogue of lovers is described as a kind of mirroring, most particularly that mimetic love by which the soul transforms itself into the image of God within itself: "But we all, with open face, beholding as in a glass the glory of the Lord, are changed into that same image from glory to glory" (2 Cor. 3.18).

As a last footnote here, we should add that the description of the snake becoming man in part recalls Ovid's account of Io (I. 583–746), one of the few instances in *Metamorphoses* of a transformed victim's return to human shape. The recollection is most interesting, perhaps, because Ovid anticipates Dante's own interest in the fate of language during metamorphosis, for the Latin poet plays wonderfully on Io's inability to form anything but mute ciphers or bestial noises when in bovine shape, and her dread that on being restored she will only low. Now after all of the extended, paired limbs of Buoso Donati shrink up or fuse into the linear form of the serpent, his singular tongue ironically divides, and he moves away hissing, no longer capable of articulate speech. But unlike Io—whose second transformation the *Ovide Moralisé* reads as an emblem of sin redeemed by divine Grace—Guercio da Cavalcanti does not fare any better for being restored to human form. For in collapsing together the downward and upward phases of metamorphosis in this episode, Dante has perversely neutralized any positive affect that might attach itself to the soul's return to human shape. The double change has indeed emphasized in painful detail the formal differences between man and snake. But in the infernal condition all such natural distinctions are highly equivocal; the human and the serpentine may even be levelled into one, as the earlier mixed monster shows more grotesquely. So the new human figure, far from being raised to a higher plane of being, at the end only points to his basic identity with the snake—for he still does not truly speak, but only spits after the other (though he now presumably possesses an unforked tongue):

> L'anima ch'era fiera divenuta,
>   suffolando si fugge per la valle,

> e l'altro dietro a lui parlando sputa.
>
> (XXV, 136–38)[41]

My speculations regarding the counterpass, metamorphosis, and conversion can be brought full circle by looking at the apostrophe to Lucan and Ovid which immediately precedes the episode just examined. Both of these classical poets, Dante says, told stories of strange transformations. But Lucan must now be silent, though his (purportedly) historical narrative gave an account of how one man crumbled and dissolved away, and another virtually exploded, because of snakebite. And Ovid, who gives us supernatural fables about the metamorphosis of Cadmus into a serpent and Arethusa into a fountain, must also speak no more. Though he was able to describe such wonders, "Io non lo 'nvidio,"

> ché due nature mai a fronte a fronte
>   non trasmutò sì ch'amendue le forme
>   a cambiar lor matera fosser pronte.
>
> (XXV, 100–02)[42]

Dante claims he is witnessing a phenomenon totally unavailable to classical, non-Christian poets. Figures which recall this uncanny exchanging or sharing of form between two distinct creatures we have encountered elsewhere in the *Inferno*. These include Minos; the centaurs; the Minotaur; the doubly monstrous Cacus; the "imagine perversa" of Canto XXIV; and even Bertran, who is described as "due in uno e uno in due."[43] The significance of many of these has already been discussed, especially as examples of what I have called infernal metamorphosis, symbolic incarnations of cupiditas and the parodic *conversio* of sin. In the present episode, the important point is that Dante's boast is not merely that of a traveller coming upon, say, a hitherto undiscovered reptile or lusus naturae. Rather, in this bizarre event the pilgrim confronts a new realm of spiritual being. What he in fact sees in this double exchange of forms is metamorphosis under the new religious and poetic dispensation of Christ, the Word made Flesh.[44] The Incarnation is what valorizes the marriage of Lucan's history with Ovid's mythology. And just as infernal metamorphosis is a demonic parody of true conversion, the terrifying flux of two and one in Canto XXV has its divine antitype in the double nature of Christ, man and God in one, the brazen serpent lifted up in the wilderness, the fountain of living waters. The *Inferno* examines paradoxes of duality and unity in various moral, spiritual, and symbolic forms, but their true measure is revealed only at the end of the *Purgatorio*. There, in Canto XXXI, Dante sees a procession in the terrestrial paradise made up of allegorical figures based largely on the Book of Revelation. But at its center, drawing the chariot of the Church, surrounded by the symbols of the four Evangelists, is a wholly un-Biblical griffin, the "animal binato," image of Christ, the final type of all conversion:

Mille disiri più che fiamma caldi
   strinsermi li occhi a li occhi rilucenti,
   che pur sopra 'l grifone stavan saldi.
Come in lo speccio il sol, non altrimenti,
   la doppia fiera dentro vi raggiava,
   or con altri, or con altri reggimenti.
Pensa, lettor, s'io mi maravigliava,
   quando vedea la cosa in sé star queta,
   e ne l'idolo suo si trasmutava.

                                   (*Purg.* XXXI, 118–26)[45]

    The two natures of this creature do not blot out but rather clarify each other, making the whole more splendid. Its radiance as an allegorical mirror of true divinity might even suggest that Dante is somehow curing the demonic, parodic character of earlier metamorphoses, not only in terms of their Christian meanings but as instances of a certain representational mode. The griffin, that is, as the only non-demonic monster of the poem, is by rights a literary redemption of the poetry of the grotesque. For while the invention of strange, mixed, two-in-one creatures is common enough in mythological imagery, the griffin suggests a crucial lesson about the decorum that guides Dante's own reinvention of such beings. As opposed to such infernal figures as Dante's Cerberus, who is given a strangely human beard and hands, or the serpent-tailed Minos, the griffin is composed of two creatures of similar ontological and symbolic status. The lack of a symbolic *human* figure means that each component will impose considerably less limitation of being on the other, and so it is in the ideal union of divinity and humanity which the griffin must represent. The double nature of the griffin, as well as Dante's shifting perception of each half, suggests that man, made in the image of God, is in no way deformed in becoming part of divinity, indeed that in this composite each stands fully independent of the other. Not so with the transformations and composites of Hell, as we have seen. Allegorical works like the *Ovide Moralisé* may suggest that a centaur like Chiron or even Hermaphroditus are mythic types of the Incarnation.[46] But not unlike the modern reader who is disturbed by the perverse excesses of such a work's imposed allegory, Dante can see the centaur as at best a parody, and a devilish one at that, of such a miracle.[47] Since the body, even the equivocal one possessed by the damned, is at least a potential revelation of the divine and human soul, we can only react with horror at seeing this visible form of humanity sink downward into the shape of a beast, however noble, or transformed into a limiting symbol, however vivid and distinct.

    The griffin provides an elegant but perhaps not inevitable way of tying together the Ovidian themes I have been discussing. The Christian symbolic and theological patterns by which Dante ironically reclaims the classical fiction of metamorphosis are already implicit in the *Inferno*, as for instance in the use of the

Phoenix image analyzed above. That the Ovidian elements are, strictly speaking, "fulfilled" by being included in the Apocalyptic pageant is perhaps too much to ask. But the contrast between the griffin and the episodes considered in this essay is useful in more general terms. For at the top of Purgatory, in the realm of the fully realized and liberated *imaginativa*—resulting from a "libero, dritto e sano arbitrio"—Ovid and Augustine can consort without irony. Divine mystery is still glimpsed through images, "corporeal similitudes," as the image of the sun shining in a mirror suggests, but the mingled love and wonder with which Dante contemplates the simultaneous transmutation and stability of the griffin is wholly different from the experience of metamorphosis in *Inferno* XXIV and XXV. There, too, the mode of change, the mode of metaphor, the mode of seeing, and the mode of understanding all seem to entail one another. But instead of the gentle intensities of *Purgatorio* XXXI there is only violence, disjunction of awareness, change that is both ugly and painful, divinity that collapses, metaphors that work by dissimilitude rather than by direct likeness, and images which are preternaturally vivid yet continue to point toward a ground of spiritual death that only the pilgrim—and the reader—will be able to transcend. On the other hand, the ethereal bodies of the souls undergoing purgation, though not eternal, are still fully human, and not subject to deforming metamorphoses. They bear the traces of the accidents of earthly life, for instance Manfred's scar (*Pur.* III, 111), but only such as give evidence of the spiritual crisis through which they obtained salvation. (Typologically speaking, such bodies are like the incorporeal but visibly wounded form which Christ possessed after his Harrowing of Hell and Resurrection, but prior to his Ascension.)

Although allusions to Ovid are still common in the *Purgatorio*, they tend to occur in the form of unironic and straightforward moral exampla, often paired with Biblical references (a device used by both Bersuire and the author of the *Fulgentius Metaphorialis*): Aglauros stands for Envy (Canto XIV); Procne, Haman, and Virgil's Amata for Wrath (Canto XVII); Pasiphae and the Cities of the Plain for Lust (Canto XXVI); and so on. In the *Paradiso*, Dante once again gives his Ovidian allusions a more paradoxical and violent turn, but with an irony—if that is the correct word—quite opposite from that which they possess in the *Inferno*. For in this last of the *Commedia's* three books, in the realm of wholly unbodied, intellectual vision, Dante is able to provide even degrading transformations with a divine value by a kind of transcendent, visionary allegoresis, evident in his use of the myths of the "transhumanized" Glaucus and the flayed satyr Marsyas (Cantos I), and that of the exiled Hippolytus (Canto XVII).[48]

Because of the simplified moral structure of Purgatory, based on the traditional seven deadly sins, and because of the different spiritual condition of the souls which ascend the mountain, the hermeneutic foci of the poem are located elsewhere than in the *Inferno*. The sufferings are still highly significant, as I have suggested. But the problematic poetry of the counterpass no longer has any place. The imagination of the poet must abandon the severe, fantastic system of punishments and its associated dilemmas of interpretation. Instead, that imagination devotes itself to the less corporeal, less ironic, and less restricting pattern of dreams and visions which the pilgrim experiences during his ascent (culminating in the procession already discussed). The endless serpentine monstrosities of sin and the mythic representations of the power of the Old Adversary shrink into the single snake that approaches at nightfall and is quickly driven off by the guardian angels (*Purg.* VII). In Purgatory, the human understanding is still divided from its divine object. But there are no longer such severe and tragic gaps as those between what a damned soul—still caught in illusion and ignorance—says of himself and his changes and the darker truths which the reader alone can divine. In lieu of this sort of split we have the more poignant but mutually recognized division between the Mantuan Virgil, a great poet condemned to Limbo, and the Mantuan Sordello, a lesser artist allowed Grace; or else the subtler chasm between Dante's dream of being rapt by an eagle into the sphere of Fire, and Virgil's "true" report that the gentle Lucia had carried him sleeping from one cornice to the next.

NOTES

1. A useful summary of traditional discussions of the counterpass can be found in the *Enciclopedia Dantesca* (Rome, 1970), 2:181–83.

2. "Because I parted persons thus united, I carry my brain parted from its source, alas! Thus is the retribution [*contrapasso*] observed in me." All citations and translations are from the edition of Charles S. Singleton, 6 vols. (Princeton, 1970).

3. See F. D'Ovidio, "Sette chiose alla 'Commedia'," *Studi Danteschi* VII (1923), pp. 27–34; cited by Singleton, *Inferno*, Part II, p. 523.

4. *Summa Theologica*, II-II, q. 61, a. 4; trans. Fathers of the Dominican Province, 2 vols. (New York, 1947).

5. *Summa Theologica*, II-II, q. 61, a. 4.

6. See Singleton. *Dante Studies 2: Journey to Beatrice* (Cambridge, 1958), pp. 47–69. Singleton's discussion of Aquinas's use of Aristotle in his reading of Conversion, Grace, and Justice is much more detailed than my brief summary can suggest. Perhaps because Singleton is mainly interested in defining the complex roles played by Virgil and Beatrice in guiding the pilgrim through his journey, the Aquinian materials he refers to are not as useful for an interpretation of the counterpass. Augustinian conversion theology, with its use of the Christ figure and its peculiar rhetorical subtleties, has been more helpful for this purpose.

7. Singleton, *Dante Studies 2*, p. 59.

8. The soul may of its own free will turn away from the Divine Justice which

is its true form, but if it does turn inward toward that Justice, neither the preparation for nor the reception of that form can be accomplished without the gratuitous help of God. See *Summa Theologica* I-II, q. 109, a. 6, resp.; and q. 112, a. 2, resp.

9. Kenneth Burke, *The Rhetoric of Religion* (Berkeley and Los Angeles, 1961), pp. 63–64, 86–117, and *passim*. Burke *is* concerned mainly with Book II of the *Confessions*, which meditates on the origins and nature of sinful perversity, and with Books VI and VII, which dramatize and define the problem of conversion. As to the interaction of human free will and the necessary offering of Divine Grace in the process of conversion, Burke notes the importance for Augustine of Jer. 31:18, "Turn thou that I may be turned."

10. Cf. John Freccero, "Dante's Firm Foot and the Journey without a Guide," *Harvard Theological Review* LII (1959), p. 273.

11. See Burke, p. 99: "All things imitate God perversely (*perverse te imitantur*)—the clearest evidence for our proposed equation: "perversity" equals "parody" when they put themselves apart from God and raise themselves up against him (*adversum te*)."

12. Joseph Mazzeo, "Hell vs. Hell: From Dante to Machiavelli," *Renaissance and Seventeenth-Century Studies* (New York, 1964), p. 97.

13. Augustine, in Book II, Chapter vi of the *Confessions*, asserts that the sheer gratuitousness of his stealing of the pears was merely a counterfeit or parody of true liberty, which is presumably shown in God's free turning of Grace toward man, an act which still does not impose necessity on that freedom of will that allows man to return to love of the Good. See *The Confessions of Saint Augustine*, trans. William Watts, Loeb Classical Library (Cambridge, 1912), pp. 86–88.

14. See Note 11. It seems to me that the ironic structure of many of the punishments in Hell exactly corresponds to that of much satiric imagery, although Dante provides his characters with a pathos and psychological depth that make it impossible to maintain the kind of stylization and distance necessary for a purely satiric humor to operate. Nevertheless, it is worth noting that satirists since Lucian have used the fiction of a journey to the underworld for the supernatural imagery and expanded moral perspective that an account of such a realm allows (not to mention the implicit figuration of human life as a species of damnation).

15. See Marianne Shapiro, "The Fictionalization of Bertran de Born (*Inf.* XXVIII)," *Dante Studies* XCII (1974), pp. 107–15. An intriguing gloss on Shapiro's essay is provided by Ezra Pound's meditation on Bertran, Love, War, and Poetry, entitled "Near Perigord," *Collected Shorter Poems* (London. 1952), pp. 171–77.

16. *Franz Kafka: The Complete Stories*, ed. Nahum N. Glatzer (New York, 1971), p. 150.

17. Of course, the damned are not completely depersonalized or reduced to mere symbol. Dante's symbolic and allegorical precision coexists with a determined dramatic realism in his presentation of individual souls. But the tension between these two ordinarily antithetical modes of representation is, appropriately, most acute and ironic in the narrative of the *Inferno*. For instance, it is painful though fitting that two souls at once so moving, so individual, and so different as Ulysses and Guido da Montefeltro should be so indistinguishable from the point of view of Divine justice, since both are equalized by being closed within the same sort of tongue-like flames.

18. I am summarizing the reading contained in Pierre Bersuire's fourteenth-century *Ovidius Moralizatus*. The text is reproduced as a marginal gloss to an important early edition of Ovid (Lyon, 1518), folios XXV–XXVIII, recently reprinted by the Garland Press, ed. Stephen Orgel (New York, 1976). I have here aligned a number of details which Bersuire treats separately. See also the *Ovide Moralisé*, ed. C. de Bour (Amsterdam, 1919–1938), Tome I, pp. 145–147, where Mercury is glossed as a preacher of Scripture, rather than as a figure of Christ himself, and Io becomes a type of Mary Magdalene, "cele d'Egipte."

19. Rosemond Tuve, in her *Allegorical Imagery* (Princeton, 1966), pp. 309–11, argues superbly that it is misguided to ask for such literary values as metaphoric proportion and coherent, dramatic narrative in a form of allegorical discourse which aims at setting forth sublime doctrinal mysteries such as the Incarnation and Salvation. "All the vehicles in allegorical images are in a way unsuitable; they are grossly, disproportionately trivial to carry their great tenor, and an inescapable radical distance characterizes the relations between terms" (310). But Tuve uses the *Ovide Moralisé* as a limiting case for medieval allegory, rather than as a great literary achievement in itself, so that her strictures do not wholly apply to the *Divine Comedy*, which seeks for the highest poetic as well as doctrinal authority.

20. The following taxonomy does not, of course, exhaust the possible meanings of metamorphosis in Ovid; indeed, since I am attempting a retrospective interpretation of the idea of metamorphosis from the point of view of the counterpass, I have emphasized or distinguished certain elements which are perhaps less crucial or less distinct in Ovid himself.

21. Skulsky, *Metamorphosis: The Mind in Exile* (Cambridge, 1981), pp. 1–9.

22. *Spiritus Mundi: Essays on Literature, Myth and Society* (Bloomington, 1976), p. 122.

23. As I have said in Note 17, Dante's "realism" is as intensely presented as his allegory. The effect of this is that the damned souls, rather than losing their individual characters in the process of metamorphosis—as they do in Ovid—have their warped selfhoods brilliantly, even cruelly, fixed for all eternity. Erich Auerbach has dealt with this aspect of Dantesque realism in detail, in *Dante: Poet*

of the Secular World (1929, trans. 1961), and in the essay, "Figura," in *Scenes from the Drama of European Literature* (New York, 1959). The epigraph to the former of these, which Auerbach takes as a schematic summary of Dante's eschatological presentation of the human world, is the Heraclitean aphorism, "A man's character (*ethos*) is his fate (*daimon*)." However, as Ernst Cassirer has pointed out (in *The Philosophy of Symbolic Forms*, Volume 2: *Mythical Thought* [1955], pp. 155–74), the word *daimon* retains the more archaic memories of a supernatural power, demon, or genius, which determines the shape of human personality and action from the outside. Fascinatingly, Angus Fletcher (in *Allegory* [1964]) has taken the "daimonic agent" as a paradigm for the creatures of all allegorical fiction, figures operating as if under the compulsion of an *idée fixe*. This would suggest that Heraclitus's apothegm might serve equally as a key to the very un-"realistic" structures of the counterpass, the fatal transformation of a man's soul into the allegorical—hence daimonic—form of his own characteristic sin. (In this regard, one must consider the Fable of Er at the end of Plato's *Republic*, which also applies a scheme of emblematic or daimonic metamorphosis to an eschatological myth.) This problem goes beyond that of literary technique, for on the ambiguous meanings of *daimon* are centered not only the interrelation of mimetic and allegorical representational modes, but the mysteries of fate and free will, compulsion and character.

24. For medieval treatments of the Pygmalion myth as a fable about human self-love and idolatry, see Tuve, *Allegorical Imagery*, p. 262.

25. Cf. Albert Cook, *Myth and Language* (Bloomington, 1980), p. 205.

26. *Met..* X. 233. Her words are included in my first epigraph.

27. "The thief, when he plies his trade, abdicates his human nature and transforms himself into a sly, creeping snake. The serpent, then, is the symbol of thievery." *La Divina Commedia*, ed. C. H. Grandgent, rev. Charles S. Singleton (Cambridge, 1972), p. 210. Also see T. H. White's translation of a twelfth-century *Physiologus*, *The Bestiary* (New York, 1954), p. 165: "Serpent gets its name because it creeps (*serpit*) by secret approaches and not by open steps."

28. Because of its habit of shedding its old skin and then growing a new one each spring, the snake *might* suggest a positive image of regeneration (for instance in the political symbolism of a Romantic poet like Shelley). But the snake lore of the Middle Ages, as represented by the Bestiaries or books like Brunetto's *Tresor*, tended to associate serpents such as the viper with especially self-destructive modes of reproduction and generation. According to popular belief, the male viper mated with the female by sticking his head down her throat, only to have it bitten off as soon as his part in the work of reproduction was completed. The infant snakes, in their turn, came into the world by tearing a fatal passage through their mother's side. Thus each generation was cut off from the next by its violence in fulfilling the primary instincts of life. See White, *op. cit.*, p. 170.

29. Cf. Skulsky, p. 116.

30. "And when he was thus destroyed on the ground, the dust drew together of itself and at once resumed the former shape; thus by great sages it is affirmed that the Phoenix dies and is born again when it approaches its five-hundredth year. In its life it feeds not on herb or grain, but only on tears of incense and amomum; and nard and myrrh are its last winding-sheet."

31. Ovid's account of the Phoenix occurs in Book XV of the *Metamorphoses*, lines 392–402. For the Christological reading, see *Ovide Moralisé*, Tome V, p. 343:

> Jhesus, vrais phenis sans pareil
> Qu'il per notre redemcion
> Voit souffrir mort et passion
> En l'arbre de la cross mori.

The palm tree, in which the Phoenix makes his final nest of nard, cinnamon and myrrh, is interpreted not only as the cross but as the Virgin Mary (Christ's Incarnation and Nativity being themselves types of his Death and Resurrection). Bersuire makes no mention of the myth, but cf. White, *Bestiary*, pp. 125–28, as well as Brunetto Latini's *Tresor*, Book V, Ch. xxvi. Dante may also have had in mind the most famous retelling of the myth in the Middle Ages, Lactantius's *Carmen de Ave Phenice*, which, although it contains no explicit passages of allegory, was always read as referring to Christ. See the edition of the poem with translation and commentary by Mary Cletus Fitzpatrick (Philadelphia, 1933).

32. Cacus does not appear in the *Metamorphoses*, but Virgil describes his battle with Hercules in *Aen.* VIII, 193–267, as does Ovid in *Fasti* 1. Singleton (*Inferno*, Part II, p. 432) notes that Dante had no classical precedent for making Cacus a centaur, though this might have been due to a misunderstanding of Virgil, who calls the monster "semihominis," or half-human (*Aen.* VIII, 194).

33. Cf. Singleton's analysis of this episode in "The Irreducible Vision," an essay introductory to *The Illustrated Manuscripts of "The Divine Comedy"*, ed. Peter Brieger, Millard Meiss, and Charles S. Singleton, Bollingen Series LXXXI, 2 vols. (Princeton, 1969), Vol. 1, pp. 1–30.

34. *Metamorphoses*, 2 vols., Loeb Classical Library (Cambridge, 1977), Vol. 1, p. 202.

35. *Ovid's Metamorphoses*, trans. Mary M. Innes (London, 1961), p. 103.

36. Cf. *Summa Theologica*, II-II, q. 66, a. 6.

37. *Ovid's Metamorphoses*, p. 104.

38. "Neither the one nor the other now seemed what it was at first: even as in advance of the flame a dark color moves across the paper, which is not yet black and the white dies away. The other two were looking on, and each cried, 'Oh me, Agnello, how you change! Lo, you are already neither two nor one.'"

39. "I saw the arms drawing in at the armpits, and the brute's two feet, which were short, lengthening out in proportion as the other's arms were shortening. Then the hind paws, twisted together, became the member that man conceals, and from this the wretch had put forth two feet. While the smoke veils the one and the other with a new color, and generates hair on the one part and strips it from the other, the one rose upright and the other fell down, but neither turned aside the baleful lamps beneath which each was changing his muzzle."

40. Skulsky, *Metamorphosis*, p. 120.

41. "The soul that was become a brute flees hissing along the valley; and the other, speaking, spits after it." Singleton's isolation of the participle "speaking" between commas misses the confusion or contamination of two actions in Dante's phrase "parlando sputa," which might be better rendered as "he spits speaking," or "he spittingly speaks."

42. "I envy him not; for two natures front to front he never so transmuted that both forms were prompt to exchange their substance."

43. Perhaps one should include among these examples of infernal two-in-oneness the sempiternal pairings of many of the damned within a single counterpass. For instance, there are the lovers Paolo and Francesca; the allies Ulysses and Diomede ("due dentro ad un fuoco" [*Inf.* XXVI, 79]); the deadly enemies Ugolino and Ruggiero; and Cavalcanti and Farinata, whose cohabitation is less comprehensible. These interlocked eternities are uncommon in the *Purgatorio* and the *Paradiso*. Especially in the case of Paolo and Francesca and Ugolino and Ruggiero—the first and the last souls Dante sees within Hell proper—these pairings are ironic marriages; they indicate the horrific symbiosis by which two humans can elicit sin in one another. Furthermore, the exclusive relation of two souls in such a condition implies the impossibility of any full participation in the larger community of God's love.

44. As I argue, Dante's "dismissal" of Lucan and Ovid turns on the problem of the Incarnation. His apostrophe to these pagan poets is thus exactly analogous to Augustine's comment that although he found many truths in the writings of the Platonists that agreed with Christian doctrine, "that the Word was made flesh and dwelt among us, did I not read there" (*Confessions*, p. 367).

45. "A thousand desires hotter than flame held my eyes on the shining eyes that remained ever fixed on the griffin. As the sun in a mirror, so was the twofold animal gleaming therewithin, now with the one, now with the other bearing. Think, reader, if I marveled when I saw the thing stand still in itself, and in its image changing."

46. On Chiron, see *Ovide Moralisé*, Tome I, pp. 239–40. On the problems of allegorical decorum, see Tuve, *Allegorical Imagery*, pp. 218–33.

47. This impression might support Skulsky's intriguing idea (*Metamorphosis*, pp. 118 and 223n) that an "imagine perversa" like the snake-man of Canto XXIV

might be seen as parodically literalizing heretical theories about the muddling mixture of divinity and humanity in the incarnate Christ, or of the Father and Son in the Holy Trinity.

48. Although both Bersuire and the *Ovide Moralisé* read Hippolytus as a type of Christ, Dante is closer to Ovid in focusing on the more purely human tragedy of his forced exile from his family and native land. Hippolytus's death and rebirth into the semi-divine Virbius ("twice a man") is no doubt of great importance in understanding the higher aspirations expressed in Dante's comparison of himself to Hippolytus, but by suppressing any direct reference to these details the poet gains both a greater dramatic power and a subtler prophetic resonance.

GIUSEPPE MAZZOTTA

The Light of Venus and the Poetry of Dante:
"Vita Nuova" and "Inferno" XXVII

My title refers to the passage in *Convivio* in which Dante classifies the seven liberal arts according to a conventional hierarchy of knowledge. Grammar, dialectic, rhetoric, music, geometry, arithmetic and astronomy are the disciplines of the *trivium* and *quadrivium*, and each of them is linked to one of the planets in the Ptolemaic cosmology. Venus is the planet identified with Rhetoric because the attributes of Venus, like those of rhetoric, Dante says, are:

> the brilliancy of its aspect which is more pleasant to behold than that of any other star; the other is its appearing at one time in the morning, at another time in the evening. And these two properties exist in Rhetoric, for Rhetoric is the pleasantest of all the Sciences, inasmuch as its chief aim is to please. It "appears in the morning" when the rhetorician speaks directly of the surface view presented to his hearer; it "appears in the evening," that is, behind, when the rhetorician speaks of the letter by referring to that aspect of it which is remote from the hearer.

The definition alludes, as is generally acknowledged, to the traditional double function of rhetoric, oratory and the *ars dictaminis* or letter-writing. What the definition also contains is the notion of the *ornatus*, the techniques of style or ornamentation whereby rhetoric is said to be the art that produces beautiful

From *Modern Critical Views: Dante*. © 1986 by Chelsea House Publishers.

appearances. The term, "chiarezza," one might add, translates *claritas*, the light that St. Thomas Aquinas conceives to be the substance of beauty and the means of its disclosure.

In *Convivio*, Dante does not really worry the issue of the beautiful as an autonomous esthetic category. Although the beautiful can be an attribute of philosophy (Dante speaks, for instance, of "la bellissima Filosofia") or the synonym of morality, the importance of both the beautiful and of rhetoric is decisively circumscribed in this speculative text of moral philosophy. To grasp the reduced value conferred on rhetoric in *Convivio*, where it is made to provide decorative imagery, one should only remember its centrality in the *De Vulgari Eloquentia*. The treatise, which straddles medieval poetics and rhetoric, was written with the explicit aim of teaching those poets who have so far versified "casualiter" to compose "regulariter," by the observance of rules and by the imitation of the great poets of antiquity. This aim reverses, may I suggest in passing, Matthew of Vendôme's judgement. In his *Ars Versificatoria* Matthew dismisses the lore of the ancient poets, their rhetorical figures and metaphors as useless and unworthy of emulation. But for Dante rhetoric, which begins with the Greeks, is the very equivalent of poetry. The concern with style and taste, which occupy a large portion of the *De Vulgari Eloquentia*, dramatizes the identification of rhetoric and poetry. At the same time, as the art of discourse, the art of pleading political or juridical causes, rhetoric is also in the *De Vulgari Eloquentia* the tool for the establishment of political, legal and moral authority. In this sense, Dante's notion of rhetoric reenacts the concerns of a cultural tradition that ranges from Cicero to Brunetto Latini.

It comes as something of a surprise that scholars, who have been remarkably zealous in mapping the complex implications of rhetoric in the *De Vulgari Eloquentia* have not given equal critical attention to its role in Dante's other major works. In the case of the other texts rhetoric is treated as a repertory of figures, but not as a category of knowledge, with unique claims about authority and power. The statement, in truth, ought to be tempered somewhat in the light of the extensive debates to which the question of allegory in both *Convivio* and the *Divine Comedy* has been subjected. Yet even then the relationship between rhetoric and the other arts or the way in which rhetoric engenders reliable knowledge and may even dissimulate its strategies is not always adequately probed. It is not my intention to retread here the research that scholars such as Schiaffini, Pazzaglia, Tateo, Baldwin and others have carried out about the various influences on Dante's thinking about rhetoric, or their systematic analyses of the places in Dante's *oeuvre* where rhetoric is explicitly mentioned. I shall focus instead on *Convivio*, *Vita Nuova* and *Inferno* xxvii to show how rhetoric works itself out in these texts, but I will also submit some new evidence that might shed light on Dante's position in the liberal arts, namely, the thirteenth century polemics which involved the secular masters of theology at the University of Paris and the anti-academism of the early Franciscans.

There is no significant trace of this polemic in *Convivio*. The point of departure of this unfinished treatise, and the principle that shapes its articulation, is the authority of Aristotle, who in his *Metaphysics*, which Dante calls "la Prima Filosofia," states that "all men naturally desire to have knowledge." The reference to Aristotle may well be the enactment of the technique of exordium which rhetorical conventions prescribe. But the reference also announces what turns out to be the central preoccupation of the four books: namely, that knowledge is made available by and through the light of natural reason. This recognition of man's rationality allows Dante to argue that it can be the choice of man to pursue the way to achieve the good life on this earth. In spite of the initial *sententia*, the *Convivio* is explicitly modeled not on Aristotle's *Metaphysics*, which deals with pure theoretical knowledge, such as the knowledge of spiritual entities, but on Aristotle's *Ethics*. This is, as Isidore of Seville refers to it, the practical "art of living rightly," which casts man in the here and now of his historical existence and which demands that man exercise the choices (without which no ethics can be conceived) appropriate to a moral agent.

It is this philosophical optimism about human rationality that accounts for the thematic configuration of *Convivio*. The narrative is punctuated, for instance, with references to one's own natural language to be preferred to Latin, which is at some remove from one's own life; it is clustered with insistent discussions on the moral virtues and on nobility, whether or not it is contingent on birth, wealth or customs; it focuses on the value of political life and the justice which the Roman Empire, a product of human history, managed to establish in the world. What sustains the textual movement, above all, is the belief in the allegory of poets as a technique that affords the thorough interpretability of the indirections of poetic language. Running parallel to the notion that poetry can be the object of a full philosophical investigation, there is an insistence on the knowability of the moral and rational operations of man.

This acceptance of the natural order is the principle that lies at the heart of two related and crucial gestures which shape the intellectual structure of *Convivio*. The first, as Gilson has argued, is the revolutionary re-arrangement, within the confines of *Convivio*, of the dignity of aims: ethics rather than metaphysics is placed as the "highest good." The second is the subordination of rhetoric to ethics. The statement needs clarification. The first treatise, actually, begins by explaining Dante's own shift away from the *Vita Nuova* to *Convivio*:

> The teachers of Rhetoric do not allow any one to speak of himself except on ground of necessity. And this is forbidden to a man because, when any one is spoken of, the speaker must needs either praise or blame him of whom he speaks.... I affirm ... that a man may be allowed to speak of himself for necessary reasons. And among necessary reasons there are two specially conspicuous. One may be urged when without discoursing about oneself great disgrace and

danger cannot be avoided.... This necessity moved Boethius to speak
of himself in order that, under the pretext of finding consolation, he
might palliate the lasting disgrace of his exile.... The other necessity
arises when from speaking about oneself great advantage to others
follows in the way of teaching. This reason moved Augustine to
speak of himself in his *Confessions*, because by the progress of his life
... he gave us example and teaching.

The passage is primarily a dismissal of what is known as epideictic rhetoric, one of
the three classical divisions, along with the deliberative and the forensic, or rhetoric
proper. Epideictic rhetoric, says Cicero in *De Inventione*, is the branch of oratory
"... quod tribuitur in alicuius certae personae laudem aut vituperationem; ..." This
epideictic mode, quite clearly, is identified with the autobiographical writing of
Boethius and St. Augustine. But for all the acknowledgement of the utility and
exemplariness of the *Confessions*, Dante's passage is overtly anti-Augustinian: the
point of *Convivio* is that the natural order, of which St. Augustine had too narrow
an appreciation, is the locus of a possible moral-social project. More importantly,
the passage marks an anti-Augustinian phase in Dante because it signals the
limitations of autobiographical writing in favor of a philosophical discourse that
would transcend private concerns and squarely grapple, as *Convivio* will do, with
the issue of the authority of intellectual knowledge and its relationship to
political power.

   The departure from the *Confessions* is, in reality, a way of taking distance
from Dante's own Augustinian text, the *Vita Nuova* and its rhetoric. It could be
pointed out that in the *Vita Nuova* there is an occasional resistance to the excesses
of self-staging. Yet the rhetoric of the self remains the path through which the
poet's own imaginative search is carried out. The exordium of the *Vita Nuova*,
consistently, stresses the autobiographical boundaries of the experiences about to
be related:

   In that part of the book of my memory before which little could be
   read is found a rubric which saith: *Incipit Vita Nova*. Beneath which
   rubric I find written the words which it is my purpose to copy in this
   little book, and if not all, at least their substance.

   The exordium is a poem, as Dante will call it later in the narrative, in the
technical sense of a *captatio benevolentiae*. What one could also point out is the
technical resonance of the term "sententia." Though the *Glossarium* of Du Cange
refers only to the juridical sense of the word and neglects the meaning of moral
lesson, which one can find in the *Rhetorica ad Herennium*, it hints that the text is
also a plea for oneself in the presence of one's beloved. But what is central in the
poem is the textual presence, which had gone unnoticed by the editors, of Guido
Cavalcanti's *Donna me prega*.

As is known, Cavalcanti wrote his poem in response to the physician Guido Orlandi's query about the origin of love. Orlandi's sonnet, "Onde si move e donde nasce amore?" proceeds to ask where is it that love dwells, whether it is "substance, accident or memory," what is it that feeds love and climaxes with a series of questions as to whether love has its own figural representation or it goes around disguised. Cavalcanti replies that love takes its dwelling place in that part where memory is, a formulation which Dante's exordium unequivocally echoes.

The echo compels us to place the *Vita Nuova* as conceived from the start in the shadow of Cavalcanti's poetry, but it does not mean that the two texts are telling the same story. The most fundamental difference between them is their antithetical views of rhetoric and the nature of the esthetic experience. For Guido memory, which is in the sensitive faculty of the soul, is the place where love literally resides. In his skeptical materialism there is no room for a visionariness that might relieve one's dark desires. The deeper truth, so runs Cavalcanti's argument, is imageless and Guido's steady effort in the poem is to unsettle any possible bonds between poetic images and love, or love and the order of the rational soul. The scientism of *Donna me prega* literalizes desire and makes it part of the night: its poetry, with its overt anti-metaphysical strains, turns, paradoxically, against poetry and assigns truth to the idealized realm of philosophical speculation.

For Dante, on the contrary, the truth of love is to be the child of time—as Venus is—and, hence, under the sway of mutability and death. The temporality of desire links it unavoidably to memory, but memory is here—and this is the main departure from Cavalcanti—a book or the "memoria artificialis," which is one of the five parts of rhetoric. The parts are usually identified as *inventio, dispositio, elocutio, memoria* and *pronuntiatio* and memory is defined as "a strong perception of things and words by the soul." The rhetoricity of memory makes the quest of the *Vita Nuova* into an interrogation of the value of figures. More precisely, memory is not the refuge of a deluded self, the a-priori recognition of appearances as illusive shapes, the way Cavalcanti would have it. For Dante, memory is the visionary faculty, the imagination through which the poet can question the phenomena of natural existence and urge them to release their hidden secrets. It can be said that Cavalcanti makes of memory a sepulcher and of death the cutting edge of vision: he broods over the severance death entails and it thwarts his imagination. He is too much of a realist, too much of a philosopher to be able to soar above the dark abyss into which, nonetheless, he stares.

But the poet of the *Vita Nuova* is impatient with this skepticism, this dead literalism, and from the start he seeks to rescue visionariness out of the platitudes of the materialists. The figures of love are not irrelevant shadows or insubstantial phantoms in the theatre of one's own mind as Cavalcanti thinks when he ceaselessly beckons Dante to join him on the plain where the light of ideas endures. Nor are women part of an infinite metaphorization, always replaceable (hence never necessary), as the physician Dante da Maiano, who tells Dante that his dream of love is only lust that a good bath can cure, believes.

The contrivance of the lady of the screen, related in chapter four, which literally makes a woman the screen on which the lover projects and displaces his own desires, is rejected because it casts doubt on Beatrice's own uniqueness. At the same time, chapter eight, which tells of the death of one of Beatrice's friends, allows Dante's sense of poetry in the *Vita Nuova* to surface. The passage is undoubtedly meant to prefigure Beatrice's own future death. Retrospectively, however, it is also another put-down of the materialists' belief that love is reducible to the mere materiality of bodies. Dante refers to the dead woman as a body without a soul. The poem he then proceeds to write is "Piangete, amanti, poi che piange Amore," which turns out to be, quite appropriately, a lament over the dead figure, "la morta imagine." But this poet can glance heavenward, "where the gentle soul was already located ..." In short, Dante installs his poetry at the point where Cavalcanti's poetry, where most poetry, for that matter, stops: between the dead body and the soul's existence. Images are not, a-priori, mere simulacra of death, and the "stilo de la loda," which re-enacts the principles of epideictic rhetoric, strives for a definition of Beatrice's felt but unknown essence.

This concern with metaphysics, with the links between rhetoric and the soul, comes forth in chapter twenty-five, where metaphor is said to be the trope that animates the face of the world. The meditation on metaphor, which is the burden of the chapter, is carried out as an attempt to grasp the nature of love. Here we see why Venus should be coupled to Rhetoric. The question Dante raises has a stunning simplicity: is love a divinity, as the Notaro suggests, or is it a mere rhetorical figure as Guido Cavalcanti in his *pastorella*, "In un boschetto," states. Dante defines love, in only partial agreement with Cavalcanti, for whom love is "un accidente-che sovente-è fero," as "accident in substance." The metaphoricity of love is then discussed in terms of a movement from the animate to the inanimate and vice-versa. Metaphor is given in the guise of *prosopopeia*, the orphic fiction whereby that which is dead is given a voice or, more correctly, a face.

With the actual death of Beatrice, related from chapter twenty-eight on, the fiction that poetry is capable of providing a simulation of life is no longer sufficient. To be sure, Beatrice was described as the living figure of love, but now that she is physically dead, the metaphors for her seem to be another empty fiction. If the question, while Beatrice was alive, was whether she is and how she is unique, now that she is dead, the question is finding the sense of metaphors that recall her. Dante's imaginative dead-end at this point (it induces tears, but Dante records no poetry) narrows in the prose to the vast image of general darkness, the death of Christ. An analogy is established between Beatrice and Christ in the effort to invest the memory of Beatrice with a glow of material substantiality. As is known, Charles Singleton views this analogy as the exegetical principle of the *Vita Nuova*, the aim of which is to portray the lover's growing awareness of the providentiality of Beatrice's presence in his life.

But the tension between the Christological language, the status of which depends on the coincidence between the image and its essence, and the poetic imagination, which in this text comes forth in the shifty forms of memory and desire, is problematic. There is no doubt that the poetic imagination aspires to, achieve an absolute stability which only the foundation of theology, which has its own visionariness, can provide. But Dante marks with great clarity the differences between his own private world and the common theological quest. The penultimate sonnet of the *Vita Nuova* addresses exactly this predicament.

> Ah ye pilgrims, that go lost in thought, per
>   chance of a thing that is not present to you,
>   come ye from folk so far away as by your
>   aspect ye show forth?
>
> For ye weep not when ye pass through the
>   midst of the sorrowing city, even as folk who
>   seem to understand naught of her heaviness.
>
> If ye tarry for desire to hear it, certes my heart
>   all sighing tells me, that ye will go forth
>   in tears.
>
> She hath lost her Beatrice; and the words that
>   a man can say of her, have power to make
>   one weep.

The sonnet is an apostrophe to the pilgrims who are going to Rome there to see the true image, literally a *prosopopeia*, Christ has left on the veil of the Veronica. The pilgrims are unaware of the lover's own heart-sickness and, in effect, the poet's mythology of love, that Beatrice is an analogy of Christ, comes forth as too private a concern. More precisely the sonnet is built on a series of symmetrical correspondences: the pilgrims are going to see Christ's image and are caught in an empty space between nostalgia and expectation, away from their homes and not quite at their destination; the lover is in his own native place, but like the pilgrims, away from his beatitude. But there is another contrast in the sonnet which unsettles the symmetries: the motion of the pilgrims, who are on their way, is in sharp contrast to the poet's invitation that they stop to hear the story of his grief. In the canzone, "Donne ch'avete intelletto d'amore," the Heavens vie with the lover to have Beatrice; now the terms are reversed: the lover seeks to waylay the pilgrims, begs them to stop for a while, a gesture that is bound to remind us of the repeated temptations the pilgrim himself eventually will experience in *Purgatorio*.

The vision of the pilgrims' journey to Rome triggers the last sonnet, "Oltre la spera" ["Beyond the sphere"], which tells of the poet's own pilgrimage. This is an imaginative journey to the separate souls, which the intellect cannot grasp. In this most visionary text, at the moment when a revelation is at hand, the eye is dazzled by the sun and the essences remain hidden behind their own inapproachable light. The perplexing quality of the image is heightened by the fact that it was used by both Averroes and Aquinas to describe the separate souls. Doctrinally, the text evokes and is poised between two opposite metaphysical systems. More poignantly, the phrase, "the sigh that issues from my heart" echoes another phrase which is patterned on a line in a sonnet by Cavalcanti. In this sonnet Cavalcanti restates the absolute separation of desire and its aim; Dante, instead, yokes rhetoric to metaphysics, makes of rhetoric the privileged imaginative path to metaphysics, though rhetoric can never yield the spiritual essence it gropes for.

Convivio picks at the very start the reference to Aristotle's *Metaphysics* on which the *Vita Nuova* comes to a close. But Dante challenges, as hinted earlier, the traditional primacy of metaphysics and replaces it with ethics. The move is so radical that Dante dramatizes in the first song, "Voi che 'ntendendo il terzo ciel movete" the shift to ethics. Written in the form of a *tenso*, a battle of thoughts within the self, and addressed to the angelic intelligences that move Venus, the planet of Rhetoric, the poem tells the triumph of the "donna gentile," Philosophy over Beatrice. With the enthronement of Philosophy, rhetoric is reduced to an ancilliary status: it is a technique of persuasion, the cover that wraps within its seductive folds the underlying morality.

The confinement of rhetoric to a decorative role in philosophical discourse is not unusual. From Cicero to Brunetto Latini rhetoricians are asked to link rhetoric to ethics because of rhetoric's inherent shiftiness, its power to argue contradictory aspects of the same question. In a way it is possible to suggest that the voice of Dante in *Convivio* is a Boethian voice, for like Boethius, who in his *De Consolatione Philosophiae*, banishes the meretricious muses of poetry to make room for the appearance of Lady Philosophy, under whose aegis poetry is possible, Dante, too, makes of poetry the dress of Philosophy.

This analogy with the Boethian text stops here, for unlike Boethius, Dante does not seek consolation for too long. Philosophy, says Isidore of Seville, is "meditatio mortis." Dante has no intention to be trapped in the grief that the shadow of Beatrice's death caused in him. He turns his back to the past in *Convivio* and ponders ethics, which is not the land of the dead, but the "ars bene vivendi." As a matter of fact, his voice is that of the intellectual, who, exiled and dispossessed, asserts the authority of his knowledge and seeks, by virtue of that knowledge, power. This claim for power by an intellectual does not, obviously, start with Dante. Its origin lies in the revival of another sphere of rhetoric, the *artes dictaminis* elaborated by Alberic of Montecassino and the Bologna school of law and rhetoric where the intellectuals would shape and argue the political issues of the day.

Yet Dante's project in *Convivio* to cast the philosopher as the advisor of the Emperor utterly fails. Many reasons have been suggested by Nardi, Leo and others as to why the project collapsed. The various reasons essentially boil down to Dante's awareness that a text expounding a system of values cannot be written unless it is accompanied by a theory of being. The text that attempts the synthesis is the *Divine Comedy*.

The point of departure of the poem is the encounter with Vergil whose "parola ornata," an allusion to the *ornatus* of rhetoric, has the power, in Beatrice's language, to aid the pilgrim in his quest. But if rhetoric is unavoidably the very stuff of the text, rhetoric's implications and links with the other disciplines of the encyclopedia are explicitly thematized in a number of places. One need mention only *Inferno* xv, where rhetoric, politics, grammar, law and their underlying theory of nature are all drawn within the circle of knowledge; or even *Inferno* xiii, the canto which features the fate of Pier delle Vigne, the counsellor in the court of Frederick II.

I shall focus, however, on *Inferno* xxvii because this is a canto that inscribes Dante's text within the boundaries of the XIII century debate on the liberal arts and, more precisely, on the Franciscan attack against logic and speculative grammar. The canto is usually read in conjunction with the story of Ulysses that precedes it. The dramatic connections between the two narratives, however superficial they may be, are certainly real. It can be easily granted that *Inferno* xxvii is the parodic counter to *Inferno* xxvi and its myth of style. In the *De Vulgari Eloquentia*, in the wake of Horace's *Ars Poetica* and of the *Rhetorica ad Herennium*, Dante classifies the tragic, elegiac and comical styles in terms of fixed categories of a subject matter that is judged to be sublime, plain or low. The canto of Ulysses, with its "verba polita," to use Vendôme's phrase, moral aphorisms and grandiloquence, stages the language of the epic hero whose interlocutor is the epic poet, Vergil. Ulysses' is a high style and it makes his story a tragic text, for Ulysses is, like all tragic heroes, an over-stater and hyperbole is his figure: he is one who has staked everything and has lost everything for seeking everything.

As we move into *Inferno* xxvii there is a deliberate diminution of Ulysses' grandeur. His smooth talk is replaced by hypothetical sentences, or, later, parenthetical remarks swearing, colloquialisms and crude idioms. From the start, Guido's speech draws the exchange between Vergil and Ulysses within the confines of the dialect:

> O thou to whom I direct my voice and who just now spoke in Lombard, saying: "Now go thy way, I do not urge thee more."
>
> (ll. 19–21)

Vergil allows Dante to speak to Guido, "Parla tu, questi e latino" (l. 33), because Vergil, too, observes the rhetorical rules of stylistic hierarchy. There is a great deal of irony in shifting from Ulysses' high ground to the specifics of the Tuscan

Appennines or Urbino and Ravenna. But from Dante's viewpoint the irony is vaster: degrees of style are illusory values and Ulysses and Guido, for all their stylistic differences, are damned to the same punishment of being enveloped in tongues of fire in the area of fraud among the evil counsellors. Even the image of the Sicilian bull within which its maker perishes (ll. 7–9), while it conveys the sense that we are witnessing the fate of contrivers trapped by their own contrivances, it also harks back to Ulysses' artifact, the Trojan horse.

It could be said that Guido is the truth, as it were, of Ulysses. If the pairing of their voices, however, can be construed as a confrontation between the epic and the mockheroic, style is not just a technique of characterizing their respective moral visions. Guido's municipal particularity of style introduces us to the question of political rhetoric—the rhetoric by which cities are established or destroyed—which is featured in the canto. What we are shown, to be sure, is an obsessive element of Dante's political thought: Guido da Montefeltro, as the advisor of Pope Boniface VIII, counselled him on how to capture the city of Palestrina, and this advice is placed within the reality of the temporal power of the Papacy. From this standpoint *Inferno* xxvii prefigures St. Peter's invective in *Paradiso* xxvii and it also echoes *Inferno* xix, the ditch of the Simonists where Pope Boniface is expected.

As in *Inferno* xix, here too, we are given the cause of the general sickness: just as Constantine, the text says (ll. 94–99), sought out Pope Sylvester to cure his leprosy, so did Boniface VIII seek Guido da Montefeltro to cure his pride. If leprosy suggests the rotting away of the body politic, pride is the fever of the mystical body and the origin of both is the Donation of Constantine. The chiasmus that the comparison draws (Boniface is equated to Constantine) points to the unholy mingling of the spiritual and secular orders and to the role-reversal of Pope and his advisor.

But there is in the canto an attention to political discourse that goes beyond this level of generality. In a way, just as there was a theology of style, we are now allowed to face the politics of theology. We are led, more precisely, into the council chamber, behind the scenes, as it were, where "li accorgimenti e le coperte vie" (l. 76), the art of wielding naked political power is shown. Here big deals are struck, so big that they focus on destruction of cities and salvation of souls. These are the terms of the transaction: by virtue of his absolute sovereignty (an authority that depends on the argument of the two keys which he quotes [ll. 103–105]), the Pope promises absolution for Guido's misdeed. Guido's advice is simply to make promises without planning to keep them (ll. 110–111).

This advice, I would like to suggest, textually repeats and reverses Brunetto Latini's formulation in *La rettorica*. Commenting on Cicero's statement that the stability of a city is contingent on keeping faith, on observing laws and practicing obedience to one another, Brunetto adds that to keep faith means to be loyal to one's commitments and to keep one's word: "e dice la legge che fede e quella che promette l'uno e l'altro l'attende." The deliberate violation of the ethical perspective, which alone, as Brunetto fully knows, can neutralize the dangerous simulations that rhetoric affords, brings to a focus what the canto on Ulysses unveils: that ethics is the set of values rhetoric manipulates at will. From Dante's viewpoint, however, the arrangement between the Pope and his counselor is charged with heavy ironies that disrupt the utilitarian calculus of the principles.

The Pope begins by taking literally what is known as his *plenitudo potestatis*, the fullness of spiritual and temporal powers given to him by God, yet he is powerless to act and seize a town. He believes in the performative power of his words, that by virtue of his office his words are a sacramental pledge. Yet, he takes advice to say words that do not measure up to his actions. There is irony even in Dante's use of the word "officio"—a term which for Cicero means moral duty and its appearance in line 91 only stresses duty's dereliction. On the other hand there is Guido, who knows that in the tough political games men play there is a gap between words and reality. Yet he believes in the Pope's "argomenti gravi" (weighty arguments) 91. 106—a word that designates probable demonstration according to logical rules—without recognizing that the Pope does not deliver what he promises, which, after all, was exactly Guido's advice to him.

The point of these ironies is that Boniface and Guido thoroughly resemble and deserve each other. Both believe in compromises, practical gains and moral adjustments, as if God's grace could be made adaptable to their calculus and to the narrow stage of the goings-on of everyday politics. And both are two sophists, of the kind St. Augustine finds especially odious in *De Doctrina Christiana*, those who transform the world of political action to a world of carefully spoken words. As a sophist, Boniface entertains the illusion that he can control the discourse of others and ends up controlling Guido while at the same time being controlled by him. As a sophist, Guido is the character who is always drawing the wrong logical inference from his actions: he mistakenly believes Dante is dead because he has heard that nobody ever came alive from the depth of Hell (ll. 61–66); he becomes a friar believing that, thus girt, he could make amends for his past (ll. 66–69).

What does it exactly mean to suggest, as I am doing, that Guido is portrayed as if he were a logician? And how does it square with the textual fact, that to the best of my knowledge has so far not been probed by commentators, namely that he is a Franciscan, or, as he calls himself a "cordigliero" (l. 67)? The fact that Guido is a Franciscan has far-reaching implications for the dramatic and intellectual structure of the canto. The tongues of fire in which the sinners are wrapped are an appropriate emblem more to a Franciscan like Guido than to Ulysses. The tongues of fire are usually explained as the parody of the Pentecostal tongues, the gift of prophecy that descends on the apostles at the time of the origin of the Church. It happens, however, that in the Constitution of the Franciscans it was established that the friars would convene at the Porziuncola every four years on the day of the Pentecosts. The reason for this ritual is to be found in the Franciscans' conscious vision of themselves as the new apostles capable of reforming the world.

Guido's language perverts the Pentecostal gift and the perversion puts him in touch with the fierce enemies of the Franciscans, the logicians. The possibility for this textual connection is suggested by the canto itself. At Guido's death there is a *disputatatio* between one of the "neri cherubini" and St. Francis over Guido's soul (ll. 112–117). The devil wins the debate and speaks of himself as a "loico" (l. 123). The debate between a devil and St. Francis is not much of a surprise, for as a fallen angel—one of the cherubim—the devil is the direct antagonist of Francis, who is commonly described in his hagiographies as "the angel coming from the east, with the seal of the living God." Further, the reference to the devil as one of the cherubim, which means "plenitudo scientiae" and is the attribute of the Dominicans, seems to involve obliquely in Dante's representation both orders of friars. But this is not a hidden allegory of a *quaestio disputata* between Dominicans and Franciscans. What is at stake, on the contrary, is the long debate in which the two fraternal orders were engaged in the XIII century—and in which they end up on the side of their opponents, as Dante implies. The debate centered on the value of the Liberal Arts at the University of Paris.

In historical terms the debate saw the preachers and the mendicants opposed by the secular masters of theology. The Dominicans, to be sure, adapted quickly to the pressures of the university circles because they were founded with the explicit intellectual aim of combatting heresies. The Franciscans, on the other hand, in response to the call for evangelical practice, believed that their homiletics had to retrieve without any sophistry the essence of the good news. Francis is an "idiota," given to the cult of *simplicitas* and Paris, the city of learning, is made to appear the enemy of Assisi.

This stress on simplicity did not mean that the Franciscans kept away for too long from the world of learning. There is a strong Augustinian strand, in effect, in their attitude toward academic knowledge. St. Augustine, it will be remembered, encourages Christians in *De Doctrina Christiana* to make good use of pagan rhetoric in order to communicate effectively the message of the Revelation. Secular wisdom, which is crystallized in the liberal arts and which St. Augustine rejected in the *Confessions*, is now viewed as a treasure to be booted by the Christians the way the Hebrews booted the "Egyptian gold."

The Franciscans, figures such as Alexander of Hales, St. Bonaventure and Duns Scotus did move into the universities, but by virtue of their voluntarism they adhered to an essential anti-Aristoteleanism. The formal edifice of Aristotelean logic, as a theory of abstract reasoning and as a doctrine that the universe is a logical system of numbers and mathematically measurable order is severely challenged. In *Inferno* xxvii, as the devil is identified as a logician, logic comes forth as the art that deals with judgements about the logical consistency or contradictions within the structure of an argument, but radically lacks an ethical perspective. Appropriately, Guido, who has betrayed his Franciscan principles is now claimed by one of the very logicians the Franciscans opposed.

But the debate between Franciscans and the secular masters is not left in the canto entirely on this academic level. There are political extensions to it which Dante absorbs in his representation. Guillaume de Saint-Amour, a leader of the secular masters had unleashed an attack in his *De Periculis Novissorum Temporum* against the Franciscans as the pseudo-apostles and heralds of the anti-Christ; in their purely formal observance of the externals of faith they are identified as the new Pharisees, who from under the habit of holiness connive with Popes to deceive the believers. As Y. M. J. Congar suggests, the polemic was a clear attempt to contain the power of the Pope, for the mendicants, by being under the Pope's direct jurisdiction, weakened the *potestas officii* of the local bishops. Largely at stake was the issue of confessions, a source of controversy between local priests and friars, which, ironically, was given a firm solution in the bull *Super cathedram* by Boniface VIII.

In *Inferno* xxvii Boniface is "The prince of the new Pharisees" (l. 85); he makes a mockery of confession, "Do not let thy heart mistrust; I absolve thee" (ll. 100–101), and his potestas appears as only temporal power. By the same token, Guido, who as a Franciscan should believe in the power of confession, settles for a pharisaic formula, "Father, since thou dost cleanse me from this sin into which I must now fall" (ll. 108–109). He seeks absolution before the commission of sin—an act that makes a mockery of his prior contrition and confession (l. 83). And, finally, he is throughout the Pope's conniver.

In effect, Guido da Montefeltro never changed in his life. The emblem he uses for himself, "my deeds were those, not of the lion, but of the fox" (ll. 74–75) gives him away. The animal images, to begin with, are consistent with the unredeemed vision of the natural world in terms of mastiff, claws and young lion (ll. 45–50). More to the point, the metaphor of the lion and the fox echoes Cicero's *De Officiis* (I, xiii, 41) and it may be construed in this context as a degraded variant of the *topos* of *fortitudo et sapientia*. But the fox, Guido's attribute, has some other symbolic resonances. In the *Roman de Reynard*, the fox goes into a lengthy confession of his sin and then relapses to his old ways; for Jacques of Vitry, more generally, the fox is the emblem of confession without moral rebirth. More importantly for *Inferno* xxvii is the fact that Rutebeuf, who wrote two poems in support of Guillaume de Saint-Amour, uses the fox as the symbol of the friars; in *Renart-le-nouvel* the fox is a treacherous Franciscan.

These historical events and symbols are brought to an imaginative focus in the digression of the deceits of False Seeming in the *Roman de la Rose* of Jean de Meung. Absorbing the anti-fraternal satire of Guillaume, Jean presents Faussemblant as a friar, a "cordelier," who has abandoned the evangelical ideals of Francis and lives on fraud. Reversing Joachim of Flora's hope that the fraternal orders were providentially established so that history would hasten to a close, Jean sees the mendicants as symptoms of decay: "fallacious is the logic of their claim: religious garment makes religious man." This sense of the friars' deceptiveness ("now a Franciscan, now a Dominican," as Jean says) re-appears in *Il Fiore*, where Falsembiante's steady practice of simulation comes forth as metaphoric foxiness. The sonnet conveys what was Jean's insight: namely, that the only fixed principle in False Seeming's shifty play of concealments (which in the sonnet the technique of enumeration and the iterative adverbs of time mime) is falsification itself.

To turn to the anti-fraternal satirists such as Guillaume and Jean is not equivalent, from Dante's viewpoint, to granting assent to their statement or even giving them the seal of a privileged authority. In *Inferno* xxvii Dante endorses the anti-fraternal rhetoric, for Guido da Montefeltro has clearly betrayed the paradigm of Franciscan piety. But Dante also challenges, as the Franciscan intellectuals did, the logicians' categories of knowledge. When the devil, at the triumphant conclusion of his dispute with St. Francis, appeals to logic's principle of non-contradiction (ll. 119–120), the devil is using logic only rhetorically: his is a sophistical refutation by which he sways the opponent. But logical conceptualizations, as has been argued earlier, are delusive because they are not moored to the realities of life and because they establish a *de facto* discontinuity between the order of discourse and the order of reality. More importantly, the devil is claiming as his own Guido da Montefeltro, whose very experience in the canto unveils exactly how the principle of non-contradiction is a fictitious abstraction: like Faux-Semblant, the Pope and the Devil himself, Guido is Proteus-like, to use Jean de Meung's metaphor for the friars, shifty and always unlike himself.

This rotation of figures and categories of knowledge is the substance of a canto in which, as this paper has shown, prophecy is twisted into rhetoric, theology is manipulated for political ends, politics and ethics are masks of desire for power, and logic is deployed rhetorically. From this perception of how tangled the forms of discourse are comes Dante's own moral voice, both here and in his attacks against the sophistry of syllogisms immediately after the Dominican St. Thomas Aquinas celebrates the life of St. Francis.

Because of this movement from theory to practice and back again to theory and from one order of knowledge to another, it appears that the liberal arts can never be fixed in a self-enclosed autonomous sphere: each art unavoidably entails the other in a ceaseless pattern of displacement. Ironically, what, from a moral point of view, Dante condemns in Guido da Montefeltro, becomes, in Dante's own poetic handling, the essence of knowledge itself, whereby the various disciplines are forever intermingled. The idea that the arts cannot be arranged in categorical definitions is not only a poet's awareness of how arbitrary boundaries turn out to be. Medieval textbooks and compendia are consistent, so to speak, in betraying the difficulty of treating each of the liberal arts as crystallized entities. If Isidore views dialectic as logic, John of Salisbury in his *Metalogicon* considers *logica* an encompassing term for "grammatica" and "ratio disserendi," which, in turn, contains dialectic and rhetoric. For Hugh of St. Victor, who follows St. Augustine in the *City of God*, *logica* is the name for the *trivium*.

These references are valuable only if we are ready to recognize that what is largely a technical debate never loses sight of the spiritual destination of the liberal arts. What the technicians may sense but never face, however, is that which rhetoricians and poets always know: that knowledge may be counterfeited. Small wonder that Dante in *Convivio* would repress, in vain, rhetoric. But in the *Vita Nuova* and the *Divine Comedy* we are left with the disclosure that rhetoric, in spite of its dangerous status and, ironically, because of its dangerousness, is the only possible path the poet must tread on the way to, respectively, metaphysics and theology. Whether or not the poet delivers genuine metaphysical and theological knowledge or dazzles us with luminous disguises is a question which lies at the heart of Dante's poetry.

JAROSLAV PELIKAN

The Otherworldly World
of the Paradiso

$\mathbf{A}$s even the cursory examination of a bibliography on Dante or of a library card catalog will suggest, the third and final cantica of the *Divine Comedy* by Dante Alighieri, the *Paradiso*, has, for whatever reason, received considerably less attention than the other two. On the other hand, the *Inferno* is the most prominent—perhaps because it is the first, or possibly because it is the most vividly dramatic, or probably because it is existentially the most accessible to the reader. Yet the *Paradiso* is in many ways the cantica of most interest to the history of Christian theology and dogma. Thomas Bergin has trenchantly summarized its doctrinal import: "For Dante, paradise was clearly the place where one learned things, so that there is more overt didactic matter in the *Paradiso* than in the other *cantiche*. It is not entirely fanciful to find significance in the fact that the word '*dottrina*' occurs twice in the *Inferno*, four times in the *Purgatorio*, and six times in the *Paradiso*; nor to note that the *Inferno* begins with a straightforward narrative statement, the *Purgatorio* with a metaphor, and the *Paradiso* with a statement of dogma. And with dogma, clearly and forcefully put, the *Paradiso* is replete."[1] It is, then, with that cantica that the present study in the history of theology deals— surely an ambitious undertaking, if not indeed a presumptuous one.

For a scholar, there is some consolation to be derived from the awareness that any presumption involved in this assignment falls far short of that entailed by the composition of a work of literature whose author dares to assert, already in its second sentence and its second tercet:

From *Eternal Feminines: Three Theological Allegories in Dante's Paradiso*. © 1990 by Jaroslav Pelikan.

I was within the heaven that receives more of His light; and I saw
things that he who from that height descends, forgets or can not
speak.[2]

In those lines the poet is echoing, no doubt consciously,[3] the words of another
visionary. As most interpreters ancient and modern would agree, the apostle Paul
was speaking about himself when he wrote to the Corinthians: "I will come to
visions and revelations of the Lord. I knew a man in Christ above fourteen years
ago (whether in the body, I cannot tell; or whether out of the body, I cannot tell:
God knoweth); such an one caught up to the third heaven. And I knew such a
man (whether in the body, I cannot tell; or whether out of the body, I cannot tell:
God knoweth); how that he was caught up into paradise, and heard unspeakable
words, which it is not lawful for a man to utter."[4] (Of course, although Saint
Paul, at any rate most of the time, leaves such "unspeakable words [ἄρρητα
ῥήματα]" unspoken, Dante does go on for the next thirty-three cantos of the
Paradiso to describe, from among the things he saw, at least all those which he
that descended from the light does have both the knowledge and the power to
tell again.) It is, fortunately, not the task of the scholar to reenact, or to
participate in, the visions of an ancient seer—be it Saint Paul in the third heaven
or Saint John the Divine in the Apocalypse, or Virgil in hell and purgatory, or
Dante in paradise—but only to give a faithful account of the text of the *Paradiso*
and to put it into context, specifically its broader historical context in the
theology and piety of the late Middle Ages, or what we are calling in this chapter
"the otherworldly world of the *Paradiso*." The *Paradiso* belongs to the late Middle
Ages first of all, of course, because that is when its author lived.[5] Dante Alighieri
was born in Florence sometime between 21 May and 21 June[6] in 1265—thus,
exactly fifty years after the greatest church council of the Middle Ages, the
Fourth Lateran held in 1215. Dante's birth came just one year after Roger
Bacon's composition of the *De Computo Naturali* [On Natural Computation], one
year after Thomas Aquinas's *Summa contra Gentiles*, and two years after the
founding of Balliol College. And he died in exile, at Ravenna, in 1321, nineteen
years before the birth of Geoffrey Chaucer. Thus, it was during Dante's lifetime
that Pope Boniface VIII, indelibly pictured in Canto XXVII of the *Inferno*[7] (as
well as in other passages, though he is named only once),[8] ascended the throne
of Saint Peter in 1294, and during his lifetime that Pope Clement V moved the
papacy from Rome to Avignon. John Wycliffe, moreover, was born only seven
years after Dante died. In anyone's chronology, therefore, Dante belongs to the
Middle Ages, much as he is connected also to the Renaissance.[9]

Yet it is in far more than a literal chronological sense that Dante's *Divine
Comedy*, and specifically the *Paradiso*, belongs to the Middle Ages. As Thomas
Bergin has said, the images of the poem "cover all kinds of human activities,
giving us such a richness of objective correlatives as to bring into the, great 'hall
of the Comedy' all forms and features of the medieval world." At the same time,

Bergin observes, "Dante's great work is concerned with matters not of this world; his subject is the afterlife, his pilgrimage takes him into realms which cannot be charted on physical maps, and his interests are in things eternal and not temporal."[10] For that is the world of the *Divine Comedy*, even and especially of the *Paradiso*: the otherworldly world view of Western Christendom at the end of the thirteenth and the beginning of the fourteenth century. "World view" here does refer, of course, to cosmology, and from time to time we shall have occasion to examine Dante's universe. But "world view," *Weltanschauung*, includes as well the vision of life and of reality with which the entire poem is suffused. For the *Paradiso*, that means first and foremost a view of this world in the light of the world to come, of *Terra* in the light of *Inferno* and *Purgatorio* and *Paradiso*, of time in the light of eternity, *sub specie aeternitatis*. To read the poem intelligently, it is not necessary to share, but it is necessary to try to imagine and thus to understand, a conception of reality in which the very definition of being, the "is-ness" of what "is," has been set by the Ultimate Reality and Ultimate Being that is God. Thus when Dante, addressing the apostle Peter, paraphrases the Nicene Creed and quotes its opening words, "Io credo in uno Dio," he declares:

> For this belief I have not only proofs
> both physical and metaphysical;
> I also have the truth that here rains down
> through Moses

and others of the Old and the New Testament.[11] As his earlier reference to "your dear brother," the apostle Paul, makes clear, Dante is referring to the celebrated definition of faith in the Epistle to the Hebrews (regarded as having been written by Paul): "Faith is the substance of things hoped for, the evidence of things not seen."[12] The "proofs both physical and metaphysical" should probably be taken as more or less equivalent to the familiar "five ways" of proving the existence of God set down by Saint Thomas Aquinas on almost the first page of the *Summa*.[13] But the reference to "Moses" is an echo of the saying of God quoted by Thomas in that discussion and addressed to Moses from the burning bush, "I am that I am,"[14] which Dante, together with the consensus of thinkers Jewish and Christian, takes to mean that God is Being itself, while all other "being," whether visible or invisible, angelic or inanimate, as the same Creed affirms, is the creation of that God and hence possesses its being derivatively and dependently.

The "world of the *Paradiso*," however, must mean even more specifically what cannot be called anything except its "otherworldly world." As the striking epigram of Shirley Jackson Case put it, "The sky hung low in the ancient world,"[15] and it continued to do so in Dante's medieval world. For not only does Dante present the Being of God as the Ultimate Reality in relation to which all other "being" has a secondary reality, thus providing what Arthur Lovejoy has called "a fairly unequivocal expression of the principle of plenitude";[16] but the primacy of the divine reality of God the Creator is, in a mysterious fashion, shared with all the creaturely dwellers of paradise as well, transforming their very existence into another order of being. That applies in a special way to the angels, but perhaps the most dramatic (and almost certainly the most enigmatic) case of such transformation is Beatrice. Whatever may be the status of "the quest of the historical Beatrice," she is, here in the *Paradiso* and above all in its closing cantos, beyond time and space and almost (though not quite) beyond creatureliness itself. "If that which has been said of her so far," Dante summarizes,

> were all contained within a single praise [*in una lodes*],
> it would be too scant to serve me now.
> The loveliness I saw surpassed not only
> our human measure—and I think that, surely,
> only its Maker can enjoy it fully.[17]

Therefore, the intuition of Gertrud Bäumer is correct when she relates Dante to the closing lines of Goethe's *Faust*.[18] Its final line, "*Das Ewig-Weibliche zieht uns hinan* [The Eternal Feminine draws us above]," unforgettably set to music by Gustav Mahler in his Eighth Symphony, does echo Dante's apotheosis of Beatrice; and it was therefore natural for it to provide the title for this book. In present-day English usage, however, the term "otherworldly" usually means "spectral" (or "spooky") and therefore suggests something "unreal," while in the *Paradiso* it is precisely the "otherworldliness" that is "really real." As A. Bartlett Giamatti put it, "all the landscapes of Hell and Purgatory are either defective or incomplete versions of the terrestrial paradise. But the terrestrial paradise is itself only an image of the celestial paradise. The garden of Eden simply reflects the City of God."[19]

At the same time, this "otherworldliness" of the *Paradiso* must not be taken to mean that Dante's consideration of this world of time and space, the world of politics and of human history, is confined to the *Inferno* and the *Purgatorio*, in both of which (as even the most casual reader can recognize) it is so prominent. On the contrary, it is possible to argue that in those first two cantiche Dante could treat politics and history as incisively and as severely as he did for the very reason that even then he had his eye on a rule of measurement beyond the here and now. That becomes strikingly evident, for example, in the portrait of the emperor Justinian which occupies all of Canto VI of the *Paradiso*, with a prelude at the conclusion of Canto V and a curious liturgical cadenza (employing a mixture of Latin and quasi-Hebrew words) in the opening three lines of Canto VII.[20] Justinian introduces himself to the poet as the lawgiver of Rome, the one

> who, through the will of the Primal Love I feel,
> removed the vain and needless from the laws.[21]

According to this definition of jurisprudence, what the law expresses is not the harsh reality of moral ambiguity in the world of politics (an ambiguity that Dante knew well from his own Florentine experience, and about which he repeatedly speaks with great bitterness in the *Divine Comedy*), but the will and purpose of the *primo Amor*, which embodies itself in natural and positive law, even though, as in the empyrean,

> where God governs with no mediator [*sanza mezzo*],
> no thing depends upon the laws of nature,[22]

much less upon the positive legislation of human societies. Justinian's introduction is followed by a remarkable survey of the history of Rome, in which one Caesar after another passes in review, from the original Caesar, Julius, to the Holy Roman Emperor Charlemagne. "Caesar I was and am Justinian [*Cesare fui e son Iustiniano*]," the emperor declares,[23] setting the criterion of law and justice as an absolute standard by which to measure all his predecessors—and all his successors as well, up to and including the political parties and partisans of Dante's own time in the empire. "Let Ghibellines," the emperor Justinian asserts as, speaking from the sixth century, he addresses himself to the problems of the fourteenth,

> pursue their undertakings
> beneath another sign, for those who sever
> this sign and justice are bad followers.[24]

It is this medieval otherworldliness of the *Paradiso* that, far from having abstracted Dante out of the real world of politics and concrete choice, enables him to pass specific judgment on conditions in the empire past and present.

That applies a fortiori to his treatment of the Church, to which we shall be returning in greater detail but which is appropriate here as a prime illustration of the otherworldly world that is the context of the *Paradiso*. The century of the *Paradiso* is also the century of Boniface VIII and of the "Babylonian captivity" of the Church under the Avignon papacy and, on the other hand, the century of John Wycliffe at Oxford and then (beginning in the fourteenth century but continuing into the fifteenth) of Jan Hus in Prague. Dante was caught up passionately in the agitation for the reform of the Church, of its hierarchy, and of the papacy itself. This is evident from Dante's other writings, above all from the *De Monarchia*, which it is a mistake to read only as a treatise on secular politics, as though there were no difference between Dante's *De Monarchia* and the *Defensor Pacis* of Marsilius of Padua; for, as a leading student of Marsilius has pointed out, "even Dante, despite his, dedication of the 'temporal monarchy' to intellectual activity, also finally apportions the papal function to caring for man's incorruptible soul, and the temporal imperial function to man's corruptible body."[25] The passage cited earlier from the *Inferno* indicates what Dante thought of Pope Boniface VIII. But all of that denunciation of corruption in the Church and in the papacy does not, as one might have expected, come to its crescendo in the hell or in the purgatory to which so many of the past occupants of the throne of Saint Peter have been consigned by Dante (and, presumably, by God), but here in heaven, where it is Saint Peter himself,

> that ancient father
> of Holy Church, into whose care the keys
> of this fair flower were consigned by Christ,[26]

who pronounces their judgment upon them—just as it is from the vantage point of heaven that its former inhabitant, "the first proud being [*'l primo superbo*]" who was "the highest of all creatures,"[27] Satan the fallen angel, must be judged. Beginning with an Italian metric version of the Latin Gloria Patri, Canto XXVII goes on to these stinging words from Peter, the Prince of the Apostles. Three times Saint Peter plaintively cries out "my place [il luogo mio]," just as, fulfilling Christ's grim prophecy, he had denied his Lord three times:[28]

> He who on earth usurps my place, my place, my place that in the
> sight of God's own Son is vacant now, has made my burial ground a
> sewer of blood, a sewer of stench, so that the perverse one who fell
> from Heaven, here above, can find contentment there below.[29]

Apparently, as the Church is viewed by none other than Saint Peter himself in the light of the other world, such a corrupt Church could provide a more comfortable domicile for Satan than it could—or, at any rate, than it should—for any legitimate successor of Peter.

The "otherworldly" criterion in the *Paradiso*'s treatment of the Church and its reform makes itself visible also in the prominent role that the *Paradiso* assigns to monks and to monasticism. For, in the vocabulary of the Middle Ages, the monastic life was often called "the angelic life [*vita angelica*]." In the Gospel, Christ had said that "in the resurrection [human beings] neither marry, nor are given in marriage, but are as the angels of God in heaven."[30] Saint Gregory of Nyssa used the saying from the Gospel to argue that since "the resurrection promises us nothing else than the restoration of the fallen to their ancient state," virginity was characteristic of "the life before the transgression" of Adam and Eve, which for that reason was "a kind of angelic life."[31] On that basis, virginity and therefore monasticism had been referred to as "angelic" by Gregory's brother, the father of Eastern monasticism, Saint Basil of Caesarea, as well as by Saint John Chrysostom.[32] Perhaps from such Greek sources, Rufinus of Aquileia, who knew the Greek Christian authors well and translated some of them into Latin, spoke of monasticism as the *vita angelica*, as did other Latin writers.[33] And in the supplement to Part III of the *Summa Theologica* the term is explained this way: "Virginity is said to be an 'angelic life,' insofar as virgins imitate by grace what angels have by nature. For it is not owing to a virtue that angels abstain altogether from pleasures of the flesh, since they are incapable of such pleasures."[34] It seems plausible that "the bread of angels" of which Dante speaks in the *Paradiso*[35] refers to the wisdom of the angels who, because they did not fall from grace with their fellows,

> were modestly aware
> that they were ready for intelligence
> so vast, because of that Good which had made them.[36]

But the "angelic life" in the usage of his time is a way of speaking about monasticism, a usage that Dante does reflect here in the *Paradiso* when—alluding to the traditional distinction according to which "the cherubim have the excellence of knowledge and the seraphim the excellence of ardor" in their charity[37]—he says that Saint Dominic was "cherubic" whereas Saint Francis was "seraphic."[38]

Even without running a detailed and precise statistical analysis, moreover, it is striking to note how often monastic figures and monastic themes appear throughout the entire third cantica of the *Divine Comedy*.[39] For example, the words of Piccarda Donati in Canto III, "We have neglected vows,"[40] are followed by the poet's question at the end of Canto IV:

> I want to know if, in your eyes, one can
> amend for unkept vows with other acts.[41]

This is followed in turn by Beatrice's response about vows at the beginning of Canto V.[42] All of this carries echoes of the most extensive discussions of vows in medieval thought, which were addressed to monastic vows. Therefore, the interpreters who have detected a note of irony in Beatrice's explanation that "the Holy Church gives dispensations"[43] are probably correct. For a vow, in Beatrice's (and Dante's) view, is not merely an agreement between two human beings, even if one of them is a priest or prelate, but ultimately a sacred contract between creature and Creator. That vertical dimension is what makes the betrayal of a vow such a crime, as can be seen also in the various cases of marital infidelity, "the force of Venus' poison,"[44] that appear in the *Inferno* and the *Purgatorio*. Here in the *Paradiso* the crime of betraying monastic vows evokes from the eleventh-century reformer of monasticism and of the Church, Saint Peter Damian, this lament:

> That cloister used to offer souls to Heaven,
> a fertile harvest, but it now is barren—
> as Heaven's punishment will soon make plain.[45]

For throughout the Middle Ages, as R. W. Southern has put it, "those who set themselves a standard higher than the ordinary looked to the monasteries for their examples,"[46] because the monasteries were the outposts of the other world here in this world, the models of authentic community, the seedbeds of holiness, and the sources of renewal. If they themselves became corrupt, as they did with such depressing regularity—

> The flesh of mortals yields so easily;
> on earth a good beginning does not run
> from when the oak is born until the acorn

is Dante's one-sentence lament[47]—the result was that not only the monks but everyone would suffer. In the familiar maxim of the Roman poet Juvenal, "*Sed quis custodiet ipsos custodes?* [But who is to guard the guards themselves?]"[48]

Or, in the complaint that Dante puts into the mouth of the sixth-century founder of Western monasticism, Saint Benedict of Nursia,

> my Rule is left
> to waste the paper it was written on.[49]

But that complaint is voiced by one who is already in heaven, as Beatrice is obliged to remind Dante about himself.[50] Indeed, he is not only in heaven, but (as she also reminds him) Dante has, at the point of encountering Benedict, come very "near the final blessedness."[51] At that exalted position, moreover, Benedict speaks as "the largest and most radiant"[52] of the hundred pearls or "little spheres [*sperule*]" to which Beatrice directs Dante's gaze. With the kind of spiritual boasting of which the apostle Paul speaks,[53] Benedict describes the achievements of his monastic foundation on Monte Cassino, built on the site of a pagan temple: "Such abundant grace had brought me light," he says,

> that, from corrupted worship that seduced
> the world, I won away the nearby sites.[54]

In so doing, Benedict established a pattern that was to become an essential component of monastic life throughout the rest of Christian history, as over and over the monks in both East and West were to be the shock troops of the Catholic and Christian faith, in the vanguard of its march across the continents. It was for this reason, among others, that in the twentieth century Saint Benedict and Saints Cyril and Methodius, the apostles to the Slavs, have been designated co-patron saints of Europe. From Dante's celebration of monastic heroism and from his lament over monastic vice, it is clear that in Dante's eyes the history of monasticism since the age of Benedict contained some of the most glorious chapters of Christian heroism, and some of the most degenerate chapters of

Christian betrayal. Yet it is undeniable that for Dante the monks were among the leading citizens of both the Church on earth and the Church in paradise.

Despite the high praise for Saint Benedict, the father of Western monasticism, the pride of place among the monks in the *Paradiso* is reserved for another monk who was not a Benedictine but a Cistercian, the monastic reformer who was also a reformer of the Church, Saint Bernard of Clairvaux.[55] In the final three cantos, which may well be the most powerful hymn ever written in praise of the Blessed Virgin Mary, the speaker is Bernard the "holy elder [*canto sere*]."[56] He describes himself as "Mary's faithful Bernard [*suo fedel Bernardo*]."[57] As Masseron has suggested, that title applies to Dante as well as to Bernard.[58] In this closing scene Bernard has left

> the sweet
> place where eternal lot assigns [his] seat,[59]

in order to expound to Dante the historical typology of Eve the mother of humankind and Mary the Second Eve. The speeches about Mary that Dante places into the mouth of Bernard are in fact a compendium of his rich and varied works devoted to her praises. Other works of Bernard of Clairvaux, particularly his letters and his treatise *On Consideration*, written for his pupil Pope Eugenius III, were likewise a source upon which Dante and his fellow reformers of church and empire drew for their denunciation of the Church's corruption.[60] In addressing such an essay as *On Consideration* to the pope, Bernard had clearly risen above the corruption of his time to carry out the historic responsibility of the monks as the conscience of the medieval Church.[61]

In Dante's own time it was neither the Benedictines nor the Cistercians, but the Franciscans and the Dominicans who had assumed much of the responsibility for the spiritual life of the Church—and who had, yet again, manifested the universal tendency to corruption through "their decadence, and sudden passion for the material goods their masters had taught them to abandon, [which] destroyed many of the spiritual gains made by Francis and Dominic, and reduced the Orders to a state little better than that of the Church their founders had begun to rebuild."[62] The founders of these two orders are the subject of Canto XI of the *Paradiso*:

> two princes, one
> on this side, one on that [*quinci e quindi*], as her [the Church's]
> guides[63]—

one of them, as noted earlier, "all seraphic in his ardor" and the other "the splendor of cherubic light on earth."[64] In his miniature biography of Francis, in which scholars have found a remarkably "symmetrical construction,"[65] Dante describes how Francis had, after an interval of "some eleven hundred years,"[66] restored the primitive Christian ideal of poverty when he took Lady Poverty as his spiritual bride. Although this bizarre act brought upon him the "scorn and wonder [*maraviglia*]"[67] of most of his contemporaries, he did manage to extract from Pope Innocent III the approval of the Rule of the Franciscans, or, as Dante calls it, "the first seal of his order."[68] What Dante then goes on to call "the final seal [*l'ultimo sigillo*]," which "his limbs bore for two years,"[69] came in the form of the stigmata, the marks of the Passion of Christ on the body of Saint Francis. Francis was and still is a controversial figure, indeed a revolutionary one. The implications of his doctrine and practice of poverty came to be seen by many of his followers, particularly the Spiritual Franciscans, as a radical attack upon the institutional Church as such, earning for them the condemnation of the Church's leaders. Nevertheless at his death this "second Christ," as he came to be known, issued a Testament (now generally acknowledged to be genuine) to his Franciscan brethren, in which

> Francis commended his most precious lady,
> and he bade them to love her faithfully.[70]

The official biographer of Saint Francis and the most eminent theological mind of the Franciscan Order (at least until Duns Scotus, who was born in the same year as Dante, 1265) was Bonaventure, who speaks in Canto XII of the Paradiso.

But it is one of the most striking of the many transpositions in the entire *Divine Comedy*, as many readers have noted and as a Dominican scholar has recently explained in some detail, that Bonaventure speaks not about Saint Francis but about Saint Dominic, founder of the Order of Preachers, just as it is the Dominican Thomas Aquinas who speaks in such glowing terms about Francis, founder of the Order of Friars Minor.[71] Writing at a time when the rivalry between the two orders and the general state of the monastic life had become a scandal throughout Western Christendom,[72] Dante employs this device to remind his readers—and any Franciscans or Dominicans who might be listening—that the two emphases, the "seraphic" celebration of the supremacy of love associated with the Franciscans and the "cherubic" cultivation of wisdom and scholarship identified with the Dominicans, are by no means mutually exclusive, but in fact need each other to be rescued from exaggeration. They are like two wheels of the chariot of Holy Church,[73] both of them indispensable to her journey on this earthly pilgrimage to the otherworldly paradise. Therefore, after Aquinas has begun by pointing to Dominic as "our patriarch [*il nostro patriarca*],"[74] it is Bonaventure who takes over to draw a vivid portrait of Dominic as "the holy athlete," whose valiant efforts as a formidable champion in defense of the truth of the Catholic faith made him "kind to his own and harsh to enemies."[75] In Dominic, it was above all the power of his intellect[76] that equipped him for his special ministry:

Then he, with both his learning and his zeal,
and with his apostolic office, like
a torrent hurtled from a mountain source,
coursed, and his impetus, with greatest force,
struck where the thickets of the heretics
offered the most resistance.[77]

For an appreciation of "the otherworldly world of the *Paradiso*," the angelic world of cherubim and seraphim, the most important accent in Dante's treatment of the Franciscans and the Dominicans here in the *Paradiso* is his use of angelic metaphors for both: Francis "was all *seraphic* in his ardor," Dominic was endowed with "the splendor of *cherubic* light on earth"[78]—"on earth," because such light and such ardor were ordinarily part of the other world, but in these two "princes" they had appeared in this world as well.

In this connection, however, it is necessary to examine one suggestion of a possible historical connection of Dante with the Franciscan Order, and to evaluate the suggestion of another historical connection between Dante and the Dominican Order. It is clear from the presentation in Cantos XI and XII just summarized that Dante was striving to be evenhanded in his treatment of the two orders, of their two founders, and of the shameful condition into which both of the orders had fallen by his own time. Yet that evenhandedness, which was apparently quite sincere and surely quite successful, must not be permitted to obscure Dante's special personal bond with the Franciscans. For like many late medieval figures—it should be noted, for example, that in June 1496, upon arriving in Cádiz, Spain, at the end of his second voyage, Christopher Columbus "assumed the coarse brown habit of a Franciscan, as evidence of repentance and humility"[79]—Dante had identified himself with Saint Francis. In Canto XVI of the *Inferno* Dante says of himself: "Around my waist I had a cord as girdle [*una corda intorno cinta*],"[80] a cord that Virgil borrows to use as an enormous fishing line for catching the monster Geryon.[81] Although this could be a purely symbolic allusion—for which there is a parallel, for example, in the words of the *Purgatorio* about Charles of Aragon as one who "wore the cord of every virtue [*ogne valor portò cinta la corda*]"[82]—the Franciscan cord did have a special significance for Dante, which some scholars have seen expressed by his reference, here in the description of Francis and his retinue in the *Paradiso*, to "the lowly cord already round their waists."[83] The reference to the "cord" in Canto XVI of the *Inferno* has given rise to the theory that Dante had once, as a young man, briefly joined the Franciscan Order.[84] John D. Sinclair thinks it "may well be true,"[85] while Charles S. Singleton insists that "these speculations are without documentary evidence" and that "it is in no way certain that D[ante] ever joined the Order, even as a tertiary."[86] Whatever may be the truth of such reports about Dante's early life, it does seem certain that when he died on the night of 13 September 1321, after a journey to Venice, he was buried at Ravenna in a small chapel near San Piero Maggiore (which is now, appropriately enough, called San Francesco)—and that he was "buried with honors, and in the costume of the Franciscan order."[87]

On the other hand, the intellectual content of the *Divine Comedy* has often been identified (in perhaps too hasty and facile a conclusion on the basis of evidence that is at best tenuous) not with the Franciscans at all, but with the Dominicans and specifically with Saint Thomas Aquinas. This issue was brought to the fore in the book *Dante le théologien*, published in 1935 by the Dominican scholar and distinguished editor of the *Commentary on the Sentences* of Thomas Aquinas, Pierre Mandonnet, who is perhaps best known to students of the history of philosophy for his pioneering research on Siger of Brabant and Latin Averroist philosophy.[88] The most important response to Mandonnet's thesis is that of Etienne Gilson, whom many would regard as the most eminent historian of medieval thought in the past hundred years.[89] In addition to many incisive comments on the standing issues of Dante interpretation, above all on the tangled problem of whether Beatrice has become more than human by the time Dante gets to the final cantos of the *Paradiso*, Gilson reviews the alleged dependence of Dante on Thomas in a section entitled "Dante's Thomism."[90] And despite his own standing as a Thomist scholar and despite the prominent place occupied by Saint Thomas in the *Paradiso*,[91] Gilson concludes that it is a mistake to read Dante as a partisan and disciple of Thomas in any but the most general sense.

He must rather be seen as a disciple of Saint Augustine—which is, after all, how Thomas also saw himself even when he was criticizing Augustine.[92] Many of the phrases and tropes that a student of Aquinas seems to recognize as Thomistic upon reading the *Divine Comedy* are in fact Augustinian.[93] Thomas Aquinas and Dante Alighieri were drawing upon a common source, who was likewise the source for most of medieval theology, and for much if not most of medieval philosophy as well. It is rather curious, then, that Augustine himself occupies a relatively small place in the *Comedy*.[94] He appears together with Saint Francis and Saint Benedict in the Tenth Heaven,[95] but he does not function as one of the dramatis personae in the way that Thomas and Bonaventure and, above all, Bernard of Clairvaux do; nor does the narrative of his life story receive any special place in the poem. Yet that very obscurity can be taken to mean that the presence and influence of Augustine are so pervasive throughout the *Purgatorio*, especially throughout the *Paradiso*, that he does not have to be one of the characters in the play, since he has provided so many of its lines—including what may well be the most familiar line it the entire work, the words of Piccarda Donati, "And in His will there is our peace [*E 'n la sua volontade è nostra pace*],"[96] words that seem to be an unmistakable echo of the words of Augustine in the *Confessions*, "In Thy good will is our peace."[97] Similar parallels abound throughout the *Divine Comedy*, above all perhaps in the *Paradiso*. All of these Augustinian, medieval, and "otherworldly" qualities of the world of the

Paradiso come together in its employment of allegory, especially of theological allegory.

NOTES

1. Bergin 1965, 274.

2. *Par.* I.4–6.

3. Mazzeo 1958, 84–110.

4. 2 Cor. 12:1–4.

5. Vossler 1929 continues to be an indispensable introduction to the entire world of Dante.

6. That is the conclusion most scholars draw from Dante's words (*Par.* XXII.111–120) about "the sign that follows Taurus," that is to say, Gemini, the "constellation steeped in mighty force [*gran virtù*]," as his "fated point of entry," to which all of his genius looks as its source.

7. *Inf.* XXVII.67–129.

8. *Inf.* XIX.53.

9. On this latter connection, it is instructive to note that throughout *The Civilization of the Renaissance in Italy* Jacob Burckhardt celebrated Dante as the embodiment of his major themes. What he said in chapter 3 of Part II could have been said of each part: "Here, again, as in all essential points, the first witness to be called is Dante" (Burckhardt 1958, 1:151).

10. Bergin 1965, 286 and 1.

11. *Par.* XXIV.130–141.

12. *Par.* XXIV.61–66, quoting Heb. 11:1.

13. *S.T.* I.2.3.

14. Exod. 3:14.

15. Case 1946, 1.

16. Lovejoy 1936, 68–69.

17. *Par.* XXX.16–21.

18. Bäumer 1949, 149; also Newman 1987, 262.

19. Giamatti 1966, 116.

20. *Enc. Dant.* 3:231–233.

21. *Par.* VI.10–12.

22. *Par.* XXX.122–123.

23. *Par.* VI.10.

24. *Par.* VI.103–105.

25. Gewirth 1951, 100, n. 54.

26. *Par.* XXXII.124–126.

27. *Par.* XIX.46–48.

28. Matt. 26:34, 69–75.

29. *Par.* XXVII.22–27.

30. Matt. 22:30.

31. Gregory of Nyssa *On the Making of Man* xvii.2.

32. Lampe 1961, 9; on "Chrysostom the metropolitan," see *Par.* XII.136–137

33. Blaise and Chirat 1954, 81.

34. *S.T.* III, Sup.96.9. *ad* 1.

35. For example, *Par.* II.11.

36. *Par.* XXIx.58–60; see also the Epilogue below.

37. *S.T.* 1.108.5. *ad* 6.

38. *Par.* XI.37–39.

39. As Palgen 1940, 66–67, has noted, the only two souls who speak to Dante in the Heaven of Saturn are both monks, Saint Benedict and Saint Peter Damian.

40. *Par.* III.56.

41. *Par.* IV.136–137.

42. *Par.* V.13–15.

43. *Par.* V.35–36.

44. *Purg.* XXV.132.

45. *Par.* XXI.118–120; see the discussion of Dante's use of medieval legends about Peter Damian in Capetti 1906.

46. Southern 1953, 158.

47. *Par.* XXII.85–87.

48. Juvenal *Satires* VI.341–348.

49. *Par.* XXII.74–75.

50. *Par.* XXII.7–8.

51. *Par.* XXII.124.

52. *Par.* XXII.28.

53. 2 Cor. II:16–33.

54. *Par.* XXII.43–45.

55. See the long footnote discussing the question "Why Saint Bernard?" in Rabuse 1972, 59–61.

56. *Par.* XXXI.94.

57. *Par.* XXXI.102.

58. Masseron 1953, 71–143.

59. *Par.* XXXII.101–102.

60. *Ep.* X.28.

61. Kennan 1967.

62. Needler 1969, 21.

63. *Par.* XI.36.

64. *Par.* XI.37–39.

65. Santarelli 1969, 37.

66. *Par.* XI.65.

67. *Par.* XI.90.

68. *Par.* XI.93.

69. *Par.* XI.107–108.

70. *Par.* XI.113–114. Although some interpreters have taken this "most prycious lady" to be Poverty, the tenor of my argument here seems to point to the conclusion that she is the Catholic Church.

71. Foster 1987, 229–249.

72. On the state of monastic life and monastic reform in the later Middle Ages, see the helpful summary of Oakley 1979, 231–238.

73. *Par.* XII.106–107.

74. *Par.* XI.121.

75. *Par.* XII.57.

76. *Par.* XII.59: "la sua mente di viva virtute."

77. *Par.* XII.97–102.

78. *Par.* XI.37–39.

79. Morison 1955, 102.

80. *Inf.* XVI.106.

81. See the review of recent critical scholarship on this passage in D'Amato 1972.

82. *Purg.* VII.114, apparently a reference to Isa. 11:5.

83. *Par.* XI.85–87.

84. On the entire question of Dante and the Franciscans, see the studies of Needler 1969, Santarelli 1969, and Foster 1987.

85. Sinclair 1961, 1:213.

86. Singleton in Toynbee 1965, 48.

87. Bergin 1965, 44.

88. Mandonnet 1935.

89. Gilson 1949.

90. Gilson 1949, 226–242.

91. *Par.* X.82–138, XI.16–XII.2, XII.110–111, 141, XIII.32–XIV.8.

92. Gilson 1926.

93. Mazzotta 1979, 147–191.

94. *Enc. Dant.* 1:80–82.

95. *Par.* XXXII.35.

96. *Par.* III.85.

97. Augustine *Confessions* XIII.ix.10.

MARÍA ROSA MENOCAL

Synchronicity

III

The momentous break that marks the beginning of lyric poetry in the European vernaculars has been an obsessive fascination for critics since Dante himself first made it a legitimate object of study in his *De vulgari eloquentia*. It is one of a number of literary-historical subjects about which the braggart claim can be made that more has been written about it than about any other. Of the many entangled issues in this domain, I wish to single out the two major metaliterary ones that seem to me to have been of greatest concern to Dante the author of the *Vita nuova*: the issue of the "new life" or new beginning for poetry that is so starkly raised by the conspicuous establishment of the vernaculars of eleventh- and twelfth-century Europe as a new beginning in literary cycles, and the deeply solipsistic nature of that newly minted poetry itself.

One can, paradoxically, dispense with any extended review of the "origins" debate(s), for when and where the story of lyric poetry in the European vernaculars "actually" begins (a matter, of course, of some considerable dispute) is not nearly so important in this discussion as the fact that it does have a discernable beginning, that it is and was perceived as a major rupture vis-à-vis its "classical" antecedents. Indeed, whatever the provocations and contingencies at its beginning, the dénouement of the story invariably includes the remarkable invention that did indeed take place as part of the cluster of innovations conveniently tagged as "twelfth century": the vernaculars were born and

From *Writing in Dante's Cult of Truth From Borges to Boccaccio*. © 1991 by Duke University Press.

prospered as literary languages, as the prime matter of a literature perceived (then, as well as now) as "new." It is difficult to overestimate the importance, difficulty, and implications of such an event, and it is supremely important to remember that, unlike the biological analogy that gives rise to the "birth" metaphor, a death is the implacable contingency of such creation: the displacement and substitution of a new language almost invariably constitutes, despite the wishes of many, the death of the one being replaced. Even more dramatically and with greater pain, of course, a number of paternal figures are supplanted by others. Dante, of course, was not only fully aware of these issues but both disturbed and fascinated by them: even his discussion of Latin as never having been a natural language at all but rather a *koine*, an artificial construct, smacks of self-justification, the defense against some unheard but deeply sensed reproach. His discussion of the inevitable evolution of natural and living languages, as opposed to those that are dead in their immutability—and the embarrassing but lurking hint that the same may hold for the poetry of such languages—leaves in no doubt his sensitivity to the issues of transitions and replacements that are both birth *and* death.[5]

Thus, the specific historical conditions of the rupture are by and large irrelevant here. Almost any of the models that have been proposed for such origins share the characteristics that are critical for the perspective necessary for this reading of the *Vita nuova*: a linguistic rupture that involves the canonization of a language previously spoken but not canonized, and the concomitant invention of poetic norms for a complex written poetry springing, in different measures and ways, from both an oral tradition (the spoken and probably sung vernacular languages and songs) and a written tradition or traditions. Dante's descriptive metaphors of heritage are unambiguous: the mother's language (her lullabies and love songs alike, those models of sung and unwritten literature) is being elevated to the status of what is otherwise the father's, and the father's, the classical, is then, of course, replaced as the model by the child's, by this "new" language of poetry.[6] Of course, there is an important paradox in all of this: the establishment of this new form, when it is sufficiently entrenched to be considered canonical (as was certainly the case soon enough with both Provençal and Mozarabic lyrics, for example), itself becomes a new norm, a new canon, a new father figure to be either followed or replaced. Thus, a Dante acutely aware of the literary history of which he is a product (and out of which, in many ways, he is trying to write himself) has not one but two major ancestral historical forms that have given him birth as a poet: firstly, the classical, since he is still, of course, a reader of that tradition; and secondly, and no less critically, those first several centuries of the vernacular or "troubadour" writings which, by the turn of the fourteenth century, are themselves quite legitimately a tradition. Historical foreshortening should not obscure the fact that the latter was in its own right no less oppressively canonical for a writer like Dante. Dante, then, stands at what may be a unique kind of crossroads in terms of poetic ancestry: because he is still remarkably close to the Latin tradition, certainly enough so that it is a fundamental part of his linguistic and poetic upbringing, it has paternal authority and will constitute, when he writes in Italian, a model he is rejecting. But—and this is the peculiarity and perhaps the paradox—he has imbibed a considerable and powerful vernacular tradition as well (certainly the *De vulgari* is an homage, among other things, to that part of his ancestry), one which was itself eminently canonical and well established, in many crucial ways decaying and at an end, dead in the death of static and artificiality, by the time Dante began his writing career. Thus, although the extant vernacular tradition also defined itself, in great measure, as breaking from that same classical patronage, it too was a past for Dante; it too has been indispensable in his creation, and it too, inevitably, must be left behind.

If Dante embraces the first of the two salient characteristics of the troubadours, the substitution and recreation of a new poetic language deriving from the maternal tongue, ultimately he is deeply troubled by its second distinguishing feature, by what we insist on calling "courtly love" but is far more advantageously described as poetic solipsism. Dispensing, once again, with the seemingly interminable discussions of many often irrelevant ancillary aspects of the "courtly love" debate, and focusing on those readings that coincide with Dante's own interpretations of his antecedents, one can indulge in the simple assertion that the greatest obsession of troubadour poetry is itself. The poetry appears, on the first level, to be about an inaccessible love object; but when one apprehends, as most poets have, that the love is inaccessible because only then can the poetry be generated, then the true, the consummated objects of love are revealed: language itself and the music and poetry that are its receptacles. Given the historical nature of the dramatic linguistic break that is being executed and the new language that is being forged and molded as one goes along, it is scarcely surprising—perhaps even inevitable—that the creator will be more intrigued by his own creation than even normally. The circular and solipsistic (and some would eventually say sterile and pristine) nature of the poetic ideology is striking: since the generation and writing of the poem itself depends on lack of fulfillment, only an unfulfilled love can exist within the borders of this poetry—since poetry itself is the real desired object. The circle is a tightly closed one (as Zumthor has so well pointed out), the poetry often starkly hermetic, the love perforce a dead end, "sans issu," as the *Tristan* poet will tell us, and the ultimate adoration is of the lyrical form per se, of this poetic language quite literally in the making. While these features are abundantly clear from the earliest Provençal examples (one need only remember Guillaume's "Farai un vers de dreyt rien" [I will make a poem from absolutely nothing]), the phenomenon reaches its peak and glory in what is called, appropriately and in full recognition of the tight hermetic circle, the *trobar clus*, perhaps best rendered as "*self*-enclosed poetry." The master craftsman here is, of course, Arnaut Daniel, who, among other things, appears to have invented what is certainly one of the most difficult of lyrical forms, the *sestina*. The essence of Arnaut's accomplishment is best conveyed by the high priest of his cult in the modern period, Ezra Pound, who first learned about him in his truncated studies in Romance philology at the University of Pennsylvania, but who, shortly after abandoning that formal academic training, expended considerable independent effort on the translation of most of Arnaut's eighteen known extant songs, writing in 1918, "I have completely rewritten, or nearly finished completely rewriting all Arnaut Daniel" (quoted in Wilhelm 1982:64). Two years later Pound published his essay of admiration on "il miglior fabbro," delighting there in Arnaut's two salient characteristics: the stunning musicality of his verses and their hermeticism. Pound's translations, which are not, in fact, as complete as he had claimed, in turn also feast on these qualities of Arnaut's poetry (the very qualities which make him so perfect an exemplar, because of the high pitch of focus and the distillation—some might say exaggeration—of obsession with self and lyricism), and Pound's renditions are sparkling mosaics of almost meaningless beautiful sounds. As one critic of those translations has put it: "One winds up with the opposite of a literal trot: a free rendering that corresponds more with the original in terms of sound than in sense of imagery."[7]

That, then, distilled through the later, far more iconoclastic philologist-become-poet, is the ancestor whom Dante too would hold up, in the considerably different, retrospective light of the *Purgatorio*, as exemplary of the tradition that had preceded him and molded him, although, crucially, the *tone* of Dante's apparent praise has not been much listened to—a problem I will return to in a later chapter. But no matter, for the time being: Dante's high estimation of Arnaut's craftsmanship and of the essential apprenticeship provided by the full range of the vernacular traditions is everywhere apparent. The *De vulgari*, certainly, makes it abundantly clear that the Provençal corpus, and the Sicilian one closely linked to it, constitute explicit role models, and from the opening pages of the *Vita nuova* there is no doubt that a crucial part of the story told is that the young Dante Alighieri has apprenticed himself to the rich (and by then venerable, over two centuries old) traditions of the highly self-reflective love lyrics of the Romance vernaculars. His own earliest efforts are so unmistakably (and self-consciously) a part of that tradition that they include, among other things, *sestine* to equal Arnaut's own best examples of the *trobar clus*. But the young artist ends up being far from satisfied with the poetics of predecessors who were once attractive, in part, because they stood as revolutionaries with respect to their, ancestors (who were Dante's own, at the same time), predecessors who taught him, quite literally, how to write in the *parlar materno*, the mother tongue. His conversion from their poetics to his own thus becomes the meticulously chronicled story of the *Vita nuova*; this follows the archetypical structures of autobiographies in beginning at the end of the story, a story which is that of how the author came to be able to understand what he had already written and then go on to write his new kind of literature—that literature of the New Life.[8]

The confusion here, in part, is that of the occasional doubling between historical author and the author who is the poet of the story of the *Vita nuova*. The role played out by the protagonist is that of authorship itself, and this conflation, a making explicit of what is always implicit, is part of Dante's kabbalistic enterprise: what is written is literally true and precedes any other reality. Among other things, that mysterious book from which the author Dante is taking his text is very much the kabbalistic text of reality. As in the *Commedia*, there is a tension between author and protagonist, the younger author, which is parallel to the tension between poet and pilgrim in the later text. After all, one is bent on usurping the other, quite literally taking his place, and the reader too suffers at least some of the anxieties and fears that naturally attend to such mergers of personalities within the self as we follow the not always gradual merger—at times a death struggle—between the two.[9] At the end, after an apparently full assimilation of the implications of the conversion, we have the new author as he sits down to—in this case—rewrite, copy, recount, the story of how the old life came to be the New Life—all, of course, inevitably, from the light of the New Life which has recast the meanings and intentions of what was read and written in the old. All, of course, rooted in the death of the old. Freccero, in words about the *Commedia* which are no less applicable to the *Vita nuova*, notes that "the paradoxical logic of all such narratives is that the beginning and end must logically coincide in order for the author and his persona to be the same" (Freccero 1986a: 263). In the case of the *Vita nuova* it is critical to note that the coincidence or convergence that unifies the beginning and end of the text is, furthermore, a congruence of emphasis on the process of writing: the first chapter gives us the author sitting down with a "book of memory" at hand and about to give the reader what we may best call a version of that text, and the last chapter ends with an invocation of a text to come, the text that is the logical and necessary result of the conversion just recounted—as it turns out, the *Commedia*.[10] And in the *Vita nuova*, it is worth repeating, the persona of the author, most markedly at the points of resolution and convergence, is the Poet. The conversion which is the fulcrum of change involves the movement, at least in theory a radical one, from poetry that serves itself primarily and a solipsistic love in the process, poetry as music and verbal hermeticism, in other words, to a poetry whose meaning and unequivocal truth exists a priori outside itself and its own frame of reference, a poetry preinscribed in the cosmos. The poet in this new universe is not the creator but the agent of revelation, at times even unknowingly so: the meaning of magic and sequences and visions may not be known until a startling revelation makes it transparent. This, of course, is exactly what is indicated in the recounting of the *Vita nuova*'s seemingly impenetrable first dream and in the author's annoying denial of an explanation for his puzzled readers, saying: "Lo verace giudicio del detto sogno non fue veduto allora per alcuno, ma ora è manifestissimo a li più semplici" (The true meaning of the dream I described was not perceived by anyone then, but now it is completely clear even to the least sophisticated [chapter 3]).[11] This is, from certain necessary perspectives, the story of a Platonic conversion: the harnessing of the primitive power of music—Poetry—to serve the needs of a kind of reason—Truth. But this is thus a species of reason that would be easily dismissed by almost any Platonist, for it is a reason which reflects not only transcendental Truths—which may or may not be true in an Aristotelian paradigm—but which is grounded in a shocking belief in the necessary truth of textuality itself and in the synchronicity that more traditional rationalists squirm away from uneasily.[12]

IV

The major dramatic turn of events, what can be fairly described as the literary conversion, in the *Vita nuova* is drawn out over nine chapters, from 19 to 28, thus beginning just before the midpoint of this text of forty-two chapters.[13] The first two of these contain two of the poems generally described as "stilnovistic," "Donne che avete intelletto d'amore" and "Amor e 'l cor gentil son una cosa," and even if we had no other indicators, we might well suspect we are on the threshold here of an important shift or event, because these are the poems in which Dante's immediate poet-ancestors most starkly reverberate. If the poems, as well as the actions narrated, of the first eighteen chapters are reflexes of the earlier "courtly" traditions of Provence and Sicily, these two poems, following both chronology and taste, approach Dante himself: they are kissing cousins to and resonances of the poet's contemporaries and near-contemporaries, Guinizelli and especially the powerful and enigmatic Cavalcanti, to whom the *Vita nuova* is dedicated and who is called here the "primo amico." In the chronology of a poetic autobiography, then, the alert reader would anticipate a threshold: narrator and protagonist must soon merge, since the last of the poetic antecedents, those still lurking about in the authorial present, are rapidly falling behind.

But from a narrative, structural point of view the text is still at this point adhering to the initially established (preconversion) format. One must pause here to consider carefully the peculiar structure of this text: "Everyone knows" that the *Vita nuova* is a prose-poetry text—and it is then described as either a hybrid or a *sui generis*. But far fewer seem to have noticed that what is of utmost importance is the variable nature of the prose–poetry relationship, the shifting relationship of three different voices vis-à-vis each other that is of interest, since in fact a major formal conversion will occur in this central cluster of chapters as well. The first part of the text is composed so that those chapters that contain poems (not all of them do, of course) include two very different prose voices which frame the lyric voice between them. There is the initial narrator, who has been telling us the story all along and is the generally unchallenged voice in the structurally simpler chapters that contain no poetry. This is the voice which is the autobiographical "I," necessarily already knowing the outcome but attempting to narrate the events "innocently" as he goes along, with a sense of fidelity to his preinscribed text. (This narrator appears also to have an often acute sense of the reader's expectations of suspense and dramatic outcome from something that has been marked off in the preexisting text and announced as the point at which a new life began.) This Dante narrates the events which, in these chapters at least, occasion or inspire a poem, introduced at the end of that chapter's events and following immediately thereafter. And these poems are—and here lies, finally, some considerable strangeness—in turn followed by a brief and usually completely straightforward and formal description of the poem itself, that poem that has just been presented. This second prose section of the chapter is normally called a *divisione*.[14]

Thus, in the first movement of the text, roughly its first half, in each chapter that presents a poem (or more than one poem, as is the tease in some chapters), there are three formally distinct presentations of what might be crudely described as the "same material": a prose narration of "what happened"; the poem(s) that formed the lyrical reaction to the event(s); and finally, and most mysteriously for almost all critics, a pseudoscientific and remarkably banal explication of the poem's structure and "divisions" (i.e., its formal fundamental formal characteristics—that is why these blurbs are called *divisioni*, of course). In the invariable order of these three components, this last is a miniature and accurate, but essentially quite primitive, *explication de texte*. The first problem in knowing just what to make of these little expositions of the poems that precede them is their transparent limitations: they rarely go beyond telling the reader what he can see for himself (even "li più semplici," as Dante would have it). Traditional criticism has scarcely gone beyond pointing out the conspicuous similarity these *divisioni* bear to mechanical scholastic procedure—and Boccaccio, as editor of the *Vita nuova*, acts out this reading by shifting these highly formal and starkly positivistic glosses to the margins.[15] But there is a no less puzzling feature, one that seems largely to have gone by the wayside in most readings: these unadorned little expositions, beginning about halfway through the text, are either eliminated altogether or are fully integrated into the quite different voice of narration that *precedes* the poem. The text's second movement is thus substantially altered, structurally and tonally, from its first: after chapter 27, in which the *canzone* stands starkly alone, without any *divisione*, each chapter that houses a poem finishes with that poem—and the voice of mock Scholasticism, that droning voice of the self-evident gloss, the simple student at his rote best, is either gone altogether or transformed, absorbed into the "crowd of Dantes" of the storyteller. But I am getting ahead of the story here.

In chapters 19 and 20 we are still playing by the old rules: Dante has given us his remarkable "philosophical" or *stilnovista* poems and the reader is still given a *divisione* after each. The subsequent chapter, 21, exists almost exclusively to give us yet a third sonnet in what would be called the "sweet new style" in the retrospective clarity of the *Purgatorio*, and it too is followed by an exposition of its outward form. But the action of the story starts to pick up again in chapter 22 when Beatrice's father dies, a prefiguration of the more significant death that is to follow. If, however, Beatrice alive is in part an emblem of the old poetry, then her father's death is much more than mere foreshadowing of her own, since the death of the old poetry's father is a literalization of transparent significance. In chapter 23, Dante dreams that Beatrice herself has died, and once again there are at least two layers of textual truth that mark events: the "annunciation" of what is "really" to happen and the literalization of the dream itself, the synchronicity playing itself out. And, in a relentless accumulation of images destroying the past, Dante's multiple literary pasts, there is yet another death—or, more appropriately, a disappearance—in chapter 24, in which we see for the last time the figure of Love.

Love had played a significant role in the first half of the book, the literally personified metaphor for Love as a separate entity and persona.[16] His fourth and last appearance here is both spectral and explicitly intended to clarify that he is disappearing because there is no longer any need for him, no longer any call, in the development of the artist's poetic ideology, for this kind of poetic prop. The narrator tells us that Love himself clarifies his own insufficiency, and quotes him as saying: "E chi volesse sottilmente considerare, quella Beatrice chiamerebbe Amore per molta simiglianza che ha meco" (Anyone of subtle discernment would call Beatrice Love, because she so greatly resembles me [chapter 24]). It is of considerable significance that this revelation comes on the heels of Beatrice's first death, so to speak, for that is what one must make of Dante's first knowledge of her death in a dream. Beatrice herself is no longer that dying kind of love poetry any more, the kind that needed agents like Love, elaborate and mediated poetic imagery, to be meaningful. It is crucial to remember here that the older, the first, the now-vanishing Beatrice had such needs, and in that purposefully cryptic first dream, with that engaging but teasingly difficult sequence of the burning and then eaten heart, she had exhibited some awareness of the nature of her limitations, at least in life. It is perhaps at this point, and not at the end of chapter 3, when Dante taunts us with the "obviousness" of the meaning of that numerically critical dream, that we can speak with some modicum of assurance about what it might in fact have so "obviously" signified. But again I get ahead of the story, for the meaning of the dream is explicitly dependent on the revelations of the conversion.

Returning, then, to the dismissal of Love from the story, the reader is left to conclude that mediation and metaphor in poetry have flown out the window—and in case it was not clear from Love's dramatic last annunciation and bowing out of the scene, Dante devotes the following chapter, the liminal twenty-fifth, to a clear prose discussion of the nature and purposes of poetry. It is a passage which includes a round dismissal of his vernacular antecedents, saying, "E la cagione per che alquanti ebbero fama di sapere dire, è che quasi fuoro li primi che dissero in lingua di si" (The reason why a few ungifted poets acquired the fame of knowing how to compose is that they were the first who wrote poetry in the Italian language [chapter 25]). Even more to the point, the chapter ends with the following succinct statement on what real poetry ought to be: "Però che grande vergogna sarebbe a colui che rimasse cose sotto vesta di figura o di colore rettorico, e poscia, domandato, non sapesse denudare le sue parole da cotale vesta, in guisa the avessero verace intendimento" (For, if anyone should dress his poem in images and rhetorical coloring and then, being asked to strip his poem of such dress in order to reveal its true meaning, would not be able to do so— this would be a veritable cause for shame [chapter 25]). Once again, one is compelled to remark on the extent to which the Dante of the *Vita nuova* is cultivating varieties of transparency; here, certainly, masking is not only dropped, it is denounced. (There is thus some irony in noting that so much criticism of the work has remained attached to the language of metaphor that is being banished from the "new life": in fact, the details of the "love story" paradoxically, start to fade and are increasingly subservient to the reflections on the nature of writing and literature that are at the core of this story of the "new life".) At this critical turning point we glimpse a Dante who has figured out the simplest solution to an impossibly complicated problem: how to limit and control the insufficiency and treachery of poetic language. The "solution" is, however, not an invention but a revelation, the kabbalistic insight that Truth is already there to be read and then rewritten—and it is only then that poetry can have any kind of exactitude of meaning, that it can say the Truth.

This revelation goes a very long way to explaining the meaning of the mysterious *divisioni* themselves, which, like the figure of Love, are no longer necessary in the new life. The last of the old-life *divisioni*, in fact, will appear in the next chapter, 26. (This, of course, is the number that will resonate strongly in the cantos of the *Purgatorio* devoted, once again explicitly, to poetic theory. It seems to me an exemplary case of the kind of synchronicity, as opposed to numerology, that Dante is involved with, for chapter 26 is important in the texts because of their internal harmony and correspondence, rather than because of any externally determined other "meaning.") The narrator tells us, from his perspective of knowing how it all came out and how it all fit together, things he could barely discern while he was living through them: Beatrice actually dies while Dante is writing the *canzone* that will stand alone in chapter 27—and we remember that in its transparency this becomes the first poem in the book not to have to be followed by a simple gloss, a poem that seems itself to reject the empty formal conceits of Scholasticism. Chapter 28, when Dante finds out about Beatrice's death in the original sequence of events, follows, and this is the last of the nine in this liminal and conversionary sequence. It is followed, appropriately, by the famous chapter that sets out the meaning of the number nine and concludes with the observation, rather precious for the modern reader, that Beatrice *is* a nine:

Ma più sottilmente pensando, e secondo la infallibile veritade, questo numero fue ella medesima ... questa donna fue accompagnata da questo numero del nove a dare ad intendere ch'ella era uno nove, cioè uno miracolo.... Forse ancora per più sottile persona si vederebbe in ciò più sottile ragione; ma questa è quella ch'io ne veggio, e che più mi piace.

If anyone thinks more subtly and according to infallible truth, it will be clear that this number was she herself ... then this lady was accompanied by the number nine so that it might be understood that she was a nine, or a miracle.... Perhaps someone more subtle than I could find a still more subtle explanation, but this is the one which I see and which pleases me the most. (chapter 29)

It is thus that in this seemingly bizarre chapter we find what is perhaps the most direct, the most unabashed and naked presentation not only of "what Beatrice means to me" (to paraphrase Eliot's famous essay on Dante) but, far more importantly, of what Dante has become; he has become a simple reader of the simplest truths inscribed, preinscribed, in a universe that can make sense only when we can become such readers. Then, at that point of breakthrough, the sense is complete, almost too simple, for the good reader—he who is not subtle, who has discarded the mediations and the conceits of all those other poetics. Initially, in fact, Beatrice's death leaves the Dante trained in the classical traditions, that earlier poet, stunned and poetryless. As Mazzotta has noted, "Now that she is physically dead, the metaphors for her seem to be another empty fiction. If the question while Beatrice was alive was whether she is and how she is unique, now that she is dead the question is finding the sense of metaphors that recall her" (1986b:156). Once again, the problem can be reduced, at least initially, to one of the nature of expression chosen and the rejection of an expressive mode, a poetics, that was insufficient to deal with fundamental truths that are inscribed in texts we must first learn how to even read. What Mazzotta is calling rhetoric here I have called poetics, but the fact that they might indeed be taken for the same thing is exactly what Dante has in mind: the elimination of both or either as a category of expression separate or separable from other categories of truth and knowledge. There is a certain pathos, I think, in realizing that it is exactly when the poet's soul is most naked, when he reveals the most outrageous of truths, that his readers, at least in this century, have thrown the most elaborate of veils on his simple revelations. She was a nine, she was a miracle—no likes about it.

The differences, then, between the old life and the new life include the fact that poems in the new life, after the living Beatrice's death, need no divisions or pseudoscientific explication, as did those in the old, now discarded days and poems once reigned over by an inaccessible love object, the living Beatrice, and a mediating Love figure. In those old days the author was just like all the other poets, in other words, all those in the tradition from which he came, a tradition within which, according to the *Vita nuova* (and as a follow-up of sorts to the *De vulgari*), poems need the prop of commentary in order to have any really unassailable "truth value"—those things that are measurable and provable such as the number of stanzas and the kind of rhyme and where the first part ends and the next begins. The old poetry adored that empty glossing of form, but in the aftermath of death and its revelations, in the aftermath of the conversion—and in some great measure that is the conversion—it is clear that for him who can read and then rewrite the universe the poems themselves have absolute truth value, they are stripped of the trappings that begged for that kind of commentary and made it necessary, and they are so simply and so clearly about transcendental other truths that they can and must stand by themselves. Beatrice *is* love. Poetry is truth. The old Beatrice is dead, and the new writer, forged by the pain of the failure of his first Beatrice, will now revel in the vision of a Beatrice who will need no Love as a figure to mediate between her and the absolute value of love itself. And just as she *is* a nine, as the newly converted Dante loses no time in telling us, so poetry, real and worthwhile poetry, is as rationally true as what others call scientific language. Here, clearly, is the merger between the disparate components characterized in the preconversion part of the text by the three different and incomplete voices: the narrative, the lyric, and the commenting. These observations, of course, have been made by a number of critics vis-à-vis the *Commedia* and its development of the notion of the inseparability of theology and poetry, but the *Vita nuova*'s explicit turning to the primary truth of (certain kinds of) texts has been far less recognized, although, oddly enough, it is expressed with an embarrassing directness that has faded in the *Commedia* itself. Freccero's observation that, contrary to what Auerbach maintained, "the theological principles that seem to underlie Dante's formal pattern are themselves in turn derived from literary principles" (1986a: 269) is, if anything, even more applicable to the *Vita nuova*, where at the most literal level—which is the level now invested with absolute truth value—the writer and his literary texts are invariably primary. This, then, is a new life indeed, and in the last half of the book, in the chapters remaining after the banishment of the past, we see an author preparing for the full significance, only partially divined (for that is the very nature of such belief in the kabbala of writing), of his newfound faith and practice. This is succinctly put in the famous last paragraph, of course, as "io spero dicer di lei quello che mai non fue detto d'alcuna" (I hope to write of her that which has never been written of any other woman [chapter 42]). Here all the components come together in the terseness and incantatory repetition of a synchronistic text: the hope that the revelations will continue and that the writing, the saying of the truths of the universe that is the poetry, will flow from that.

NOTES

5. Ironically, perhaps, the classicization of a language—i.e., the fixing of a language such as Latin as an essentially unchanging entity—is a very distinct form of language death, although the language does not necessarily disappear, at least not immediately. In the *De vulgari*, Dante classifies Latin as an "artificial" language, a concept not far removed from (although considerably more delicate than) that of death; they are in comparable juxtaposition to the ever-shifting qualities of a vernacular, which is, by the fact that it does constantly evolve, a living language. Dante's observation about the artificiality of Latin has been of great interest to linguists, particularly in recent years when the very nature of "Latin" has been scrupulously questioned and largely redefined to the point where Dante's notion, once discarded as fanciful, can now be regarded as far more adequate a representation than the one that used to be commonly held, i.e., that the written literary language was, in some living and functional way, the normal spoken language of the Roman Republic and Empire. In the context of the *Vita nuova*, however, it is perhaps a key observation to remember, for it is, of course, Latin that Love speaks, at least some of the time—a fact that has led some critics to dismiss Singleton's valid assertion that he (Love) is a "troubadour." Singleton says that the Latin is meant to signify that his pronouncements are oracular, but at the same time, the Latin is perhaps meant to indicate the artificiality and inaccessibility of much troubadour poetry, poetry that had, paradoxically (and certainly ironically, from Dante's perspective), broken away from a dead Latin and was written in a "vernacular"—a *koine*, of course, one to which he thought literary Latin had, in fact, been comparable. But, clearly, the major thrust in the context of the *Vita nuova* is not the oracularity of the earlier poetry per se, but rather its unintelligibility (the two often being confused) and obscurity or hermeticism. It is this hermeticism, coupled with explicit falsehood (the gist of the second appearance of Love, where he is mediating for the different false lovers), that is finally repudiated in Love's third appearance: Dante accusingly and despairingly asks him point-blank why he speaks so obscurely, and Love, finally, replies in Italian. For more extended discussions see Singleton 1945 and 1946, Shaw 1947, and, more recently, Brownlee 1984.

6. It is, at a minimum, a revelatory coincidence that in the genesis and articulation of the Hispano-Arabic poetry (which some believe is an important model for the other new Romance poetries), the poetic voice in Classical Arabic is male, the vernacular (Romance) voice is female (and taken, explicitly, from the oral tradition), and the whole is, precisely because of the admixture of poetic types, a radically new hybrid that challenges the canonical standards that had previously excluded the vernacular voice altogether.

7. Wilhelm 1982: 119. The essay "Il miglior fabbro" is part of Pound's famous and often-quoted *The Spirit of Romance*, which is Pound's version, in the throes of a heady rebellion against the academic philological tradition recently

abandoned, of the birth-from-death history of the Romance literary tradition. Although it is probably almost never used in that way, Pound's text is nothing less than a new literary history to correspond to (and supplant) those from the formidable, no-nonsense Germanic tradition of *romanische Philologie* he had no doubt been fed as a budding philologist at Penn.

8. Here lies, I sense, one of the crucial differences between my own reading of this central aspect of the text and others', rooted, once again, in my acceptance of the implied truths of the literary story line. Barolini, for example, in a number of ways the most sophisticated of critics to deal with the issue of the historical layers of writing present in the text, writes: "The lyrics thus chosen undergo not only a passive revision in the process of being selected for inclusion, but also an active revision at the hand of the prose narrative, which bends them into a new significance consonant with the poet's 'new life.' The violations of original intention that occur result in certain narrative reversals; poems written for other ladies in other contexts are now perceived as written for Beatrice ..." (1984:15). In a comparable tone, Holloway describes the procedure as: "In the *Vita nuova* Dante is deconstructing his own earlier poetry, finding deeper layers of meaning to it than he at first suspected were there ... like some manuscript palimpsest" (105). In these cases, as in many others far less noteworthy, there is a reluctance to believe in (or at least voice belief in) Dante's naked statements of poetic revelation that made him realize that, to take the critical example at hand, poems he thought he had written for other women turn out, in fact, to have been (unsuspectingly) written for Beatrice. Words and phrases such as "revisions," "bends," "violations of original intention," "deconstruct," and "palimpsest" all work to distance the modern critic from the very issue of belief in the Truth of revelation vis-à-vis literature itself that Dante is focused on. The problem with this kind of distancing is that it effectively denies the possibility of sincerity on the part of Dante (he didn't "really" believe those poems were magically or mystically or kabbalistically prewritten for Beatrice, he just cleverly constructed a text that says that because that is an allegory for something else)—and perhaps it is in part the result of the notion that in the acknowledgement and articulation of sincerity the critic would be suspected of holding the same belief herself. It is also interesting that while a critic may safely proclaim and document an author's belief in a canonical religious Truth (no one, I'm sure, has ever thought twice about whether Charles Singleton believed in the Christ himself), the language of both Barolini and Holloway illustrates the typical critical aversion to Dante's statements about the Truth of a literary revelation within which the real meaning of a text is never clear until the reality it describes has been played out and consummated.

9. The problem of the multiple Dantes in this text is most charmingly described as "a small crowd" by Stillinger (55, n. 31), and in the expression lies a significant insight: which voice is speaking from out of the crowd is, at times, not at all a sure thing.

10. It is perfectly just that the temporal authenticity of the extant text of the *Vita nuova* has always been a matter of (seemingly unresolvable) contention. See Harrison's final (fittingly, of course) chapter, "Vision and Revision," for a detailed discussion of the problem of the "original" ending of the *Vita nuova*—briefly, whether the text does originally end with the famous final lines announcing a new work devoted to Beatrice, or whether these are instead a *rifacimento*, a "touch-up" written some dozen years later. In the *rifacimento* view of the text, the original *Vita nuova* ends with Dante finding consolation for his grief from Beatrice's death in philosophy, allegorized in the *Donna gentile*. But this was an ending that had to be revised when Dante in fact found philosophy an inadequate consolation, abandoned the *Convivio*, and turned to the *Commedia*. In fact, as Harrison notes, we do not have to decide (on the philological plane of pseudoscientific discourse) on the issue of *rifacimento* itself, only on its possibility—and, of course, one could practically describe the *Vita nuova* as being about *rifacimento*: "Revision remains a fundamental and always already operative principle.... The possibility of a later revision ... remains plausible because of the revisionary agenda that sustains the work.... And what does the 'story' dramatize if not a series of corrections and revisions in the poet's search for adequate idiom?" (150). Again, I sense a difficulty of belief in critical language such as "the poet's search for adequate idiom," which seems to render both rational and linear a process which in the *Vita nuova* is both visionary and kabbalistic—but clearly Harrison's analysis of the thematic congruity of the *rifacimento* is very much congruent with my own reading.

11. All quotations from the *Vita nuova* are from Chiappelli, ed., and from the English version of Musa. Hereafter they will be referred to by chapters only.

12. Even Jung finally squirmed away and was uncomfortable with the discrepancy between apparent versus provable truths, especially with the issue of causality; for the latter problem, see Popp, forthcoming. Still, his lucid expository statements would not have made Dante uncomfortable: "No reciprocal causal connection can be shown to obtain between parallel events, which is just what gives them their chance character. The only recognizable and demonstrable link between them is a *common meaning*, or equivalence. The old theory of correspondence was based on the experience of such connections—a theory that reached its culminating point and also its provisional end in Leibniz's idea of *pre-established harmony*. Synchronicity is a modern differentiation of the obsolete concept of *correspondence, sympathy and harmony*. It is based not on philosophical assumptions but on empirical evidence and experimentation" (emphasis mine). "On Synchronicity," 518, quoted here from the edition in *The Portable Jung*, ed. Joseph Campbell.

13. See Harrison, 7–9, for a critique and reevaluation of the Singletonian reading that places Beatrice's death at the mathematical center of the text. My own interest is not in any external mathematical correspondence (i.e., in number

symbolism or numerology) but rather in the synchronistic correspondences, which derive their coherence principally from internal correspondence.

14. Almost all studies of the *Vita nuova*, including the major ones discussed in the preceding notes, include at least some attention to the structural properties of the work, including the disposition of narrative prose, framed lyric, and *divisioni*. Other studies that focus more specifically on this aspect of the work include Hollander 1974 (with a characteristically exhaustive bibliography) and D'Andrea, which sees scholastic commentaries as the source of the *divisioni*. See also Barolini 1989, where the structure of the *Vita nuova* is explored in terms of that of Petrarch's *Canzoniere*. Pipa makes the unusual revisionist argument, based on a strongly politicohistorical reading of the work, that the heart of the *Vita nuova* is not the poetry but the prose, which is read in part as political allegory. Most recently, the Stillinger dissertation includes a lengthy and lucid chapter devoted to the formal structures of the work, a formal structure which is "governed throughout by divergent formal principles" (61) and within which ever-variable *divisioni* play different kinds of roles. Although in great measure this work (which only came to my attention when this book was in its final stages of preparation) is quite different from my own in approach and conclusions, at least one aspect of Stillinger's reading of the *Vita nuova* seems to me to be harmonious with my own: he believes that the relationship between poetry and narrative prose in the text may be understood according to the text's own internal model, i.e., the poetry is Beatrice, the narrative prose is Dante. As he notes, this model is appealing because "it is satisfyingly concrete. It is strange, too, in a way that I think is faithful to the spirit of the *Vita nuova*.... My own similitude might be expressed with similar cryptic boldness: in the *Vita nuova*, the prose is Dante and the poetry is Beatrice" (70). I differ from Stillinger here, however, in that he identifies what seems to me the unflinching equation of the literal truth of textuality and being of the "Beatrice is a nine" revelation as a part of "sweeping[ly] analogical thought" and a "personification of abstract thought."

15. See Stillinger, especially 83–113, for a full and provocative discussion.

16. Love has appeared four times in the *Vita nuova*, in chapters that, retrospectively, have alluded to the harmony with Beatrice's own "nineness": 3, 9, 12, 24 [1,3,4,6]. In his first three appearances, all of which, of course, precede the conversion, Love is explicitly and emphatically the protagonist's master—the young writer, the poet, is portrayed by the older and wiser author, the narrator, as having been pathetically at Love's mercy. Provisionally, it is also worth noting that this Love first appears in chapter three (and, of course, at synchronistically appropriate hours) and is thus the provocation not only for Dante's first poem (a love poem, of course) but also for his establishment of a relationship with Cavalcanti and other poets which, within the parameters of the story we are told, consists exclusively of exchanges of poems and opinions on the same. That first poem is that "recounting" or lyrical version of the vision in which Love has held

Beatrice in his arms, held her flaming heart in his hand, forced her, apparently against her will, to eat it, and then dissolved in tears before disappearing, with Beatrice still in his arms, into the heavens. The confusing (and one might add, confused) dream, lyricized, is sent out for reactions from other poets, to no avail—and it is then that Dante, who clearly wishes to prolong the reader's confusion, ends the chapter with the maddening, "The true meaning of the dream I described was not perceived by anyone then, but now it is completely clear even to the least sophisticated," quoted above, and this persistently enigmatic dream will be discussed further below. It is nevertheless true that a considerable amount of ink has been spilled on the question of just exactly who this Love is, although I think the question is only a complicated or difficult one as long as one is assuming the issues at hand are theological rather than primarily poetic. See the extended discussions in Shaw, Singleton and Musa. Singleton's identification of him as the "Troubadour god of Love" is certainly the closest, although the use of the word "god" here is problematic and ultimately probably misleading. If we do assume that in his retrospective on his period of poetic training Dante is dealing with literary issues and history principally, then the figure of Love personified that appears four times in the text is that poetic *conceit* of Love which, indeed, the troubadours canonized. It is a Love defined in such a way in the cumulative canon that it is, as we have noted above, highly solipsistic. Musa's argument that in Provençal poetry love is never personified misses the point: Dante, in some measure for the sake of an acting out of his conversion, personifies the earlier lyrical construct of love that emerges from the poetry from which he is himself evolving. Hollander 1974 also grapples with the issue: "One of the aesthetic and rational problems of the *Vita Nuova* is Dante's rather confusing treatment of Amore. It is a problem which he himself partly acknowledges in the brilliant if self-serving twenty-fifth chapter of the work" (6).

TEODOLINDA BAROLINI

Purgatory as Paradigm: Traveling the New and Never-Before-Traveled Path of This Life/Poem

> *Fr.* Nulla me deinceps accusatione turbaveris. Dic
> ingenue quicquid est, quod me transversum agat.
> *Aug.* Rerum temporalium appetitus.
>
> (Petrarch, *Secretum*)

The narrative of the *Commedia* is a line intersected by other lines; it is a "vedere interciso da novo obietto," a seeing interrupted by new things, the *novi obietti* or *cose nove* that do not trouble angels. It is a voyage intersected by other voyages; each time the pilgrim meets a soul, his lifeline intersects another lifeline. In hell he encounters failed voyages, journeys that have ended in failure. Ulysses' special stature within the poem derives in no small measure from the fact that his lifeline concludes with a literal voyage that has literally failed, so that he, alone among the souls Dante encounters, unites the poem's formal and thematic values: he both represents a failed voyage (one among many), and he recounts a failed voyage (uniquely). While in *Inferno* and *Paradiso* the moving pilgrim encounters perfected voyages, voyages that have achieved either the stasis of failure or the peace of success, in *Purgatorio* all the intersecting lifelines are in motion, voyaging in time—just as on earth all parties in any encounter are moving forward along their respective lines of becoming. (In fact, because the *Purgatorio* swerves so fundamentally from the *Commedia*'s basic narrative structure, whereby a moving figure encounters stationary ones, the poet compensates by ritualizing

From *The Undivine Comedy: Detheologizing Dante*. © 1992 by Princeton University Press.

the narrative components of the seven terraces, so that, if the pilgrim does not meet fixed souls, he does meet a fixed pattern of angels, encounters, and examples.)[1] Given its temporal dimension, the narrative of the second canticle is most akin, in its rhythm, to the narrative of life; its *cammino* is most similar to the "nuovo e mai non fatto cammino di questa vita" described in the *Convivio*, in a passage that provides the clearest exposition of life as voyage to be found in Dante's oeuvre:[2]

> ... lo sommo desiderio di ciascuna cosa, e prima da la natura dato, è lo ritornare a lo suo principio. E però che Dio è principio de le nostre anime e fattore di quelle simili a sé (sì come è scritto: "Facciamo l'uomo ad imagine e similitudine nostra"), essa anima massimamente desidera di tornare a quello. E sì come peregrino che va per una via per la quale mai non fue, che ogni casa che da lungi vede crede che sia l'albergo, e non trovando ciò essere, dirizza la credenza a l'altra, e così di casa in casa, tanto che a l'albergo viene; così l'anima nostra, incontanente che nel nuovo e mai non fatto cammino di questa vita entra, dirizza li occhi al termine del suo sommo bene, e però, qualunque cosa vede che paia in sé avere alcuno bene, crede che sia esso. E perché la sua conoscenza prima è imperfetta, per non essere esperta nè dottrinata, piccioli beni le paiono grandi, e però da quelli comincia prima a desiderare. Onde vedemo li parvuli desiderare massimamente un pomo; e poi, più procedendo, desiderare uno augellino; e poi, più oltre, desiderare bel vestimento; e poi lo cavallo; e poi una donna; e poi ricchezza non grande, e poi grande, e poi più. E questo incontra perché in nulla di queste cose truova quella che va cercando, e credela trovare più oltre.

The greatest desire of each thing, given first by nature, is to return to its beginning. And since God is the beginning of our souls and maker of those similar to himself (as is written: "Let us make man in our image and likeness"), the soul desires above all to return to him. And like the pilgrim who travels on a road on which he has never been, who thinks that every house he sees from a distance is the inn, and finding that it is not, redirects his belief to the next, and thus from house to house, until he comes to the inn; so our soul, as soon as it enters on the new and never before traveled path of this life, straightens its eyes to the terminus of its highest good, and then, whatever thing it sees that seems to have some good in it, the soul believes that it is that terminus. And because the soul's knowledge is at first imperfect, because it is neither expert nor learned, small goods seem to it to be big goods, and so from these it begins at first to desire. So we see children desire above all an apple; and then, proceeding further, a little bird; and then, further still, beautiful clothing; and then a horse; and then a lady; and then not great riches; and then great riches; and then more. And this happens because in none of these things does the soul find what it is looking for, and it believes that it will find it further on.

(*Conv.* 4.12.14–16)

This passage is virtually a blueprint for the *Commedia*. We begin with desire, the supreme desire to return to our origin; this desire provides the energy that moves the pilgrim along his road, a road on which he has never before traveled, one that is thus by definition new. In the same way that the pilgrim mistakes the houses that he sees along the road for the inn, the place of legitimate repose, so the soul on the new and never before traveled path of life mistakes the little goods that it encounters for the supreme good that it seeks. Our progress on the path of life is figured linguistically as successiveness: we desire something, "e poi, più procedendo," we desire something new, "e poi, più oltre," something new again, and so on as by virtue of a succession of *e pois* our desires grow ever greater, and we create what Dante will shortly describe as a pyramid of objects of desire. This rhythm of escalating desire figures the narrative rhythm of the poem, also a continuum in which forward progress is marked by encounters with successive new things. In particular, the *Convivio* passage figures the *Purgatorio*, where the desire to see and know new things is insistently underscored, where for the first time the pilgrim is among other pilgrims: "Voi credete / forse che siamo esperti d'esto loco; / ma not siam peregrin come voi siete" ("You think perhaps that we are experts regarding this place, but we are pilgrims as you are" [*Purg.* 2.61–63]).[3] Like their counterparts in the *Convivio*, the voyagers in the second realm are repeatedly shown to be neither *esperti* nor *dottrinati* but rather strangers in a strange land, whose ignorance triggers their frequent *maraviglia*. Most importantly, the souls of purgatory are learning to devalue the *piccioli beni* by which they were tempted as they journeyed along the path of life, to exchange such goods for the supreme good to which they are now returning. The very idea of a return to the beginning ("lo ritornare a lo principio"), of a progression forward to the past,[4] finds its precise counterpart only in purgatory, where forward motion is a way of recuperating and redeeming the past, of returning to lost innocence and our collective point of origin, the garden of Eden. Only purgatory is the place where "tempo per tempo si ristora" (*Purg.* 23.84), where time is restored to us so that we can undo in time what we did in time.[5] Indeed, the experience of purgatory is the conversion of the old back into the new. the unmaking of memory, in which the once new has been stored as old.

No episode in *Inferno* or *Paradiso* captures the essence of the earthly pilgrimage like the Casella episode at the beginning of *Purgatorio*, whose structure faithfully replicates life's—and terza rima's—continual dialectic between forward motion and backward glance, voyage and repose, illicit curiosity and necessary desire. On the one hand the poet stages Cato's rebuke, thus acknowledging the idea of a premature repose, a lapse into misdirected desire. On the other the poet valorizes the object of desire that occasions the rebuke, the lyric whose sweetness "ancor dentro mi suona" ("still sounds within me" [*Purg.* 2.114]). The authority of the present tense and the adverb *ancora* prohibits us from crudely labeling the experience "wrong"; rather we must attend to both constitutive elements within the spiral of desire, fully present only in the second realm: both the desire that functions as goad (here Cato), and the desire that functions nostalgically (here Casella's song). One could restate the above by saying that the *Purgatorio* is the most Augustinian of Dante's three canticles. The *Inferno*, by contrast, draws on the spirit of the Old Testament, while the *Paradiso* is informed by saints of both newer and older vintage, such as Francis and Peter (though Benedict belongs to Augustine's middle period). Perhaps the much debated absence of Augustine from Dante's poem is related to the Augustinian basis of the second realm: Augustinianism—like memory itself—is a presence in purgatory more than in paradise, but there is in purgatory, as we shall see, another vigorous spokesperson for the saint's thought, namely Beatrice. In other words, Dante uses Augustinian doctrine in the realm where separation from earthly objects of desire is still problematic, to provide the philosophical basis for such separation, much as Petrarch uses Augustinus in the *Secretum*; however, the Augustinus role is assigned to Beatrice, who in a sense therefore becomes a substitute Augustine.[6]

Purgatorio is the canticle in which the restless heart of the Christian pilgrim is most literally dramatized, embodied not only by Dante but by all the souls he meets. Its "plot" hinges on an Augustinian view of temporal goods as inherently dissatisfying because of their mortality, as necessarily dissatisfying even when they are (in Augustine's words) "things perfectly legitimate in themselves, which cannot be relinquished without regret."[7] The tension between the legitimacy of the object of desire on the one hand and the need to relinquish it on the other is the tension that sustains the second canticle of the *Commedia*, the tension that Dante maximizes and exploits in order to create the bittersweet elegiac poetry of *Purgatorio*: "biondo era e bello e di gentile aspetto, / *ma* l'un de' cigli un colpo avea diviso" ("blond he was and beautiful and of gentle aspect, *but* a blow had divided one of his eyebrows" [*Purg.* 3.107–8]). The first verse renders Manfredi's desirability, which is the desirability of what Petrarch calls the "cosa bella mortal"; we want him as we want on earth, without thought of sublimation. Then, after evoking nostalgically the earthly object in its earthly beauty, the second verse, beginning with the adversative, tells us the problem: it is wounded, imperfect, fallen; or, to complete Petrarch's thought, "cosa bella mortal passa, et non dura" ("the beautiful mortal thing passes, and does not last" [*Canzoniere* 248.8]). The second verse brings us back to why there need be a purgatory, to the fact that even the most beautiful of earthly things is always compromised, wounded, mortal, that therefore we must learn to love different things, in a different way. The spiral of conversion that moves away from the noble temporal goods for which the soul feels a backward-turning love in the direction of their eternal counterparts is paradigmatically rendered in the concluding verses of *Purgatorio* 28, where the pilgrim "lapses" toward his classical poets and "converts" to Beatrice: "Io mi rivolsi 'n dietro allora tutto / a' miei poeti ... poi a la bella donna torna' il viso" ("I turned all backward to my poets; then to the beautiful lady returned my face" [*Purg.* 28.145–46, 148]).

The second canticle tells of the soul's voyage from desiring successive new things to becoming itself new: "Voi siete nuovi" says Matelda to the travelers in *Purgatorio* 28.76, and although she means "newly arrived," her words also adumbrate the souls' newly minted condition at purgatory's end. The theme of voyage is linked to the search for the new in a way that recalls the *Convivio*'s pilgrim passage, where the traveler goes successively from one *bene*—one new thing—to the next. As in the paradigmatic Casella episode, the *Purgatorio* offers us both the necessary encounter with the new, with the "altra novità ch'apparve allora" ("other novelty that then appeared" [*Purg.* 26.27]) and the refusal to be detoured by the new, like the man who "vassi a la via sua, che che li appaia" ("goes on along his path, whatever appears to him" [*Purg.* 25.5]). In typical purgatorial language, Matelda constitutes a necessary detour, a "cosa the disvia / per maraviglia tutto altro pensare" ("thing that for wonder detours all other thought" [*Purg.* 28.38–39]), while the seven virtues who escort the pilgrim in the earthly paradise stop at the water as a guide stops "se trova novitate o sue vestigge" ("if he finds a new thing or its traces" [*Purg.* 33.108]). In fact, the importance of the *cosa nova* for the *Purgatorio* is such as to strongly support Petrocchi's restoration of "novità" in place of "vanità" in *Purgatorio* 31.60, where Beatrice castigates the pilgrim for having continued to pursue, after her death, "altra novità con sì breve uso" ("another novelty of such brief use"). Thus formulated, Beatrice's rebuke resonates with the voyage of life, the "vedere interciso da novo obietto," and with the reminder that she was the pilgrim's ultimate *cosa nova*.[8] *Novità* is a temporally charged way—a profoundly Augustinian way—of saying *vanità*, a synonym of *vanità* that says everything it says and more, by adding the temporal dimension of voyage and pilgrimage that is key to this temporal realm. The Augustinian basis of the second canticle is rooted in its temporality, its overwhelming concern to trace the will's transition—in time—from mortal to immortal objects of desire, from objects of "brief use" to objects that the soul can "enjoy" indefinitely. Beatrice's "con sì breve uso" is strikingly coincident with Augustine's injunction to use earthly things rather than enjoy them.[9] The dimension of time, transition, successiveness—so fundamental to Augustine's analysis of the human condition that even eating is analyzed from a temporal perspective (it spreads its snares of concupiscence in the transition, "in ipso transitu," from hunger to satiety)[10]—is the dimension in which the purgatorial soul undertakes what is an essentially Augustinian pilgrimage.

The Augustinian aspect of Dante's thought finds its gloss in the pilgrim passage of *Convivio* 4.12, which echoes *Confessions* 1.19: "non haec ipsa sunt quae a paedagogis et magistris, a nucibus et pilulis et passeribus, ad praefectos et reges, aurum, praedia, mancipia, haec ipsa omnino succedentibus maioribus aetatibus transeunt" ("For commanders and kings may take the place of tutors and schoolmasters, nuts and balls and pet birds may give way to money and estates and servants, but these same passions remain with us while one stage of life follows upon another"). Augustine's *passer* becomes Dante's *augellino*, Augustine's *aurum* becomes Dante's *ricchezza*; both authors are concerned with the transitoriness ("transeunt") of life and the successiveness of human desire, which remains constant in its inconstancy as it passes to the "succeeding older ages" of our lives—the "succedentibus maoribus aetatibus." The pilgrim passage of *Convivio* 4.12 is translated into verse at the very heart of the *Purgatorio*, in canto 16's description of the newborn soul which, sent forth by a happy maker upon the path of life ("mossa da lieto fattore" [*Purg.* 16.89]), willingly turns toward all that brings delight ("volontier torna a ciò che la trastulla" [90]).[11] The voyage is perilous, and the simple little soul that knows nothing, "l'anima semplicetta che sa nulla" (16.88),[12] is distracted by the very desire that also serves as necessary catalyst and propeller for its forward motion: "Di picciol bene in pria sente sapore; / quivi s'inganna, e dietro ad esso corre, / se guida o fren non torce suo amore" ("First the soul tastes the savor of a small good; there it deceives itself and runs after, if guide or curb does not twist its love" [91–93]). The spiritual motion of the soul that runs after little goods—"piccioli beni" is the expression used in both the treatise and the poem—is explained in the *Convivio*, where we learn that this errancy occurs because, to the inexperienced soul, "piccioli beni le paiono grandi, e però da quelli comincia prima a desiderare." The crucial point at which the soul is deceived, the node where desire and spiritual motion meet free will and justice, provides the point of departure for the anatomy of desire that dominates the *Commedia*'s "mezzo del cammin," an analysis that responds to the following queries: to whom is the blame of the soul's self-deception to be charged, to the stars or to itself, and is there any guidance to help it on its way? (canto 16); in what different forms can the soul's self-deception manifest itself, i.e., what forms can misdirected desire assume? (canto 17); what is the process whereby such self-deception occurs, i.e., what is the process whereby the soul falls in love? (canto 18).

At the end of canto 17 we learn that love is the seed of all human activity, whether it be good or evil ("amor sementa in voi d'ogne virtute / e d'ogne operazion che merta pene" ["love is the seed in you of every virtue and of every act that merits suffering" (*Purg.* 17.104–5)]); this principle—which implies that love is the foundation for hell as well as purgatory—is restated at the outset of canto 18: "amore, a cui reduci / ogne buono operare e 'l suo contraryo" ("love, to which you reduce all good action and its contrary" [*Purg.* 18.14–15]). In other words, desire is the motive force for all our actions. Again, the struggling traveler of *Convivio* 4.12 provides the model for the purgatorial meditation; in the *Convivio* too the seeker is driven by his desire from one "good" to the next, in search of the object of desire that will finally bring desire to an end: "Ciascun confusamente un bene apprende / nel qual si queti l'animo, e disira; / per che di giugner lui ciascun contende" ("Each of us confusedly apprehends a good in which the soul may rest, and this it desires; to reach this good each of us contends" [*Purg.* 17.127–29]). This view of life as a struggle along the pathway of desire, a view that profoundly informs the *Commedia*'s narrativity, is elaborated in canto 18, where we learn that the soul, seized by love, begins to desire, that desire is precisely the motion of the soul as it follows after the object it craves (which it seeks to apprehend, to possess), and that such motion will never cease— the soul will never rest—until the beloved object gives it joy: "così l'animo preso entra in disire, / ch'è moto spiritale, e mai non posa / fin che la cosa amata il fa gioire" (*Purg.* 18.31–33).

The second canticle's Augustinian thematic of spiritual motion finds its peculiarly Dantesque focus in canto 19's evocation of Ulysses.[13] It is here that the *dolce serena* of the pilgrim's dream, later exposed as a stinking, stuttering hag and thus the embodiment of the false and misleading desires expiated on purgatory's top three terraces, boasts that she was able to detour Ulysses from his path: "Io volsi Ulisse del suo cammin vago / al canto mio" ("I turned Ulysses, desirous of the journey, with my song" [*Purg.* 19.22–23]). This alignment of the Greek voyager with the *dolce* serena is of great significance within the poem's anatomy of desire. The terraces of avarice, gluttony, and lust purge affective inclinations toward goods that are false because, having seduced us with promises of full satisfaction (like the siren, who claims "sì tutto l'appago!" [19.24]), they are not in fact capable of delivering the ultimate satisfaction—*quies*, peace, freedom from craving—that we seek. Because of their mortality, these "beni" cannot make us truly happy, cannot offer us true repose, but only more time on the treadmill of desire, the treadmill of the new: "Altro ben è che non fa l'uom felice; / non è felicità, non è la buona / essenza" ("There is another good that does not make man happy; it is not true happiness, not the good essence" [*Purg.* 17.133–35]). The desiring purged on the top three terraces is characterized by excessive abandon vis-à-vis these seductive but misleading goods: "L'amor ch'ad esso troppo s'abbandona, / di sovr'a not si piange per tre cerchi" ("The love that abandons itself too much to it is lamented above us in three circles" [*Purg.* 17.136–37]). The key word here is *troppo*, which echoes the original partition of love, capable of erring "per malo obietto / o per troppo o per poco di vigore" ("through an evil object or through too much or too little vigor" [*Purg.* 17.95–96]). The figure who stands within the *Commedia*'s metaphoric system for excess, abandonment of limits, transgression, trespass—in short, for *troppo di vigore*—is Ulysses.

I am suggesting that there is a programmatic reason for the insertion of Ulysses' name into the economy of *Purgatorio* at this point. Rather than focus on the siren/*femmina balba* and the identity of the lady who rudely unveils her, I believe that we can profitably consider this passage from the vantage of its provocative and unexpected naming of Ulysses, posing the question "Why Ulysses here?"[14] The siren's invocation of the Greek wayfarer serves first to remind us of what we already know, namely that he can be characterized in terms of his own false craving, the misplaced and misleading *ardore*—burning desire— that causes him to burn as a tongue of flame in hell. More importantly, the presence of Ulysses serves to characterize the desire of the top three terraces as Ulyssean, to metaphorize avarice, gluttony, and lust, so that we see these sins in the light of their root cause: excessive desire, the pursuing of objects with *troppo di vigore*. As validation of the Ulyssean thrust here conferred upon the final three terraces, we note the presence of a tree upon the terrace of gluttony whose parent is none other than the tree that Ulysses desired—metaphorically—to eat, the tree from which Adam and Eve did indeed eat: "Trapassate oltre sanza farvi presso: / legno è più sù the fu morso da Eva, / e questa pianta si levò da esso" ("Pass onward without drawing near; further up is a tree that was bitten by Eve, and this plant was taken from that one" [*Purg.* 24.115–17]). This graft from the tree of knowledge enjoins the souls in Ulyssean language ("Trapassate oltre") against Ulyssean trespass ("sanza farvi presso"), an injunction that is built into the tree's very shape, which is inverted so that its branches taper not toward the top but the bottom, "perché persona sù non vada" ("so that none will go up it" [*Purg.* 22.135]). A generalized interdict of this sort was uttered with respect to the pillars of Hercules, which were placed where they are "acciò che l'uom più oltre non si metta" ("so that man will not go beyond" [*Inf.* 26.109]). And what is the root cause of *trapassare oltre*? What caused both Ulysses and Eve to ignore the interdicts they encountered? According to the analysis of human motivation provided by the second canticle, they were spurred by twisted love, by misshapen desire—by variants of the desire felt so keenly and underscored so emphatically on the terrace of gluttony, as the souls gather around the graft from the tree "that was bitten by Eve":

> Vidi gente sott'esso alzar le mani
>   e gridar non so che verso le fronde,
>   quasi bramosi fantolini e vani
> che pregano, e 'l pregato non risponde,
>   ma, per fare esser ben la voglia acuta,
>   tien alto lor disio e nol nasconde.

I saw people under it raising their hands and crying out I know not what toward the leaves, like avid and desiring children who beg, and he whom they beg does not answer but—to make their longing more acute—holds high the object of their desire and does not hide it.

(24.106–11)

Dante handles gluttony in such a way as to deliteralize it; by invoking the tree of knowledge and the restraints that Eve did not tolerate he forces us to associate the sin purged on the sixth terrace with Eve's metaphorical gluttony— her eating of the tree of the knowledge of good and evil, her *trapassar del segno*— and thus to see gluttony in a Ulyssean light anticipated by the siren of canto 19. This expanded reading of the sins of concupiscence (for what I have said about gluttony can easily be applied to avarice and lust as well)[15] is confirmed in the *Purgatorio*'s final cantos, where Beatrice's view of the fallacy of earthly desire recalls both Augustine and the *dolce serena*: "e volse i passi suoi per via non vera, / imagini di ben seguendo false, / che nulla promession rendono intera" ("he turned his steps along a not true path, following false images of good that satisfy no promise in full" [*Purg.* 30.130–32]). The basic plot of the *Purgatorio*, like that of the *Vita Nuova*, is a courtly medieval inflection of the Augustinian paradigm whereby life—new life—is achieved by mastering the lesson of death. Because of the courtly twist, the pilgrim's original desire for Beatrice was not in itself wrong; indeed his desire for Beatrice led him to love "the good beyond which there is nothing to aspire" ("i mie' disiri, / che ti menavano ad amar lo bene / di là dal qual non è a che s'aspiri" [*Purg.* 31.22–24]).[16] What was wrong was his failure, after her death, to resist the siren song of the new, the *altre novità* that are false if for no other reason than that they are mortal, corruptible, confined to the present and doomed to die: "Le presenti cose / col falso lor piacer volser miei passi" ("Present things with their false pleasure turned my steps" [*Purg.* 31.34–35]).[17] Having encountered the lesson of mortality once, he should not have needed to be taught it again; like Augustine after the death of his friend, he should have learned the error of "loving a man that must die as though he were not to die"—"diligendo moriturum ac si non moriturum" (*Conf.* 4.8). Having learned, when Beatrice died, that even the most beautiful of mortal things, the most supreme of earthly pleasures, will necessarily fail us, Dante should have known better than to ever desire another "cosa mortale": "e se 'l sommo piacer sì *ti fallio* / per la mia morte, qual cosa mortale / dovea poi trarre te nel suo disio?" ("and if the supreme pleasure thus *failed you*, with my death, what mortal thing should then have drawn you into desire?" [*Purg.* 31.52–54]). A similar theologizing of courtly topoi along Augustinian lines is already evident in the *Vita Nuova*, whose protagonist is converted from desiring Beatrice's "mortal" greeting, which fails him, to desiring only "quello che non mi puote venire meno" (18.4), a phrase that will be punctually recast in the *Purgatorio*'s "sì ti fallio." "Beatitudine," as he calls it in the *libello*, is spiritual autonomy, the ability to relinquish even the best and most beautiful of earthly things—such as Beatrice's greeting, Casella's song, Manfredi's beautiful aspect. Not the cessation of desire, but the mastery of an infallible desire, is the goal; and indeed the pilgrim enters the earthly paradise full of a questing desire ("Vago già di cercar dentro e dintorno" ["Desirous already to search inside and about" (*Purg.* 28.1)]) that cannot go wrong.

So, the paradigm of the quest remains, but the quester can no longer err. Within this conceptual node, we can identify the purgatorial valence that will be assigned to the figure of Ulysses, the shadings particular to the only canticle in which everyone is questing, in which everyone must needs fly "con l'ale snelle e con le piume / del Bran disio" ("with the slender wings and with the feathers of great desire" [*Purg.* 4.28–29]). We note that the verb *volgere*, used by Beatrice to indict the pilgrim ("e volse i passi suoi per via non vera"), and then by the pilgrim as he acknowledges the legitimacy of her rebuke ("Le presenti cose ... volser miei passi"), is the same verb used by the siren in her boast regarding Ulysses: "Io volsi Ulisse del suo cammin vago." In fact, the Ulyssean twist that Dante gives his Augustinian thematic is made explicit by Beatrice in her summation, where she says she intends to strengthen the pilgrim in any future encounters with sirens, any future exposure to their seductive songs: "e perché altra volta, / udendo le serene, sie più forte" ("and so that another time, hearing the sirens, you may be stronger" [*Purg.* 31.44–45]). Here we find the *Purgatorio*'s ultimate synthesis of the Ulyssean model (a man—in this case Dante—tempted by sirens) with Augustine's critique of false pleasure. Given that the sirens of verse 45 may be interpreted in the light of Cicero's *De finibus* as knowledge,[18] resistance to the sirens constitutes not only resistance to the false pleasures of the flesh but also resistance to the false lure of philosophical knowledge, a lure embodied in Dante's earlier itinerary by the *donna gentile*/Lady Philosophy of the *Convivio*,[19] the text that begins with the Ulyssean copula of desire and knowledge: "tutti li uomini naturalmente desiderano di sapere." As the pilgrim has learned restraint before the sweet siren in all her guises, so, in the earthly paradise, the griffin is praised for having resisted the sweet taste of the tree of knowledge: "Beato se', grifon, che non discindi / col becco d'esto legno dolce al gusto, / poscia che mal si torce il ventre quindi" ("Blessed are you, griffin, who do not tear with your beak from this tree sweet to the taste, for by it the belly is evilly twisted" [*Purg.* 32.43–45]). By resisting the temptation of knowledge, the griffin refuses to challenge God's interdict (the *interdetto* of *Purgatorio* 33.71, where the tree is glossed precisely in terms of the limits it represents, the obedience it exacts, and the consequent justice of the punishment meted to those who transgress). The temptation to which Adam/Ulysses succumb is the temptation that the griffin resists.

All the threads are tied in these cantos—the threads connecting gluttony, concupiscence, pride, curiosity, questing, loving, transgressing, Ulysses, the siren, Adam, and Eve[20]—as the Augustinian critique of misplaced desire proper to the *Purgatorio* converges with the theme of limits and transgression central to the poem as a whole, the theme embodied by Dante not only in the canonical figures of Adam and Lucifer but also in the more idiosyncratic and personal mythography of Ulysses. It is worth noting that the system of values that finds expression in the tied threads of *Purgatorio* was already, to a significant degree, present in the earlier works. We have seen that the purgatorial journey toward spiritual autonomy is adumbrated in the *Vita Nuova*; so too, the *Convivio* explores the desire for knowledge in ways that portend the *Commedia*. Let us consider, for instance, the passage in *Convivio* 4.13 where Dante compares the desire for riches to the desire for knowledge. (It should be noted that riches, *le ricchezze*, are characterized in the *Convivio* in terms that strikingly anticipate the *dolce serena* of *Purgatorio* 19, as "false traditrici" and "false meretrici" who make promises of satisfaction they cannot fulfill, and who lead not to repose but to renewed desire.)[21] This being the *Convivio*, Dante's assessment of man's desire to know is comparatively sanguine and untroubled, and the successiveness of the desire for knowledge, with its many scaled opportunities for reaching "perfection," is sharply disjoined from the unilaterality of the desire for wealth, which leads only to increased desire:

> E così appare che, dal desiderio de la scienza, la scienza non è da dire imperfetta, sì come le ricchezze sono da dire per lo loro, come la questione ponea; chè nel desiderare de la scienza successivamente finiscono li desiderii e viensi a perfezione, e in quello de la ricchezza no.

> And so it appears that, on the basis of the desire for knowledge, knowledge itself is not to be called imperfect, as riches instead are to be called on the basis of the desire for riches, as the question posed; for in the desire for knowledge successively our desires conclude and come to perfection, and in desiring riches this does not happen.
>
> (*Conv.* 4.13.5)

Similarly, in an earlier passage on desire in *Convivio* 3.15, Dante invokes the miser to explain what the seeker after knowledge is not; the miser is doomed to failure, since, by pursuing the unattainable, he desires always to desire: "e in questo errore cade l'avaro maladetto, e non s'accorge che desidera sé sempre desiderare, andando dietro al numero impossibile a giugnere" ("and into this error falls the accursed miser, and he does not realize that he desires himself always to desire, going after a number impossible to reach" [*Conv.* 3.15.9]).[22] By contrast, the seeker after knowledge will satisfy his desire and fulfill his quest, in part because his quest is measured rather than gluttonously insatiable, and he realizes that there is a line he cannot cross: "E però l'umano desiderio è misurato in questa vita a quella scienza che qui avere si può, e quello punto non passa se non per errore, lo quale è di fuori di naturale intenzione" ("And so human desire is measured in this life by that knowledge which here can be had, and it does not pass that point except by error, which is outside of natural intention" [*Conv.* 3.15.9]).[23]

One could describe the distance between the *Convivio* and the *Commedia* in terms of the poet's growing concern about our Ulyssean lack of measure, our failure to respect the line that cannot be crossed, "quello punto [che l'umano desiderio] non passa se non per errore." Even in the treatise, Dante concludes his defense of the desire for knowledge by quoting St. Paul on the need for limits: "E però Paulo dice: 'Non più sapere che sapere si convegna, ma sapere a misura'" ("And so Paul says: 'Do not know more than is fitting, but know with measure'" [*Conv.* 4.13.9]). Moreover, the fact that Dante sees a basis of comparison between the desire for wealth and the desire for knowledge is significant, indicating the conceptual foundation for his mature ideology of an intellectual as well as a material cupidity and pointing forward to the *Commedia*'s composite image of Ulysses on the one hand and the wolf on the other. The *lupa* of *Inferno* 1 illuminates the negative side of the basic human condition whereby "disire è moto spirituale" and recalls Augustine's own reduction of all desire to spiritual motion, either in the form of "charity," desire that moves toward God, or "cupidity," desire that remains rooted in the flesh.[24] As cupidity, our dark desire, the *lupa* is quintessentially without peace, "la bestia sanza pace" (*Inf.* 1.58). Her restlessness and insatiability denote unceasing spiritual motion, unceasing desire: heavy "with all longings" ("di tutte brame" [49]), "her greedy craving is never filled, and after eating she is more hungry than before" ("mai non empie la bramosa voglia, / e dopo 'l pasto ha più fame che pria" [98–99]). Her limitless hunger is both caused by unsatisfied desire and creates the condition for ever less satisfaction, since, in Augustine's words, "When vices have emptied the soul and led it to a kind of extreme hunger, it leaps into crimes by means of which impediments to the vices may be removed or the vices themselves sustained" (*De doct. Christ.* 3.10.16). When the "antica lupa" is recalled as an emblem of cupidity on purgatory's terrace of avarice (again indicating the common ground that underlies all the sins of inordinate desire), her "hunger without end" is once more her distinguishing characteristic: "Maladetta sic tu, antica lupa, / che più che tutte l'altre bestie hai preda / per la tua fame sanza fine cupa!" ("Cursed be you, ancient wolf, who more than all the other beasts have prey, because of your deep hunger without end! [*Purg.* 20.10–12]). The "antica lupa," the "bestia sanza pace" of the poem's first canto, prepares us for *Purgatorio*'s rooting of all sin in desire and for the coupling of Ulysses, a wanderer who makes the mistake of enjoying the sights and sounds that he should merely use, with the "dolce serena": it is impossible to separate in categorical fashion avarice from greed, greed from lust, or any of the three from desire—including the desire for knowledge—that has become immoderately transgressive, that has gone astray.[25]

The *Convivio*'s assessment of the possibilities for human desiring is not so positive as to preclude the figure of the errant voyager. Thus, Dante offers the parable of the path that is shown and then lost ("e pongo essemplo del cammino mostrato [e poscia errato]"),[26] a story whereby one man makes his way across an arduous and snowy plain, leaving his tracks for those behind him, only to be followed by one who is incapable even of keeping to the path laid out by his predecessor, and so loses himself: "e, per suo difetto, lo cammino, che altri sanza

scorta ha saputo tenere, questo scorto erra, e tortisce per li pruni e per le rume,
e a la parte dove dee non va" ("and, through his own fault, the path that another
without guidance knew how to follow, this one with guidance loses, and wanders
wrongly through the bushes and down the steep slopes, and to the place where
he should go does not go" [*Conv.* 4.7.7]). Still, despite the Ulyssean presence of
the *cammino errato*, it should be noticed that the parable puts great emphasis on
the cammino mostrato as well, devoting attention to the industry and skill of the
guide who "per sua industria, cioè per accorgimento e per bontade d'ingegno,
solo da sé guidato, per lo diritto cammino si va là dove intende, lasciando le
vestigie de li suoi passi diretro da sé" ("by his own industry, by observation and
the resources of intellect, guided only by himself, goes where he intended,
leaving the traces of his steps behind himself" [4.7.7]). Particularly striking is the
proto-Vergilian image of the tracks left for those who come behind, which
anticipates the description of the Roman poet as one "che porta il lume dietro e
sé non giova, / ma dopo sé fa le persone dotte" ("who carries the light behind and
helps not himself, but after himself makes people wise" [*Purg.* 22.68–69]). While
in the *Convivio* the guide is able to benefit from his own *industria*, the *Commedia*
will recombine the parable's elements so that the guide fails, and instead the
follower benefits from the guide's proffered help and reaches his goal. Indeed, in
the poem the very idea of being able to make one's way "per bontade d'ingegno,
solo da sé guidato" will be suspect.

Even more telling than the parable of the *cammino errato* is the predictive
value of our pilgrim passage from *Convivio* 4.12; here we already find the
association between misdirected desire and the voyager who will never reach his
goal. As we proceed from desire to desire, as our desires grow ever larger and we
quest more and more insatiably for the prize that eludes us, we may deviate from
the straight and truest path:[27]

> Veramente così questo cammino si perde per errore come le strade
> de la terra. Che sì come d'una cittade a un'altra di necessitade è una
> ottima e dirittissima via, e un'altra che sempre se ne dilunga (cioè
> quella che va ne l'altra parte), e molte altre quale meno allungandosi
> e quale meno appressandosi, così ne la vita umana sono diversi
> cammini, de li quali uno è veracissimo e un altro è fallacissimo, e
> certi meno fallaci e certi meno veraci. E sì come vedemo che quello
> che dirittissimo vae a la cittade, e compie lo desiderio e dà posa dopo
> la fatica, e quello che va in contrario mai nol compie e mai posa dare
> non può, così ne la nostra vita avviene: lo buono camminatore giugne
> a termine e a posa; lo erroneo mai non l'aggiugne, ma con molta
> fatica del suo animo sempre con li occhi gulosi si mira innanzi.

> Truly thus this path is lost through error like the roads of the earth.
> For just as from one city to the other there is by necessity one best

and straightest road, and another road that instead gets always
further away (that is, which goes in another direction), and many
others of which some get further and others come nearer, so in
human life there are different paths, of which one is the truest and
the other the most false, and some less false and some less true. And
as we see that the path that goes most directly to the city fulfills
desire and gives rest after weariness, while the one that goes in the
contrary direction never brings fulfillment and can never bring rest,
so it happens in our life: the traveler on the right path reaches his
goal and his rest; the traveler on the wrong path never reaches it, but
with great weariness of soul always with his greedy eyes looks ahead.

(*Conv.* 4.12.18–19)

In the figure of the traveler on the wrong path who never reaches his goal, never
fulfills his quest and his desire, never finds peace but strains forward as with
"great weariness of soul always with his greedy eyes he looks ahead," we have a
full-fledged anticipation of the Ulysses figure within the *Commedia*: the *erroneo
camminatore* whose greedy desire and ever forward-looking "occhi gulosi" lead
him fatally to his death.[28] On the other hand, in the *buono camminatore* who
reaches his goal and finds repose ("giugne a termine e a posa"), we find
anticipated all the pilgrims of the *Commedia*, all the souls in the second realm.
Given this realm's intimate tie to the concepts of pilgrimage and voyage, it is not
surprising to find at its outset a particularly lucid synthesis of the *Convivio's* two
types of voyagers.

The presence of Ulysses as mariner saturates the first canto of *Purgatorio*,
from the opening image of the poem as the "little ship of my intellect," to the
closing cadenza about the deserted shore "that never saw any man navigate its
waters who afterward had experience of return" ("che mai non vide navicar sue
acque / omo, the di tornar sia poscia esperto" [*Purg.* 1.131–32]). No human
navigator has ever seen these waters and returned to tell the tale; the pilgrim, on
the other hand, looks "a l'altro polo" ("altro polo" is used only here in *Purgatorio*
1, twice, and in *Inferno* 26) and sees "quattro stelle / non viste mai fuor ch'a la
prima gente" ("four stars never seen save by the first people" [23–24]). How can
it be that, in the course of Ulysses' journey, "the night saw *all* the stars already of
the other pole" ("*Tutte* le stelle già de l'altro polo / vedea la notte" [*Inf.*
26.127–28]), while now the other pole shows the pilgrim four stars that no one
has seen since Adam and Eve? Whether the contradiction is meant to indicate
the purely symbolic nature of these four purgatorial stars,[29] or whether the night
somehow saw what Ulysses himself did not see, the dialectic between vision
denied and vision vouchsafed is essential to this canto, whose themes of
castigated pride and potentially broken laws ("Son le leggi d'abisso così rotte?"
["Are the laws of the abyss so broken?"] asks Cato in line 46) link it to its
predecessor, *Inferno* 34, as surely as its style and tonality disjoin it. In the same

way, the pilgrim—of whose previous *follia* Vergil speaks in what the poem has coded as a Ulyssean lexicon—is purposely linked to the Greek sailor, only to be just as purposely disjoined: although his backward descent to the base of the mountain makes him appear a man who travels in vain until he returns to the road he has lost ("com'om the torna a la perduta strada, / che 'nfino ad essa li pare ire in vano" [119–20]), in fact this backward motion will serve to dissociate him from Ulyssean pride, bringing him to the reeds of rebirth rather than to the "perduta strada" of hell.[30]

Throughout these opening cantos of *Purgatorio* recur the images of travel: Dante and Vergil are "come gente che pensa a suo cammino, / che va col cuore e col corpo dimora" ("like people who think of their path, who go in heart and remain in body" [*Purg.* 2.11–12]); the souls dispersed by Cato move off toward the mountain's slope "com'om the va, né sa dove riesca" ("like a man who goes, nor knows where he may come forth" [*Purg.* 2.132]). Throughout these cantos, also, runs the leitmotif of limits, of the non-Ulyssean humility that distinguishes our travelers from the *erroneo camminatore*. The newly arrived souls of purgatory are "rustic" ("selvaggia" [*Purg.* 2.52]) rather than "urbanely" self-confident;[31] not being "esperti d'esto loco," they look around "come colui che nove cose assaggia" ("like one who tastes new things" [*Purg.* 2.54]). In contrast to Ulysses, who sought to conquer the *nova terra*, to make it no longer new, these souls accept their status as "nova gente" (*Purg.* 2.58). In contrast to Ulysses, who in trying to reach purgatory was striving to be a new thing in the sense of something not envisioned by God, something not written into the divine script (the periphrasis for the shore, "che mai non vide navicar sue acque," anticipates the periphrasis for God, "Colui che mai non vide cosa nova"), these souls are new things in the sense that they will be made new, will be "remade like new plants, renewed with new leaf" at the canticle's end. Like the souls, the pilgrim too is God's "cosa nova": not an attempt to abrogate the laws and surprise God but a sign of God's providence, as Sapìa indicates when she exclaims that the pilgrim's journey is "sì cosa nuova ... the gran segno è che Dio t'ami" ("such a new thing that it is a great sign that God loves you" [*Purg.* 13.145–46]).[32] This contrast is sustained in canto 3 through Vergil's discourse on human intellectual limits ("State contenti, umana gente, al *quia*" ["Content yourselves, human folk, with the fact that certain things are" (*Purg.* 3.37)]), through the description of the purgatorial souls as timid sheep, who are content to act without knowing the reason why ("e lo 'mperché non sanno" [84]), and finally through the temporal ban—the "divieto" of verse 144—that punishes the "presumption" ("presunzïon" [140]) of those who die excommunicate. In canto 4 we learn that to scale purgatory we must fly with the wings of great desire and then find contrasted the immoderate zeal of Phaeton's flight with the immoderate torpor of the negligent Belacqua;[33] at the same time, there is also the suggestion that Belacqua's negligence partakes of humility and might have something to teach the pilgrim, who—unlike Phaeton—will have to accept his limitations before climbing to the top of this mountain. Belacqua's friendly taunt, "Forse / che di sedere in pria avrai distretta!" ("Maybe before then you'll need to sit!" [*Purg.* 4.98–99]), will be picked up by Sordello's sterner reminder of limits—"sola questa riga / non varcheresti dopo 'l sol partito" ("not even this line would you cross after the sun's departure" [*Purg.* 7.53–54]), where the use of the verb *varcare* carries a Ulyssean reverberation.

In the *Purgatorio*, then, Dante takes great pains to establish the paradigm of the *erroneo camminatore* versus the *buono camminatore* and to associate the pilgrim with the latter. He sets up an implied model, a scale that measures various approaches to the divine and indicates the wide range of right movement, of acceptable—non-Ulyssean—flight. But, in a text whose fiction is that it is no fiction, and whose strategy is that there is no strategy, the matter is never so simple. Thus, in canto 3, the theme of human limits is allowed to embrace the ecclesiastical establishment, up to and including the pope: had the bishop of Cosenza, instructed to hunt Manfredi by Clement IV, been able to "read" the face of God that is his infinite mercy ("avesse in Dio ben letta questa faccia" [*Purg.* 3.126]), Manfredi's bones would not have been disinterred. The bishop, and with him his superior, was proved incapable of "reading," understanding and interpreting, the divine will.[34] In the same way, in canto 5, the mystery of divine predestination will baffle not only human agents, like the pope, but a devil, who will be infuriated by the inexplicable intervention of an angel on Bonconte's behalf: "Io dirò vero, e lo 'l ridì tra' vivi: / l'angel di Dio mi prese, e quel d'inferno / gridava: 'O to del ciel, perché mi privi?'" ("I will tell the truth, and you retell it among the living: the angel of God took me, and the one from hell cried, 'O you from heaven, why do you deprive me?'" [*Purg.* 5.103–5]). What Bonconte recounts cannot be logically explained or comprehended, since it belongs to the mystery of providence; it must be accepted on faith, as the truth: "Io dirò vero," says Bonconte. And, indeed, it must be the "truth," or else Dante would not be sanctioning what Bonconte said to him ("e lo 'l ridì tra' vivi"), or else—in fact—Bonconte would not be where he is, in purgatory. In this fiction a soul, in this case Bonconte, tells the pilgrim that he is telling the truth; the poet repeats what the soul "said" to the pilgrim, along with the injunction to repeat it, and thereby presents it as the truth rather than as fiction. Ultimately, however, the fiction is a fiction, no matter how skillfully deployed, and the choice to save Manfredi, thereby branding the pope an incompetent reader of the divine text, like the choice to save Bonconte, is Dante's. Thus we come back to the word *presunzione* inscribed into the conclusion of canto 3: whose presumption is really at stake here, if not the poet's? The textual language employed in these episodes—not only the failure to read but also calling the Archiano's convergence with the Arno the place where the river loses its name, where its signifier is emptied of significance, "Là 've 'l vocabol suo diventa vano" (*Purg.* 5.97)—serves to highlight the metatextual implications: does Dante read God correctly, as he claims, or does he read like Clement, composing a text whose *vocaboli* are therefore *vani*?

I submit that the terms *presunzione* and *presumere* may be said to carry a Ulyssean charge in all Dante's works, that indeed they were invested by Dante with a special significance as early as the *Convivio* and the *De vulgari eloquentia*, before such a thematic could properly be dubbed "Ulyssean."[35] In other words, Dante has a history of using these words in contexts that indicate his ongoing concern with the problem of intellectual arrogance, the problem to which in the *Commedia* he gives dramatic and poetic shape with the figure of Ulysses. In the *De vulgari eloquentia* we find the first and programmatic use of the adjective as a qualifier for Eve, *presumptuosissima Eva*, who, in replying to the devil, became the first human to speak (1.4.2).[36] The sin of human presumption ("culpa presumptionis humane" [1.6.4]) leads to mankind's "third" fall; following the expulsion from the garden of Eden and the flood, in our foolish pride we presume yet a third time: "per superbam stultitiam presumendo" (1.7.3). The participle "presumendo" is immediately picked up by the next word, "Presumpsit," which powerfully begins the paragraph dedicated to the discussion of the linguistic diaspora occasioned by Nimrod's hubristic attempt to construct the tower of Babel: "Presumpsit ergo in corde suo incurabilis homo, sub persuasione gigantis Nembroth, arte sua non solum superare naturam, sed etiam ipsum naturantem, qui Deus est" ("So uncurable man, persuaded by the giant Nimrod, presumed in his heart to surpass with his art not only nature, but also nature's maker, who is God" [1.7.4]). The connection between pride and human endeavor—human "art" as it is called here and in a related passage in *Inferno* 11[37]—is a striking feature of this passage, and one that anticipates the *Commedia*; Nimrod's attempt to surpass not only nature but nature's maker will cause him to be remembered in each canticle of the poem, as part of an "artistic" constellation that also includes Ulysses and Phaeton.[38] Not surprisingly, then, in the *Commedia presumere* is invested with enormous self-consciousness; on both occasions in which Dante employs the verb (the noun occurs only in *Purgatorio* 3), he is referring to himself.[39] It appears in *Paradiso* 33, in the supreme moment of the pilgrim's nontransgressive transgression, where the verb's prideful connotations are redeemed through the grace of God: "Oh abbondante grazia ond'io presunsi / ficcar lo viso per la lute etterna" ("O abundant grace whereby I presumed to thrust my face through the eternal light" [82–83]). If the point here is the legitimate presumption that propels us toward our maker, the poem's other usage recoups its previous history in Dante's works; in answer to the pilgrim's query as to why Peter Damian alone was predestined to welcome him to the heaven of Saturn, the saint replies that the mystery of predestination is hidden in the abyss of God's will and that human beings should not presume to tackle such a question: "E al mondo mortal, quando tu riedi, / questo rapporta, sì che non presumma / a tanto segno più mover li piedi" ("And to the mortal world, when you return, bring back this message, so that it will not any longer presume to move its feet toward such a goal" [*Par.* 21.97–99]).

Here the poet advises himself, through the medium of Peter Damian, to advise the world not to seek presumptuously to know what cannot be known; like the passage in *Paradiso* 13 in which Dante, the great judger, condemns hasty judgments through the agency of St. Thomas, this passage betrays a protective awareness of the *Commedia's* own Achilles' heel. As a self-proclaimed prophecy, the *Commedia* is a text whose basic program of revealing the state of souls after death participates in the very presumption it is supposed to warn the world against. Indeed, the *Commedia's* only defense against such presumption is its aggressive assumption of the mantle of truth, its vigilant assertions that it is a true prophecy, vouchsafed by God in a vision. Dante is aware that he is only preserved from presumption by the divine investiture that he alone knows he received, and that only his ability to persuade us of this investiture's historicity (or of his sincerity in claiming its historicity) prevents us from considering him fraudulently self-deluded and self-promoting: as self-deluded and self-promoting as, for instance, the false prophets of *Inferno* 20, or the mendacious preachers of *Paradiso* 29.[40] This awareness dictates both the connection between artistry and pride that runs through his work and the (defensive) aggression he directs at any others—like the false prophets and the lying preachers—whose art it also is to present themselves as tellers of truth. This aggression toward rival claimants was first directed, in the course of Dante's career, against poets whose pretensions surpassed their abilities. Thus, when, in the *De vulgari eloquentia*, Dante condemns the Tuscan poets for their mad arrogance, he uses language that anticipates the *Commedia's* lexicon of Ulyssean hubris;[41] the key word, *praesumptuositas*, used in adjectival form earlier in the treatise for Eve, now describes poets who try to go beyond their natural limits. They should desist from such presumption, and if nature or laziness has made them ducks, they should accept their lowly status (likewise Nimrod should have accepted the low position of human art in the mimetic hierarchy) and cease to imitate the star-seeking eagle: "et a tanta presumptuositate desistant, et si anseres natura vel desidia sunt, nolint astripetam aquilam imitari" (2.4.11). Poets like Guittone d'Arezzo, in other words, should not seek to imitate supreme poets, poets who seek the stars, poets like Dante; their (false) claims to tell truth should not interfere with his (true) claims.[42] The question of presumption is thus intimately connected to the question of access to truth, as Peter Damian tells us in the *Commedia* and as Dante had already clarified in this passage from the *Convivio*:

> ché sono molti tanto presuntuosi, che si credono tutto sapere, e per questo le non certe cose affermano per certe; lo qual vizio Tullio massimamente abomina nel primo de li Offici e Tommaso nel suo Contra li Gentili, dicendo: "Sono molti tanto di suo ingegno presuntuosi, che credono col suo intelletto poter misurare tutte le cose, *estimando tutto vero quello che a loro pare, falso quello che a loro non pare.*"

for there are many who are so presumptuous that they think they know everything, and on this basis they treat matters that are not certain as certain; which vice Cicero greatly abominates in the first book of the *De officiis* and Thomas in his *Contra gentiles* saying: "There are many so presumptuous in their intelligence that they think with their minds to be able to measure all things, *believing everything to be true which seems to them to be true, and false that which seems to them false.*"

(Conv. 4.15.12)

The *Convivio* foreshadows the dialectical bind in which the author of the *Commedia* is caught, as he either ferociously condemns those who fail to accept their limits[43] or wards off the possibility that he himself may not be accepting his limits, that the authority of his authorship may cause him to transgress against other authorities: "E prima mostrerò me non presummere [contra l'autorità del Filosofo; poi mostrerò me non presummere] contra la maiestade imperiale" ("And first I will demonstrate that I have not presumed [against the authority of the Philosopher; then I will show that I have not presumed] against the imperial majesty" [*Conv.* 4.8.5]).[44] Looking again at the episode in *Paradiso* 21 where Peter Damian denounces the pilgrim's curiosity regarding predestination, we note that the pilgrim beats a retreat from his daring original query to the humbler "Who are you?": "Sì mi prescrisser le parole sue, / ch'io lasciai la quistione e mi ritrassi / a dimandarla umilmente chi fue" ("So did his words impose a limit that I left the question and drew back to asking humbly who he was" [*Par.* 21.103–5]).[45] But the episode gives us a counter signal as well, in the form of the rhyme words *abisso* and *scisso*, which send us back to one of the most daringly transgressive passages in the poem and remind us that the pilgrim's retreat cannot be simplistically equated with the poet's. Peter Damian tells the pilgrim that the seraph whose eyes are most fixed on God would not be able to answer his question, "for what you ask is so far advanced in the abyss of the eternal decree that from every created vision it is cut off": "però che sì s'innoltra ne to *abisso* / de l'etterno statuto quel che chiedi, / che da ogne creata vista è scisso" (*Par.* 21.94–96). This same rhyme occurs elsewhere only in *Purgatorio* 6, where *abisso* also refers to the inscrutability of the divine will ("abisso / del tuo consiglio" as compared to "abisso / de l'etterno statuto"), where our awareness is also cut off—"scisso"—from understanding, and where the recollection of our eternal shortsightedness follows a query, addressed to God, of enormous presumption:

> E se licito m'è, o sommo Giove
> che fosti in terra per noi crucifisso,
> son li giusti occhi tuoi rivolti altrove?
> O è preparazion che ne l'*abisso*

> del tuo consiglio fai per alcun bene
> in tutto de l'accorger nostro *scisso*?

And if it be lawful for me, o supreme Jove who was crucified for us on earth, are your just eyes turned elsewhere? Or is it a preparation that in the *abyss* of your counsel you make for some good that is completely *cut off* from our perception?

> (*Purg.* 6.118–23)

The new and never before traveled path of this poem entails bizarre reversals: on the one hand, we have a poet who invents a special penalty to castigate the presumption of anyone who challenges the authority of the church, a temporal ban ("divieto") of thirtyfold the amount of time passed by such a soul "in sua presunzion"; on the other hand, this same poet presumes to ostentatiously include in the community of the saved, by his own—that is, "God's"—fiat, a soul who was notoriously cast out by one of God's chosen vicars. And, were questioning a pope not problematic enough, this poet presumes to question God himself, wondering all the while if it is licit so to do—"se licito m'è"—because he knows perfectly well that it is not.[46]

Purgatorio 6 is a canto in which the narrator steps out of bounds—both ideologically, in the lengthy invective that escalates into the questioning of divine justice, and narratologically, in that the invective is couched in the form of a digression: a literal swerving away from the narrative confines and off the narrative path. Ideological *transgressio* thus elicits narratological *digressio*.[47] Beginning in verse 76, the digression finds its pretext in the civic embrace of Vergil and Sordello and preempts the rest of canto 6; not until canto 7 does the interrupted encounter between the two Mantuan poets resume (the willed and programmatic nature of the interruption is further emphasized by its coincidence with the canto break).[48] There are signs of the coming disruption in the first part of the canto: the narrator has already slipped out of harness in lines 22–24, when he suggests to the still living Marie de Brabant that she begin to provide for her immortal soul;[49] the encounter with Sordello also elicits a brief apostrophe that momentarily arrests the narrative flow in midverse: "Venimmo a lei: o anima lombarda, / come ti stavi altera e disdegnosa" ("We came to him; O Lombard soul, how you were proud and disdainful" [*Purg.* 6.61–62]). Of particular importance is the attack on the integrity of Vergil's text that is staged between lines 28 and 48: the poet has the pilgrim wonder why it is that in the *Aeneid* prayer does not help Palinurus to cross the Acheron, while in purgatory prayer is a force for spiritual advancement; Vergil is forced to confront the fact that he was writing about souls whose prayers are disjoined from God, while the pilgrim is experiencing the requests of souls whose prayers have access to divine justice. In Vergil's murky explanation (the fact that he tells us that his text is clear on this point, "La mia scrittura è piana" [34], only highlights the obscurity of his gloss), the justice that will so exercise the poet later on in this canto is already present: "ché cima di giudicio non s'avvalla / perché foeo d'amor compia in un punto / ciò che de' sodisfar chi qui s'astalla" ("for the summit of judgment is not lowered because the fire of love fulfills in one moment that which he who stays here must satisfy" [37–39]). Vergil has thus already posed, indirectly, the question of how justice can be bent by love without ceasing to be just (or how, by implication, it can fail to be bent by love without ceasing to be just).[50] He further anticipates the poet by inserting into his address a little authorial signpost: Vergil's "se ben si guarda con la mente sana" ("if with sound mind you consider well" [36]) will be echoed in the course of the digression by the poet's own "se bene intendi ciò che Dio ti nota" ("if you understand well what God tells you" [93]). These anticipations serve to underscore the disjunction between Vergil and Dante, *Aeneid* and *Commedia*. Prior to his great invective, an invective that is licit—if indeed it is, *se licito m'è*—precisely because he is one who interprets God's notations correctly, the poet stretches a textual cordon between his text and the *Aeneid*, confirming the latter in its errors and thus creating the space, the liminality, in which the *Commedia* can receive its mandate for prophetic transgression, for the literal trespass of the sign ("trapassar del segno") that is his "digression."

In the *Commedia* Dante uses the terms *digressione* and *digredire* only twice, on both occasions to usher in a full-fledged change in subject matter:[51] in *Purgatorio* 6 he uses the noun, congratulating Florence on "questa digression che non ti tocca" ("this digression that does not touch you" [128]); while in *Paradiso* 29 the poet concludes the invective against fraudulent preachers by announcing that it is time for us to turn our eyes back to the straight road (in this case, the straight road, the narrative path, is a discussion of the nature of angels), since we have digressed enough ("Ma perché siam digressi assai, ritorci / li occhi oramai verso la dritta strada" [127–28]). If we consider that the brunt of *Paradiso* 29's critique is that there exist unscrupulous preachers who tell falsehoods, inventions, and lies, we begin to discern the consonance between the poem's two self-proclaimed digressions: they are both metatextual moments, concerned with situating the text from which they pretend to depart with respect to other texts; in a word, far from being extraneous, they are integrally connected to Dante's campaign to be seen as a teller of truth. In his condemnation of false preachers, Dante's strategy is the fairly straightforward attack on other pretenders that we have already noted to be a staple of his career. The invective of *Purgatorio* 6, on the other hand, offers the more delicate dialectic between the author's awareness of his own potential for transgression and the express declaration of his status as a teller of truth, one whose words are corroborated by events, by history itself: "S'io dico 'l ver, l'effetto nol nasconde" ("If I tell the truth, the facts do not hide it" [*Purg.* 6.138]). The truly remarkable nature of the rupture in *Purgatorio* 6, moreover, is suggested by the steps that Dante takes to restore the fictive status quo that he has so emphatically sundered. In canto 7 Sordello will guide the

pilgrim to the valley of the princes, showing him its denizens, in the same way
that in canto 6 the poet offers to guide the emperor, exhorting him to "look" at
what he has to show in the thrice repeated formula, "Vieni a veder" ("Come to
see");[52] as the poet apostrophizes Albert I of Austria, accusing him of abandoning
the garden of the empire, so Sordello notes that Albert's father, Rudolf I, could
have healed the wounds that have been the death of Italy. Sordello might almost
be said to "imitate" the poet, self-consciously drawing attention to his narrative
role as Dante did in the digression: "Anche al nasuto vanno mie parole / non men
ch'a l'altro" ("My words apply to the large-nosed one no less than to the other"
[*Purg.* 7.124–25]). However, when Sordello echoes the poet in his use of "licito,"
it is not to suggest the possibility of transgression but rather the need to accept
one's limits: "licito m'è andar suso e intorno; / per quanto ir posso, a guida mi
t'accosto" ("it is permitted me to go up and around; as far as I am able, I will
accompany you as guide" [*Purg.* 7.41–42]).

Sordello restores narrative normalcy and ideological humility, leading us
back within the limits, both narratologically and theologically. Rather than
attend to the unveiled voice of the poet, we once more learn our lessons at the
hands of a figure within the fictive construct, one, moreover, who does not
question the workings of providence: thus Sordello explains that if nobility is
rarely passed on from father to son, it is because God wills it so (*Purg.* 7.121–23).
Another figure within the fictive construct, Nino Visconti, refers to the mysteries
of providence in a periphrasis that wonderfully literalizes the limits to our mental
voyaging: God is "the one who so hides his first cause that there is no fording
thereto" ("colui che sì nasconde / lo suo primo perchè, che non là è guado"
[*Purg.* 8.68–69]). Nino is drawing attention to the singular grace that has brought
the pilgrim to purgatory while alive, a grace that he effectively posits as the only
answer to the poet's anguished query of canto 6; the text's reply to its author's
"Vieni a veder" is Nino's echoing call to Currado to "come and see what God
willed in his grace": "vieni a veder che Dio per grazia volse" (*Purg.* 8.66). And so
we are folded back within the fiction; so *di-gressio*, trespass without the bounds,
is channeled within, becoming the "trapassar dentro" of the author's address to
the reader in canto 8: "Aguzza qui, lettor, ben li occhi al vero, / chè 'l velo è ora
ben tanto sottile, / certo che 'l trapassar dentro è leggero" ("Reader, here sharpen
well your eyes to the truth, for the veil is now so thin that certainly to pass within
is easy" [19–21]). The digression has been righted by the restoration of the
fiction (somewhat "thinner" than usual, perhaps, as a result of the preceding
rupture): truth is under the veil, within the fiction, not only outside it, in the
space of digression. And yet, finally, is not the fiction more transgressive than
that which it corrects? What is more transgressive than Nino's call, when we
consider that the object of God's grace whom Currado is summoned to see is
none other than our author? The poet addresses us again, in canto 9, to alert us
to the exalted nature of his theme and therefore of his art: "Lettor, tu vedi ben
com'io innalzo / la mia matera, e però con più arte / non ti maravigliar s'io la

rincalzo" ("Reader, you see well how I raise my matter, and therefore do not marvel if with more art I sustain it" [70–72]). The episode that follows is not known for its linguistic or poetic virtuosity, for its hold on the reader or its dramatic power; indeed, the description of the ritual encounter with the angel at purgatory's gate would hardly seem to qualify as an example of "più arte." To the extent, however, that art is measured by its access to truth, this passage may indeed be of the "highest," if, as Armour claims, it constitutes a supreme example of figural polysemy.[53] Apparently simple writing may not be so simple, may even be "exalted," if the literal veil covers not a fictitious truth, a metaphorical truth, but the actual—incarnate—truth. If the fiction tells truth then the retreat from the trespass of the digression is in fact not a retreat but an advance. The implications of the digression, with respect to *praesumptuositas*, are thus more intact than ever, as we—and the poet—approach the terrace of pride.

NOTES

1. For the basic narrative structure of each terrace and the variations applied to it, see Enrico De' Negri, "Tema e iconografia del *Purgatorio*," *Romanic Review* 49 (1958): 81–104.

2. Michelangelo Picone writes a brief history of the pilgrimage metaphor in *Vita Nuova e tradizione romanza* (Padua: Liviana, 1979); see chapter 5, "*Peregrinus amoris*: la metafora finale," where he concludes his resume with this passage from the *Convivio*, in which the metaphor is presented "al massimo delle sue potenzialità espressive" (152). The importance of this passage for the *Commedia* is noted by Bruno Basile, "Il viaggio come archetipo: note sul tema della 'peregrinatio' in Dante," *Letture classensi* 15 (1986): 9–26.

3. The typology of Exodus, of pilgrimage, is further signaled by the psalm, "In exitu Israel de Aegypto" in *Purg.* 2. As Peter Armour explains, this typology applies in a unique way to purgatory: "the *Inferno* and the *Paradiso* do not actually refer to the Exodus, for the souls there are not going anywhere"; "the path of purification is a single, continuous road to be started in this life and completed in the next" ("The Theme of Exodus in the First Two Cantos of the *Purgatorio*," *Dante Soundings*, ed. David Nolan [Dublin: Irish Academic Press, 1981], 59–99; quotations, 77, 79). Pilgrimage motifs in the *Vita Nuova* and the *Commedia* are treated by Julia Bolton Holloway, *The Pilgrim and the Book* (New York: Peter Lang, 1987), chapter 3, and John G. Demaray, *Dante and the Book of the Cosmos* (Philadelphia: The American Philosophical Society, 1987).

4. Giovanni Cecchetti uses the happy expression "nostalgia del futuro" to describe the condition of the souls in purgatory in "Il *peregrin* e i *navicanti* di *Purgatorio*, VIII, 1–6: saggio di lettura dantesca," *A Dante Symposium in Commemoration of the 700th Anniversary of the Poet's Birth*, ed. W. De Sua and G. Rizzo (Chapel Hill: University of North Carolina Press, 1965), 159–74;

quotation, 168. I disagree with Cecchetti's insistence that nostalgia for the past is completely absent from the verses at the beginning of *Purg.* 8, and from the *Purgatorio* in general; the poetic tension of the second canticle, carefully manipulated by the poet, is generated from the interplay between the souls' double nostalgia. They do, as Cecchetti says, want to return home, but they are not yet completely sure where home is.

5. The importance of the verse "dove tempo per tempo si ristora" is discussed by Ricardo J. Quinones, *The Renaissance Discovery of Time* (Cambridge: Harvard University Press, 1972), 72, and by me in *Dante's Poets: Textuality and Truth in the "Comedy"* (Princeton, N.J.: Princeton University Press, 1984), 46–47. See also Luigi Blasucci, "La dimensione del tempo nel *Purgatorio,*" *Studi su Dante e Ariosto* (Milan: Ricciardi, 1969), 37–64, and Franco Masciandaro, *La problematica del tempo nella "Commedia"* (Ravenna: Longo, 1976), chapter 5.

6. A balanced discussion of Augustine's role in the works of both Dante and Petrarch is provided by Carlo Calcaterra, *Nella selva del Petrarca* (Bologna: Cappelli, 1942). Recently, Augustine's absence from the *Commedia* has been taken up by Peter S. Hawkins, "Divide and Conquer: Augustine in the *Divine Comedy,*" *PMLA* 106 (1991): 471–82. Hawkins focuses on the intertextual presence of Augustine in Vergil's discourse of *Purg.* 15. Interestingly, he too concentrates on a purgatorial presence, which he also sees as mediated through a substitute figure, who in his more political reading is Vergil.

7. The passage from the *Enchiridion* is cited by Jacques Le Goff, *The Birth of Purgatory,* trans. Arthur Goldhammer (1981; Chicago: University of Chicago Press, 1984), 71. Le Goff does not relate Augustine's analysis to Dante's purgatory; in fact, his chapter on Dante, the weakest in the book, makes very little use of the material that his own previous chapters provide.

8. See above, chapter 2, for Beatrice as a *cosa nova*. In his edition, Petrocchi supports "novità nel senso di 'giovanile esperienza,' 'immatura passione,' o magari 'altra passione per donna giovine'" (*La Commedia secondo l'antica vulgata* 3:538). While these meanings are certainly legitimate, I think this passage provides a key example of the benefits of taking Dante's use of *novo* more literally, as in "nuovo e mai non fatto." *Purgatorio* 10's periphrasis for God as "Colui che mai non vide cosa nova" is also profoundly Augustinian, considering Augustine's struggle to "dismiss any idea of 'newness' in the will of God" (Paul Ricoeur, *Time and Narrative,* trans. Kathleen McLaughlin and David Pellauer [1983; Chicago: University of Chicago Press, 1984], 26).

9. "Some things are to be enjoyed, others to be used, and there are others which are to be enjoyed and used. Those things which are to be enjoyed make us blessed. Those things which are to be used help and, as it were, sustain us as we move toward blessedness" (*On Christian Doctrine* 1.3.3; trans. D. W. Robertson, Jr. [Indianapolis: Bobbs-Merrill, 19581, 9).

10. *Confessions* 10.31: "But the snare of concupiscence awaits me in the very process; of passing from the discomfort of hunger to the contentment which comes when it is satisfied" (trans. R. S. Pine-Coffin [London: Penguin, 1961]). The Latin is from the Loeb edition, 2 vols. (Cambridge: Harvard University Press; London: Heinemann, 1977).

11. Voyage imagery to describe the unfolding of the human soul is also found in *Purg.* 25; a human fetus is still in transit when a plant has already arrived: "questa è in via e quella è già a riva" (54).

12. Points of contact between authors frequently spell out their divergences as well, and it should be noted that Dante's beautiful image of the newborn soul as a little girl, "che piangendo e ridendo pargoleggia" (*Purg.* 16.87), expresses a relative innocence that is certainly not Augustinian. Indeed, the very passage in *Confessions* 1.19 cited above begins with a disclaimer of the innocence of childhood.

13. Giorgio Padoan brings together Augustine and Dante's Ulysses in "Ulisse 'fandi fictor' e le vie della sapienza," 1960, rpt. in *Il pio Enea, l'empio Ulisse* (Ravenna: Longo, 1977), 170–204; drawing attention to the medieval tradition whereby wandering at sea signifies the soul's inclination toward false goods, Padoan cites, among other texts, a passage from Augustine's *De beata vita* (181–84). John Freccero points to resemblances between Augustine's allegory of voyage and *Inf.* 26 in "The Prologue Scene," 1966, rpt. in *Dante: The Poetics of Conversion*, ed. Rachel Jacoff (Cambridge: Harvard University Press, 1986), esp. 20–23.

14. Robert Hollander's reading, which leads to the conclusion that "Ulysses was precisely such a sailor; Dante is so no longer," is representative of a prevalent approach toward this episode, whereby the siren and Ulysses are situated within the poem's moral allegory but the question of their local significance, of why Ulysses is invoked here, is never really posed. See *"Purgatorio* XIX: Dante's Siren/Harpy," in *Dante, Petrarch, Boccaccio: Studies in the Italian Trecento in Honor of Charles S. Singleton*, ed. Aldo S. Bernardo and Anthony L. Pellegrini (Binghamton, N.Y.: Medieval and Renaissance Texts and Studies, 1983), 77–88; quotation, 86.

15. Petrarch engages in a metaphorically expanded reading of the sins of concupiscence in his Augustinian *Secretum*, where he treats ambition and the desire for glory as forms of avarice.

16. Augustine does not conceive of erotic objects of desire as vehicles toward God, a fact that Petrarch (more attuned to the historical Augustine than Dante) dramatizes in the *Secretum*: the Augustinus figure consistently refutes Franciscus's courtly rationalizations of his love for Laura as a path toward virtue.

17. Dante's use of *falso* as qualifier for *piacer* recalls Augustine's invocation of God as "dulcedo non fallax, dulcedo felix et secura" in *Confessions* 2.1.

18. "It is knowledge that the Sirens offer, and it was no marvel if a lover of wisdom held this dearer than his home" (*De fin.* 5.18; trans. H. Rackham [Cambridge: Harvard University Press; London: William Heinemann, 1971]). The *De finibus* is brought to bear on Dante's sirens by Joseph Anthony Mazzeo, "The 'Sirens' of *Purgatorio* XXXI, 45," *Medieval Cultural Tradition in Dante's Comedy* (1960; rpt., New York: Greenwood Press, 1968), who shows that the two terms of Beatrice's rebuke (the sirens of 31.45 and the *pargoletta* of 31.59) stand "for the temptations of the mind as well as the temptations of the flesh" (209). For the literary and autobiographical implications of the *pargoletta* qua temptation of the flesh, see Sara Sturm-Maddox, "The Rime *Petrose* and the Purgatorial Palinode," *Studies in Philology* 84 (1987): 119–33.

19. The connection between the siren of *Purg.* 19 and Lady Philosophy is elaborated by Colin Hardie, "*Purgatorio* XIX: The Dream of the Siren," *Letture del "Purgatorio"*, ed. Vittorio Vettori (Milan: Marzorati, 1965), 217–19.

20. Among the threads that are tied is the one linking Dante's two key sins: *superbia* (the crucial sin in the private sphere) and *cupidigia* (the crucial sin in the public sphere) are both forms of *il trapassar del segno*. Hardie stipulates, I believe correctly, that the siren "should turn out to be complex and comprehensive": "She should personify the whole range of seven [sins], just as the sin of Adam can be shown to include elements of the whole gamut from superbia to luxuria" ("*Purgatorio* XIX," 236–37).

21. See *Convivio* 4.12, and note the adjective *nuovo*, always part of Dante 's discourse of desire: "Promettono le false traditrici sempre, in certo numero adunate, rendere lo raunatore pieno d'ogni appagamento; e con questa promissione conducono l'umana volontade in vizio d'avarizia.... Promettono le false traditrici, se bene si guarda, di torre ogni sete e ogni mancanza, e apportare ogni saziamento e bastanza; e questo fanno nel principio a ciascuno uomo, questa promissione in certa quantità di loro accrescimento affermando: e poi che quivi sono adunate, in loco di saziamento e di refrigerio danno e recano sete di casso febricante intollerabile; e in loco di bastanza recano *nuovo termine*, cioè maggiore quantitade a desiderio e, con questa, paura grande e sollicitudine sopra l'acquisto. Sì che veramente non quietano, ma più danno cura, la qual prima sanza loro non si avea" (4–5). Referring generically to "quanto la verace Scrittura divina chiama contra queste false meretrici" (8), Dante underlines the social ills caused by a desire that can never be satisfied, that is always new: "E che altro cotidianamente pericola e uccide le cittadi, le contrade, le singulari persone, tanto quanto lo nuovo raunamento d'avere appo alcuno? Lo quale raunamento *nuovi desiderii* discuopre, a lo fine de li quali sanza ingiuria d'alcuno venire non si può" (9).

22. The *Convivio*'s *avaro maladetto* also figures in the fourth strophe of the canzone "Doglia mi reca," where Dante writes of a miser who follows a "dolorosa strada," and to whom the pursuit of gain will bring no peace (note the Ulyssean cast to the lexicon, e.g., "folle volere"):

Corre l'avaro, ma più fugge pace:
oh mente cieca, che non pò vedere
lo suo folle volere
che 'l numero, ch'ognora a passar bada,
che 'nfinito vaneggia.

The miser is cursed for having desired what can only be desired in vain, for having hungered without finding satisfaction, for having accomplished nothing:

dimmi, che hai tu fatto,
cieco avaro disfatto?
Rispondimi, se puoi, altro che "Nulla."
Maledetta tua culla,
che lusingò cotanti sonni invano;
maladetto lo tuo perduto pane,
che non si perde al cane:
ché da sera e da mane
hai raunato e stretto ad ambo mano
ciò che sì tosto si rifá lontano.

For the importance of this canzone in forecasting the moral basis of the *Commedia*, see my "Dante and the Lyric Past," *Cambridge Companion to Dante*, ed. Rachel Jacoff (Cambridge: Cambridge University Press, 1993).

23. On *Convivio* 3.15's assessment of the desire for knowledge, in comparison to that of St. Thomas, see Bruno Nardi, *Dal "Convivio" alla "Commedia": Sei saggi danteschi* (Rome: Istituto Storico per il Medio Evo, 1960), 66–75. In *La felicità mentale* (Turin: Einaudi, 1983), Maria Corti makes too much of the alleged theological orthodoxy of the treatise's fourth book in comparison to its predecessors, basing herself in part on the issue of the desire for knowledge. The distance between *Convivio* and *Commedia* on this topic remains much more striking than the distance between *Convivio* 3 and *Convivio* 4.

24. "I call 'charity' the motion of the soul toward the enjoyment of God for His own sake, and the enjoyment of one's self and of ones neighbor for the sake of God; but 'cupidity' is a motion of the soul toward the enjoyment of ones self, one's neighbor, or any corporal thing for the sake of something other than God" (*On Christian Doctrine* 3.10.16).

25. Anthony K. Cassell makes the point that the "*lupa* suggests something including, yet more encompassing than, the fully realized sin of *avaritia* or *cupiditas* in its extreme manifestations: the wolf represents the temptation of the sins of incontinence or concupiscence in the broadest sense" (*"Inferno" 1*, Lectura Dantis Americana [Philadelphia: University of Pennsylvania Press, 1989], 68).

26. For this passage I have followed the edition of G. Busnelli and G. Vandelli (2d ed., rev. A.E. Quaglio, 2 vols. [Florence: Le Monnier, 1964]), in order to use

their bracketed emendation. In his edition Cesare Vasoli comments that "Busnelli e Vandelli aggiungono [*e poscia errato*], richiamandosi al testo della canzone ('cui è scorto il cammino e poscia l'erra'). Ma l'aggiunta non sembra indispensabile" (598).

27. Despite the fact that men take different paths ("ché l'uno tiene uno cammino e l'altro un altro"), there is only one true path: "Sì come dice l'Apostolo: 'Molti corrono al palio, ma uno è quelli che 'l prende,' così questi umani appetiti per diversi calli dal principio se ne vanno, e uno solo calle è quello che noi mena a la nostra pace" (*Conv.* 4.22.6).

28. The theme of "occhi gulosi" is recalled in the pilgrim's own *occhi vaghi* of *Purg.* 10 ("ch'a mirare eran contenti / per veder novitadi ond'e' son vaghi" [103–4]), which echo an earlier passage where his *mente* is similarly *vaga*, desirous of new sights: "la mente mia, che prima era ristretta, / lo 'ntento rallargò, sì come vaga" (*Purg.* 3.12–14).

29. This is Charles Singleton's position in *Journey to Beatrice* (1958; rpt., Baltimore: Johns Hopkins University Press, 1977), 141–203; he mentions Ulysses as one who may have seen the stars (147) but does not elaborate.

30. Backward motion is forced upon the false prophets of *Inf.* 20; likewise the proud Christians addressed by the poet in the apostrophe of *Purg.* 10 have faith in their "retrosi passi" (123). Like flight on the wings of desire, therefore, backward motion can be coded positively or negatively. This double coding is typical of *Purgatorio* (where the poet frequently assigns a positive valence to what had seemed like an exclusively negative code): in the verses cited above, for instance, the "perduta strada" is in fact positive, the road that the traveler has lost and hopes to find, and partakes only contrastively of the negative "perduto" of *Inf.* 26.84.

31. The similes of *Purg.* 26.67–69 and *Par.* 31.31–36 are based on the same contrast between "humble" countryside and "expert" *urbs*.

32. The pilgrim's status as a legitimate non-Ulyssean *cosa nova* is underscored in the next canto by Guido del Duca, for whom the grace accorded to Dante is a "cosa che non fu più mai" (14.15).

33. Dante uses a periphrasis for the sun's path to introduce Phaeton into the discourse, referring to "la strada / che mal non seppe carreggiar Fetòn" (*Purg.* 4.71–72).

34. The simoniac pope Nicholas III uses similar textual language when he expresses his wonder at the presumed early arrival of Boniface in hell: "Di parecchi anni mi mentì lo scritto" (*Inf* 19.54).

35. The entries "presumere," "presuntuoso," "presunzione" in the *ED* by Francesco Vagni speak, correctly, of "una temerarietà di ordine intellettuale" but fail to elaborate in terms of Dante's longstanding concern with this problematic. In a *quaestio* entitled "De praesumptione," *ST* 2a2ae.21 (Blackfriars 1966, ed. and

trans. W.J. Hill), Aquinas comments that presumption "occurs by turning towards God in ways that are inordinate, much as despair takes place by turning away from God" (33:103), and that the sinner suffers from a lack of moderation, "hoping to obtain pardon without repentance or glory without merits" (105). Noting the fine line between genuine hope and presumption ("'Presumption' is sometimes used to describe what really is hope, because genuine hope in God when looked at from the vantage point of the human situation almost seems like presumption" [107–9]), Aquinas concludes by making the connection between presumption and pride: "presumption appears to spring directly from pride; implying, in effect, that one thinks so much of himself that he imagines God will not punish him nor exclude him from eternal life in spite of his continuing in sin" (113). Augustine offers a Ulyssean description of presumption in the *Confessions*, commenting on "the difference between presumption and confession, between those who see the goal that they must reach, but cannot see the road by which they are to reach it, and those who see the road to that blessed country which is meant to be no mere vision but our home" (7.20).

36. In "Dante's Biblical Linguistics," *Lectura Dantis: A Forum for Dante Research and Interpretation* 5 (1989): 105–43, Zygmunt G. Baranski notes that Dante rewrites Genesis in proposing that Eve was the first to speak and suggests that "the reference to Eve as the first speaker is a smokescreen ... a pseudo-problem introduced to give a veneer of logical legitimation and the appearance of a valid philosophical *quaestio* to the ensuing discussion" (118). I would suggest, rather, that Eve is introduced as the epitome of *praesumptuositas*, Dante's overriding concern at this point in the treatise; indeed, for whom else could he so legitimately employ the redolent superlative, *presumptuosissima Eva*? I would add, moreover, that the issue of female speech is an obsessive one with Dante, who will end up reversing the silence of the lyric lady and the mis-speech of Eve with that most loquacious of literary ladies, the *Beatrix loquax* of *Paradiso*. Once more Dante's path is anomalous: the traditions he inherits boast female abstractions like Boethius's *Filosofia* who speak authoritatively, in a voice that is coded as non-gender-specific, i.e., masculine, and female nonabstractions who either do not speak or speak within the province of the gender-specific. In Beatrice Dante creates a historicized object of desire—not a personification—who yet speaks, indeed, in the *Paradiso*, speaks "like a man," unconstrained by the content or modality normatively assigned to female speech. In this ability to at least imaginatively reconcile the woman as a sexual and simultaneously intellectual presence, Dante was not followed by the humanists, who, in the accounts of recent feminist scholarship, were not particularly generous to their female counterparts, according them a voice only at the price of their sexuality.

37. The *De vulgari eloquentia* stresses Nimrod's failure to respect the mimetic hierarchy, whereby human "art" follows nature, which in turn follows God (*Inf.* 11.99–105). Rather than be content with the position of human art at the bottom

of the hierarchy, Nimrod seeks to make it surpass not only nature, but also God, thus lifting it to the top of the ladder.

38. See chapter 3, note 13 for this grouping. Joan M. Ferrante, in "A Poetics of Chaos and Harmony," *Cambridge Companion to Dante*, points out that *arte* is the most used noun "core rhyme" in the *Commedia* (core rhymes are "rhyme groups in which one of the rhyme words is contained within the other two as if it were their core"); suggestively enough, the last appearance of *arte* in the poem shortly follows the last reference to Phaeton in *Par.* 31.125. Also suggestive, from the point of view of Dante's "Ulyssean" art, is the fact that, according to Ferrante's data, the second most present noun core rhyme word is *ali*.

39. The adjective appears once, with reference to Provenzan Salvani, who was "presuntüoso / a recar Siena tutta a le sue mani" (*Purg.* 11.122–23), in a context redolent of poetic pride.

40. With respect to the false prophets, and Dante's perception of the fundamental similarity between their calling and his own, leading to the defensiveness that therefore dictates his handling of them, see my "True and False See-ers in *Inferno XX*," *Lectura Dantis: A Forum for Dante Research and Interpretation* 4 (1989): 42–54.

41. "Post hec veniamus ad Tuscos, qui propter amentiam suam infroniti titulum sibi vulgaris illustris arrogare videntur. Et in hoc non solum plebeia dementat intentio" (1.13.1).

42. Guittone d'Arezzo, because of the religious pretensions of his postconversion poetry became, for Dante, the example par excellence of the poet who goes beyond his limits, who "fishes for the truth and has not the art" (*Par.* 13.123); for Dante's views of Guittone, see *Dante's Poets*, 85–123.

43. "E oh stoltissime e vilissime bestiuole che a giusa d'uomo voi pascete, the presummete contra nostra fede parlare e volete sapere, filando e zappando, ciò che Iddio, the tanta provedenza hae ordinata! Maladetti siate voi, e la vostra presunzione, e chi a voi crede!" (*Conv.* 4.5.9). In the *Questio de aqua et terra* as well, Dante writes that certain questions "proceed either from much foolishness or from much presumption, because they are above our intellect" ("vel a multa stultitia vel a multa presumptione procedunt, propterea quod sunt supra intellectum nostrum" [75]), and that we must desist from trying to understand the things that are above us, and search only as far as we are able: "Desinant ergo, desinant homines querere que supra eos sunt, et querant usque quo possunt" (77). Also in the *Questio* Dante defines the habitable earth as extending from Cadiz, on the western boundaries marked by Hercules, to the Ganges ("a Gadibus, que supra terminos occidentales ab Hercule positos ponitur, usque ad hostia fluminis Ganges" [54]), thus evoking Ulysses both through the Herculean interdict of *Inf.* 26 and the mad flight beyond Cadiz of *Par.* 27. In the *Epistole*, the Florentines are cast as mad and presumptuous transgressors (Dante uses the

very word "transgredientes" for those "who transgress divine and human laws" [*Ep.* 6.5]), puffing themselves up in their arrogant rebellion ("presumendo tumescunt" [*Ep.* 6.4 and passim]); by contrast, the poet is endowed with a prophetic mind that does not err ("si presaga mens mea non fallitur" [*Ep.* 6.17]).

44. Other examples of this authorial concern are the passage in which Dante argues that it would be presumptuous to discuss ("presuntuoso sarebbe a ragionare") the limit that God put on our imaginations (*Conv.* 3.4.10), as it is also presumptuous to attempt to speak of Cato ("O sacratissimo petto di Catone, chi presummerà di to parlare?" [*Conv.* 4.5.16]). On questions of authority in the *Convivio*, see Albert Russell Ascoli, "The Vowels of Authority (Dante's *Convivio* IV.vi.3–4)," in *Discourses of Authority in Medieval and Renaissance Literature*, ed. Kevin Brownlee and Walter Stephens (Hanover, N.H.: University Press of New England, 1989), 23–46.

45. Sapegno's comment on "prescrisser" ("imposero un freno alla mia voglia di sapere") clarifies the passage's Ulyssean component, as does the consonance between "a tanto segno più mover li piedi" (*Par.* 21.99) and "il trapassar del segno." Daniello's gloss situates the *segno* toward which we are not to move within the context of the *trapassar del segno*: "*Prescrivere* propriamente significa assegnar termine ad alcuna cosa, il quale da essa non si possa trapassare" (quoted by Sapegno, *La Divina Commedia*, 3 vols. [Florence: La Nuova Italia, 1968], 3:267).

46. Dante frequently registers a high level of defensive anxiety in the vicinity of his critiques of the Church. Thus, in the Epistle to the Italian cardinals we find him defending himself from the charge of being infected with the presumption of Uzzah ("Oze presumptio" [*Ep.* 11.12]). For further discussion of Uzzah, see chapter 6.

47. Giuseppe Mazzotta notes the importance of the digression, reading it however as an index not of transgression but of alienation, as a sign that "a rupture exists between history and the text" (Dante, *Poet of the Desert* [Princeton, N.J.: Princeton University Press, 1979], 136).

48. Mark Musa notes that "the interruption that is part of the narrative (when Sordello prevents Virgil from finishing his sentence) is followed by an interruption of the narrative itself" and that Dante "has interpolated between the first and second stages of Sordello's embrace the longest auctorial intervention in the whole of the *Divine Comedy*, interrupting narrative time with auctorial time" (*Advent at the Gates: Dante's "Comedy"* [Bloomington: Indiana University Press, 1974], 97–98).

49. Marie is warned lest she find herself, after her death, in a worse flock than the one to which her treachery consigned Pierre de la Brosse; the brief "digression" is occasioned by the sight of Pierre among the group of souls who died violent deaths: "Pier da la Broccia dico; e qui proveggia, / mentr'è di qua, la donna di Brabante, / sì che però non sia di peggior greggia" (*Purg.* 6.22–24).

50. Both questions will be reprised in the heaven of justice, a heaven whose subtext is, to a great degree, the justice of Vergil's own damnation. See *Par.* 20.94–99, where the eagle will articulate the paradox of the dialectic between God's love and God's justice, already touched upon by Vergil in *Purg.* 6.

51. Sergio Corsi, "Per uno studio del 'modus digressivus,'" *Studi di italianistica: In onore di Giovanni Cecchetti*, ed. P. Cherchi and M. Picone (Ravenna: Longo, 1988), 75–89, argues that Dante conceived of the *modus digressivus* according to the wider canons of classical and medieval rhetoric (as encompassing formal shifts, like similes or descriptions of place and time), rather than in the more limited modern sense of major shifts in content. By contrast to the *Commedia*, the term digressione appears with some frequency in the *Convivio* (see the *ED* entry by Fernando Salsano). For Dante's self-conscious use of metaphors of departing and returning with respect to the voyage of discourse, see chapter 2, note 1.

52. The anaphoric "Vieni a veder" (in lines 106, 112, 115; repeated four times if we count "Vien, crudel, vieni, e vedi la pressura" in 109) derives from the Apocalypse, where it is also repeated four times: "Veni, et vide" is the command that each of the four beasts issues to St. John (Apoc. 6:1, 3, 5, 7). Dante's presentation of himself as a prophetic truth-teller thus gains from an implicit alignment of his text with the Book of Revelation; in fact, since Dante is the speaker, the analogy is between him and the four beasts on the one hand and between the negligent emperor and John as visionary witness on the other. More often, as we shall see in chapter 7, Dante is content to align himself with the author of the Apocalypse, whose four beasts figure prominently in the procession of the earthly paradise.

53. See Peter Armour, *The Door of Purgatory: A Study of Multiple Symbolism in Dante's "Purgatorio"* (Oxford: Clarendon, 1983), who points out that, because the episode of *Purg.* 9 "involves symbols and not personalities, [it] is one of the purest examples of polysemy in the *Comedy* and as such is one of the simplest episodes technically, if not conceptually" (144). One could propose an additional metapoetic polysemy with respect to the three steps leading up to purgatory's gate: each step could be taken to represent one of the *Commedia*'s canticles, associating *Inferno* with the self-knowledge of the mirroring step, *Purgatorio* with the penitential suffering of the cracked and burned step, and *Paradiso* with Christ's redemptive blood and flaming passion as reflected in the third step. This reading, whereby the poet has inscribed a reference to his poem into the canto's figural symbolism, would further support Armour's case for the importance of this passage vis-à-vis the *Commedia* as a whole.

GIUSEPPE MAZZOTTA

Imagination and Knowledge
(Purgatorio XVII–XVIII)

In *Purgatorio* XVII the pilgrim is passing through the circle of wrath, and we are told that because of the hour of the day (it is dusk) and because the terrace is covered by a cloud of black smoke—an overt literalization of the biblical cloud of wrath—his physical vision is blurred. The difficulties the pilgrim experiences in seeing are presented in the opening lines of the canto in an address to the reader:

> Ricordati, lettor, se mai ne l'alpe
> ti colse nebbia per la qual vedessi
> non altrimenti che per pelle talpe,
> come, quando i vapor umidi e spessi
> a diradar cominciansi, la spera
> del sol debilmente entra per essi;
> e fia la tua imagine leggera
> in giugner a veder com'io rividi
> lo sole in pria che già nel corcar era.
>
> *(Purg.* XII, 1–9)

(Recall, reader, if ever in the mountains a mist has caught you, through which you could not see except as moles do through the skin, how when the moist dense vapors begin to dissipate, the sphere

From *Dante's Vision and the Circle of Knowledge.* © 1993 by Princeton University Press.

of the sun enters feebly through them, and your imagination will quickly come to see how, at first, I saw the sun again, which was now at its setting.)

The address is marked by a series of metaphorical symmetries. The image of the Alpine heights, which, ever since St. Augustine, have been conceived of as a spot of possible vision, is reversed into the picture of the mole burrowing into the depths of the earth. The heavy solidity of the natural world bends into the immateriality of mist and sky, just as the mist and dying light of day are countered by the appeal to the reader's memory. For memory, as the traditional iconographic motif has it, is the *oculus imaginationis*, the eye of inner vision cutting through the shadows and airy shapes of this twilight landscape.[1] This inner eye of vision is, in turn, counteracted by a discrete double figuration of blindness. One is the blindness of a mole, "the blind laborious moles," in the language of Vergil (*Georgics* I, 183), which "dig out chambers" underground (*sub terris*). The other is the allusion to the eye blinded by wrath. This blindness, which finds its authoritative text in Psalm 30, "conturbatus est in ira oculus meus," extends a number of direct references to the perplexed and impaired sight of the sinners in the preceding cantos of *Purgatorio*, and it also characterizes the moral substance of this ledge where the sin of wrath is purged. Even the initial address to the reader, which signals the will to a bond between the reader's ordinary perception of daily life and the lonely experience of the pilgrim, is balanced by another apostrophe. As soon as the poet has evoked the misty scene, he appeals to the imagination, the "imaginativa" (13), as the visionary faculty which leads the mind astray from the perception of the material world:

> O imaginativa che ne rube
> talvolta sì di fuor, ch'om non s'accorge
> perchè d'intorno suonin mille tube,
> chi move te, se 'l senso non ti porge?
> Moveti lume che nel ciel s'informa,
> per sé o per voler che giú lo scorge.

(13–18)

(O imagination, that do sometime so snatch us from outward things that we give no heed, though a thousand trumpets sound around us, who moves you if the sense affords you naught? A light moves you which takes form in heaven, of itself, or by a will that downwards guides you.)

This elaborate set of figurative symmetries, parallels, and antitheses conveys a sense of impasse in which Dante as a poet is caught. The formal polarities of the passage, which aim at picturing the landscape within which the pilgrim finds himself, in fact, arrest the narrative flow. But it is also the pilgrim who is at a standstill here: "Noi eravam dove più non saliva / la scala sù, ed eravamo affissi, / pur come nave ch'a la piaggia arriva.... Se i piè si stanno, non stea tuo sermone" (*Purg*. XVII, 76–84) (We stood where the stair went no higher and were stopped there, even as a ship that arrives at the shore.... If our feet are stayed, do not stay your speech). The pilgrim's deadlock, however, is only provisional, for, in dramatic terms, the apostrophe to the power of the imagination introduces a series of three images of punished wrath that appear in the mind, which is said to be restrained within itself.

From a formal viewpoint, the downward movement of the imagination from a light above—the word deployed is "giù" (downward)—harks back, one might add, to the figure of the setting sun, its rays already dead on the low shores, and of the mole underground. But it also reverses the upward movement suggested by the picture of mountain climbing at the exordium of the canto. More substantively, the imagination discloses, first, the image of Procne avenging the violation of Philomela by Tereus (19–21); second, that of Haman, who was hanged on the gallows he had prepared for Mordecai (25–30); and, finally, the image of Amata, who flew into a fit of grief and rage on hearing the news of Turnus's death, and hanged herself (33–39). The three images quickly fade out as soon as the pilgrim's face is struck by the light, the way, to paraphrase the text, sleep is broken when light strikes closed eyes (40–45).

I shall have occasion in the next chapter to muse again on the metaphor of sleep as the state that prepares and allows visionary experiences. I shall stress here, where the narrative focuses on the abrupt interruption of sleep, that sleep designates the mind's state of passivity, and that the simile the poet deploys for the pilgrim's sudden vision underscores the fact that the images he perceives are not mere objects of ordinary experience, which Dante mimetically duplicates or evokes, nor are they figures of his rational will. The mind is acquiescent and nonresistant as it surrenders to the imperious powers of the "imaginativa." In the opening lines of the canto the pilgrim's gaze hovers over the materiality of a landscape which is at the edge of becoming invisible. Now the "imaginativa" has no contact either with the reality of sense experience or with the claims of the will, and it triggers an inner vision which has the effect of swiftly seizing the mind away from the outside reality.

The power of the mind's self-absorption and removal from the surrounding contingencies and sensory impressions, because of its complete bondage to one of the senses, has been highlighted a few cantos earlier in *Purgatorio* IV (1–18). The pilgrim, who has just met Manfred and has been absorbed by the marvel of this encounter, has not noticed the passage of time. The experience prompts Dante to ponder (and this is the brunt of his meditation at the opening of canto IV) the question of the unity of the three powers of the soul—vegetative, sensitive, and rational—which are all involved when a faculty receives pain or pleasure. The view reflects Aristotle's ideas from his *De anima*, and it also echoes Dante's explication of *De anima* in *Convivio*.[2] But the only time that the "imaginativa" is invested with the attribute of autonomy from the world of the senses occurs in *Purgatorio* XVII, a strategic point if there ever was any, for this is the central canto of the *Divine Comedy*.

Traditionally, scholarly glosses on the passage point out that the "imaginativa" renders the *vis imaginativa* or *phantasia*, the imagination as the passive or receptive faculty of the mind.[3] More recently the apostrophe has been taken to be the basis, along with other features of the purgatorial canticle, such as dreams and art images, for a description of Dante's mode of vision. The dramatic articulation of *Inferno* takes place through a *visio corporalis*; *Paradiso*'s through a *visio intellectualis*; *Purgatorio*'s through a *visio spiritualis*, a vision, that is, achieved through sensible forms and images.[4] But these glosses do not begin to account for Dante's central claim for the power of the imagination, nor do they address the complex set of interrelated problems which hinge around the issue of the imagination. These are problems of moral knowledge which Dante develops from canto XVI to XVIII of *Purgatorio*, and I will give a quick synopsis of them.

Purgatorio XVI focuses on the question of free will ("libero arbitrio," 70–72). To the pilgrim's query about the cause of iniquity in the world, whether it is to be sought in the stars or in man (58–63), Marco Lombardo responds by upholding the principle of moral responsibility. The thesis of astral influence on man's will is clearly incompatible with the tenet of the freedom of the will resolutely affirmed by Christian doctrine, and Bishop Tempier condemned in 1277 the proposition that "voluntas nostra subiacet" to the power of celestial bodies (art. 154; cf. also art. 156).[5] The belief in astral determinism has been associated by Giles of Rome with Alkindi and, more generally, with Averroes, while Siger of Brabant and Aquinas believed, as Dante did, in the indirect influence of the stars on the will.[6] Accordingly, Marco Lombardo asserts that man is given an inner light of choice between good and evil, and thus he dismisses the belief in material determinism and in the direct influence of the stars on the actions of men. If the heavens were to move all things by necessity, Marco Lombardo explains, then free will would be destroyed and there would be no justice in happiness for good nor grief for evil. By a powerful ludic image to which I shall return in chapter 11, the soul at its creation is said to be like a child that sports and goes astray if its inclinations are not guided or curbed.

By a paradoxical formulation human beings, then, are free subjects ("liberi soggiacete") (80). From this paradoxical premise of a necessary combination of freedom and restraint, which defines the essence of laws, Marco Lombardo consistently moves on to evoke the crisis of the law. By the logic of the exposition laws are identified as moral principles binding each individual's moral autonomy to the stability and order of the general body politic. But because the laws are neither enforced nor observed, the unity of the polity is mutilated; the two "suns" of Rome (106)—the two institutions ordained by God, church, and state—have eclipsed each other, that is, have confused the spheres of their respective operations (127–29) and have left the world blind. As is common with the *Divine Comedy*, general moral concerns—figured, as they are, through the same metaphorical language of curbs, blindness, and so on—are transposed into the historical and political realm, which is the locus where abstract propositions are tested. More than that, Marco's historical awareness makes the questions of free will and imagination not just issues of individual psychology and morality but also central concerns of history.[7]

In *Purgatorio* XVII, after the apostrophe to the imagination, Vergil expounds the theory of love shaping the moral order of *Purgatorio*. The problem of free will figures prominently in his discourse. Love, which is the principle and seed of every action, is said to be either instinctive or elective. Whereas instinctive love, the natural impulse that binds all creatures, never errs, the love of choice entails the possibility of moral error. One sins because of excessive or defective attachment to the objects one chooses to love or because one chooses the wrong object. Vergil's exposition triggers new perplexities in the pilgrim: How do we know, in effect he asks, what to love? Or, to put it in the terms of the philosophical debate between voluntarists and rationalists in the thirteenth century, what is the relationship between desire and knowledge? Must one love so that one may know, or must one first know an object in order that one may then love it? To answer this question Dante etches in *Purgatorio* XVIII what amounts to a theory of knowledge whose foundation lies in the imagination.

The mind, Vergil says, quick to love, naturally seeks happiness and is drawn to those objects that promise it. The mechanism of the mind in love starts off when the faculty of perception takes from the material world of objects an image and unfurls it within, so that the mind inclines to it. This inclination is love. In the words of the poem, "Vostra apprensiva da esser verace / tragge intenzione, e dentro a voi la spiega, / sì che l'animo ad essa volger face; / e se, rivolto, inver' di lei si piega, / quel piegare è amor, quell'è natura / che per piacer di novo in voi si lega" (*Purg.* XVIII, 22–27) (Your perception takes from outward reality an impression and unfolds it within you, so that it makes the mind turn to it; and if the mind, so turned, inclines to it, that inclination is love, that is nature, which by pleasure is bound on you afresh).

The mind, then, perceives particular objects through the "intenzione," a term which has the force of a cliché: it alludes to the "intentiones imaginatae," an object of thought in Aristotle's *De anima* and its Scholastic commentaries.[8] On the face of it, Dante's definition of the process of knowledge can be brought within the parameters of St. Thomas's theories. "Nihil est in intellectu quod non sit prius in sensu"—the intellect knows nothing except by receiving sense impressions, Aquinas says in the *De veritate*, and he adds that the intellect reaches understanding only through the mediation of the materiality of the imagination. Aquinas's phrase, may I add, which is of Aristotelian origin (*De anima* 432a, 7–8) occurs also in a variety of Dante's texts.[9]

This view of the role the imagination plays in the production of knowledge in no way disrupts man's moral sense; the imagination, actually, is the ground on which the possibility of conceptualization as well as the exercise of moral judgment rest. Such a formulation, which is Dante's, ushers in a logically consistent query by the pilgrim: If love is an inclination toward an object of pleasure, a ceaseless movement of desire which acquiesces only when "la cosa amata il fa gioire" (33) (the thing loved makes it rejoice)—a phrase which is the reversal of Cavalcanti's love anguish—how can man judge and determine what is good or bad love? The predicament is self-apparent, since love is kindled in us by the perception of an outside reality and is offered to the intellect by the workings of the imagination. The argument circles back to *Purgatorio* XVI and centers on the principle of free will, which Dante now calls both "innata libertate" (*Purg.* XVIII, 68) (innate freedom) and "libero arbitrio" (*Purg.* XVIII, 73–75), freewill, the faculty that counsels and holds the threshold of assent.

So obsessive is Dante with questions of moral choices and their consequences throughout the *Divine Comedy* that this insistence on free will cannot come as a complete surprise. As is known, "liberum arbitrium" is acknowledged to be the substance of the whole poem in the *Epistle to Cangrande*: "Si vero accipiatur opus allegorice, subiectum est homo prout merendo et demerendo per arbitrii libertatem iustitie premiandi et puniendi obnoxius est" (par. 11) (If the work is taken allegorically, the subject is man according as by his merits or demerits in the exercise of his free will he is deserving of reward or punishment by justice).[10] The assertion of free will in *Purgatorio* XVIII marks primarily the dismissal of the blindness of those people (34–39), the Epicureans one infers, who hold every love praiseworthy in itself because its matter appears to be always good. This charge against the Epicureans, against whom Dante articulates his conviction that man has the power to exercise intellect and will, cognition and desire, the conjunction of which is "libero arbitrio," rehashes Cicero's critique in *De finibus* (I and II). More precisely, the Epicurean claim about the sameness of all loves is for Dante "blind": it is a delusory figment of the mind, a style of thought which effaces all distinctions of value and the possibility of moral choice.[11] But as the centrality of moral choice is unquestionably vindicated, the origin of the two faculties of the intellective soul, intellect and will, remains unknown, just as always unknown in the *Divine Comedy* are the first causes: "Però, là onde vegna lo 'ntelletto / de le prime notizie, omo non sape / e de' primi appetibili l'affetto" (55–57) (Therefore whence comes the knowledge of first ideas and the bent to the primary objects of desire, no man knows).

I have been referring to "liberum arbitrium" as an intellectual operation involving the power of both judgment and choice (free will), and as an operation of the will. The two terms are not interchangeable. The decision to adopt either entails a prior decision as to whether freedom is an act of rational knowledge or an act of the will. In *Monarchia*, in the wake of Boethius, Dante refers to "liberum arbitrium" as "de voluntate iudicium."[12] The definition means that free will is the free judgment about the will, or, to state it clearly, free will does not reside in the will, as the Franciscans believe; rather, it resides in the intellect, which can make determinations about what one wills. Such an understanding of the intellect's primacy over the will means the will's servitude to reason. In the light of this text from *Monarchia*, historians of philosophy have argued that Dante, against Duns Scotus, sides with the Averroists in holding that the *liberum arbitrium* is the "free judgement of reason, unimpeded by the appetites, about actions to be undertaken."[13] More than that, on the basis of this very passage in *Monarchia*, Nardi has argued that Dante doubts the existence of free will in *Paradiso* IV, the canto where, as has been shown in chapter 4, the pilgrim is caught in a provisional impasse and his will is inert in making judgments.

Nardi's suggestion depends on his espousal of the Augustinian theologians who asserted the primacy of the will in the act of knowledge. From their perspective St. Thomas Aquinas's own orthodoxy was questioned, and, along with Averroes' theses, he was condemned in 1277 (art. 157, 158, 159).[14] Aquinas had no doubts that "choice is an act of the will and not of reason; for choice is accomplished in a certain movement of the soul toward the good which is chosen. Hence it is clearly an act of the appetitive power."[15] He even wrote that it is the will that moves the intellect, since the will's aim is action. But he also believed that will and reason are always interacting, that election is a desire proceeding from counsel, and that the intellect provides deliberation and judgment about the objects of the will. Such a moderate rationalism made him vulnerable to charges of heresy by the voluntarists.[16]

In his formulation of how the mind comes to know and judge its desires, Dante largely follows, as I have said before, Aquinas. Like Aquinas he is rigorously empirical in the conviction that all knowledge derives from the materiality of sense experience and that objects produce images in the mind. For all its apparent flatness, however, the statement that the imagination follows empirical perception and is contained within and subdued to the sovereign authority of reason is a radical reversal of a number of positions Dante previously staked.

It is, quite clearly, a reversal of the "imaginativa," the faculty that in *Purgatorio* XVII is said to have no bondage to the realm of nature and has the trait of an illumination coming from above. It also alters the concerns of the *Vita nuova*, a narrative which starts off under the aegis of memory, seeks to recapture its sensuous signs, probes the opaque folds of the mind, and is punctuated by hallucinations, dreams, ghostly appearances, and seizures. These fits constitute the dramatic counterpart of memory's effort to resurrect the past, for they lie outside of the will, and, however refractory they may appear to be to reason's decipherment, they are objects of the poet's sustained rational inquiry. More generally, by recalling the Thomistic perspective that the intellect cannot reach understanding without the mediation of phantasms and images, Dante focuses on the issue which is crucial to him as a poet: the value of the representations of the imagination—a question which is the pivot of the debate between St. Thomas and Siger of Brabant.

The text which is central to this discussion is the *De unitate intellectus contra Averroistas*, a polemical tract St. Thomas wrote during his second stay in Paris, where he was teaching as a master (1268–72). Though it is not clear whether St. Thomas was opposing Siger of Brabant—who, as we have seen in the preceding chapter, was the leader of the so-called radical Aristotelians in Paris—or some other prominent figure of Siger's philosophical school, the burden of the treatise is to refute two views which Averroes put forth in his commentary on Aristotle's *De anima*. One is the view of the possible intellect as an incorruptible and separate substance. The other is the view of the possible intellect as one for all men. This is to say that the intellect is not a substantial form of the body and, thus, cannot be thought of as an individualized entity. The logical consequence of this doctrine is the denial of personal immortality, for only the one, general intellect survives death. It also denies the existence of a free will, since the act of judgment is a rational operation entailing the conjunction of will and reason. As I have indicated earlier in this chapter, these inferences were drawn, along with other propositions, by Bishop Tempier in the condemnations of 1277.[17]

Aquinas's quarrel with the Averroists springs from a variety of concerns. He objects to the view that the intellect is a simple and incorporeal substance, whose function is to grasp universal and not concrete entities. From Aquinas's perspective, Averroes' theory of separateness, in short, precludes the possibility of individualized knowledge, or, to put it differently, Averroes makes man the object of the intellect's knowledge and not the subject of knowledge. It also precludes the possibility of moral life. More important, the positing of the unity of the possible intellect appears to Aquinas as patently absurd, because it does not account for diversity of opinions, rational disagreements, and, generally, the fragmentation and subjectivity of knowledge. Were the possible intellect one, it would then follow that there must be one common act of understanding and of willing and, paradoxically, free choice would be the same for all. "If, therefore, there is one intellect for all," Aquinas writes, "it follows of necessity that there be one who understands and consequently one who wills and one who uses according to the choice of his will all those things by which men are diverse from one another. And from this it further follows that there would be no difference among men in respect to the free choice of the will, but it (the choice) would be the same for all, if the intellect in which alone would reside pre-eminence and dominion over the use of all other (powers) is one and undivided in all. This is clearly false and impossible. For it is opposed to what is evident and destroys the whole of moral science and everything which relates to the civil intercourse which is natural to man, as Aristotle says."[18]

In response to Aquinas's critique, Siger of Brabant insists that epistemological differences between men are to be attributed not to the intellect but to the diverse and contradictory experiences men have of phantasms, to the "intentiones imaginatae," which mediate between the separate intellect and the diverse individual acts of knowledge: "It is by these phantasms that the knowledge of this man and the knowledge of that man are diverse, in so far as this man understands those things of which he has phantasms, and that man understands other things of which he has phantasms." Aquinas quotes these lines of Averroes and challenges their validity. For him "the phantasms are preparations for the action of the intellect, as colors are for the act of sight. Therefore the act of the intellect would not be diversified by their diversity in respect to one intelligible.... But in two men who know and understand the same thing, the intellectual operation itself can in no way be diversified by the diversity of the phantasms."[19] The source of the Averroists' problem lies in their failure, finally, to distinguish between the things that are outside of the mind and their phantasms.

It is clear that such a debate shapes Dante's theory of knowledge and moral choices in *Purgatorio* XVIII, where he underwrites sundry notions about the imagination. The first is that the imagination, which is the property of the sensitive soul, is neither corporeal nor incorporeal but shares in corporeality and incorporeality. The second is that the imagination by itself neither inquires nor knows if the shadows of objects it apprehends are true or false. It is the office of the understanding to know and judge their truth or falsehood. But it is also clear that for all their ideological divergences, Dante unveils the fact that Averroes, Siger of Brabant, and Aquinas actually agree that the imagination is the central path to knowledge. Yet they circumscribe the powers of the imagination within the perimeter of reason. Their insight into the imagination, which speculative philosophers and theologians share but from which they turn away, forces Dante, who always installs himself imperiously at the center of the most complex intellectual debates of the thirteenth century, to reflect on the value and threatening powers of the imagination. Lest this be seen as an idealistic claim about the privilege and uniqueness of poetry over the mode of knowledge made available by the discourses of theology and philosophy, let me stress that each of these theoretical discourses reveals particular aspects of and has access to the imagination. Dante's poetry does not bracket or elide these particular viewpoints; rather, it is the all-embracing framework within which theological and philosophical discoveries about the imagination are grounded and are given a concrete focus. By themselves, neither theologians nor philosophers are especially equipped to make pronouncements about the imagination, which is the province of aesthetics, the path of knowledge, and the home, as it were (and the import of the metaphor will be evident later), of the poet.

The claim is not unwarranted for the *Vita nuova*, which, moving around the double focus of love and intellect, delves into the seemingly limitless horizon of the imagination as well as the effort of binding it. It is a story of nightmares, apparitions, rapid alterations of the mind, deliriums—all shapes and seductive images that turn out to be erratic, but to which the poet-lover succumbs—and these together are the *terra incognita* of love and poetry themselves. The text is also organized around what the poet calls "ragioni," prose chapters which attempt to grasp rationally the sense of the ghostly landscape his poems obsessively conjure up.[20] The prescriptions of reason are steadily observed throughout the narrative as a way of making both poetry and the lover's experiences, which are beyond ordinary paradigms, intelligible. But the lyrical essence remains elusive, as images are neither memories nor thoughts, and the world is the theater of solitary fantasies in which matter vanishes, in which bodies are astral bodies and dazzling emanations of light. Written as a visionary account of love for Beatrice, the *Vita nuova* is directed to Guido Cavalcanti, whose poem "Donna me prega" casts love as a tragic circle under the cloud of unknowing.[21] Deploying Averroistic and scientific-medical materials, Guido conceives of love as a child not of Venus but of Mars, as a violent experience which vanquishes the mind. The mind, in turn, separated from the shadows of desire, understands only the abstract essence of love which has been purified of all individualized concreteness (figures, colors, shapes).

As I have argued earlier, the *Vita nuova* takes to task Guido's literalization of the spirits as material substances and asserts, on the contrary, the visionary power of the imagination. By the end of the work memory, which is an interrogation of the past, is reversed into an expectation of the future. The reversal of memory takes place in the light of the vision of Beatrice sitting in glory that the lover has at the end of the narrative. One sense of this "libello" is available from a sonnet Dante wrote to Cino da Pistoia which can be understood as a recapitulation of the dramatic experience related in the *Vita nuova*: "Io sono stato con Amore insieme / da la circulazion del sol mia nona, / e so com'egli affrena e come sprona, / e come sotto lui si ride e geme. / Chi ragione o virtù contro gli sprieme, / fa come que' che 'n la tempesta sona, / credendo far colà dove si tona, / esse le guerre de' vapori sceme. / Però nel cerchio de la sua palestra / libero arbitrio già mai non fu franco, /sì che consiglio invan vi si balestra. / Ben può con nuovi spon' punger lo fianco, / e qual che sia 'l piacer ch'ora n'addestra, / seguitar si convien, se l'altro è stanco" (I have been together with love since my ninth circulation of the sun and I know how love spurs and bridles, and how under his sway one laughs and wails. He who urges reason or virtue against him, he acts like one who raises his voice in a storm, thinking to lessen the conflict of the clouds, there where the thunder rolls. Thus within his arena's bounds free will was never free, so that counsel loses its shafts in vain there. Love can indeed prick the flank with new spurs; and whatever the attraction that is now leading us, follow we must, if the other is outworn).

If in this sonnet moral knowledge and free will are shown to be overwhelmed by love's passion, and in the *Vita nuova* the imagination of love is its incandescent core, in *Purgatorio* XVII and XVIII Dante centers on the moral value of love. The vibrations of the heart, every virtue, every good action and sin are reduced to love, the substantial and formal principle joining together heart and mind, sensitive and rational souls, in an intuition of the good. In strictly Thomistic terms Dante's doctrine holds that the natural appetite tends to a good existing in a thing, and the will tends to what is apprehended as good, for evil is never loved except under the aspect of good. The mind inclined to love is a captive of pleasure (*Purg.* XVIII, 25–27), yet there is always a free will to make choices.

Vergil's rational exposition of love exemplifies, in itself, the vision of an intelligible order governing creation: his discourse displays a recognition of the availability of such an order to the mind of natural man. Yet, the apostrophe to the imagination in *Purgatorio* XVII, "O imaginativa che ne rube / talvolta sì di fuor," disrupts, on the face of it, the rational scheme Vergil puts forth. More precisely, the apostrophe acknowledges the imagination as a power, a figure of personification that arrives like a thief ("che ne rube"), dispossessing one of one's consciousness of the world outside of experience. There is also an implied violence (it is the *vis imaginatitiva*) in the operation of the imagination, which Dante mutes by the omission of the vis in the phrase. For all its violence, however, the imagination does not have a spontaneous motion: the power is said to come from God or from the stars. But what exactly is the "imaginativa"? And what does the disjunction "or" mean in the reference (18) to the origin of the imagination (a light moves the imagination, which takes form in heaven, by itself or by a will that guides it downward)?

In technical terms the *imaginatitiva* is one of the five interior senses that Aristotelean psychology (the textbook for subsequent speculation is Aristotle's *De anima*) locates in the sensitive part of the soul. The arrangement is not uniform, but the order of faculties and functions of the mind most consistently repeated is Avicenna's. In the structure he envisions there is (1) *fantasia sive sensus communis*, which occupies the first chamber of the brain and which receives the impressions conveyed by the five senses; (2) *imaginatio*, which is located in the anterior chamber and retains the impressions; (3) *imaginativa sive cogitativa*, which is known as *virtus formalis* and composes images; (4) *aestimativa*, whose role is to apprehend impressions; and (5) *memorialis sive reminiscibilis*, which is in the posterior chamber of the brain and represents in the mind, from the storehouse of impressions, that which has been absent.[22]

The phrasing of *Purgatorio* XVII effectively blurs the mechanical, clear-cut distinctions of traditional psychology. The canto opens with an address to the reader's memory and imagination ("Recall, reader, if ever in the mountains ... and your fancy [*imagine*] will quickly come to see") (1–9); there is immediately after a reference to the "imaginativa" (13), which is followed further down by a reference to the "alta fantasia" (25) (high fantasy). These terms are traditionally understood as different inner senses, but they are deployed by Dante (as they are by Aquinas) to describe various aspects of the same process of representation. To be sure, Dante maintains throughout the poem a hierarchy of imaginative states, and the hierarchy of vision, it can be said, is the life principle of the *Divine Comedy*. Such an assertion of an imaginative hierarchy is for Dante a way of restoring connections between diverse areas of human psychology. It is also a way of challenging specific philosophical theories about rational moral freedom to be attained by affirming the empire of reason over the forces and impulses of the imagination. Dante's contention is that psychologists and theologians, who claim that moral freedom can be reached by reason's overcoming of the sensuous realm of passions, in fact restrict the sphere of the imagination's powers and circumvent the possibility of imagination's dialogue both with experiences that lie above the grasp of reason and with those that he assigns to the darkness of unreason.

The theologians' concern is to safeguard the operations of reason from the erratic intrusions of the imagination, to subdue this vagrant faculty, always impatient of restraint, under the authority and rigor of moral sense. This concern is so generalized that it involves prominent figures such as St. Bonaventure and Albert the Great as well as Hugh and Richard of St. Victor. All of them, and especially Richard of St. Victor in his *Benjamin Minor*, acknowledge the visionariness of the imagination, such as in mystical experiences, though they never confront its contradictory powers.

St. Bonaventure urges that the imagination be not allowed to go astray and to take over at the expense of reason, because "it is likely to disturb the freedom of the will." Albert the Great in *De apprehensione*, which draws heavily from Aristotle, Augustine, and Avicenna, understands the imagination as a faculty of retention and preservation of images, and it is said to differ from fantasy, which is the free play of the imagination, in that it enables one to imagine, say, a man with the head of a lion. Because it is the locus of vain imaginings and chimeras, because it is a faculty that may preclude or corrupt the workings of the mind by involving it in immoderate absorption with the "intentiones" it affords, fantasy, so the argument goes, must submit to reason.

In these texts the general insight is that imagination, insofar as it depends on material perception of reality, is to reason as shade is to light, as Hugh of St. Victor puts it. But in the *Benjamin Minor* by Richard of St. Victor (whom Dante acknowledges, as will be shown more extensively in chapter 8 below, in the *Epistle to Cangrande* as one of his authorities) the imagination is not simply excluded from the arc of light shed by reason, nor is it banished to the peripheral activity of manufacturing dark delusions of the heart. Richard of St. Victor's point of departure is an allegory of reason and imagination, which are related as a mistress and a handmaiden who keeps in contact with the servants, the senses. But the imagination is an "evagatio," a pilgrim spirit, always capable of error and coming into play when the mind fails to realize its highest goal of contemplation:

> it is manifestly concluded that reason never rises up to the cognition
> of the invisible unless her handmaiden, imagination, represents to
> her the form of visible things.... But it is certain that without

imagination she would not know corporeal things, and without knowledge of these things she would not ascend to contemplation of celestial things. For the eye of the flesh alone looks at visible things, while the eye of the heart alone sees invisible things.... Bala (imagination) is garrulous; Zelpha, drunken. For not even Rachel, her mistress, can suppress Bala's loquacity, and not even the generosity of her mistress can completely quench Zelpha's thirst. The wine that Zelpha drinks is the joy of pleasures. The more of it she drinks, the greater is her thirst. For the whole earth does not suffice to satisfy the appetite of sensation.... Now the imagination makes noise in the ears of the heart with so much importunity, and so great is its clamor, as we have said, that Rachel herself can scarcely, if at all, restrain her. It is for this reason that often when we say psalms or pray we wish to banish phantasies of thoughts or other sorts of images of things from the eyes of the heart, but we are not able to do so. Since even unwillingly we daily suffer a tumult of resounding thoughts of this sort, we are taught by daily experience of what sort and how great is the garrulity of Bala. She calls to memory everything, whether seen or heard, that we ourselves have done or said at some time or another.... And often when the will of the heart does not give assent to hearing her, she herself nevertheless unfolds her narrative although, as it were, no one listens.[23]

The allegory continues with a distinction between a rational imagination and a bestial imagination. The imagination is rational when from those things which we know by means of bodily sense we fabricate something else; for instance, we have seen gold and we have seen a house, and we picture a gold house. The imagination is bestial, on the other hand, when "with a wandering mind we run about here and there without any usefulness, without any deliberation concerning those things which we have seen or done."[24] This type of imagination will not be consulted by Rachel. Valued by Richard, however, are the two children of Bala, Dan and Naphtalim; Dan knows nothing save through the corporeal and can bring before the eyes of our hearts infernal torments; Naphtalim can see the walls of the heavenly Jerusalem made of precious stones.

　　Richard's notion of the double power of the imagination, which can deal with the satanic and the heavenly, which wanders off or attends on the needs of reason, may well be construed as an ideal anticipation of Dante's sense of the ambivalence of the imaginative faculty. Dante's sense of the imagination's ambivalence can only in part be accounted for in doctrinal terms. It is certainly true that for Dante the origin of the "imaginativa," for instance, is not clearly stated. The images are said to descend into the mind either from God, whose will directs them downward, or from a light formed in the heavenly intelligences. The disjunction has forced scholars to solve the issue of causality either in astrological terms of dream visions, of a natural origination (and this is Nardi's view), or in supernatural terms (as Singleton does), since God is the maker of the ecstatic visions the pilgrim beholds.[25] But the imagination is ambivalent for Dante in a more essential and radical way.

In *Purgatorio* XVII, 13–18, the "imaginativa" is represented in a language that suggests simultaneously its passive and active traits: it is moved from above, and yet it has the power to snatch us from outward things; it is personified as if it were an alien feminine force, yet it is contained in the mind; it is the eye that sees when, paradoxically, all the lights of the natural world have gone or are going out. The mind's cognitive process in *Purgatorio* XVIII depends on imagination's power to represent objects to the point that imagination is the ground of all knowledge. But in *Purgatorio* XVII the imagination is not the ground; it dislodges us, rather, from the ground. It is within this context that we can begin to understand the figurative discrepancies that characterize the exordium of canto XVII, which I have analyzed at length at the beginning of this chapter. The temporal dislocation figured by memory, the spatial dislocations figured by the Alps, the reversal of the mountain heights into the mole's depth and of light into darkness, the metaphoric interplay of vision and blindness, which actually starts in *Purgatorio* XIII—all show that the imagination is a figure of reversals in which immobility turns into action and actions are frozen as images. It is a trope that is always other than what it seems to be.

The logical and conceptual implications of imagination's steady displacement and self-displacement can be gauged by considering its narrative function in *Purgatorio* XVII. Why does Dante address the imagination directly as he introduces the sins of punished wrath? What does this proximity between *ira* and the imagination disclose about either? *Ira*, as one gathers from Aquinas's discussion of vices, is a passion of the sensitive appetite, which is swayed by the irascible and which, as it flares up, dims the light of understanding and impedes the judgment of reason.[26] "Ira per zelum turbat rationis oculum," says St. Gregory the Great, and the *ira caeca*, a formula that obviously accounts for the blindness of the purgatorial ledge, does not differ from madness. John Chrysostom, for instance, refers to anger as *furor* and *insania*.[27] In the analytic of the passion the heart is said to be inflamed with the stings of its own anger, the body trembles, the tongue stammers, the face is fired, the eyes blaze; more precisely, anger is accompanied by a fervor, the heat of the blood around the heart, and this is the opposite of the heat produced in love. Since all sins in *Purgatorio* are forms of perverted love, the sins of anger are cases of mad love.

The first tragic figuration of anger represents what medical authorities starting from Avicenna to Bernard of Gordon in his *Lilium medicinale* have called *amor hereos*, literally the disease of the imagination, a love that alters reason's judgment, for it corrupts the *vis aestimativa* which presides over and binds the imagination.[28] The examples of punished wrath the pilgrim beholds (*Purg.* XVII, 19–39) bear out this claim. The details of the Ovidian story of Procne and

Philomela are well known: Tereus is a descendant of Mars, and his marriage to Procne takes place under the aegis of the Furies. When Tereus meets his sister-in-law, Philomela, he is taken with her, schemes to possess her, and rapes her. Philomela accuses Tereus of confounding all natural feelings, of making her her sister's rival. Angered by her words, and to prevent her from revealing his transgression, he cuts out her tongue. Philomela reappears years later at the feast of Bacchus and weaves a pictogram telling the story of the violation she had suffered. When Procne discovers the horror, in a fury of madness she kills Tereus's son and serves him up as a meal.

The story can certainly be taken as Ovid's poetic parable of the relationship between art and violence. Art for Ovid reveals and displaces violence, for it relates the shift from voice to vision back to voice, as the three principals are metamorphosed into nightingale, swallow, and hawk. The shift, more to the point, discloses how the melic lure of the birds' song transfigures and possibly conceals a plot of madness. The metaphor of metamorphosis, finally, conveys the essence of the image as a figure of dislocation and of alterations of identity.

There are other dimensions of meaning common to these three images. Much as the story of Tereus, the other two stories—of Haman, who was hanged on the gibbet he had prepared for Mordechai, and of Amata, who not to lose Lavinia to Aeneas commits suicide on hearing the false news of Turnus's death—dramatize the element of foreignness, the intrusion of a stranger as a figure throwing into havoc one's familiar world. And in all three cases the stability of the social world is crushed by the destructiveness of the characters' unaccommodated imaginings. More important, all three images are traversed by the shadow of Mars: Tereus is Mars's descendant; Haman plots the destruction of the Jews; and Amata's raving madness ("mad she utters many wild things in moaning frenzy") is triggered by the madness of war. The implicit reference to Mars in the three examples of punished anger must be accounted for in terms of the traditional links existing between Mars and the irascible appetite, the faculty of action seeking to possess the object it desires. In this context one should add that the angel's voice the pilgrim hears as soon as the images vanish, "*Beati/pacifici*, the son sanz'ira mala" (*Purg.* XVII, 68–69) (*beati pacifici* who are without sinful anger), seals, by contrast, the imaginative bond Dante envisions between war and wrath. By this link Dante draws wrath into the dark night of desire or, to put it in the vocabulary of Dante's own poetic experience, into the space celebrated by Guido Cavalcanti and the Epicureans wherein love is war. He also draws it into the public world of political realities, which the fury of war annihilates.

To link wrath and war as versions of mad love, as the *Purgatorio's* moral system explicitly enables the reader to do, means to root them in the inconsistency of the phantasms which seize and darken one's own judgment and social values. The madness of Tereus, Procne, Haman, and Amata lies in their transgression of reason's bounds as they will to control events and to impart to them the direction of their desires. But they are above all mad because they have yielded to the *vis*, as it were, to the violence of their phantasms; they have literalized the phantasms and have succumbed to them by suppressing reason and, in the case of Procne, language itself. In this sense wrath, which is an active appetite and leads to action, is the passion that mediates between the imagination (of which it is a form gone astray) and the *liberum arbitrium*, which is a principle of action. Small wonder that Dante discusses imagination, love, and moral knowledge in the context of wrath, for wrath is their metonym and their threat, in the sense that it mimes and distorts the individual operations of each one of them.

But there is another, more fundamental reason why Dante should discuss the mysterious workings and origins of the poetic imagination in the context of wrath. The proximity between divine madness and inspired poetry is a given for Plato; and Dante, to put it at its most general, recognizes that the poet, in treading the paths of knowledge, needs both the flight of the imagination and the ceaseless dialogue between imagination and reason. This link is not kept at the level of mere abstraction. The loop between wrath and poetry is suggested by Dante himself in *Inferno* VIII. In this infernal scene, against the stoical ideals of the imperturbability of the sage, he pits the *laudabilis ira*, the just indignation that the pilgrim, like an angry prophet, voices against the savage violence of the "ombra ... furiosa" (48) (furious shade) of Filippo Argenti.

Dante's own wrath in the canto where wrath is punished (*Inf.* VIII) is consistent with his commitment to his visionary calling, to his steady impulse to yoke moral knowledge and vision. Unlike the images of punished wrath—where the characters surrender to the sovereign call of the imaginings that possess them and, thereby, enter the strange and demonic world of unreason—Dante yields to the imperious summons of the imagination free from restraint and yet, at the same time, yearns to bring his vision within the compass of reason and the demands of reality. By the same token, the world of reality is transposed into the light of visionary figurations. This convergence of visionariness and reality, which is the equivalent of the quandary of freedom and necessity articulated by Marco Lombardo in the oxymoron "liberi soggiacete" (*Purg.* XVI, 80), is the work of art itself, which is the outcome of imagination and the rules of reason and which, inasmuch as it is work and production, entails the desire to engage in a dialogue with others and is, thus, the negation of destructive madness. Central to Dante's work of art is the resolute conviction that his own moral knowledge is rooted in and flows from the extraordinary vision that has been granted to him.

The aesthetic-moral unity of the *Divine Comedy* effectively depends on the poet's astonishing power to hold together two principles that, on the face of it, are irreconcilable. At the very center of the *Divine Comedy* Dante presents the imagination variously as a dazzling poetic faculty autonomous from the rigors of the discourse of reason, as inseparable from the tragic errors of madness, as the path to love, and as the instrument of reason's judgments. To exert a moral judgment, which is simultaneously will and knowledge translated into action, imagination's excesses must be sacrificed and held at bay. To yield to the unrestrained promptings of the imagination is to lapse into the fantastic realm of mad violence. Yet, sacrificing the excesses of the imagination to the order of rationality is tantamount, by the inexorable logic of Dante's text, to renouncing the very visionariness which shapes the poem.

There is, then, at the heart of the *Divine Comedy* a doubleness which is deeper than the determination of how much of St. Thomas Aquinas or how much of Averroes' value systems get absorbed in the text. This doubleness is that of the imagination, as has been described above—a complex, forever ambivalent, and protean faculty which theologians and philosophers never confront in all its problematic implications. Dante is not alone, however, in confronting the doubleness of the imagination as both the portal to a knowledge of reality and as exceeding the domain of material reality. Another poetic text, one that is legitimately viewed as the foundation of Dante's own poetic-moral apprenticeship, directly confronts the question of the ambiguity and potential deceptiveness of images.

The poem is Guinizelli's "Al cor gentil," which is an extended meditation on the effort to establish analogies between the secret essence of love and the world of nature. More to the point, Guinizelli's song seeks to cast much as Dante does in the *Vita nuova*—the figure of a woman as an irreplaceable and unique image of love. The poem ends with an imagined encounter between God and the poet. God chides the poet for his presumptuous claim about the woman's divinity and for comparing her to God. The comparison, from God's view, is a sin of pride, but the poet replies that he should not be held accountable for the fault: to him the woman does have the semblance of an angel.

Dante goes well beyond Guinizelli's insight into the deceptive effects of images, just as he goes beyond Aquinas's and Siger's formulations. Dante's sense of the primacy of the imagination, in fact, allows him to draw their respective perceptions within a space where ideological contradictions and differences of opinion can be harmonized, for in his construction the apparent contradictions depend on something prior to them: the doubleness of the imagination. This doubleness Dante, who is the visionary poet of history, makes the core of his work.

The awareness of the two operations of the imagination accounts for the vital tension in the *Divine Comedy* between the uncertain vision in the world of immanence and the clarity of knowledge the pilgrim incessantly pursues. In *Purgatorio* XVI the origin of evil is said to rest in the confusion of the secular and spiritual orders:

> Dì oggimai che la Chiesa di Roma,
> per confondere in sè due reggimenti,
> cade nel fango, e sè brutta e la soma.

> (127–29)

(Tell henceforth that the Church of Rome, by confounding in itself two governments, falls in the mire and befouls both itself and its burden.)

In *Purgatorio* XVII Vergil, after his exposition of the nature and power of love, turns the issue of confusion around:

ciascun confusamente un bene apprende
nel qual si queti l'animo, e disira.

(127–28)

(Each one apprehends confusedly a good wherein the mind may find rest.)

In the first passage the confusion in the social and moral structures of the world is unequivocally condemned. Political order depends on the observance of hierarchical differences and distinctions between institutions. Yet the imagination apprehends confusedly the objects of desire: this confused apprehension of the good textually recalls the Augustinian opening statement of the *Confessions* "inquietum est cor nostrum donec requiescat in te" (Restless is our heart till it rests in thee). The Augustinian echo places us in history as the land of longing, where all knowledge is—to put it in the metaphors that introduce the apostrophe to the imagination in *Purgatorio* XVII—a *cognitio vespertina*, a twilight knowledge.

The double value the word "confusion" acquires in these two cantos draws attention to Dante's obstinate assertion of the moral necessity of order in the world of man. It also conveys his insight into the confused perceptions the imagination makes available to reason's judgment. In this world veiled by fogs of desire we see as does the mole in its winding maze. Dante, the poet of vision, knows well both the role blindness plays in arriving at knowledge (this is the myth of Tiresias) and how blind knowledge can be. But even as we are in a world of confused shadows, we also can see, in the language of the first letter to the Thessalonians, as the children of light and of the day do, for we belong neither to darkness nor to the night. This mode of vision is rendered by Dante's understanding of contemplation. Such an understanding affords him the notion that poetic vision is not simply the outcome of the pilgrim's journey toward knowledge; vision precedes and gives a shape to that outcome. The primacy of vision, as chapter 8 will show, depends on the pilgrim's intuition, the form of immediate cognition in which the imagination incorporates and yet exceeds the mode of knowledge supplied by the rational faculties.

NOTES

1. The motif of memory as the eye of the imagination has been studied by Yates 1972. On the role of the poetic imagination in medieval literature see Wetherbee 1976.

2. In *Convivio* II, xiii, 24, Dante acknowledges the power of music to draw to itself man's minds, "che quasi sono principalmente vapori del cuore, sì che quasi cessano da ogni operazione: sì e l'anima intera, quando l'ode, e la virtù di tutti quasi corre a lo spirito sensibile che riceve lo suono." Elsewhere Dante wills to probe the sense of the word "mente," and he writes: "Dico adunque che lo Filosofo nel secondo de l'Anima, partendo le potenze di quella, dice che l'anima principalmente hae tre potenze, cioè vivere, sentire e ragionare: e dice anche muovere; ma questa si può col sentire fare una, però che ogni anima che sente, o con tutti i sensi o con alcuno solo, si muove; sì che muovere è una potenza congiunta col sentire. E secondo che esso dice, è manifestissimo che queste potenze sono intra sè per modo che l'una è fondamento de l'altra; e quella che è fondamento puote per sè essere partita, ma l'altra, che si fonda sopra essa, non può da quella essere partita. Onde la potenza vegetativa, per la quale si vive, è fondamento sopra 'l quale si sente, cioè vede, ode, gusta, odora e tocca; e questa vegetativa potenza per sé puote essere anima, sì come vedemo ne le piante tutte. La sensitiva sanza quella essere non puote, e non si trova in alcuna cosa che non viva; e questa sensitiva potenza è fondamento de la intellettiva, cioè de la ragione: ... E quella anima che tutte queste potenza comprende, e perfettissima di tutte l'altre, è l'anima umana, la quale con la nobilitade de la potenza ultima, cioè ragione, participa de la divina natura a guisa di sempiterna intelligenza; ... e però è l'uomo divino animale da li filosofi chiamato" (*Conv.* III, ii, 11–15). "Mente" is defined as that power of the soul capable of "virtù ragionativa, o vero consigliativa."

3. In *Convivio* II, ix, 4, Dante briefly discusses optics and modes of visions, and he writes: "E qui si vuol sapere che avvegna che più cose ne l'occhio a un'ora possano venire, veramente quella che viene per retta linea ne la punta de la pupilla, quella veramente si vede, e ne la imaginativa si suggella solamente. E questo è però che 'l nervo per lo quale corre lo spirito visivo, è diritto a quella parte, e però veramente l'occhio l'altro occhio non può guardare, sì che esso non sia veduto da lui." The editors of *Convivio* gloss the passage by quoting Aristotle's *De anima* (III, 7, 431a, 16–17; 8, 432a, 8–9), where the "imaginativa" or "fantasia"—from which the intellect draws the material for its knowledge—is discussed. For Aristotle's theory of mind and imagination see Wedin 1988. More generally see Watson 1986 and the brilliant study by Wolfson 1935. Of great interest for the link between Avicenna's idea of imagination and Aristotle is Portelli 1982. See also Hoorn 1972; cf. also Blaustein 1984.

4. Newman 1967 applies convincingly to Dante's text the Augustinian paradigm suggested by Bundy 1927.

5. Hissette 1977, pp. 239–41.

6. In addition to the texts mentioned by Hissette (note 5 above) see Blaustein 1984. Cf. St. Augustine, *City of God* V, 1–8, on free will and the influence of the stars.

7. It is possible to suggest, given the political context of the discussion on free will and determination, that astrology is to Dante a suspect science because it can be used to legitimize the political authority of tyrants, who, having no dynastic or popular source of legitimacy, would avail themselves of the justifications provided by astrologers such as Guido Bonatti at the court of Ezzelino da Romano (1237–56) at Padua.

8. An excellent review of the range of meanings of *intenzione* is by Gregory in *Enciclopedia dantesca* 1970–78, 3:480–82. See also Nardi 1985, "La conoscenza umana," especially pp. 138–41. In *Convivio* III, ix, 7, Dante writes: "Queste cose visibili, sì le proprie come le comuni in quanto sono visibili, vengono dentro a l'occhio—non dico le cose, ma le forme loro—per lo mezzo diafano, non realmente ma intenzionalmente, sì quasi come in vetro transparente." The passage echoes Aristotle's *De anima* III, 8, 431b. Averroes in his commentary on *De anima* II, 4, t. c. 49, understands "intentio" as the material representation of an object. See also Aquinas's *Summa contra Gentiles* I, 53, quoted by Singleton in his notes to *Purgatorio* XVIII, 23. I found the study of Pegis 1983 compelling.

9. Cf. *Paradiso* IV, 41–42: "però che solo da sensato apprende / ciò che fa poscia d'intelletto degno." The tenet must be complemented by Beatrice's warning that "dietro ai sensi / vedi che la ragione ha corte l'ali" (*Par.* II, 56–57). In *Convivio* II, iv, 17, Dante asserts that it is from sense that "comincia la nostra conoscenza." Yet he knows that there is an intellectual knowledge that transcends the senses: "pure risplende nel nostro intelletto alcuno lume de la vivacissima loro [separate substances] essenza." In *Convivio* III, iv, 9, the limit of the intellect's power to grasp separate substances lies in the "fantasia."

10. I have slightly altered Toynbee's translation (p. 201) to fit the grammar of my sentence.

11. On Epicurean *voluptas* see Brown 1982. Cf. also St. Augustine, *City Of God* V, 9, for a critique of Cicero's understanding of free will.

12. *Monarchia* I, xii, 2. Cf. Murari 1905, pp. 318–20, for the links between Dante and Boethius.

13. I am translating from Nardi 1944, "Il libero arbitrio e la storiella dell'asino di Buridano," p. 302. Cf.: "Si ergo iudicium moveat omnino appetitum et nullo modo preveniatur ab eo, liberum est; si vero ab appetitu quocunque modo preveniente iudicium moveatur, liberum esse non potest, quia non a se, sed ab alio captivum trahitur" (*Monarchia* I, xi 4–5).

14. Hissette 1977, pp. 241–51. Cf. Lottin 1942–49, 1:274–77.

15. *Summa theologiae* I, 83, 8; cf. also I–II, 13, 1; *De veritate* XXII, 15. On the whole issue see Lottin 1942–49, "Nature du libre arbitre," 1:207–16. Cf. also Gilson 1956, pp. 252–56.

16. Cf. the account by Leff 1968, especially pp. 225–28.

17. Of great interest on the problem of the soul in the thirteenth century is Pegis 1963. Cf. also on the question of the soul and its faculties, the possible intellect (and the polemic against Averroes' interpretation of Aristotle's *De anima*), Aquinas, *Summa contra Gentiles*, chaps. 58–65.

18. Aquinas, *On the Unity of the Intellect against the Averroists*, trans. Zedler, chap. IV, par. 89, pp. 60–61. Cf. also Albert the Great, *De unitate intellectus contra Averroem*, in *Opera omnia* 10:437–76. The relation of Siger's writings to St. Thomas's treatises is far from clear. Mandonnet 1976 believed that St. Thomas attacked Siger's *De anima intellectiva*, but Van Steenberghen 1977 has refuted him. It may be that Aquinas's polemic was directed against the *Quaestiones in tertium de anima*. Cf. the remarks in the translation of the *De unitate* by Nardi 1947; cf. Gilson 1955, pp. 396–97.

19. *On the Unity of the Intellect against the Averroists*, trans. Zedler, chap. IV, par. 105, p. 61.

20. Stillinger 1992 has studied the tradition and function of the commentary in the *Vita nuova*; cf. also D'Andrea 1980; Singleton 1977, and Shaw 1976.

21. Cf. Corti 1983; see also the introduction to the translation of Cavalcanti's poetry by Nelson 1986, especially pp. xxxvi–liii.

22. *De anima* I, 5 (5 rb); IV, 1 (17 va). Avicenna's topography of the mind is referred to and opposed to St. Augustine's three modes of vision by Aquinas, *Summa theologiae* I, 78, 4. Cf. Albert the Great, *De apprehensione* and *Sum. de Creat.*, in *Opera omnia* 3 and 2, respectively. See also Bundy 1927, pp. 177ff.

23. Richard of St. Victor, *The Twelve Patriarchs*, for Benjamin Minor see chaps. V and VI, pp. 58–59.

24. Richard of St. Victor, *The Twelve Patriarchs*, chap. XVI, p. 68.

25. "Un secondo accenno all'*immaginativa* si ha nel *Purgatorio*, là dove si dice, che essa compie un lavorio nel quale non è soccorsa dalle impressioni dei sensi esterni, ma da 'lume che nel ciel s'informa,' cioè dall'influenza naturale delle sfere celesti e non, come pensano erroneamente alcuni, da specie intelligibili partecipate per grazia" (Mardi 1984, "La conoscenza umana," p. 140). Nardi goes on to stress that Dante's sense of the mind's visionary experiences (cf. *Purg.* IX, 16–18: "la mente nostra, peregrina / più da la carne e men da' pensier presa, / a le sue vision quasi è divina") is Platonic and not Aristotelian in origin. Cf. Singleton's commentary on *Purgatorio* XVII, 13–18.

26. St. Thomas Aquinas gives an extended analysis of wrath, both as a virtue (righteous indignation) and as a vice against the order of reason in the *Summa theologiae* IIa IIae, 158, 1–8. Cf. Aristotle's *Ethics* II, 5, cited by Aquinas.

27. *Summa theologiae* IIa IIae, 158, 1, r., quotes Gregory's *Moralia* V, 45 (*PL* 75:727). In article 4 Aquinas cites Chrysostom.

28. Wack 1990, especially pp. 74ff.; cf. Ciavolella 1976 and, above all, the magisterial study on medieval physicians by Nardi 1959.

HAROLD BLOOM

The Strangeness of Dante:
Ulysses and Beatrice

T he New Historicists and allied resenters have been attempting to reduce and scatter Shakespeare, aiming to undo the Canon by dissolving its center. Curiously, Dante, the second center as it were, is not under similar onslaught, either here or in Italy. Doubtless the assault will come, since the assorted multiculturalists would have difficulty finding a more objectionable great poet than Dante, whose savage and powerful spirit is politically incorrect to the highest degree. Dante is the most aggressive and polemical of the major Western writers, dwarfing even Milton in this regard. Like Milton, he was a political party and a sect of one. His heretical intensity has been masked by scholarly commentary, which even at its best frequently treats him as though his *Divine Comedy* was essentially versified Saint Augustine. But it is best to begin by marking his extraordinary audacity, which is unmatched in the entire tradition of supposedly Christian literature, including even Milton.

Nothing else in Western literature, in the long span from the Yahwist and Homer through Joyce and Beckett, is as sublimely outrageous as Dante's exaltation of Beatrice, sublimated from being an image of desire to angelic status, in which role she becomes a crucial element in the church's hierarchy of salvation. Because Beatrice initially matters solely as an instrument of Dante's will, her apotheosis necessarily involves Dante's own election as well. His poem is a prophecy and takes on the function of a third Testament in no way subservient to the Old and the New. Dante will not acknowledge that the *Comedy*

From *The Western Canon*. © 1994 by Harold Bloom.

must be a fiction, *his* supreme fiction. Rather, the poem is the truth, universal and not temporal. What Dante the pilgrim sees and says in the narrative of Dante the poet is intended to persuade us perpetually of Dante's poetic and religious inescapability. The poem's gestures of humility, on the part of pilgrim or of poet, impress Dante scholars but are rather less persuasive than the poem's subversion of all other poets and its persistence in bringing forward Dante's own apocalyptic potential.

These observations, I hasten to explain, are directed against much Dante scholarship and not at all against Dante. I do not see how we can disengage Dante's overwhelming poetic power from his spiritual ambitions, which are inevitably idiosyncratic and saved from being blasphemous only because Dante won his wager with the future within a generation after his death. If the *Comedy* were not Shakespeare's only authentic poetic rival, Beatrice would be an offense to the church and even to literary Catholics. The poem is too strong to disown; for a neo-Christian poet like T. S. Eliot, the *Comedy* becomes another Scripture, a Newer Testament that supplements the canonical Christian Bible. Charles Williams—a guru for such neo-Christians as Eliot, C. S. Lewis, W. H. Auden, Dorothy L. Sayers, J. R. R. Tolkien, and others—went so far as to affirm that the Athanasian creed, "the taking of the Manhood into God," did not receive full expression until Dante. The Church had to wait for Dante, and for the figure of Beatrice.

What Williams highlights throughout his intense study, *The Figure of Beatrice* (1943), is the great scandal of Dante's achievement: the poet's most spectacular invention is Beatrice. No single personage in Shakespeare, not even the charismatic Hamlet or the godlike Lear, matches Beatrice as an exuberantly daring invention. Only the J writer's Yahweh and the Gospel of Mark's Jesus are more surprising or exalted representations. Beatrice is the signature of Dante's originality, and her triumphant placement well within the Christian machinery of salvation is her poet's most audacious act of transforming his inherited faith into something much more his own.

Dante scholars inevitably repudiate such assertions on my part, but they live so under the shadow of their subject that they tend to lose full awareness of the *Divine Comedy*'s strangeness. It remains the uncanniest of all literary works for the ambitious reader to encounter, and it survives both translation and its own vast learning. Everything that allows a common reader to read the *Comedy* ensues from qualities in Dante's spirit that are anything but what is generally considered pious. Ultimately Dante has nothing truly positive to say about any of his poetic precursors or contemporaries and remarkably little pragmatic use for the Bible, except for Psalms. It is as though he felt King David, ancestor of Christ, was the only forerunner worthy of him, the only other poet consistently able to express the truth.

The reader who comes freshly to Dante will see very quickly that no other secular author is so absolutely convinced that his own work is the truth, all of the truth that matters most. Milton and perhaps the later Tolstoy approximate Dante's fierce conviction of rightness, but they both reflect contending realities as well and show more of the strain of isolated vision. Dante is so strong—rhetorically, psychologically, spiritually—that he dwarfs their self-confidence. Theology is not his ruler but his resource, one resource among many. No one can deny that Dante is a supernaturalist, a Christian, and a theologian, or at least a theological allegorist. But all received concepts and images undergo extraordinary transformations in Dante, the only poet whose originality, inventiveness, and preternatural fecundity actually rival Shakespeare's. A reader working through Dante for the first time, in a terza rima translation as accomplished as Laurence Binyon's or in John Sinclair's lucid prose version, loses an immensity in not reading the Italian poem, and yet an entire cosmos remains. But it is the strangeness as well as the sublimity of what remains that matters most, the utter uniqueness of Dante's powers, with the single exception of Shakespeare's. As in Shakespeare, we find in Dante a surpassing cognitive strength combined with an inventiveness that has no merely pragmatic limits.

When you read Dante or Shakespeare, you experience the limits of art, and then you discover that the limits are extended or broken. Dante breaks through all limitations far more personally and overtly than Shakespeare does, and if he is more of a supernaturalist than Shakespeare, his transcending of nature remains as much his own as Shakespeare's unique and idiosyncratic naturalism. Where the two poets challenge each other most is in their representations of love—which returns us to where love begins and ends in Dante, the figure of Beatrice.

The Beatrice of the *Comedy* occupies a position in the heavenly hierarchy that is difficult to apprehend. We have no guidelines for understanding it; there is nothing in doctrine that calls for the exaltation of this particular Florentine woman with whom Dante fell eternally in love. The most ironic commentary on that falling is by Jorge Luis Borges in "The Meeting in a Dream" (*Other Inquisitions, 1937–1952*):

> To fall in love is to create a religion that has a fallible god. That Dante professed an idolatrous admiration for Beatrice is a truth that does not bear contradicting; that she once ridiculed him and another time rebuffed him are facts rendered by the *Vita nuova*. Some maintain that those facts are symbolic of others. If that were true, it would strengthen even more our certainty of an unhappy and superstitious love.
>
> (*translated by Ruth L. C. Simms*)

Borges at least restores Beatrice to her origin as an "illusory encounter" and to her enigmatic otherness for all readers of Dante: "Infinitely Beatrice existed for Dante; Dante existed very little, perhaps not at all, for Beatrice. Our piety, our veneration cause us to forget that pitiful inharmony, which was unforgettable for Dante."

It scarcely matters that Borges is projecting his own ironically absurd passion for Beatrice Viterbo (see his Kabbalistic story, "The Aleph"). What he slyly emphasizes is the scandalous disproportion be tween whatever it was that Dante and Beatrice experienced together (next to nothing) and Dante's vision of their mutual apotheosis in the *Paradiso*. Disproportion is Dante's royal road to the sublime. Like Shakespeare, he can get away with anything, because both poets transcend other poets' limits. The pervasive irony (or allegory) of Dante's work is that he professes to accept limits even as he violates them. Everything that is vital and original in Dante is arbitrary and personal, yet it is presented as the truth, consonant with tradition, faith, and rationality. Almost inevitably, it is misread until it blends with the normative, and at last we are confronted by a success Dante could not have welcomed. The theological Dante of modern American scholarship is a blend of Augustine, Thomas Aquinas, and their companions. This is a doctrinal Dante, so abstrusely learned and so amazingly pious that he can be fully apprehended only by his American professors.

Dante's progeny among the writers are his true canonizers, and they are not always an overtly devout medley: Petrarch, Boccaccio, Chaucer, Shelley, Rossetti, Yeats, Joyce, Pound, Eliot, Borges, Stevens, Beckett. About all that dozen possesses in common is Dante, though he becomes twelve different Dantes in his poetic afterlife. This is wholly appropriate for a writer of his strength; there are nearly as many Dantes as there are Shakespeares. My own Dante deviates increasingly from what has become the eminently orthodox Dante of modern American criticism and scholarship, as represented by T. S. Eliot, Francis Fergusson, Erich Auerbach, Charles Singleton, and John Freccero. An alternate tradition is provided by the Italian line that commenced with the Neapolitan speculator Vico and proceeded through the Romantic poet Foscolo and the Romantic critic Francesco de Sanctis, culminating in the early-twentieth-century aesthetician Benedetto Croce. If one combines this Italian tradition with some observations by Ernst Robert Curtius, the distinguished modern German literary historian, an alternative to the Eliot-Singleton-Freccero Dante emerges, a prophetic poet rather than a theological allegorist.

Vico rather splendidly overstated his case when he averred of Dante that "had he been ignorant of Latin and scholastic philosophy, he would have been even greater as a poet, and perhaps the Tuscan tongue would have served to make Homer's equal." Nevertheless, Vico's judgment is refreshing when one wanders in the dark wood of the theological allegorists, where the salient characteristic of the *Comedy* becomes Dante's supposedly Augustinian conversion from poetry to belief, a belief that subsumes and subordinates the imagination. Neither Augustine nor Aquinas saw poetry as anything except childish play, to be set aside with other childish things. What would they have made of the *Comedy*'s Beatrice? Curtius shrewdly observes that Dante presents her not merely as his means of salvation but as a universal agency available to everyone of gentle heart. Dante's conversion is to Beatrice, not to Augustine, and Beatrice sends Virgil to Dante to be his guide, rather than sending Augustine.

Clearly Dante prefers Beatrice, or his own creation, to the allegory of other theologians, and just as clearly Dante does not desire to transcend his own poetry. Augustine and Aquinas have the same relation to Dante's theology that Virgil and Cavalcanti have to Dante's poetry: all forerunners are dwarfed by the poet-theologian, the prophet Dante, who is the author of the final testament, the *Comedy*. If you want to read the *Comedy* as an allegory of the theologians, start with the only theologian who truly mattered to Dante: Dante himself. The *Comedy*, like all of the greatest canonical works, destroys the distinction between sacred and secular writing. And Beatrice is now, for us, the allegory of the fusion of sacred and secular, the union of prophecy and poem.

Dante's outstanding characteristics as poet and as person are pride rather than humility, originality rather than traditionalism, exuberance or gusto rather than restraint. His prophetic stance is one of initiation rather than conversion, to adopt a suggestion of Paolo Valesio, who emphasizes the hermetic or esoteric aspects of the *Comedy*. You are not converted by or to Beatrice; the journey to her is an initiation because she is, as Curtius first said, the center of a private gnosis and not of the church universal. After all, Beatrice is sent to Dante by Lucia, a remarkably obscure Sicilian saint, so obscure that Dante scholars are unable to say why Dante chose her. John Freccero, the best living Dante critic, tells us that "In a sense, the purpose of the entire journey is to write the poem, to attain the vantage-point of Lucy, and of all the blessed."

Yes, but why Lucy? To which the answer certainly cannot be: Why not? Lucy of Syracuse lived and was martyred a thousand years before Dante and would now be totally forgotten if she had not had an esoteric importance for the poet and for his poem. But we know nothing about that importance; we do not even know who the greater female soul who sent Lucy to Beatrice was. This "lady in heaven" is usually identified as the Virgin Mary, but Dante does not name her. Lucy is called "the enemy of all cruelty," presumably an attribute shared by all the ladies of heaven. "Illuminating Grace" is the usual abstraction stuck onto Dante's Lucy by the commentators; but that, too, would hardly seem to be a unique quality of a particular Sicilian martyr whose name means "light." I labor this point to underline how sublimely arbitrary Dante insists on being. There is hidden matter in the *Comedy*; the poem undeniably has its hermetic aspects, and they can hardly be judged of secondary importance since Beatrice centers them. We always come back to the figure of Beatrice in reading the *Comedy*, not so much because she is somehow a type of Christ, but because she is the ideal object of Dante's sublimated desire. We do not even know whether Dante's Beatrice had a historical existence. If she did and can be identified with the daughter of a Florentine banker, it scarcely matters in the poem. The *Comedy*'s Beatrice matters not because she is an intimation of Christ, but because she is Dante's idealized projection of his own singularity, the point of view of his work as an author.

Let me be blasphemous enough to mingle Cervantes with Dante, so as to compare their two heroic protagonists: Don Quixote and Dante the Pilgrim. Don Quixote's Beatrice is the enchanted Dulcinea del Tobosa, his visionary transfiguration of the farm girl, Aldonza Lorenzo. The banker's daughter, Beatrice Portinari, has the same relation to Dante's Beatrice that Aldonza has to Dulcinea. True, Don Quixote's hierarchy is secular: Dulcinea takes her place in the cosmos of Amadis of Gaul, Palmerin of England, the Knight of the Sun, and similar worthies of a mythological chivalry, while Beatrice ascends into the realm of Saint Bernard, Saint Francis, and Saint Dominic. If one has a preference for poetry over doctrine, this is not necessarily a difference. Knights-errant, like saints, are metaphors for and in a poem, and the heavenly Beatrice, in terms of institutional and historical Catholicism, has no more or less status or reality than the enchanted Dulcinea. But Dante's triumph is to make my comparison seem somehow a blasphemy.

Perhaps Dante really was both pious and orthodox, but Beatrice is his figure and not the church's; she is part of a private gnosis, a poet's alteration of the scheme of salvation. A "conversion" to Beatrice can be Augustinian enough, but it is hardly a conversion to Saint Augustine, any more than a devotion to Dulcinea del Tobosa is an act of worship directed toward Iseult of the White Hands. Dante was brazen, aggressive, prideful, and audacious beyond all poets, before or since. He imposed his vision on Eternity, and he has very little in common with the flock of his piously learned exegetes. If it is all in Augustine or in Thomas Aquinas, then let us read Augustine or Aquinas. But Dante wanted us to read Dante. He did not compose his poem to illuminate inherited truths. The *Comedy* purports to be the truth, and I would think that detheologizing Dante would be as irrelevant as theologizing him.

When the dying Don Quixote repents his heroic madness, he falls back into his original identity of Alonso Quixano the Good, and he thanks God's mercy for his conversion to pious sanity. Every reader joins Sancho Panza in protesting, "Don't die! ... Take my advice and live many years.... Perhaps we shall find the lady Dulcinea behind some hedge, disenchanted and as pretty as a picture." When Dante's poem ends, there is no Sancho to join the reader in hoping that the poet's power not fail the high fantasy of the Christian heaven. I suppose there are readers who go to the *Divine Comedy* as a conduit to the divine love that moves the sun and the other stars, but most of us go to it for Dante himself, for a poetic personality and dramatic character that not even John Milton can quite equal. No one wants to transmute the *Comedy* into *Don Quixote*, but a touch of Sancho might have softened even the Pilgrim of Eternity and perhaps reminded his scholars that a fiction is a fiction, even if it itself believes otherwise.

But what kind of a fiction is Beatrice? If she is, as Curtius insisted, an emanation from God, then Dante was up to something we cannot decipher, even though we sense that it is there. Dante's revelation can hardly be termed private, like William Blake's, but not because it is less original than Blake's. It is more original, and is public because it is so successful; nothing else in Western literature, except for Shakespeare upon his heights, is nearly so fully articulated. Dante, the most singular and savage of all superbly refined temperaments, made himself universal not by his absorption of tradition, but by bending tradition until it fitted his own nature. By an irony that transcends anything I know akin to it, Dante's strength of usurpation has resulted in his being weakly misread in one mode or another. If the *Comedy* is a truthful prophecy, then its scholars are tempted to read it by the illumination of Augustinian tradition. Where else shall the proper interpretation of Christian revelation be found? Even so subtle an interpreter as John Freccero sometimes falls into the conversion of poetics, as if only Augustine could present a paradigm for self-mastering. A "novel of the self" like the *Comedy* must thus take its origin from Augustine's *Confessions*. Far more powerful than the Romantics who worshiped and imitated him, Dante invents his own origin and masters his self with his own conversionary figure, Beatrice, who does not seem to me a very Augustinian personage. Can Beatrice be the object of desire, however sublimated, in an Augustinian conversion narrative? Freccero eloquently says that, for Augustine, history is God's poem. Is the history of Beatrice a lyric by God? Since I myself am partial to finding the voice of God in Shakespeare or Emerson or Freud, depending upon my needs, I have no difficulty in finding Dante's *Comedy* to be divine. I would not speak of the divine *Confessions*, however, and I do not hear the voice of God in Augustine. Nor am I persuaded that Dante ever heard God in any voice but his own. A poem that prefers itself to the Bible can, by definition, be said also to prefer itself to Augustine.

*   *   *

Beatrice is Dante's *knowing*, according to Charles Williams, who had no sympathy for Gnosticism. By knowing he meant the way from Dante the knower to God the known. Yet Dante did not intend Beatrice to be his knowing alone. His poem argues not that each of us is to find a solitary knowing, but that Beatrice is to play a universal role for all who can find her, since presumably her intervention for Dante, via Virgil, is to be unique. The myth of Beatrice, though it is Dante's central invention, exists only within his poetry. Its strangeness cannot truly be seen, because we know of no figure comparable to Beatrice. Milton's Urania, his heavenly muse in *Paradise Lost*, is not a person, and Milton qualifies her with the warning remark that it is the meaning, not the name he calls. Shelley, imitating Dante, celebrated Emilia Viviani in his *Epipsychidion*, but

High Romantic passion did not prevail, and Signora Viviani eventually became "a little brown demon" for her disillusioned lover.

To recover something of Dante's strangeness we need to see his treatment of a universal figure. No Western literary character is so incessant as Odysseus, the Homeric hero better known by his Latin name of Ulysses. From Homer to Nikos Kazantzakis, the figure of Odysseus/Ulysses undergoes extraordinary modifications in Pindar, Sophocles, Euripides, Horace, Virgil, Ovid, Seneca, Dante, Chapman, Calderón, Shakespeare, Goethe, Tennyson, Joyce, Pound, and Wallace Stevens, among many others. W. B. Stanford in his fine study *The Ulysses Theme* (1963) sets the muted but negative treatment by Virgil against Ovid's positive identification with Ulysses, in a contrast that establishes two of the major stances that will probably always contend in the metamorphoses of this hero, or hero-villain. Virgil's Ulysses will become Dante's, but so transmuted as to make Virgil's rather evasive portrait tend to fade away. Unwilling to condemn Ulysses directly, Virgil transfers that work to his characters, who identify the hero of the *Odyssey* with guile and deceit. Ovid, an exile and an amorist, mingles himself with Ulysses in a composite identity, so bequeathing to us the now-permanent idea of Ulysses as the first of the great wandering womanizers.

In canto 26 of the *Inferno*, Dante created the most original version of Ulysses that we have, one who does not seek home and wife in Ithaca but departs from Circe in order to break all bounds and risk the un known. Hamlet's undiscovered country from whose bourn no traveler returns becomes the pragmatic destination of this most impressive of all doom-eager heroes. There is an extraordinary passage in *Inferno* 26 that is difficult to absorb. Ulysses and Dante are in a dialectical relationship because Dante fears the deep identity between himself as poet (not as pilgrim) and Ulysses as transgressive voyager. This fear may not be fully conscious, yet Dante must on some level experience it, because he portrays Ulysses as being moved by pride, and no more prideful poet than Dante has ever existed, not even Pindar or Milton or Victor Hugo or Stefan George or Yeats. Scholars want to hear Beatrice or assorted saints speak for Dante, but she and they do not share his accent. The voice of Ulysses and that of Dante are dangerously close, which may be why Virgil's explanation hardly suffices when he says that the Greek may disdain the voice of the Italian poet. Nor does Dante allow himself any reaction whatsoever to the magnificent speech that he writes for Ulysses, as a voice speaking out of the flame (I use here and throughout John D. Sinclair's 1961 prose translation):

> When I parted from Circe, who held me more than a year near Gaeta before Aeneas so named it, not fondness for a son, nor duty to an aged father, nor the love I owed Penelope which should have gladdened her, could conquer within me the ardor I had to gain experience of the world and of the vices and the worth of men; and I put forth on the open deep with but one ship and with that little

company which had not deserted me. The one shore and the other I saw as far as Spain, as far as Morocco, and Sardinia and the other islands which that sea bathes round. I and my companions were old and slow when we came to the narrow outlet where Hercules set up his landmarks so that men should not pass beyond. On my right hand I left Seville, on the other had already left Ceuta. "O brothers," I said, "who through a hundred thousand perils have reached the west, to this so brief vigil of the senses that remains to us choose not to deny experience, in the sun's track, of the unpeopled world. Take thought of the seed from which you spring. You were not born to live as brutes, but to follow virtue and knowledge." My companions I made so eager for the road with these brief words that I could hardly have held them back, and with our poop turned to the morning we made of the oars wings for the mad flight, always gaining on the left. Night then saw all the stars of the other pole and ours so low that it did not rise from the ocean floor. Five times the light had been rekindled and as often quenched on the moon's underside since we had entered on the deep passage, when there appeared to us a mountain, dim by distance, and it seemed to me of such a height as I had never seen before. We were filled with gladness, and soon it turned to lamentation, for from the new land a storm rose and struck the forepart of the ship. Three times it whirled her round with all the waters, the fourth time lifted the poop aloft and plunged the prow below, as One willed, until the sea closed again over us.

Even as English prose rather than as preternaturally strong Italian terza rima, does this extraordinary speech provoke in the common reader anything like the following reflection, written by the most gifted of Dante's critics? "What separates Ulysses' definitive death by water from Dante's baptism unto death and subsequent resurrection is the Christ event in history, or grace, the Christ event in the individual soul."

Surely an infinitely less powerful passage could prompt exactly that reflection with equal justice. There is a disproportion between a doctrine or a piety that voids every difference except assent, and a poetic text almost beyond rival. Something is plainly wrong with a way of reading Dante that yields all authority to Christian doctrine, even if Dante himself is partly responsible for such reductiveness. In Dante's arrangement of Hell, we are at the eighth level down of the eighth circle down, which is not too far away from Satan. Ulysses is a fraudulent counselor, primarily because of his craft and cunning in bringing down Troy, ancestor of Rome and so of Italy, as Virgil in particular recorded. Dante does not speak to Ulysses because in one sense he is Ulysses; to write the *Comedy* you set your course for an uncharted sea. And with great clarity Dante tells us what he will not have Ulysses recount: the death of Achilles, the Trojan horse, the theft of the Palladium, all of which are occasions for the wanderer's damnation.

The last voyage is not in that category, whatever its outcome. Himself inflamed, Dante bends toward the flame of Ulysses with desire, the longing for knowledge. The knowledge he receives is that of pure quest, made at the expense of son, wife, and father. The quest is, amid much else, a figuration for Dante's own pride and obduracy in prolonging his exile from Florence by refusing terms that would have returned him to his family. Eating another man's salt bread, going down stairs not your own, is one price paid for questing. Ulysses is willing to pay a more ultimate price. Whose experience is truly closer to Dante's—the triumphant conversion of Augustine or the last voyage of Ulysses? Legend tells us that Dante was pointed out in the streets as the man who had somehow returned from a voyage to Hell, as though he were a kind of shaman. We can assume that he believed in the reality of his visions; a poet of such force who judged himself to be a true prophet would not have regarded his descent into Hell as mere metaphor. His Ulysses speaks with absolute dignity and terrible poignancy: not the pathos of damnation, but the pride that knows how pride and courage do not suffice.

Virgil's Aeneas is something of a prig, and that is what many of his scholars turn Dante into, or would if they could. But he is no Aeneas; he is as savage, self-centered, and impatient as his Ulysses, and like his Ulysses he burns with the desire to be elsewhere, to be different. His distance from his double is greatest, presumably, when he has Ulysses speak so movingly of "this so brief vigil of the senses that remains to us." Even there we should remember that Dante, who died at fifty-six, wished to live another quarter-century, for in his *Convivio* he set the perfect age at eighty-one. Only then would he have been complete, and his prophecy perhaps fulfilled. Granted that Ulysses sets sail for the "unpeopled world," while Dante's cosmic voyages are to lands crowded with the dead, there is a distinction between these two questers, and Ulysses is certainly the more extreme. At the least, Dante's quester is a hero-villain, akin to Melville's Ahab, another ungodly, godlike man. A Gnostic or Neoplatonic hero is very different from a Christian hero, but Dante's imagination is not always moved by Christian heroism, unless he is celebrating his own crusader ancestor, Cassiaguida, who more than reciprocates with overwhelming praise of his descendant's courage and audacity. That is the undersong of Dante's vision of Ulysses: admiration, fellow-feeling, familial pride. A kindred spirit is saluted, even though he resides in the Eighth Circle of Hell. It is Ulysses who makes the judgment that his final voyage was a "mad flight," presumably in contrast to Dante's Virgil-guided flight.

Viewed strictly as a poem, no flight could be madder than that of the *Comedy*, which Dante does not wish us to view as a poem only. That is Dante's privilege, but not the privilege of his scholars, and it ought not to be the stance of his readers. If we are to see what makes Dante canonical, the very center of the Canon after Shakespeare, then we need to recover his achieved strangeness, his perpetual originality. That quality has very little to do with the Augustinian story of how the old self dies and the new self is born. Ulysses may be the old self and Beatrice the new, but Dante's Ulysses is his own, and so is Beatrice. What Augustine had done, Dante could not do better, and Dante saw to it that the *Comedy* became no more Augustinian than it was Virgilian. It is what he desired it to be: Dantean only.

Jesus Ben Sira, author of the wonderful Ecclesiasticus, which is consigned forever to the noncanonical Apocrypha, says that he comes as a gleaner in the wake of famous men, our fathers who begot us. Perhaps that is why he is the first Hebrew writer to insist upon his own proper name as author of his book. One cannot say too often that Dante did not come as a gleaner in order to praise the famous men before him. He distributes them, according to his own judgment, in Limbo, Hell, Purgatory, and Heaven, because he is the true prophet and expects to be vindicated in his own time. His judgments are absolute, ruthless, and sometimes morally unacceptable, at least to many now among us. He has given himself the last word, and while you are reading him, you don't want to argue with him, mostly because you want to listen and to visualize what he has seen for you. He cannot have been an easy person with whom to quarrel while he lived, and he has proved fierce ever since.

Though dead, white, male, and European, he is the most alive of all the personalities on the page, contrasting in this with his only superior, Shakespeare, whose personality always evades us, even in the sonnets. Shakespeare is everyone and no one; Dante is Dante. Presence in language is no illusion, all Parisian dogmas to the contrary. Dante has stamped himself upon every line in the *Comedy*. His major character is Dante the Pilgrim, and after that Beatrice, no longer the girl of the *New Life*, but a crucial figure in the celestial hierarchy. What is missing in Dante is the ascension of Beatrice; one can wonder why, in his daring, he did not also illuminate the mystery of her election. Perhaps it was because all of the precedents he had were not only heretical, but belonged to the heresy of heresies, Gnosticism. From Simon Magus onward, heresiarchs had elevated their closest female followers to the heavenly hierarchies, even as the outrageous Simon, first of the Fausts, had taken Helena, a whore of Tyre, and proclaimed her to have been Helen of Troy in one of her previous incarnations. Dante, whose Eros had been sublimated and yet remained permanent, risked no comparisons.

Still, in a poetic rather than a theological sense, Dante's myth of Beatrice is closer to Gnosticism than to Christian orthodoxy. All evidence for what might be called the apotheosis of Beatrice is not merely personal (as it has to be) but comes out of a visionary world akin to the Gnosticism of the second century. Beatrice must be an uncreated spark of the divine or emanation of Godhood, as well as a Florentine girl who died at the age of twenty-five. She does not undergo the religious categories of judgment that lead to blessedness and sainthood but seems to go directly from death to being part of the hierarchy of salvation. There is no indication, either in the *New Life* or the *Comedy*, that Beatrice was subject to sin, or even to error. Instead she was, from the start, what her name indicated: "she who confers blessing." Dante says of her that, at nine, she was "the youngest of the Angels," a daughter of God, and after she dies her poet speaks "of that blessed Beatrice who now gazes continually on His countenance, who is blessed throughout the ages."

We cannot regard Dante as indulging himself in erotic hyperbole; the *Comedy* is inconceivable without a Beatrice whose joyous acceptance in the highest regions was always assured. Petrarch, seeking to distance himself from the more than formidable poet of his father's generation, invented (as he thought) poetic idolatry in regard to his beloved Laura, but what, beyond Dante's own, scandalous authority, restrains us from seeing Dante's worship of Beatrice as the most poetic of all idolatries? By his authority, Dante integrates Beatrice into Christian typology, or perhaps it would be more accurate to say that he integrates Christian typology into his vision of Beatrice. Beatrice, not Christ, is the poem; Dante, not Augustine, is the maker. This is not to deny Dante's spirituality but only to indicate that originality is not in itself a Christian virtue, and that Dante matters because of his originality. As much as any other poet except Shakespeare, Dante has no poetic father, even though he asserts that Virgil occupies such a place. But Virgil is summoned by Beatrice and vanishes from the poem when Beatrice triumphantly returns to it, in the concluding cantos of the *Purgatorio*.

That return, extraordinary in itself, is preceded by another of Dante's grand inventions, Matilda, who is seen gathering flowers in a restored earthly paradise. The vision of Matilda was crucial for Shelley's poetry, and it is appropriate that this passage of Dante was translated by Shelley, in what may be the best version of any part of the *Comedy* in English. Here is the climax of the passage as rendered by Shelley, who went on to compose a diabolic parody of the vision in his very Dantesque death poem, *The Triumph of Life*:

> *I moved not with my feet, but mid the glooms*
> *Pierced with my charmed eye, contemplating*
> *The mighty multitude of fresh May blossoms*
>
> *Which starred that night, when, even as a thing*
> *That suddenly, for blank astonishment,*
> *Charms every sense*, and makes all thought take wing,—
>
> *A solitary woman! and she went*
> *Singing and gathering flower after flower,*
> *With which her way was painted and besprent.*

"Bright lady, who, if looks had ever power
To bear true witness of the heart within,
Dost bask under the beams of love, come lower

Towards this bank. I prithee let me win
This much of thee, to come, that I may hear
Thy song: like Proserpine, in Enna's glen,

Thou seemest to my fancy, singing here
And gathering flowers, as that fair maiden when,
She lost the Spring, and Ceres her, more dear."

In the previous canto, Dante had dreamed of "a lady young and beautiful going through a meadow gathering flowers and singing," but she identified herself as Leah, the Biblical Jacob's first wife, and contrasted herself to her younger sister, Rachel, who became the Patriarch of Israel's second wife. Leah foretells Matilda, and Rachel is the forerunner of Beatrice, but it is a little difficult to see them as a contrast between the active and the contemplative life:

> Know, whoever asks my name, that I am Leah, and I go plying my fair hands here and there to make me a garland; to please me at the glass I here adorn myself, but my sister Rachel never leaves her mirror and sits all day. She is fain to see her own fair eyes as I to adorn me with my hands. She with seeing, and I with doing am satisfied.

Has time destroyed these metaphors? Have they yielded to feminism's critique? Or is it that, in a post-Freudian era, we recoil from the exaltation of narcissism? Certainly the commentary of the usually acute Charles Williams seems a touch embarrassing at our current moment: "Dante, for the last time, dreams: of Leah gathering flowers—what else is all action? and of Rachel looking in her glass—what else is all contemplation? for now the soul may justly take joy in herself and in love and beauty."

The vision of Leah or Matilda gathering flowers as an emblem of doing or action unfortunately calls to my mind a James Thurber cartoon in which two women observe a third picking flowers, and one says to the other, "She has the true Emily Dickinson spirit except that she gets fed up occasionally." The image of Rachel or Beatrice contemplating herself in the mirror tends to summon up Freud's unfortunate moment when he compared the narcissism of women to that of cats. My associations are doubtless arbitrary, but typology, with whatever learned explanations, does not always serve Dante well. That he intended the *Comedy* to be a poem "about" his conversion, "about" his becoming a Christian, I greatly doubt. If he did, it could only be in the etymological meaning of the

English "about," which is: to be on the outside of something. On its inside, the *Comedy* is about Dante's being called to the work of prophecy.

You can become a Christian without accepting the mantle of Elijah, but not if you are Dante. The vision of Matilda replacing Proserpina in a restored earthly paradise does not come to the newly converted Christian, but to the prophet-poet whose vocation has been confirmed. Shelley, no Christian but a Lucretian poet-prophet, was transformed by the Matilda passage because it illuminated, for him, the passion of the poetic vocation, the restoration of the paradisal nature that had abandoned his great precursor, Wordsworth. Matilda is Beatrice's forerunner because Proserpina revivified makes possible the return of the Muse. And Beatrice is not an imitation of the Christ, but Dante's creativity lancing out to identify itself with an old love, whether real or largely imaginary.

The idealization of lost love is an almost universal human praxis; what is remembered across the years is a lost possibility for the self, rather than of the other. The association of Rachel and Beatrice works so beautifully not because each is a type of the contemplative life, but because each is a passionate image of lost love. Rachel matters to the Church because of its interpretation of her as contemplative emblem, but she matters to poets and their readers because a great narrator, the Yahwist or J writer, made her early death in childbirth the great sorrow of Jacob's life. In poetic typology, Rachel precedes Beatrice as the image of the early death of a beloved woman, while Leah is linked to Matilda as a vision of deferred fulfillment. Jacob served Laban in order to win Rachel and first received Leah instead. Dante longs for the return of Beatrice, but the journey to Beatrice through Purgatory takes him first to Matilda. Although it is the hour of the morning star, of the planet Venus, it brings Matilda, not Beatrice, to Dante. Matilda sings like a woman in love, and Dante walks with her, but it is only a preparation, even as Leah was a preparation for Rachel.

What bursts upon the poet is a triumphal procession rather shockingly centered upon the prophet Ezekiel's vision of "the wheels and their work," the Chariot and the Enthroned Man. Dante evades the shock by telling his readers to go to the text of Ezekiel for the more outrageous details, even as he follows the Revelation of Saint John the Divine in reading Ezekiel's Man as Christ. For Dante, the Chariot is the triumph of the Church, not as it was, but as it should be; and he surrounds this idealized militancy with the books of the two Testaments, again not to rely on them but to get them out of his way. All of this, even that Griffon symbolizing Christ, matters only because of the beauty that it heralds, the return of one's ancient love, no longer forever and irretrievably lost.

The actual advent of Beatrice in canto 20 of the *Purgatorio* involves the permanent vanishing of Virgil. She makes Virgil redundant, not because theology is replacing poetry, but because Dante's *Comedy* now wholly replaces Virgil's *Aeneid*. Although he explicitly insists otherwise, Dante (now named, by Beatrice herself, for the first and only time in his poem) celebrates his own powers as poet by enthroning Beatrice. Pragmatically, what else could he be doing? Even Charles Singleton, the most theological of major Dante exegetes, emphasizes that Beatrice's beauty "is said to surpass any created by nature or by art." If you are intent upon assimilating Dante to the allegory of the theologians (as Singleton invariably was), then only God, through the Church, could create and sustain a splendor beyond nature and art. But Beatrice, as we need to keep reminding ourselves, is altogether Dante's creation, in precisely the sense in which Dulcinea was Don Quixote's. If Beatrice is more beautiful than any other woman in literature or in history, Dante is celebrating his own power of representation.

The *Purgatorio*, in Dante's overt scheme, explores the Catholic argument that desire for God, having been displaced into wrong channels, must be restored through expiation. Dante's boldest assertion through out his work is that his desire for Beatrice was not a displaced one but always led on to a vision of God. The *Comedy* is a triumph, and so presumably must be the supreme Western instance of religious poetry. It is certainly the supreme example of a wholly personal poem that persuades many of its readers to believe they are encountering ultimate truth. Thus even Teodolinda Barolini, in a book professedly written to detheologize Dante, allows herself to say that "the *Commedia*, perhaps more than any other text ever written, consciously seeks to imitate life, the conditions of human existence."

The judgment is puzzling. Do the *Inferno* and the *Purgatorio*, let alone the *Paradiso*, seek to "imitate life" more consciously than *King Lear* or even the Dante-influenced *Canterbury Tales*? Whatever Dante's realism may be, it does not give us what Chaucer and Shakespeare bestow upon us: characters who change, even as actual human beings change. Only Dante changes and develops in the *Comedy*; everyone else is fixed and immutable. Indeed they have to be, because the final judgment has been made upon them. As for Beatrice, as a character in a poem, which is truly all she can be, she is necessarily even more removed from an imitation of life, for what has she to do with the conditions of human existence? Charles Williams, despite his gurulike attitudes, is sounder on this issue than the Dante scholars begin to be, when he observes of the *Comedy*, "Even that poem was necessarily limited. It does not attempt to deal with the problem of Beatrice's own salvation, and Dante's function there."

I find that claim somewhat crazy, but better such craziness than smothering Dante with doctrine or mistaking his poem for an imitation of life. As far as Dante was concerned, as a poet, there was absolutely no problem of Beatrice's own salvation. She saved Dante by giving him his greatest image for poetry, and he saved her from oblivion, little as she may have wanted such salvation. Williams muses mystically on the "marriage" between Beatrice and Dante, but that is Williams and not Dante. When she enters *Purgatorio* she speaks to her poet neither as a lover nor as a mother, but as a deity speaks to a mortal, albeit a mortal with whom she has a very special relationship. Her harshness to him is another inverted self-compliment on his part, since she is the superb mark of his originality, the trumpet of his prophecy. In effect, his own genius chides him, for what other reproof could the proudest of all poets accept? I suppose he would not have resisted a direct descent of Christ, but even Dante would not go so far as to risk such a representation.

The muse intervenes, but he names her "blessedness" and asserts a role for her that could benefit everyone else. She will not descend for and to others, except for his poetry; and so he is her prophet, a function he had been preparing since the *New Life*. Despite his complex relations to many traditions—poetic, philosophical, theological, political—Dante owes Beatrice to none of them. She can be distinguished from Christ, but not from the *Comedy*, because she is Dante's poem, the single image of images that represents not God, but Dante's own achievement. I am growing accustomed to having scholars tell me that Dante was interested in his own achievement as a way to God, and I decline to believe them. An exile from his own city, a witness to the failure of the emperor upon whom he had set his best hopes, Dante at last had only his poem to shore against his ruin.

The philosopher George Santayana in his *Three Philosophical Poets* (1910) distinguished among Lucretius, Dante, and Goethe on the basis of their Epicurean naturalism, Platonic supernaturalism, and Romantic or Kantian idealism, respectively. Santayana said of Dante that "He became to Platonism and Christianity what Homer had been to Paganism," but then added that love, as Dante "feels and renders it, is not normal or healthy love." It seems sacrilege to judge Dante's passion for Beatrice to be abnormal and unhealthy only because it offers so little resistance to a mystical transformation of the beloved into part of the divine apparatus for redemption. Still, Santayana was shrewd and refreshing in this, as also in ironically praising Dante for being ahead of his time in sustained egotism.

When Santayana added that Dante was a Platonist unlike any other, he should have gone on to a more important formulation: Dante was also a Christian unlike any other, and Beatrice is the mark of that unlikeness, the sign of what Dante added to the faith of the Church. Pragmatically, at least for poets and critics, the *Comedy* became the third Testament prophesied by Joachim of Fiore. The subtlest stand against the pragmatic test is not that made by the school of Auerbach, Singleton, and Freccero, but that by A. C. Charity in his study of Christian typology, *Events and Their Afterlife* (1966), and by Leo Spitzer, acknowledged by Charity as forerunner. Charity insists that Beatrice is an image of Christ, but is not Christ, or the Church, and he cites Kenelm Foster as saying that "she does not replace Christ, she reflects and transmits him." That may be piety, but it is not the *Comedy*, in which when Dante looks upon Beatrice, he sees Beatrice and not Christ. She is not a mirror but a person, and even Leo Spitzer in his 1988 *Representative Essays* does not altogether meet the difficulty of her individualistic status, indeed, her uniqueness:

That Beatrice is the allegory, not only of revelation, but of *personal*
revelation, is proved both by the autobiographical origin of this
figure and by her status in the Beyond: she is not an angel, but the
blessed soul of a human being that, just as it influenced Dante's life
on this earth, is called to perform for Dante in the course of his
pilgrimage services of which she alone is capable; she is not a saint,
but a *Beatrice*, not a martyr, but one who died young and was allowed
to stay on earth only in order to show Dante the possibility of
miracles. The dogmatic license here taken by Dante appears less
daring if we consider the fact that revelation may come to the
Christian in an individual form, suited to him personally.... She is ...
the counterpart of ... those historical persons born before the
Redeemer who foreshadow him.

Resourceful as Spitzer was, this will not do, and it in no way diminishes
Dante's "daring." According to Dante, Beatrice is much more than a merely
personal or individual revelation. She has come initially to her poet, Dante, but
through him she comes to his readers. Virgil says to her in the *Inferno*, "O lady
of virtue, through whom alone (*sola*) the human kind surpasses everything within
the smallest circle of the heavens," which Curtius expounds as "Through
Beatrice alone, mankind surpasses everything earthly, whatever this may mean:
Beatrice has a metaphysical dignity for all men—Beatrice alone." Spitzer also
gets too quickly from the difference between being a *prefiguration* of Christ and
an *imitation* of Christ. Had Beatrice come *before* Christ, you might argue that she
was another forerunner, but, of course, she comes after, and what Dante fell in
love with, in her and as her, was not the imitation of Christ. At the least she is,
as Santayana observed, a Platonizing of Christianity, which has never stopped
being Platonized, before and since Dante. At the most she is what Curtius
insisted she was: the center of a poetic gnosis, of the vision of Dante.

That returns us to her as the sign of Dante's originality, the heart of his
power and his strangeness. Pride is not a Christian virtue, but it has always been
a crucial virtue in the greatest poets. Shakespeare may be the grand exception, as
he is in so many things. We never will know what his attitude was in regard to
having written *Hamlet* or *King Lear* or *Antony and Cleopatra*. Perhaps he required
no attitude, because he never lacked acknowledgment and commercial success.
He must have known, quite consciously, how original and enormous his
achievement was, but we search the plays in vain for self-compliments, and the
sonnets, though they contain some, also express considerable modesty. Could
Shakespeare unironically have spoken of any rival poet's gift or scope, or believed
in the "proud sail" of George Chapman's "great verse"? Dante proudly sets sail
for Paradise, and celebrates himself for celebrating Beatrice. In *Paradise Lost*
Satan's pride, however it is related to Milton's, brings him down. In the *Comedy*,
Dante's pride carries him up, to Beatrice and beyond.

Beatrice emanates from Dante's pride but also from his need. Scholars interpret what she stands for or represents; I suggest we begin to consider what it was that Beatrice enabled Dante to exclude from his poem. Vico charmingly deplored Dante's extensive knowledge of theology. Dante's spiritual erudition is not the problem; that of his exegetes is. Remove Beatrice from the *Comedy*, and Virgil would have to yield to one saint or another as Dante's guide from the Earthly Paradise up to the Celestial Rose. A reader's religious resistance, which can already be rather more considerable than the Anglo-American scholars of Dante ever want to acknowledge, would certainly be heightened if Saint Augustine took the place of Beatrice. More important, Dante's resistance to received doctrine would have been heightened also. There is more apparent than actual concurrence between Dante's vision and the Catholic faith, but Dante centers on Beatrice partly to avoid having to waste his imaginative energies on a needless quarrel with orthodoxy.

It is Beatrice whose presence and function transform Augustine and Aquinas into something figuratively much richer, adding strangeness to truth (if you think it is the truth) or to fiction (if you regard it as that). I myself, as a student of gnosis, whether poetic or religious, judge the poem to be neither truth nor fiction but rather Dante's *knowing*, which he chose to name Beatrice. When you know most intensely, you do not necessarily decide whether it is truth or fiction; what you know primarily is that the knowing is truly your own. Sometimes we call such knowing by the name of "loving," almost invariably with the conviction that the experience is permanent. Most often it departs and leaves us bewildered, but we are not Dante and cannot write the *Comedy*, so all we finally know is loss. Beatrice is the difference between canonical immortality and loss, for without her Dante would now be another pre-Petrarchan Italian writer who died in exile, a victim of his own pride and zeal.

I have considerable distaste for Charles Williams whether he writes Christian fantasy, rather grotesque poetry, or unabashed Christian apologetics as in *He Came down from Heaven* and *The Descent of the Dove*. Nor is Williams what I regard as a disinterested critic of literature. He is, in his way, as much an ideologue as the neo-Feminists, pseudo-Marxists, and Francophile reductionists who make up our current School of Resentment. But Williams has the almost solitary distinction of reading Dante as primarily the creator of the figure of Beatrice:

> The image of Beatrice existed in his thought; it remained there and was deliberately renewed. The word, image, is convenient for two reasons. First, the subjective recollection within him was of something objectively outside him, it was an image of an exterior fact and not of an interior desire. It was sight and not invention. Dante's assertion was that he could not have invented Beatrice.

A poet's assertion is a poem, and Dante is neither the first nor the last great poet to insist that his invention was a clearing of sight. Perhaps Shakespeare might have said the same of Imogen in *Cymbeline*. Williams compares Beatrice to Imogen, but Beatrice, unlike Dante the Pilgrim and Virgil the Guide, unlike the Ulysses of the *Inferno*, is not quite a literary character. She has dramatic qualities, including some flashes of high scorn; but being herself more the whole poem than a personage in it, she can be apprehended only when the reader has read and absorbed the entire *Comedy*, which perhaps accounts for a curious opacity (by no means here an aesthetic flaw) in the figure of Beatrice. Her remoteness, even toward her poet-lover, is far greater than Williams acknowledges and is carefully orchestrated by Dante, culminating in the poignant moment in the *Paradise* when he sees her, now from afar:

> I lifted up my eyes and saw her where she made for herself a crown, reflecting from her the eternal beams. From the highest region where it thunders no mortal eye is so far, were it lost in the depth of the sea, as was my sight there from Beatrice; but to me it made no difference, for her image came down to me undimmed by aught between.
>
> "O Lady in whom my hope has its strength and who didst bear for my salvation to leave thy footprints in Hell, of all the things that I have seen I acknowledge the grace and the virtue to be from bondage into liberty by all those ways, by every means for it that was in thy power. Preserve in me thy great bounty, so that my spirit, which thou hast made whole, may be loosed from the body well-pleasing to thee." I prayed thus; and she, so far off as she seemed, smiled and looked at me, then turned again to the eternal fount.

Commenting on this amazing passage in a previous book, I noted that Dante refused to accept his cure from the hand of any man, however saintly, but only from the hand of his own creation, Beatrice. One Catholic literary critic chided me for not understanding the faith, and at least one Dante scholar said that my observation was Romantic-Satanic (whatever that can mean, this late in the day). My reference was clearly to Freud's plangent and eloquent summa, "Analysis Terminable and Interminable," the lament of the founder of psychoanalysis that his patients would not accept their cure from him. Dante, prouder than any of us, would accept his cure only from Beatrice, and it is to Beatrice that Dante prays. His prophetic audacity is not Augustinian, just as his Imperial politics repudiates Augustine's sense that the church had replaced the Roman Empire. The *Comedy* is an apocalyptic poem, and Beatrice is an invention possible only for a poet who expected his prophecy's fulfillment before his own death. What would Augustine have thought of Dante's poem? I would guess that his largest objection would have been to Beatrice, a private myth that carries the heavens before it, even as Dante bears away the Kingdom of God.

What precedent, if any, was there for Beatrice? She is a Christian muse who enters the poem's action and so fuses herself with the poem that we cannot conceive of it without her. Dante's designated precursor was Virgil, and if there is a parallel to Beatrice in the *Aeneid*, it has to be Venus. Virgil's Venus, as Curtius emphasizes, is much more an Artemis or Diana figure than an Aphrodite. She is severely restrained, strangely Sibyl-like, and scarcely the mother of Eros, as compared to the half-god, Aeneas. Himself both Epicurean and Stoic, the actual Virgil (as opposed to Dante's strong misreading) hardly longs for grace and redemption, only for respite from the endless vision of suffering and its meaninglessness. If Dante had been more accurate, Virgil would be with the superb Farinata in the sixth circle of hell, reserved for the Epicureans and other heretics.

Virgil's own precursor was Lucretius, the most powerful of all materialist and naturalistic poets, and more Epicurean than Epicurus. Dante had never read Lucretius, who was not revived until the closing decades of the fifteenth century. I regret this enormously, as it would have given Dante an opponent altogether worthy of his strength. Whether Lucretius would have horrified Dante, we cannot know, but Dante would have been outraged to learn that Virgil was far closer in spirit, if not in sensibility, to Lucretius than to Dante. Certainly Virgil's Venus is a deliberate swerve away from the Lucretian Venus, so we have the irony that Lucretius is Dante's wicked grandfather as it were, if I am at all correct in surmising that the Virgilian Venus is the direct ancestor of Beatrice. George Santayana has an apt characterization of the Venus of *On the Nature of Things* as an Empedoclean Love existing in dialectical tension with Mars:

> The Mars and Venus of Lucretius are not moral forces, incompatible with the mechanism of atoms; they are this mechanism itself, insofar as it now produces and now destroys life, or any precious enterprise, like this of Lucretius in composing his saving poem. Mars and Venus, linked in each other's arms, rule the universe together; nothing arises save by the death of some other thing.

The Empedoclean-Lucretian formula "dying each other's life, living each other's death" delighted W. B. Yeats, pagan mystagogue that he was, but it would have been rejected, with contempt, by Dante. Virgil's undoubted reaction, on the basis of his own Venus, was ambivalent. He took from Lucretius, whose poem he clearly studied closely, the idea that Venus's truest life-giving was to the Romans, through her son Aeneas, their ancestor and founder. But his Venus does not engage in perpetual embraces with Mars. Weirdly, for she is after all the goddess of love, Virgil's Venus is as chaste as Beatrice. Virgil himself, unlike Dante, was not passionate toward women and probably (in Dante's scheme) deserved to be not only in canto 10 of the *Inferno* with Farinata the Epicurean, but also in canto 15 with Brunetto Latini the sodomite, Dante's honored teacher.

It is an exquisite irony that Beatrice, the supreme Christian muse, may find her likely origin in a Venus figure who is Diana-like partly as a reaction-formation against the lustful Epicurean Venus and partly because Dante's forerunner did not desire women. The dominant female in Virgil's epic is the frightening Juno, a nightmare of a goddess and the counterpoise to Virgil's Venus, indeed, a countermuse to Venus. Does Dante have a countermuse? Freccero locates her in the Medusa of *Inferno*, canto 9, and in turn relates this figure to the Lady Petra of Dante's "stony rhymes," including the great sestina that Dante Gabriel Rossetti translated so powerfully: "To the dim light and the large circle of shade." Freccero contrasts Dante to Petrarch, his dissenting successor in the next generation, whose Laura is in effect both muse and countermuse, Beatrice and Medusa, Venus and Juno. For Freccero, the comparison favors Dante, since Beatrice points beyond herself, presumably to Christ and God, and Laura remains strictly within the poem. Pragmatically, I would suggest that this is a difference that makes no difference, despite Freccero's Augustinian severities:

> Like Pygmalion, Petrarch falls in love with his own creation and is in turn created by her: the pun *Lauro/Laura* points to this self-contained process which is the essence of his creation. He creates with his poetry the Lady Laura who in turn creates his reputation as poet laureate. She is therefore not a mediatrix, pointing beyond herself, but is rather enclosed within the confines of his own being as poet, which is to say, the poem. This is precisely what Petrarch acknowledges when he confesses in his final prayer to the sin of idolatry, adoration of the work of his hands.

If one is not persuaded theologically by Dante, and most of us no longer are, what supports Freccero's sense that Dante is somehow free of Petrarch's inescapable aesthetic dilemmas? Is it that Petrarch, as ancestor of both Renaissance and Romantic poetry, and so of modern poetry as well, must share in the supposed sins of those who arrive after the medieval synthesis has dissolved? Dante, like Petrarch, falls in love with his own creation. What else can Beatrice be? And since she is the *Comedy*'s greatest originality, does she not in turn create Dante? Only Dante is our authority for the fiction that Beatrice points beyond herself, and she is certainly confined within the *Comedy*, unless you believe that Dante's personal gnosis is true not only for him, but for everyone else as well.

Does anyone pray to Beatrice, except Dante the Pilgrim of Eternity? Petrarch was happy to confess to idolatry because, as Freccero himself has splendidly shown, the confession helped to distance him from his overwhelming precursor. But does Dante not adore the finished *Comedy*, the astonishing work of his own hands? Idolatry is a theological category and a poetic metaphor; Dante, like Petrarch, is a poet and not a theologian. That Dante was a greater poet than Laura's victim, Petrarch doubtless recognized; but of the two it is Petrarch who has been even more influential on later poets. Dante vanished until the nineteenth century; he was scarcely esteemed during the Renaissance and the Enlightenment. Petrarch took his place, thus fulfilling his shrewd program of embracing poetic idolatry or inventing the lyric poem. Dante died when Petrarch was seventeen, in 1321. When Petrarch, about 1349, prepared the first version of his sonnets, he seems to have known that he was inaugurating a mode that transcended the sonnet form, and that shows no signs of waning six and a half centuries later. A second *Comedy* was not possible, any more than tragedy has been possible since Shakespeare ceased to write it. The canonical greatness of Dante, for a final time, has nothing to do with Saint Augustine, or with the truths, if they are truths, of the Christian religion. At our present bad moment, we need above all to recover our sense of literary individuality and of poetic autonomy. Dante, like Shakespeare, is an ultimate resource for that recovery, provided we can evade the sirens that sing to us the allegory of the theologians.

JOHN KLEINER

Finding the Center

In 1836, in a private letter to a sympathetic friend, Gabriele Rossetti reported a remarkable discovery he had made while studying the *Vita nuova*. This early work of Dante's was, he realized, much more highly structured than any reader had hitherto noticed. If one stripped away the *Vita nuova*'s prose and paid close attention to the arrangement of the remaining lyric poems, one could see that the work possessed a hidden symmetry: the three major canzoni in the collection divide the shorter poems into four evenly balanced groups. The organization of the collection is not random or casual; it is, rather, mathematically exacting:[1]

Ten Minor Poems
Canzone
Four Sonnets
—Central Canzone—
Four Sonnets
Canzone
Ten Minor Poems.

A discovery like Rossetti's invites many different responses. To readers who view secrecy as a writerly virtue, the central pattern might well appear to be evidence of a brilliantly executed reticence: in the *Vita nuova*, Dante strives for

From *Mismapping the Underworld: Daring and Error in Dante's 'Comedy'*. © 1994 by the Board of Trustees of the Leland Stanford Junior University.

and achieves a poetic architecture so subtle that it defeats detection by nearly all his readers. This elusiveness, they might suggest, matches the methods of erotic concealment the lover practices in the pursuit of his beloved—it is the formal equivalent of Dante's outwardly disguised yet inwardly unwavering passion for Beatrice. Other readers, more engaged by notions of poetic control than by secrecy, might choose to focus on the way the Rossettian schema imposes order on an apparently unruly gathering. For such readers, the pattern demonstrates Dante's persistent interest in symmetry. It is, they might suggest, a foretaste of the grander, more complex numerological schemes built into the *Comedy*. For still other readers whose tastes run toward allegoresis, the pattern offers a different kind of promise: here, in the arrangement of the poems, is a key to unlocking the work's meaning. By establishing a center for the work—the canzone "Donna pietosa"—Dante determines the proper course of our interpretive trajectory.

To my mind, these are all promising responses. Whether we choose to focus on the pattern's subtlety, its orderliness, or its message, Rossetti's discovery helps us to appreciate the wonderful strangeness of Dante's enterprise. And yet there are many readers who have staunchly refused to interest themselves in the Rossettian schema. From as early as the turn of the century, critics have repeatedly sought to warn readers against it.[2] These skeptics have denied that the pattern is important, questioned its deliberateness, and cast doubt on the perspicacity of its interpreters. They have argued that the symmetry of the *Vita nuova* is not Dante's creation, but the work of unself-critical critics: it is, they have claimed, little more than a numerologist's fantasy.

This chapter is about this debate and will present what is, I hope, an objective analysis of the competing arguments. My purpose is not, however, to settle the matter in favor of one side or the other; I am less interested in arguing for a final secure reading of the Rossettian pattern than in using it to plot readerly motives and assumptions. The debate over the *Vita nuova*'s hidden symmetry reveals, I shall suggest, the difficulty of interpreting patterns that promise more than they achieve—patterns that seem as if they should be perfectly executed but are not.

Of the many scholars to endorse the Rossettian schema, none has been more eloquent or influential than Charles Singleton. His *Essay on the "Vita nuova"* has long been recognized as a watershed in the history of Dante studies, and it is in the pages of this work that the typical American reader is likely to have first learned of the *Vita nuova*'s symmetric structure. Though Singleton's aims are distinctive, his *Essay* nonetheless provides a useful model for seeing what can be made of a pattern. His claims about the Rossettian pattern's importance are greater in scope than those of any critic except, perhaps, Rossetti himself.

At the heart of Singleton's *Essay* is a theological theory of poetic form. Based on citations from Bonaventure, Augustine, and Aquinas, Singleton argues that during the Middle Ages the art of poetry was understood as an extension of divine art. It was generally accepted, he claims, that "poems ought to resemble the creation" and that "poets ought to be like God."[3] In Dante's case, this imitative impulse manifests itself in two types of analogy: Dante writes poetry that he hopes will reflect the formal order of the cosmos and the hermeneutic order of sacred scripture.

Both types of analogy help to explain, and are in turn confirmed by, the *Vita nuova*'s hidden pattern. Since symmetry is a prominent feature of medieval cosmology, it is logical that a theomimetic poet should wish to order his poems symmetrically.

> At a time when this universe of ours revealed to the contemplative eye of man an order and a harmony expressing the substantial order and harmony of its Creator, it cannot be insignificant that the microcosmic vision of the poet should reveal a symmetry resembling that of the greater artifact, the cosmos. Our human art is grandchild to God's. Being this, it can reflect that light by which all that is intelligible comes from him. (Singleton, p. 7)

Symmetry also functions as a hermeneutic principle because of the peculiar structure of Christian history. In the Christian library, there are essentially two kinds of text corresponding to two distinct historical periods: there is the prospective text of the Old Testament and the retrospective of the New. At the dividing line stands the single critical event—the Crucifixion—to which all biblical narratives are supposed to refer. If a poet is to imitate this structure, then he should locate at the center of his work an event of comparable importance-an event that grants his narrative meaning and direction.[4] In Singleton's account of the *Vita nuova*, this "central" event is Beatrice's death as recorded in the central canzone, "Donna pietosa."

> Even as (in the medieval view) the death of our Lord Jesus Christ stands at the center of the whole Christian universe, saying what now is and what then is; and even as all things that come before His death look forward to it and all things that come after His death look back upon it: just so is the death of Beatrice in that little world of the *Vita Nuova* where Beatrice is, as Christ in the real world whose author is God. (Singleton, p. 24)

Viewed through Singleton's eyes, the Rossettian schema is much more than an elegant decoration designed to flatter the knowing eye. Whatever pleasure Dante may have taken in perfecting his pattern is held to be less significant than his ethical responsibility to strive after order and harmony. The work's highly controlled form is treated as if it were a sign of the poet's high moral seriousness. This reading of the *Vita nuova* is powerfully predictive. For if the *Vita nuova* reflects a theological pressure toward symmetry, then that same pressure should be apparent whenever and wherever Dante exercises his creative faculty. Form, in Singleton's account, does not merely express a particular artist's sensibility at a particular moment in his career; it expresses a worldview shared by an entire community.

The prediction implicit in Singleton's reading of the *Vita nuova* has, in fact, been tested with remarkable success. Since the *Essay's* publication, scholars have discovered dozens of numerical patterns and symmetries unsuspected by previous generations of readers. These range from relatively accessible insights—the realization that like-numbered cantos of the *Inferno*, *Purgatorio*, and *Paradiso* have important thematic ties—to truly abstruse discoveries about the positions of critical words or rhymes.[5] Singleton himself is responsible for bringing to light one of the subtlest of these structures. In 1965 he realized that by counting the number of lines contained in different cantos of the *Purgatorio*, one could reveal a symmetrical pattern centered on the *Purgatorio's* central canto.[6]

Canto	14	15	16	17	18	19	20
No. of lines	151	145	145	139	145	145	151

One may or may not be attracted to this kind of canto-counting, but one can hardly doubt that Singleton and his followers are responding to something real. They have shown that the *Comedy* exhibits patterns and symmetries that are strikingly inventive and subtle, and that demanded immense labor for their realization. It is clear from their research that structure plays a role in Dante's work far beyond that to which modern readers are accustomed.

But if the *Essay* has pushed critics to make significant discoveries and to rethink their assumptions, the numerological arguments proposed in it are nonetheless seriously flawed, and it is these flaws that I now wish to consider.

As I noted earlier, the Rossettian schema depends on division of the *Vita nuova's* lyrics into two basic groups: major canzoni on the one hand, sonnets and other "minor" poems on the other. Once we accept this division, demonstrating the pattern's deliberateness is relatively simple. Let us assume, for the moment, that the *Vita nuova* contains 28 poems of one type (26 sonnets and 2 non-canzoni) and 3 poems of another (3 canzoni). How likely is it that these 31 poems should fall purely by chance into a symmetrical arrangement? A moment's thought shows that there are fifteen possible symmetrical arrangements: one canzone must go in the middle of the collection and the other two canzoni must go in one of fifteen paired positions on either side. The number of random asymmetrical arrangements is clearly much greater. In fact, the total number of ways of ordering the poems approaches 4,500:

$$N_{total} = \frac{31!}{(28!)(3!)} = \frac{(31)(30)(29)}{(3)(2)(1)} = 4,495.$$

Symmetry could conceivably emerge without any prodding from the poet, but such a felicitous accident is extremely unlikely—the odds against it are roughly 300 to 1.

This clear and simple calculation would settle the matter were it not for a problem glossed over in the preceding paragraph: The calculation depends on assigning each poem to one of two groups, yet several of the poems resist such simple classification. The most problematic poems are the collection's three lyric fragments: the unfinished canzoni of chapters 27 and 33 and the sonnet fragment of chapter 34. In order to reveal (or impose) a symmetric pattern, one must handle these fragments very delicately: the unfinished canzone of fourteen lines must be labeled a sonnet; the unfinished canzone in two stanzas must be labeled a non-canzone; and the brief sonnet fragment must be ignored altogether.[7]

The lyric fragments defy simple classification, and their fragmentary condition itself casts doubt on Singleton's approach. One of the principal contentions of the *Essay* is that medieval poets in general, and Dante in particular, felt a theological compulsion to present finished works. According to Singleton, the completeness of a poem is a sign that it is "designed to reflect God's work in its completeness and perfection."[8] If this is the case, then why does Dante admit lyric fragments into the collection? And why does he place them so near the work's end? Reading through the *Vita nuova*, one increasingly confronts poems that seem imperfect and incomplete. The climactic confrontation occurs in the final chapter, where Dante alludes to a "mirabile visione" that he hopes one day to describe—if he lives long enough.

> Appresso questo sonetto apparve a me una mirabile visione, ne la quale io vidi cose che mi fecero proporre di non dire più di questa benedetta infino a tanto che io potesse più degnamente trattare di lei. E di venire a ciò io studio quanto posso, sì com'ella sae veracemente. Sì che, se piacere sarà di colui a cui tutte le cose vivono, che la mia vita duri per alquanti anni, io spero di dicer di lei quello che mai non fue detto d'alcuna. (*V.N.* 42.1–2)

> After I had written this sonnet there came to me a miraculous vision in which I saw things that made me resolve to say no more about this blessed one until I would be capable of writing about her in a nobler

way. To achieve this I am striving as hard as I can, and this she truly
knows. Accordingly, if it be the pleasure of Him by whom all things
live that my life continue for a few more years, I hope to write of her
that which has never been written of any other woman.

This promise of greater things to come, this resolution to remain silent until new
skills are achieved, turns the *Vita nuova* into a provisional project—a work whose
true end lies in the future. As Robert Harrison observes, "A dramatic failure, an
avowed authorial inadequacy, haunt the end of this work."[9]
    Another aspect of the *Vita nuova* that Singleton's analysis fails to address is
the eccentric placement of Beatrice's death. In the *Essay*, Singleton claims that
there is an analogy between Beatrice's death and Christ's: Christ dies and is
resurrected at the center of time, Beatrice dies in the canzone that comes at the
Vita nuova's center—the canzone "Donna pietosa."

> The attentive reader will come to see that the death of Beatrice holds
> a central position in the *Vita Nuova*. This is true even in point of
> outward arrangement of the poems. For there are three longer
> poems so spaced as to mark off the work into three equal parts, and
> it is the second of these longer poems, the middle one, which gives
> us Beatrice dead. We see her dead body. Women are covering her
> face with a veil. (Singleton, p. 7)

Singleton urges the attentive reader to note that Beatrice's death holds a "central
position," yet this is not actually the case. The central canzone "Donna pietosa"
does not describe Beatrice's real death, but only Dante's vision of her death; the
real event comes five chapters and four poems later. The "attentive reader"
should recognize the importance of this sleight of hand. By eliding the difference
between vision and reality, Singleton deftly avoids having to answer a difficult
question: If the center is as important as he claims, then why *doesn't* Beatrice die
there? Why should a prophetic dream occupy the formal center of the work
instead of the crucial event foreshadowed in that dream?
    Singleton speaks enthusiastically of closure and symmetry and invites his
readers to admire the medieval artist's devotion to perfectly executed patterns.
Yet when it comes to his own theory, he proves something less than a
perfectionist. The gaps in his account are so pervasive that he must surely have
noticed them and decided to suppress them. In composing the *Essay*, he appears
to have realized that the erring details were less important than his larger
message, that his theory was too elegant to be sacrificed on account of a few
irritating glitches. It is easy to smile at Singleton's compromise with error, but
hard to articulate a position that would not be equally inconsistent. Assume, for
the moment, that one decides to reject Singleton's reading based on the
anomalies and contradictions discussed above. Though such a decision might

explicitly release the poet and reader from the charge of obsessive perfectionism, it implicitly reaffirms the perfectionist impulse. To reject the Rossettian schema as imperfectly realized and *therefore* unintended is to assume, with Singleton, that authorial intent and formal perfection are coincident, that the only deliberate patterns are those executed without blemish.

In the remainder of this chapter, I shall pursue a different approach to the *Vita nuova*, partly to bring into focus certain neglected aspects of the work and partly to demonstrate a general analytic method. I propose to show that it is possible to generate an appealing, even genuinely informative reading of the *Vita nuova* in which order and disorder are viewed as complementary rather than opposing categories.

Consider, first, the question of closure. Is the *Vita nuova* a finished or a provisional project? Is Dante striving after perfect symmetry and failing, or is he merely uninterested in it? Nowhere does this question seem more pressing than in the chapters devoted to recording Beatrice's death. At the start of chapter 27, Dante announces that he wants to write a new poem dealing with a new and grander theme: Beatrice's effect on himself. It is a theme that will require, he claims, a full canzone.

> E però propuosi di dire parole, ne le quali io dicesse come me parea essere disposto a la sua operazione, e come operava in me la sua vertude; e non credendo potere ciò narrare in brevitade di sonetto, cominciai allora una canzone, la quale comincia: *Sì lungiamente.*

> Sì lungiamente m'ha tenuto Amore
> e costumato a la sua segnoria,
> che sì com'elli m'era forte in pria,
> così mi sta soave ora nel core.
> Però quando mi tolle sì'l valore,
> che li spiriti par che fuggan via,
> allor sente la frale anima mia
> tanta dolcezza, che 'l viso ne smore.

> Poi prende Amore in me tanta vertute,
> che fa li miei spiriti gir parlando,
> ed escon for chiamando
> la donna mia, per darmi più salute.
> Questa m'avvene ovunque ella mi vede,
> e sì è cosa umil, che noi si crede.

XXVIII

Quomodo sedet sola civitas plena populo! facta est quasi vidua domina gentium. Io era nel proponimento ancora di questa canzone, e compiuta n'avea questa soprascritta stanza, quando lo segnore de la giustizia chiamoe questa gentilissima a gloriare. (*V.N.* 27–28)

And so I decided to write a poem telling how I seemed to be disposed to her influence, and how her miraculous power worked in me; and believing I would not be able to describe this within the limits of the sonnet, I immediately started to write a canzone which begins: *So long a time.*

> So long a time has Love kept me a slave
> and in his lordship fully seasoned me,
> that even though at first I found him harsh,
> now tender is his power in my heart.
> But when he takes my strength away from me
> so that my spirits seem to wander off,
> my fainting soul is overcome with sweetness,
> and the color of my face begins to fade.
>
> Then Love starts working in me with such power
> he turns my spirits into ranting beggars,
> and, rushing out, they call
> upon my lady, pleading in vain for kindness.
> This happens every time she looks at me,
> yet she herself is kind beyond belief.

XXVIII

How doth the city sit solitary that was full of people! How is she become a widow, she that was great among nations! I was still engaged in composing this canzone, in fact I had completed only the stanza written above, when the God of justice called this most gracious one to glory.

For a moment, at least, we are disoriented. Dante has promised to write a full canzone, yet after he has completed only a single stanza, he suddenly starts a new chapter and shifts abruptly from Italian to Latin. Only when we read beyond the quotation from Jeremiah and learn of Beatrice's death can we make sense of what has happened: Beatrice has died while Dante was in the middle of composing "Sì lungiamente," and that tragedy has permanently deferred the canzone's completion. With Beatrice no longer among the living, the poem's original message and phrasing cease to be appropriate. The fragmentary canzone survives as the visible trace of a crisis that has forced a fundamental change in Dante's art and, one supposes, his life.

If this deployment of a lyric fragment to signal a literary and spiritual crisis is deliberate, as I believe it is, then it expresses an approach to poetic form far more sophisticated than that allowed either by Singleton or by most of Singleton's critics.[10] Fully aware that his readers will associate artistic control with formal closure, Dante deliberately introduces a confusion-producing fragment into his collection. We cannot say that the young poet is either an adept or an opponent of closed literary systems because his performance brings the categories of perfection and imperfection into a creative, meaning-engendering opposition. It is precisely the deferral of the finished lyric that communicates its author's suffering. So artful is this staging of defeat, in fact, that it raises new problems for the readers of the *Vita nuova*. To recognize the significance of the poet's failure is to recognize that his failure is strategic and thus not really a failure at all. Even as Dante announces his terrible incapacitating crisis, he demonstrates a coolheaded virtuosity in manipulating literary conventions.

The ambiguous nature of Dante's artistic failure extends even to the placement of the canzone's fracture. As we noted earlier, the unfinished canzone lasts exactly fourteen lines before being abandoned. It is thus a fragmentary *canzone* that looks uncannily like a perfect *sonnet*. In fact, it exhibits not only the right number of lines, but also essentially the right structure: its *diesis* occurs after the eighth line, and it scans and rhymes much like Dante's other sonnets.[11] Of the 21 canzoni that Dante composed during his life, "Sì lungiamente" is the only one that could suffer such a felicitous incompletion. We could, of course, claim that this is merely an accident, but if this is so, Dante goes to a surprising length to attract our attention to it. Before beginning "Sì lungiamente," Dante explicitly tells us *not* to expect that his next poem will be a sonnet. He cannot write a sonnet because the sonnet would be inadequate to his new theme ("e non credendo potere ciò narrare in brevitade di sonetto, cominciai allora una canzone"). And then, curiously enough, he delivers his sonnet look-alike.

The local shift from canzone to sonnet necessarily affects the larger work's structure. As the *Vita nuova*'s nineteenth poem, "Sì lungiamente" falls in the second group of four sonnets. Thus if it had been completed, we would need to redraw the Rossettian schema as follows:

Ten Minor Poems
Canzone
Four Sonnets
Central Canzone
Three Sonnets
Canzone

      Canzone
      Ten Minor Poems

This hypothetical arrangement of lyrics is clearly not symmetric. The canzoni and sonnets no longer balance one another, and the collection is no longer centered on the revelatory canzone "Donna pietosa." Had Dante managed to finish "Sì lungiamente," the collection as a whole would have lost its order and its center; Dante only finishes the total work by leaving part of it unfinished.

      There are at least two ways to construe Dante's complex use of fragments in the *Vita nuova*. One could claim that in this first extended work, the young poet stages the victory of order over chaos, that he allows a larger, more complete structure to be born from what appears to be a local failure. Or one could claim that the elegant order of the *Vita nuova* masks a fundamental imperfection, that Dante leaves his work, at its very center, unstable and unfinished. It is up to us to choose, but whichever path we follow we should acknowledge the dynamic interdependence of order and disorder, perfection and imperfection.

      Let us now turn to the problem of Beatrice's two deaths—one in dream and one in reality. Is there evidence that this awkward doubling is also subject to poetic control, to an art of controlling chaos? To explore this possibility let us broaden the scope of our investigation: instead of worrying solely about the arrangement and articulation of the poems, let us also consider the structure of the *Vita nuova*'s prose.[12]

      The prose of the *Vita nuova* fulfills a dual function: it propels forward the narrative of Dante's "new life" while simultaneously providing a running commentary on the poems written in the course of that "new life." As both storyteller and autoexegete, Dante is extremely consistent. To gloss his poems, he always follows the same basic procedure—he divides them into smaller and smaller semantic units that he calls "divisions" (*divisioni*). This process of dividing poems is, Dante claims, a form of revelation: "La divisione non si fa se non per *aprire la sentenzia* de la cosa divisa" (14.13; emphasis mine). Similarly repetitive is Dante's use of chapter headings. Rather than experimenting with different openings as he does in the *Comedy*, Dante builds a narrative frame based on a monotonous sequence of "then, then, then, and then." *Appresso* and *poi* are the first words in half of the *Vita nuova*'s 42 chapters.

      The insistent, even wearying uniformity of the prose chapters gives prominence to even the subtlest variations in format. Thus when Dante decides in Chapter 31 to reverse the positions of the poems and the *divisioni*, we immediately sense the change in rhythm; we have moved, it seems, from one section of the work to another. We are similarly affected by the subtle shift in the use of chapter headings: in the austere prose of the *Vita nuova*, we cannot help but notice that Dante begins by favoring *appresso* and then shifts to *poi*. I have cited these specific changes because they are both triggered by Beatrice's death.

As Figure 1 indicates, the shift from *appresso* to *poi* and the transposition of the *divisioni* mark Beatrice's death as a formal turning point.

Dante explicitly comments on one of these shifts. In chapter 31, he tells us that he is reversing the order of the poems and the explanatory "divisions" so that the poems following Beatrice's death will seem "more widowed":

> E acciò che questa canzone paia rimanere più vedova dopo lo suo fine, la dividerò prima che io la scriva; e cotale modo terrò da qui innanzi. (*V.N.* 31.2)

> And in order that this canzone may seem to remain all the more widowed after it has come to an end, I shall divide it before I copy it. And from now on I shall follow this method.

Though the precise meaning of this metaphor is by no means obvious, I think we can safely infer a connection between mourning and memory. When Dante speaks of a poem as being "widowed," he is suggesting that its orientation is essentially retrospective and memorial. This is true of all the poems following Beatrice's death insofar as they come after the "central" event of Dante's new life; every poem after chapter 31 takes its meaning from the past. The transposition of poem and gloss can also be said to represent a form of "widowing" because it establishes a new temporality of reading: in the new order, readers do not *look* forward to the gloss that will explicate the poem; instead, they are called upon to remember the gloss that they have already read.

Given Dante's willingness to interpret the positions of poems and divisions metaphorically, it seems likely that the coincident shift from *appresso* to *poi* might also be significant. Though the two terms are close in meaning, they are not identical: *appresso* has a wider, more complex range of associations. When used as an adverb, *appresso* suggests separation, but when used as a preposition, it suggests proximity and is closely related to the verb *appressare*. These conflicting senses of *appresso* mirror the complex relations between events occurring before Beatrice's death. In this period of Dante's life, events follow after one another but also point *toward* the event that will determine their meaning. *Appresso* ceases to be the proper conjunction between different chapters as soon as Beatrice's death occurs; from that point onward, the poet no longer progresses toward the future, but simply moves away from the past. The only post-Beatrice appearance of *appresso* as a chapter heading occurs, appropriately enough, in the final chapter when Dante looks *forward* to his future work.

> *Appresso* questo sonetto apparve a me una mirabile visione, ne la quale io vidi cose che mi fecero proporre di non dire più di questa benedetta infino a tanto che io potesse più degnamente trattare di lei. (*V.N.* 42.1–2)

After I had written this sonnet there came to me a miraculous vision in which I saw things that made me resolve to say no more about this blessed one until I would be capable of writing about her in a nobler way.

The signposts that mark the center of the prose narrative are certainly not obvious, and yet they are not any more obscure than the hidden numerical pattern discovered by Rossetti. If we can believe that one pattern is Dante's deliberate creation, then we might as well believe that the other is as well. The only problem is that the two patterns locate two *different* centers for the work. While the lyric center is Beatrice's visionary death, the prose center is Beatrice's actual death. From a strict Singletonian perspective, such a contradiction is very difficult to explain.[13] For if Dante is trying to imitate God's work, he should not be uncertain about his work's interpretive center. A work that has two centers is potentially unstable, ambiguous, and confusing. In such a work one does not know exactly where to look for the critical signs that will anchor its meaning.

This is an especially serious problem in the *Vita nuova* because the two centers are so different. The dream scene, as Singleton observes, is cast in the readily identifiable form of a revelation. We recognize Dante's crisis not only from his tear-stained face, but also from the heavens themselves. Borrowing the imagery of Revelation 6:12–14, Dante depicts the features of a mourning cosmos:

> E pareami vedere lo sole oscurare, sì che le stelle si mostravano di colore ch'elle mi faceano giudicare che piangessero; e pareami che li uccelli volando per l'aria cadessero morti, e che fossero grandissimi terremuoti. E maravigliandomi in cotale fantasia, e paventando assai, imaginai alcuno amico che mi venisse a dire: "Or non sai? la tua mirabile donna è partita di questo secolo" (*V.N.* 23.5–6)

> And I seemed to see the sun grow dark, giving the stars a color that would have made me swear that they were weeping. And it seemed to me that the birds flying through the air fell to earth dead, and there were violent earthquakes. Bewildered as I dreamed, and terrified, I imagined that a friend of mine came to tell me: "Then you don't know? Your miraculous lady has departed from this world."

Beatrice's actual death, by contrast, is handled with extreme reticence. Dante refuses to speak directly about the most important event in his new life on the apparently paradoxical ground that such a description would be inconsistent with his original plan for the *Vita nuova*. At the very climax of the poet's new life," Beatrice vanishes into a fold of the narrative he categorically refuses to open.

E avvegna che forse piacerebbe a presente trattare alquanto de la sua partita da noi, non è lo mio intendimento di trattarne qui per tre ragioni: la prima è che ciò non è del presente proposito, se volemo guardare nel proemia che precede questo libello. (*V.N.* 28.2)

And even though the reader might expect me to say something now about her departure from us, it is not my intention to do so here for three reasons. The first is that such a discussion does not fit into the plan of this little book, if we consider the preface which precedes it.

Though the existence of these two competing centers represents a serious problem for Singleton's theory, it is easily accommodated in an interpretive framework that admits tension and fragmentation as valid analytic categories. If there are two centers in the *Vita nuova*—one reticent and one revelatory—then one might venture that that contradiction is itself revealing. It is certainly the case that Dante presents his relation to Beatrice in contradictory ways. Although he repeatedly invokes Beatrice as the figure whose presence authenticates his work, the figure who both inspires his poetry and serves as its subject, he also repeatedly affirms his inability to write a poem adequate to her. This posture toward the beloved is, of course, not unique to Dante, but it has seldom been maintained so resolutely. Every suggestion of Beatrice's animating presence is matched by a complementary suggestion that it is her absence that in fact animates the Vita nuova's poetry. We are regularly reminded that Beatrice's power lies as much in her unbroken silence as it does in her wondrous greeting. And while the poet may never claim to fully appropriate Beatrice, he also never completely renounces his hope of finding adequate words.[14]

As the structural tensions in the *Vita nuova* help us to notice the writer's conflicted desires, so the reverse is also true: acknowledging the rift in Dante's motivations helps us to make sense of his failure to create a perfectly ordered, perfectly coherent work. Ambivalent about his project and "uncentered" as artist, he designs a work with two competing centers, a work pointing simultaneously toward reticence and revelation. In such a reading of the *Vita nuova*, Love's criticism of the "uncentered" lover applies equally well to the artist and to his artifact:

Ego tanquam centrum circuli, cui simili modo se habent circumferentie partes; tu autem non sic. (*V.N.* 12.4)

I am like the center of a circle, equidistant from all points on the circumference; you, however, are not.

The interpretation of the *Vita nuova* that I have just proposed bears obvious similarities to Singleton's. As Singleton plotted the work's structure to disclose its coherence, so have I used its structure to disclose tensions and contradictions. The form of this repetition may, I realize, trouble some readers. While Singleton can claim that the *Vita nuova*'s perfect symmetry reflects a "passion for order" demonstrated by countless medieval artifacts, my approach may appear to present the work as strange and anomalous—an oddly modern-looking experiment in dissonance. Subsequent chapters will, I hope; lessen the appearance of anachronism; one goal of this study is to clarify the roles played by error and disorder within medieval cosmology, hermeneutics, and aesthetics. An even more immediate goal is to describe disorder's role within the *Comedy*. In that later poem, the patterns are clearer and stronger than in the *Vita nuova*; there we find more complex symmetries, more numerical wizardry, and a more insistent emphasis on closure. But that work also reveals the poet's deepening interest in the perils of pretending to perfection and his widening awareness of the gap between human and divine art. On the question of poetic control, the *Comedy* is, I believe, even more ambitiously ambivalent than Dante's first youthful experiment.

NOTES

1. "The interpretation of the *Vita Nuova* depends on knowing what portions are to be taken first and what portions are to be taken last.... The central canzone, which is 'Donna pietosa,' is the head of the skein, and from that point must the interpretation begin; then one must take, on this side and on that the four lateral sonnets to the left and to the right.... On this side and on that follow the two canzoni, placed symmetrically.... And thus collating the ten compositions to the right with the ten to the left, we come finally to the first and the last sonnets of the *Vita Nuova*.... The central part, which constitutes the Beatrice Nine, consists of nine compositions." *Gabriele Rossetti: A Versified Autobiography*, trans. and supp. William Michael Rossetti (London: Sands, 1901), p. 137; also in Kenneth McKenzie, "The Symmetrical Structure of Dante's *Vita nuova*," *Publications of the Modern Language Association* 18 (1903): 342. Rossetti's description differs from the pattern sketched here in the text insofar as it encompasses 33 rather than 31 poems. Following the advice of his friend Charles Lyell, Rossetti includes a sonnet by Cavalcanti, and he counts as a poem the first unfinished version of "Era venuta." The 31-poem version of the pattern was "discovered" independently in 1859 by Charles Norton. For the circumstances of the pattern's original discovery, see E. R. Vincent, *Gabriele Rossetti in England* (Oxford: Clarendon Press, 1936), pp. 72–110.

2. Among the more vitriolic opponents of the hidden pattern is Michele Scherillo; see "La forma architettonica della *Vita nuova*," *Giornale dantesco* 9 (1902): 84–88. The objections of Scherillo and other Italian critics were answered by McKenzie, whose rhetoric was no less fiery: "He [Scherillo] declares that anyone who believes that Dante had the intention of arranging the *Vita*

Nuova symmetrically shows 'deplorable ingenuousness and lack of critical training.' It seems to me, however, that these deplorable qualities are shown rather by attempting to deny what is evident." "Symmetrical Structure," p. 349. For the history of the pattern's initial reception, see McKenzie's article and Angelina La Piana, *Dante's American Pilgrimage* (New Haven: Yale University Press, 1948), pp. 119–21. Recent American critics of the *Vita nuova* have, by and large, accepted the pattern's deliberateness and sought to interpret it. See, for example, Charles Singleton, *An Essay on the "Vita Nuova"* (Cambridge, Mass.: Harvard University Press, 1949; reprint, Baltimore: The Johns Hopkins University Press, 1977); Mark Musa, "An Essay on the *Vita Nuova*," in *Dante's "Vita Nuova"*, ed. and trans. Mark Musa (Bloomington: University of Indiana Press, 1973); and Jerome Mazzaro, *The Figure of Dante: An Essay on the "Vita Nuova"* (Princeton: Princeton University Press, 1981). One notable exception to this trend is Robert Harrison's *The Body of Beatrice* (Baltimore: The Johns Hopkins University Press, 1988), a work to which this chapter is much indebted.

3. Singleton, *Essay*, p. 50.

4. Singleton argues that even the numerical grouping of the poems has a meaning. The pattern (viewed correctly) is engineered to reveal the Beatricean nine:

10 – 1 – 4 – 1 – 4 – 1 – 10
(1 + 9) – 1 – (4 + 1 + 4) – 1 – (9 + 1)
1 – 9 – 1 –9 – 1 – 9 –1 .

"Here on the surface are ripples and eddies which are so many signs. ... signs that Beatrice is a miracle, that she is herself a number nine which, like miracles, is the product of three times three" (ibid., pp. 79–80).

5. See, for example, Giuseppe Mazzotta's analysis of the parallels among *Inferno* 7, *Purgatorio* 7, and *Paradiso* 7 in *Dante, Poet of the Desert* (Princeton: Princeton University Press, 1979), pp. 319–28. For a discussion of proportional numerology, see Thomas Elwood Hart, "The Cristo-Rhymes and Polyvalence," *Dante Studies* 105 (1987): 1–42. For a more local kind of numerical pun on perfection, closure, and the number 10, see R. A. Shoaf, "*Purgatorio* and *Pearl*: Transgression and Transcendence," *Texas Studies in Literature and Language* 32, 1 (1990): 155.

6. Singleton, "The Poet's Number at the Center," *Modern Language Notes* 80 (1965): 1–10. Since 1965 the hunting and debunking of centers has become a minor cottage industry among Dante scholars (this writer included). Singleton's discovery was first attacked by Richard Pegis in "Numerology and Probability in Dante," *Medieval Studies* 29 (1967): 370–73. It was then defended by J. L. Logan, who extends the pattern also to the *Purgatorio* and *Paradiso* by invoking a principle of "mystic" addition (i.e., 142 = 1 + 4 + 2 = 7). "The Poet's Central Numbers," *Modern Language Notes* 86 (1971): 95–98. Jeffrey Schnapp uses slightly different arguments to find a more local center associated with the

celestial cross described in *Paradiso* 16 in *The Transfiguration of History at the Center of Dante's "Paradise"* (Princeton: Princeton University Press, 1986), pp. 72–76, 158–59. Line numbers are very rarely indicated on medieval manuscripts, and there is no obvious reason why Dante should have expected his readers to go to the trouble of counting lines for themselves; the pattern would thus have seemed even more subtle to Dante's contemporaries than it does to modern readers. Singleton explains this puzzle by suggesting that Dante, like other medieval artists, composed his patterns to please God rather than man: "We know that such an edifice [Chartres] was not addressed to human sight alone, indeed not primarily to human sight at all. He who sees all things and so marvelously created the world in number, weight, and measure, would see that design, no matter where its place in the structure." "Poet's Number," p. 10.

7. In order to make the pattern work, one must not count the unfinished version of "Era venuta" as a poem at all. One must classify the unfinished canzone "Quantunque volte" as a non-canzone. And, most questionable of all, one must classify the unfinished canzone "Sì lungiamente" as a sonnet. This final point is taken up at greater length later in this chapter.

8. Charles Singleton, ed. and trans., *The Divine Comedy*, vol. 3, *Paradiso* (Princeton: Princeton University Press, 1975), p. 609.

9. Harrison, *Body of Beatrice*, p. 11.

10. One critic who suggests that truncation is managed for poetic effect is Nancy J. Vickers: "The act of writing is interrupted, and interruption ironically transforms, through abrupt truncation, the would-be *canzone* back into a perfectly crafted sonnet." "Widowed Words: Metaphors of Mourning," in *Discourses of Authority in Medieval and Renaissance Literature*, ed. Kevin Brownlee and Walter Stevens (Hanover, N.H.: University Press of New England, 1989), p. 99.

11. The proper category for the lyric "Sì lungiamente" is in fact the subject of some difference of opinion among critics. Kenelm Foster and Patrick Boyde, in *Dante's Lyric Poetry*, (London: Oxford University Press, 1967), 2: 129, summarize the points for and against its classification as a sonnet: "It has the necessary fourteen lines (in itself, not significant); the *pedes* correspond exactly to those of a sonnet (unique among canzone-stanzas by stilnovisti ...), there is no *verso chiave* (unique in Dante's canzoni, but quite common—e.g., in Cino). The differences are that 1.11 is a heptasyllable, and even if it were not (assuming that *chiamando* remained in rhyme), the resultant rhyme scheme—CDD; CEE— never occurs in any of Dante's sonnets where each *volta* always contains all the rhymes." Foster and Boyde classify the poem as a canzone-stanza, but they note the irony of Dante's presentation of his work as a fragment that is not a sonnet. "What is interesting and even amusing is that Dante protests in the prose that he did not think he could treat his subject 'in brevitade di sonetto' whereas not only is the stanza self-contained in its fourteen lines, but the theme is stated in full in

the first four." Ultimately it is not so much a question of whether "Sì lungiamente" "really" is a sonnet, but whether the play between perfection and imperfection is significant.

12. The structure of the prose is briefly discussed in Singleton's *Essay*. Singleton claims that since "Donna pietosa" is "contained in chapter twenty-three, and since the last chapter of the *Vita Nuova* is numbered forty-two, the death of Beatrice could hardly be more centrally placed" (p. 7). But as Harrison points out, 42 divided in half does not equal 23. The chapter containing "Donna pietosa" comes close to the numerical center of the prose chapters, but it does not come at the center. The prose "center" that I will be discussing is determined not numerically, but by the chapters' varying form.

13. Oddly enough, the *Comedy* presents much the same problem. In a 1954 essay, Singleton claims that Beatrice's return in the procession in Earthly Paradise (canto 30) takes place at the center of the *Comedy*—a return that mirrors Beatrice's disappearance in the *Vita nuova*: "In the *Vita Nuova*, at the center of the *Vita Nuova*, Beatrice is seen to depart from this life.... At the *center* of the *Divine Comedy*, Beatrice comes, Beatrice returns." "Pattern at the Center," in *Elements of Structure*, ed. Charles Singleton (Cambridge, Mass.: Harvard University Press, 1954), p. 57 (emphasis mine). In 1965, Singleton contradicts this claim with marvelous confidence (or perhaps self-irony?); in the lead sentence to "Poet's Number," Singleton blithely announces that "the central canto of the *Commedia* is, of course, the seventeenth of the *Purgatorio*, the central *cantica*" (emphasis mine). How can the center of the *Comedy* be located in *Purgatorio* 30 and also in *Purgatorio* 17?

14. See Harrison, *Body of Beatrice*, chaps. 6 and 7.

WILLIAM FRANKE

Dante's Interpretive Journey:
Truth Through Interpretation

HISTORICITY OF TRUTH

'... colui che 'n terra adusse
la verità che tanto ci soblima ..."
(*Paradiso* XXII.41–42)

Considered historically—for, indeed, interpretation, far from excluding
history, includes it as in its essence interpretive—the cultural project of Dante
parallels in provocative ways the currents in modern thought that have
culminated in "philosophical hermeneutics."[9] Both may be described as
radicalizations of the thinking of the historical conditionedness of all knowledge
and culture. This development in German thought may be traced from the
protohistoricism of Johann Gottfried von Herder, with his recognition that each
historical epoch has an individuality that is incommensurable with that of others
and so can be comprehended only in its own historically specific terms, through
the variously historical hermeneutics of Friedrich Schleiermacher, Johann
Gustave Droysen, and Wilhelm Dilthey, to Heidegger's analysis of the historical
character of understanding as built directly into the structure of existence in the
world. With this last thinker, lucid awareness is achieved of the historicity not
only of every possible object of understanding but also of understanding itself,
that is, of its being in every instance situated within determinate limitations and
partialities, remote from the bird's-eye view of so-called historical science.

Denied the illusion of being able to project oneself without residue into the past so as to understand its particularities exclusively from their own perspective, historians rather must recognize that they always only fuse their own inescapable horizon of understanding with that of the past world they wish to study. That historical understanding is always just such a "fusion of horizons" ("Horizontverschmelzung") is the thesis in which Gadamer has attempted to bring the whole modern development of hermeneutics to consummation as a philosophical theory.[10]

This opening up and exposing of rational and dogmatic knowledge to the crosscurrents of history, which begins taking place toward the end of the eighteenth century with the challenge to Enlightenment paradigms, recapitulates in crucial respects a break with Scholastic knowledge based on ahistorical essences of which Dante deserves to be hailed as a perhaps unwitting protagonist.[11] Dante's bringing the knowledge of his age into the midst of historical flux, most simply but decisively by his opting for the vernacular, defined in his treatise on the subject by its mutability in contrast to unchanging, rule-governed, "grammatical" language, was motivated not by a spirit of epistemological critique so much as by a prophetic spirit, bent on seeing true ideals become effectual on a broad historical basis, hence in the lives of the laity. From the time of the *Convivio*, Dante took upon himself the task of vulgarizing clerical knowledge and so of placing the nourishment of a divine *scientia* as well as of human wisdom, theretofore reserved largely for sterile fruition by the few learned in a dead language, on tables for general cultural consumption by all whose natural desire to know had survived uncorrupted.[12] Dante's championing of the vernacular, especially in his choosing it for his poem of the highest doctrinal intent and content, constitutes an emblematic gesture and a program for rendering the timeless verities of philosophy and dogmatic religion effective in history.

Dante need not be seen as an absolute innovator here. Historical consciousness had become manifest in a variety of forms in medieval Europe even centuries before Dante's time. Questions raised—often rather nervously—by theologians about the human *auctores* of various books of the Bible, for example, had generated reflection upon the possibility of some sort of historical mediation even of the sacred truth of Scripture.[13] Nevertheless, Dante's imaginative enactment of a revelation of religious truth in convincingly historical terms, bringing timeless dogma into intrinsic contact with corruptible matters of fact and language, and with the historical existence of a reader, constituted a major provocation regarding the issue of truth and history,[14] as it still does today.

It is perhaps no exaggeration to sum up the direction and import of Dante's whole life's work as a writer under the concept of *divulgazione*, which in a precise sense indicates translation into the vernacular, but also carries along in its train a thoroughgoing cultural revolution. The incidence of knowledge upon history, even were the body of knowledge vulgarized to remain self-identical (which it does not), is thereby made not a secondary effect but the primary thrust of such knowing and culture as Dante disseminates. Not knowledge per se, as an abstract, ahistorical system, but its appropriation, its event in and as originating history (what we will find it useful to think about in terms of Heideggerian "Ereignis"), becomes paramount. The very figure of the "convito" or banquet of knowledge as a "bread of angels" suggests how it is through assimilation, literally digestion, that the knowledge Dante wishes to be shared first comes into its own.

Dante attempted in his treatises to bring the medieval world's most precious reserves of knowledge into the stream of history, where their value could be exploited for the world-historical reform his prophetic sense envisioned. But the divulgation-dissemination of truth as something already fixed and finished, like the dogma of an institutionalized religion, being brought into a historical world likewise already constituted in its supporting structures and foundations, was not likely to originate fundamental change. Indeed, Dante's treatises remained for the most part uncompleted. What Dante discovered in his poem, on the other hand, was an approach to truth and to rendering it active, that is, to making it happen historically, of quite another order of power and significance. He discovered the capability of the work of art, as the site of a coming to be of truth, to open the world anew and give a new sense to history, actually founding an order of significances, or in other words a world, and originating a determinate historical dispensation. With this discovery, Dante's operative notion of truth was revolutionized.[15]

To divulgate or spread the truth is not just to make knowledge of what is taken to be true more widely available. More importantly, divulgation means actualizing truth, putting it to work. For truth becomes effectual only by happening as an event. The course of history may be influenced as intrahistorical forces are directed or redirected in consequence of the application of knowledge, by definition (presumably), knowledge of truth. But, more radically, the advent of truth in history impinges not on the component pieces of history, its separate materials and players, as it were, but on the fundamental dispensation and organizing framework of the historical world. And certainly the knowledge of truth that Dante proposes to divulgate is intended to make the world fundamentally different.

Like the *Convivio* and his other theoretical writings, Dante's *Commedia* is a massive work of appropriation. The highest and holiest offerings of classical and Christian culture are harmonized, or at least amalgamated, into an ensemble that may be entered into experientially, in the wake of the first-person experience of the protagonist. In this, the poem goes quantum leaps beyond the treatise in its receptiveness to the historicity of truth. Although continuity with the *Convivio*'s project of vulgarization is underscored by the reprise in *Paradiso* II of the figure of the "pan de li angeli" ("bread of angels"), truth is nevertheless no longer taken only as a particular "something," a metaphysical substance (an effect perhaps of "veritas" being a grammatical substantive) to be dished out and shared like "vivande" on a banquet table.

The poem is indeed full of metaphysical doctrines put forward with a paraenetic force and often staged with an artistry that promotes Dante's principles as fixed truths. But the truth Dante serves as poet rather than as ideologue, letting it occur in his poem, has rather the character of an event of disclosure. He imagines the truth about each individual as happening in puce as he meets them in the eternal world. By form and gesture, position and surrounding circumstances, as well as by utterance, Dante epitomizes the true and eternal being of the personages he encounters, the "status animarum post mortem" (Epistle to Can Grande, sec. 8), exposed for what it really is, allowing also for concealment as a background of shadow to the truth that comes to light. The essence of each individual unfolds visibly and audibly in the encounter with Dante-protagonist, being made manifest in sensory phenomena and palpable images of punishment, penance, or radiance. In this staggering act of imagination Dante apprehends truth, understood as the ultimate secret and eternal destiny of a human being, in the form of an event, a perceptible happening. Far in advance, presumably, of his own theoretical consciousness,[16] Dante's imagination grasps the eventhood of truth. Indeed, only with the present century will theoretical articulation of the intrinsic historicity of truth, here so compellingly envisioned, be fully achieved.

Although Dante still one-sidedly rehearses the rhetoric of truth as transcendental and timeless, which was handed down to him in the cultural heritage of the Middle Ages, his poetry nevertheless embodies the radical historicity of the truth of each individual as it is revealed in the immediacy of their encounters with Dante-pilgrim. It is in what happens to the *Commedia*'s characters in the present of their appearance in the poem, which essentially recapitulates the decisive event(s) of their earthly historical existence, now seen, however, in the light of an eschatological dawn, that the truth about them, the essence of their being in the sight and judgment of God, is revealed. In this sense it is in the form of history, as realized in sequences of phenomenal events, that the poem proffers its truth, in addition to the metaphysical and doctrinal truth that is also propounded in mixed discursive forms.

Dante's treating truth as disclosure in history has been famously expounded by Erich Auerbach. For Auerbach, Dante is the pivotal figure in a rejuvenation of Western culture that recuperates the earthly, historical lives and fates of humans as united with their true essences. Dante rediscovered "man as we know him in his living historical reality ... and in that he has been followed by all subsequent portrayers of man, regardless of whether they treated a historical or a mythical or a religious subject, for after Dante myth and legend also became history."[17] The representation of the other, the true, world in images and events that epitomize and eschatologically perfect individuals as they exist in this world constitutes the characteristic procedure of Dante as "Dichter der irdischen Welt" ("poet of the secular world").

Revisiting the argument developed under this title some twenty years later, Auerbach explained that he had taken over ideas broached first by Hegel, making them the basis of his own reading of the *Commedia*.[18] Hegel had written of the "changeless existence" of the denizens of the other world into which Dante "plunges the living world of human action and endurance and more especially of individual deeds and destinies."[19] Deeds, destinies, and action are of course the stuff of human history. But in the *Commedia* they represent not merely the brute fact of what actually happens: they reveal a definitive truth, that is, the divine judgment upon the individuals concerned. Dante undertakes, in Auerbach's words, "to set forth the divine judgment, to unearth the complete truth about individual historical men, and consequently to reveal the whole character and personality" (Auerbach, *Dante als Dichter*, p. 175).

The basic Hegelian insight found another powerful exponent, enormously influential especially for Italian criticism, in Francesco De Sanctis. De Sanctis celebrated the "inimitable individuality" of the *Commedia* in comparison with other medieval representations of the other world, underlining in Dante "the drama of this life represented in the other world, without detriment to its reality and gaining in grandeur" ("il dramma di questa vita rappresentato nell'altro mondo, senza scapitare di realtà e guadagnando d'altezza").[20] De Sanctis too honors Hegel as a paladin of historically incarnate truth—"Nessuno più di lui [Hegel] ti parla d'individuo e d'incarnazione, sente che là è il vero" (p. 340)— even while complaining that his disciples erroneously made form merely instrumental to the manifestation of idea.

The boldly historical nature of Dante's mode of poetic representation can be made evident, for example, by comparing the *Commedia* with other medieval works, for instance Alain de Lille's *Anticlaudianus*, an earlier poetic work with a similarly exalted claim to revealing a divine truth. Alain's celestial theophany is played out by such characters as Natura and Phronesis, abstract and remote from the historically dense and specific personages that so strongly distinguish the work of Dante.[21] To take just one example, even as abbreviated a cameo appearance as that of Pia dei Tolomei is stamped with the indelible marks of an irreducibly historical existence. Geographical place-names specify her earthly origin and terminus, while reference to the single, fatal event of her marriage suffices to adumbrate her whole life story:

> "ricorditi di me che son la Pia:
>   Siena mi fé; disfecemi Maremma:
>   salsi colui che 'nnanellata pria
> disposando m'avea con la sua gemma."
>   (*Purgatorio* V. 130–36)

("remember me who am Pia:
    Siena made me; Maremma undid me:

> he knows it who having first betrothed me
> wedded me with his gem.")

Formally, the poem positions its journey at a precise historical date in 1300, the middle of Dante's life and a year of crisis in the political history of Florence, Italy, Europe. In content, it burgeons with historical personages, so that virtually all the characters, whether they are cast as human or not, are treated as historical. It deals extensively *ad seriatem* with the various regions and rulers, families and cities, of Italy and beyond. The two great powers of universal history are relentlessly evoked and evaluated, and each receives a concentrated historical review in a prophetic perspective: the Church, especially in the allegorical representations of the Earthly Paradise in *Purgatorio* XXXII; and the Empire, most exhaustively in Justinian's narration of the vicissitudes of the sign of the eagle in *Paradiso* VI.

The historical character and consistency of Dante's poem has received extensive notice and has been widely recognized as key to Dante's significance in the history of culture. As handed down from the Auerbachian paradigm, this emphasis upon the historicity of Dante's narrative has been variously developed especially within the American school of Dante criticism. In one way or another, virtually all the most notable criticism since Singleton acknowledges the historicity of Dante's vision as its radically determinative element. In John Freccero's reading, the *Commedia* begins from Dante's break with the *Convivio's* Neoplatonic unguided ascent of the mind to truth, conceived as an escape from the body and its imprisonment in a temporal order. Dante is impeded from ascending directly toward the light over the mountain of the prologue scene by beasts representing various passions not fully sublatable into pure intellect. The "piè fermo," that is, the left foot, remains always lower, inasmuch as the will is always weaker than the intellect and drags it back from its purely intellectual love. Dante must get to the top of Purgatory by way of an "altro viaggio." For Christian conversion engages the whole human being in its full historicity, including the body and all that is least conformable to the intellectual ideals of Platonism. Thus Dante's truth cannot be reached except through a recapitulation of his whole personal and cultural history, in order that he be converted not only in his mind but in the full historical amplitude of his existence toward God. Such is the precondition for the whole journey and for its successful consummation.[22]

Even more directly, Giuseppe Mazzotta has recognized that "history is the question that lies at the very heart of the text" of the *Divine Comedy*, and he means history in a sense that makes it indissociable from the particular situatedness of interpretation, in the sense, that is, of a "theology of history" that "emphasizes, in a forceful way, the problematical character of every individual with his irreducible fund of experience and values."[23] Touching in a more oblique but interesting way on the issue, Eugene Vance's work on the history of theories of translation recognizes Dante as unique in the whole of the Middle

Ages for having been open to historical change and contingency as a possible source of enrichment rather than of inevitable loss and decline.[24] And again, Jeffrey Schnapp has shown in convincing detail for cantos XIV to XVIII of the *Paradiso* how, for all its vertical thrust, the *Commedia* always passes through history toward transcendence, transfiguring rather than annulling or escaping from the conditions of history.[25]

A common point of departure, then, for numerous major treatments of the poetics of the *Divine Comedy*, both old ones and especially the newer, has been found in the conspicuous historicity of the poem's content and form. The dense historical allusivity of the poem marks its individuality for many critics, not only specialists but those who view it in bold outline as well, for example, George Steiner.[26] Even textbook histories of literature commonly marvel at how direct and "realistic" Dante's representations of historical personages, places, and predicaments are, finding them to be quite without precedent and emphasizing the radical difference of Dante's poem from poems in the didactic-allegorical genre from which it emerges, precisely on grounds of its reversal of their ahistoricity.

In more ways than are easily reckoned, the undeniable primacy historicity assumes in Dante's interpretation of truth has been fully acknowledged. The present study aims at a more concentrated theoretical development of what, until now, has come to light as truly distinctive about Dante's poetic work primarily through the evidence of particular exegetical instances. In other words, it seeks to interrogate the philosophico-theological presuppositions and underpinnings of Dante's realization of the historicity of truth. Such a philosophical *approfondimento* can help us understand the truth Dante proposes as the correlative of interpretation rather than only as a confessional given, something to be either swallowed whole or indulged as Dante's personal *pazzia*, but in either case opaque and unpersuasive to those who do not happen to share Dante's religious beliefs.[27]

We can, of course, simply accept as part of the fiction that Dante has some sort of direct, privileged access to truth normally unavailable to mortals. This view seems especially easy to adopt in an era when we feel fairly immune to the "truths" Dante is advocating anyway. Yet to treat the truth claims as just a private madness of Dante's that may have enhanced or hampered his poetry, depending on how well we think poetry and theology mix, diminishes our understanding of his poem and its meaning. Dante is employing in this poem a way of disclosing truth through interpretation. The truth he proposes, if it is to be true for us, cannot simply be taken on his authority, the authority of one who has been there, to the other world, and has seen. This may after all, whether in the author's intention or in the reader's reception, turn out to be no more than a surface fiction. And at any rate it can distract attention from the truly extraordinary originality of Dante's poem as an interpretive act. The poem claims, as becomes explicit in direct addresses to the reader in the name of truth, to involve readers and their whole historical world in a journey of interpretation leading to a disclosure of their vital reality and final destiny. The present speculative reflection upon the *Commedia* contends that Dante has an understanding of truth and interpretation that can be appreciated more fully than ever today. He need be neither stigmatized nor patronized as a dogmatist with whom no dialogue is possible. He should rather be understood as engaged in an endeavor of interpretation that has a potentially universal message that would call all humankind to hear and heed.

2. Truth Through Interpretation and the Hermeneutic of Faith

A guisa d'uom che 'n dubbio si raccerta,
e che muta in conforto sua paura,
poi che la verità li è discoverta,
mi cambia' io ...
(*Purgatorio* IX. 64–67)

So far it has been argued that truth is revealed in the *Commedia* in and through history, where history involves immersion in the actual experience of existing individuals. Initially, however, the embrace of history creates problems for us in accepting or even in understanding the poem's claims to universal truth. The historicity of the *Commedia*'s characters and of Dante's encounters with them is all compounded by interpretation. The lives are recalled for us through the mediation of the characters' own memory and motivations; the encounters are mimetically reconstructed or invented by the interpretive art of poetry. Truth is purportedly revealed to us through a historicity that is itself the product of interpretation.

How can Dante pretend that his deeply personal convictions, not only about the providentiality of the Roman Empire but also about the individuals he knew or knew of are at the same time ultimate truths? Does not interpretation inevitably veer off into zones of opinion and personal belief remote from what can be established as "true" in the ordinary acceptation of something objectively so? It is not evident to us how truth and interpretation can live so comfortably together. Dante's *Commedia* makes extreme claims to truth of the most absolute kind; it claims to be representing some absolute—true and revealed—state of souls in an unchanging, transcendent realm. Yet at the same time, it goes to the other extreme of subjectivity in speaking the mind of Dante, replete with personal predilections and envenomed diatribes. This so-called true revelation patently consists of merely an interpretation (and a highly biased one at that) of this-worldly, historical being, which presumably can be known without revelation, but only as opinion or appearance, not as ultimate truth.

Why has it become so difficult for us today to understand how interpretation, permeated by prejudice and partiality, as it emphatically is in Dante, can lead to what may intelligibly be given the name of truth? Dante, evidently, could still take for granted that an absolute truth might very well be reached through interpretation. After all, the supreme method, the *via maestra*, for finding out truth in general in his day was through exegesis of the Divine Word, the source of all Truth, which could only be apprehended through a living and personally responsive interpretation. But this perspective has been forgotten due to a narrowing of the understanding of truth brought about through the hegemony of scientific paradigms of knowledge, in which truth tends to be opposed to "mere" interpretation. Can Dante, along with modern speculation in hermeneutic theory, help us recuperate an understanding of how interpretation can be a way of coming into the experience of truth?

Even before the Renaissance coined the term "Middle Ages" to designate somewhat contemptuously what stood between itself and the classical world, culture for the epoch consummated in Dante's poem was essentially just that, a middle, and as such a *traditio*, and inscribed within this, a *translatio*. This is one reason why the hermeneutic model is so germane to Dante's project. The Bible was held to contain the truth in its fullness for humankind, from their first beginning to their latter end; the function of knowledge and culture was principally to preserve and transmit this truth, to continue to live within its horizon and so participate in its ongoing event, rather than to discover new contents or continents. In this respect, the Middle Ages epitomizes a hermeneutic culture, in which knowledge is construed as the mediation of an experience rather than as the grasping of an object, or, in other words, as more like reading than like sense perception. It is not so surprising after all that copies and commentaries upon texts, to the exasperation of modern philologists, should have so freely altered and sometimes substantially augmented the texts even of highly revered works. For transmitting a text entailed reactualizing the whole experience sedimented within it, in such a way that the text became indistinguishable from its tradition.[28]

Dante simply brings to the fore the dynamic eventhood of this activity of mediation and transmission by his poetry articulated as personal address. Indeed, much of the burden of the ensuing chapters will be to sound the significance of Dante's employing a discourse of overt address to a reader. But this emphasis on receptivity and appropriation in the interpreter's act as intrinsic to the revelation of truth, swinging loose from strict enchainment to an objective reality to be known unaltered, which counts as the first imperative of science as classically construed, seems to us to throw the process open to individual caprice and *arbitrium*. We feel we must escape from the web of interpretation in order to attain the truth.

Yet interpretation understood hermeneutically and hence as a dynamic sort of knowing turns out to be a process of moving oneself into the event in which things are disclosed, that is, the event of truth.[29] Accordingly, the goal of Dante's whole interpretive journey is to move in perfect synchrony with the universe, in which his knowledge of ultimate being is made perfect by the conformity of his will to God's, symbolically his moving in step with the cosmos, moved concordantly by its final cause:

> ma già volgeva il mio disio e 'l velle,
>   sì come rota ch' igualmente è mossa
>   l'amor che move il sole e l' altre stelle.
> (Paradiso XXXIII. 143–45)

> (but already my will and desire were being revolved
>   as a wheel which is moved uniformly
>   by the love that moves the sun and the other stars.)

Interpretation as the transformation of the interpreter into conformity with truth, as a projective participating of the interpreter in the event in which truth is disclosed, returns to and specifies the characterization of interpretation as a form of involvement from which we began. It is a participation in the event of being in which things come to be *as* what they are, and so are revealed in their truth. Interpretation can be a way of entering into this event, a reorigination of one's own being and of all beings that has traditionally been figured as salvation, an event of dispossessing oneself of oneself in order to lend all one's being to the salvation event.[30]

The eventhood of truth and of being is presented in the *Commedia* through the eventhood of the author and also of that other author, the reader. Accordingly, the whole representation and disclosure of the poem is offered to readers in their own situated, historical particularity and this includes Dante himself as first reader of his poem and journey, internally to its event. It is the very dynamism of Dante's own personal engagement with each person and idea along the way, the conditionedness by narrative circumstance of his responses, that makes the encounters revelatory. For only so, precisely in such narrative contexts, can they be truly apprehended as event. Dante must realize his own act of interpretation as event in order for it to be authentic participation in an event of truth that becomes intelligible in and through it. And, in turn, Dante must make this truth happen for his readers as an event in their own existence, if its character as event is not going to be betrayed. It is only through the event of the interpreter that being, or whatever is interpreted, can be grasped as event.[31]

The truth, then, apprehended and promulgated by the poem, for as much as its image is that of univocal verity, eventually realizes itself in the multiplicity and dispersion of the historical particularity and ineradicable difference of readers. Dante presents a total system of theology, but his specific contribution as poet is to concretely realize this monolith, to make happen the event of its being experienced, in the actual historical existence of individuals. As an abstract symbolic system or book, the poem delineates a whole order of the cosmos enfolding within itself an ethical system. But for its truth to happen it has need of a reader; indeed, it is experienced in the first instance in correlation with Dante himself as reader, who in telling his story, and as an integral part of it, strives to understand its significance. For anything such as an event of truth can occur only in the existence of individuals and for them—whose being, moreover, comes into its own in and by this same event. This exigency is clearly recognized within the poem itself, in its addresses to the reader, which have been noticed as a peculiarly distinguishing feature of Dante's work, indeed a portentous novelty in the history of literature. Through its addresses to its reader, Dante's poem becomes veritably a divine co-mediation of truth and interpretation.

A Hermeneutic of Faith

We have dwelt on the extent to which Dante engages history, and we have seen how this has been widely acknowledged to be integral to his whole cultural project. But Dante's vision, as has already proved impossible to ignore, is equally a vision of transcendent truth. Not from history does Dante receive his assurances of imminent redress of the world's wrongs. Not from history can he acquire unshakable belief in God's providence. History seems to rudely contradict all his beliefs. His principle of interpretation is not any empirically historical principle but rather a hermeneutic of faith.[32] The interpretations he gives not only of the political past but also of the future destiny of humanity are based overtly on religious revelations and beliefs.

Conjoined, then, with his sense of the historicity of truth is Dante's vision and conviction of a transcendent revelation of truth. It is only this revelation by and from supernatural grace that makes history readable at all for him, since the truth Dante finds there is the opposite of what can be seen by an unadvised, unaided view. Does not such faith and the interpretive biases it entails prejudice any possibly historical understanding of truth? Does it not amount to a blanket acceptance of a metaphysical worldview and a dogmatic ethical-religious system as the basis for all one's subsequent interpretive endeavors, a refusal to submit to the test of history and let what happens pure and simple show the truth? Is it not to have decided what truth is in advance of all historical happenings on the basis of a message allegedly fallen out of the skies?

Such would be the case only for a shallow or at any rate intellectually unsophisticated understanding of faith. In actual fact, it is precisely the historicity of human existence and its full recognition that motivate the espousal of a hermeneutic of faith. The recognition of its historicity exposes the element of faith—of choosing to believe, for motives that may or may not be rational (and are not all reasons and motives compounded of both?)—that underlies all our "knowledge." For a historical being to judge that anything is thus and so is to overstep what can be strictly warranted on the basis of its own epistemic condition as constantly in flux; its historicity permits no simple unity and stability to human knowing.[33]

In the ground-breaking theological reflection of this century, precisely the recognition of the ineluctable historical conditionedness of the word of God in the text of Scripture, a result greatly encouraged by the generally acknowledged success of a historical-critical method of study, has led not only to the skepticism of some that there is any content to Scripture beyond that of human history abandoned to its own fate but also, paradoxically, to the sense of a new directness of encounter with the Word itself in faith. Precisely the recognition that all objective expressions and texts are only culturally relative manifestations of divinity frees faith to go beyond them—vehiculated all the same by those very words handed down through tradition—to a reality that directly illuminates the texts rather than being but a faint and dubious sort of inference from them. The directness of knowledge of God in faith thereby reached defines what is essentially a prophetic attitude that has enormous importance also for Dante.

This historic development in contemporary theology, pivoting on the step from recognition of the historical conditionedness of every actual word to the apprehension of a true Word that is not given as such, in the form of a cultural object, but may nevertheless give itself to be apprehended by apprehending the interpreter, has been concisely outlined by Robert Funk. Funk attributes especially to Rudolph Bultmann the break with the formidably empowering presupposition underlying the rise of modern biblical criticism that "when one does exegesis he is interpreting the text." It is reassuring to the scientifically-minded thus to be able to delimit the scope of inquiry even into religious matters in positive terms by reference to an objectively specifiable entity like "the text." Yet something is lost in this cleanly scientific treatment of what also has roots in the experience of religious mystery. Divorced from the actual experience in which the religious text's meaning realizes itself as event, the text as such offers to investigation what is in effect a slough. Much can be learned about the supporting structures of a form of life from such a post mortem dissection, but it is deluded to expect that the whole truth about anything living and intelligent can be grasped in this way. What really needs to be interpreted, from a theological viewpoint, is not just a textual object produced by all the accidents of human history that can be so impressively documented, or at least suggestively inferred, by textual scholars. It is the word of God itself, after all, to which human text and tradition are but instrumental, that must be the primary concern. Otherwise theology simply reduces itself to documentary history.

Funk takes Bultmann to represent the culmination of the whole development of modern biblical criticism in its revelation that "the biblical text, like any other text, is composed of human language and is therefore culturally conditioned. It was but a short step to the conclusion that the New Testament is only a relative statement of the word of God" (Funk, *Language, Hermeneutic, and the Word of God*, p. 10). And yet this discovery harbors some extraordinary implications for faith that came to be felt particularly in Karl Barth's "Word of God" theology. Barth began from the divine Word rather than from human culture and its parameters in endeavoring to account for the possibility of revelation. As explained in the preface to the second edition of the *Römerbrief*, Barth's method is to live on intimate terms with the biblical text until it becomes so familiar that it is no longer seen as such and one is confronted with the divine Word itself. "One sees emerging here the view that it is not the text that is to be interpreted—the text is already interpretation—but the word of God itself, which, of course, cannot be equated with any human formulation" (Funk, p. 11).

Funk goes on to give special emphasis to the reversal of the direction of interpretation brought about by this newfound directness: the interpreter, the exegete, becomes the interpreted, and it is the Word that does the interpreting. His formulation is indebted to the contribution of the theologians of the so-called "New Hermeneutic":

> If it is God's word that is the object of exegetical endeavors, the process is at a dead end, for this word is not accessible to the exegete as an object for scrutiny. Yet this blind alley is precisely what led Gerhard Ebeling and Ernst Fuchs to the conclusion, remarkable as it may sound, that the word of God is not interpreted—it interprets! That is to say, it is indeed the word rather than the words with which exegetes have ultimately to do, but since they are in the embarrassing position of being unable to lay hold of that word, they can only permit it to lay hold of them. With this startling insight the direction of the flow between interpreter and text that has dominated modern biblical criticism from its inception is reversed, and hermeneutics in its traditional sense becomes hermeneutic, now understood as the effort to allow God to address man through the medium of the text (p. 11).

A homologous sort of reversal is brought about in Dante's poem considered as an interpretation of the word of God. It is not the textual artifact that counts most in the end. This human work gives itself out to be merely a means of facilitating a more direct encounter with the divine Word. In effect, Dante employs poetry as a way of gaining a hearing for the Logos, a procedure he theorizes in *De vulgari eloquentia*.[34] In the *Commedia*, it is especially the addresses to the reader—but as an emblem of a much more general potential of poetry—that will effect this reversal, making the reader the one who is interpreted by the agency of the word of the text. In this way, interpretation is not an operation performed on a passive object but more essentially a rendering up, a restitution, of the interpreter's being to an event of truth in which the human interpreter is addressed by the Word speaking in the text. This inverted—

or rather rectified—relation so fundamental to the Bible as word of God can be lost and/or regained in countless culturally specific ways in every age. This study proposes to render its discovery in Dante a little more evident through bringing the *Commedia* into relation with modes of understanding the happening of religious truth that are historically nearer to us.[35]

Of course, what is nearer may be more obscure depending on what conditions and affinities prevail in a culture. Today it seems especially difficult to understand how the postulate of providence, for example, operative a priori in interpretation, could possibly serve the ends of historical truth. Does it not rather foreclose real discovery and search by fixing a conclusion, and in fact presupposing a whole metaphysical teleology, in advance? This is how faith has often appeared to modern humanity's rationality. But that is because it has not really had a hermeneutic point of view on knowledge and understanding. And yet if modernity and its "enlightenment," radiated by such luminaries as Nietzsche, Freud, Marx, teaches us anything, it is that no knowledge is neutral, unbiased, purely objective. All our understanding and knowledge of the world take shape within our projections involving our own way of being, that is, within projections of possibilities that form the basic structure of a world as we can experience it.

It is precisely because of our historical predicament that we turn to faith, recognizing that all our "knowledge" is in any case of the nature of faith, that any stability or adequacy in representation that may be accepted as given, or necessary, is nevertheless predicated on that act of acceptance and consent in such a way that knowledge, however committed to being based simply on what is, can be claimed or asserted only as a mode of belief. This suggests how Dante's hermeneutic of faith can actually be continuous with his vision of historicity as constitutive of truth. The justification for faith, then, is that it is presupposed anyway. The question of *which* faith (and broadly considered this might include, for example, trust in technology) will be decided, as appropriate, by historical circumstances, those that present themselves once the openness to and disposition of faith, as no more than commensurate with the human epistemic condition, become active and conscious and ready to respond to possibilities and their occasions. To see this we need to turn to hermeneutic ontology and to Dante's investment in it. The ontological power of interpretation has been examined in an explicitly theoretical way especially in our own day,[36] though Dante already exploits it fully in practice.

The final form taken by the paradox, with which Dante presents us, of truth as belonging to interpretation rather than to "knowledge" is that of a revelation of truth of a transcendent, eternal order in the form of a historical event. Such a paradox is far from arbitrary, however, when we consider that it matches the founding paradox of Christian faith: namely, the revelation of a transcendent God in the historical man Jesus of Nazareth. Above all, Dante's interpretive revelation of truth must gain its validity from participation in this master event.[37] Interpretation is thereby revealed ultimately as an act of total existential conversion, of turning, first of all upon oneself and one's past, in answer to a claim one recognizes and the concomitant opening of a new horizon.

NOTES

9. Of this putative revolution in thought, *Wahrheit und Methode* has become a sort of manifesto. The major breakthroughs, however, are found in the works, early and late, of Gadamer's teacher, Martin Heidegger, as will be made evident throughout this study by its allusions and citations.

10. On the history of the development of hermeneutic philosophy centered on this problematic, leading up to and including Gadamer's contribution, see Franco Bianchi, *Storicismo ed ermeneutica* (Rome: Bulzoni, 1974).

11. See especially Hans Urs von Balthasar, *Herrlichkeit: Eine theologische Ästhetik*, vol. 2 (Einsiedeln, Switzerland: Johannes, 1962), particularly section 1 on Dante's conversion ("Wendung") to the vernacular, to secularism, and to history. The master design and momentous historical significance of Dante's works are often more overtly appreciated by nonspecialized scholarship, which views Dante in broader synthetic contexts. See also Karl-Otto Apel, *Die Idee der Sprache in der Tradition des Humanismus von Dante bis Vico* (Bonn: Bouvier, 1975), especially pp. 104–29.

12. "Oh beati quelli pochi che seggiono a quella mensa dove lo pane de li angeli si manuca! ... E io adunque, che non seggio a la beata mensa, ma fuggito de la pastura del vulgo, a' piedi di coloro che seggiono ricolgo di quello che da loro cade, e conosco la misera vita di quelli che dietro m'ho lasciati.... Per che ora volendo loro apparecchiare, intendo fare un *generale convivio*" (*Convivio* I. i. 7–11; emphasis mine).

13. See A. J. Minnis, *Medieval Theory of Authorship* (London: Scholar Press, 1984).

14. This registers, for example, in Zygmunt Baranski's discussions of "authority and challenge" with regard to this poetry "'truer' than history" and of Dante's compulsion to innovate generically in "'Primo tra Cotanto Seno': Dante and the Latin Comic Tradition," *Italian Studies* 46 (1991): pp. 7–8, as well as in "La lezione esegetica di *Inferno* I: Allegoria, storia e letteratura nella *Commedia*"; for background, see R. H. C. Davis and J. M. Wallace-Hadrill, *The Writing of History in the Middle Ages* (Oxford: Clarendon Press, 1991).

15. I have described Dante's poem as an effort to set up truth in originating a world and by it to institute history in terms borrowed from Heidegger's theory of art: "Die Kunst ist das Ins-Werk-Setzen der Wahrheit.... Das ist so, weil die Kunst in ihrem Wesen ein Ursprung ist: eine ausgezeichnete Weise wie Wahrheit seiend, d. h. geschichtlich wird" ("Art is the setting-into-work of truth.... This is

so because art is in its essence an origin: an outstanding way in which truth comes to be, which means becomes historical"—*Ursprung*, pp. 79–80).

16. There are some indications of a theory of truth in the Letter to Can Grande (sec. 8). The truth of a thing ("veritas de re") is conceived as truth only to the extent that it exists in a subject ("que in veritate consistit tanquam in subiecto"). This is to make truth an attribute of conceptions or propositions existing in conscious subjects rather than of the things themselves. Truth may be defined, then, in accordance with the conventional Scholastic formula (*aedequatio intellectus et rei*) as a correspondence of the ideas of the subject to their object ("similitude, perfecta rei sicut est"). Nevertheless, an understanding of truth as "aletheia" (unconcealment) would not necessarily have been inaccessible to Dante: it finds a key source text in Aristotle's *Nichomachean Ethics* (VI. 3, 4: 1140a). According to this theory, that beings be disclosed as what they are is the precondition of our being able to make true affirmations about them.

17. Auerbach, *Dante: Poet of the Secular World*, pp. 19, 175; originally published as *Dante als Dichter der irdischen Welt* (1929).

18. Auerbach, "Farinata and Cavalcante" in *Mimesis: The Representation of Reality in Western Literature*, trans. W. Trask (1953; reprint, Princeton: Princeton University Press, 1968), p. 191.

19. Georg Wilhelm Friedrich Hegel, *Hegel's Aesthetics*, trans. T. M. Knox (Oxford: Oxford University Press, 1975), p. 1103.

20. Francesco De Sanctis, *Lezioni sulla* Divina Commedia (1854; reprint, Bari: Laterza, 1955), p. 16.

21. Cf. Peter Dronke, *Dante and Medieval Traditions* (Cambridge: Cambridge University Press, 1986), pp. 8–14.

22. John Freccero, *The Poetics of Conversion*. See especially chapters 1 and 2, "The Prologue Scene" and "The Firm Foot on a Journey without a Guide."

23. Giuseppe Mazzotta, *Dante, Poet of the Desert: History and Allegory in the "Divine Comedy,"* pp. 3, 5.

24. Eugene Vance, *Marvelous Signals: Poetics and Sign Theory in the Middle Ages* (Lincoln: University of Nebraska Press, 1986), chap. 10 and p. 262. Some decades earlier, Bruno Nardi, in "Il linguaggio," chap. 4 in *Dante e la cultura medievale*, had brought out the originality of the view that Dante had gradually developed of language as in its essence historically evolving.

25. Jeffrey Schnapp, *The Transfiguration of History at the Center of Dante's "Paradise"* (Princeton: Princeton University Press, 1986).

26. See Steiner's discussion of how "context presses on text with the weight of shaping life" (p. 167) in "Dante Now: The Gossip of Eternity," in *On Difficulty & Other Essays* (Oxford: Oxford University Press, 1972).

27. This problem is focused particularly by T. S. Eliot, *Dante* (London: Faber & Faber, 1929), and is further probed by I. A. Richards, *Beyond* (New York: Harcourt Brace Jovanovich, 1974), pp. 107–8.

28. Rita Copeland, in *Rhetoric, Hermeneutics, and Translation in the Middle Ages: Academic and Vernacular Texts* (Cambridge: Cambridge University Press, 1991), develops the acknowledged fact that "Medieval arts commentary does not simply 'serve' its 'master' texts; it also rewrites and supplants them" (p. 3).

29. We have already noted in the previous section how truth in Dante's poetry is fundamentally conceived neither as accuracy of representation nor in the first instance as an entity to be grasped but rather as an event of disclosure. The conception of truth as disclosure, "aletheia," is treated by Heidegger in *Sein und Zeit*, sec. 44, and in "Vom Wesen der Wahrheit" (1930). Discussion of its applications in theology by Bultmann, Fuchs, and Ebeling can be found in Robert W, Funk, "Language as Event and Theology," pt. 1 of *Language, Hermeneutic, and the Word of God: The Problem of Language in the New Testament and Contemporary Theology*.

30. This can be described in an idiom of the later Heidegger as "appropriation" ("Ereignis") of human being to Being, revealed in the event of unconcealment. Not by making Being its own, but rather by being appropriated to it, the human being who interprets comes into the truth. Of course, this may be characterized as an event of dissonance or "rift"—as in Heidegger's "Ursprung des Kunstwerkes"—as much as of concordance, and the range of Dante's images will embrace both possibilities.

31. This aspect of the work has been fathomed in numerous oblique ways by Dante criticism, perhaps nowhere more subtly than by Gianfranco Contini (who, however, credits Charles Singleton) in "Dante come personaggio-poeta della *Commedia*": "Ogni tappa e sosta del suo viaggio olreterreno è una modalità del suo 'io'" ("Every station and stay of his supraterrestrial journey is a modality of his 'io'"—p. 361). Contini teases out the implications of Dante's "doppio 'io,'" ("double both the *agens* and the *auctor* of the poem, a transcendental but nonetheless existential "I" (p. 336), and moreover an "io' che è noi" ("I that is we"—p. 341).

32. The notion of an "herméneutique de foi" is broached by Paul Ricoeur in "Existence et herméneutique;' in *Le conflit des interprétations*.

33. Cf. Nietzsche's account of the origin of knowledge ("Ursprung der Erkenntnis") out of "Glaubenssätze" (articles of faith)—such as "dass es dauernde Dinge gebe, dass es gleiche Dinge gebe, dass es Dinge, Stoffe, Körper gebe" ("that there are lasting things, that there are similar things, that there are things, materials, bodies")—which become part of the heritage and endowment of the species for their survival value. *Die fröhliche Wissenschaft* ('*La Gaya Scienza*'), pt. 3, secs. 110, 111 (Frankfurt Am Main: Insel, 1982), p. 127.

34. Cf. Roger Dragonetti, *Aux frontières du langage poétique*. Dante's invention by the art of poetry is brought out as away of coming into ("invenire") the transcendent truth of the Logos. It is through vernacular language as a contingent human convention, and especially through poetic language as the invention of an individual's *ingenio*, that Dante, paradoxically, attempts to imitate the ordering principle at the origin of things themselves, the Logos, *per quem omnia facto sunt*. Dante seeks through the radically historically contingent and mutable language of the vernacular to recuperate an originary, absolute language of things themselves in the form of the "vulgare illustre." Through poetry, vernacular language, which is by definition agrammatical, can prove to be rule-governed in a higher sense by embodying universal harmonies and can, moreover, manifest an intrinsic order of things, all being in proportion to the One from which poetry and music alike devolve.

35. The contemporary search for religious understanding, so relevant to understanding Dante's search, beyond simply assessing this artifact as a historical and aesthetic monument, is provocatively explored by David Tracy in *The Analogical Imagination: Christian Theology and the Culture of Pluralism* (New York: Crossroad, 1981). Tracy proposes a phenomenology of "classic" expression in a sense that might help us to reinterpret the *Divine Comedy*'s status as classic. The classic makes "a claim that transcends any context from my preunderstanding that I try to impose upon it, a claim that can shock me with the insight into my finitude as finitude, a claim that will interpret me even as I struggle to interpret it. I cannot control the experience, however practiced I am in techniques of manipulation. It happens, it demands, it provokes" (p. 119). Although the immediate inspiration here must be Gadamer, this construction of the classic also overlaps with Heidegger's theory of the work of art as an origin of truth. As Werner Jeanrond, *Text and Interpretation as Categories of Theological Thinking*, comments: "According to Tracy a classic expression discloses paradigmatic knowledge, even truth, even in fact transformative truth, that is to say the kind of truth which changes the human being with whom it comes into contact" (p. 140).

36. For more on this, see the essays under the heading "Hermeneutic" in David Guerrière, ed., *Phenomenology and the Truth Proper to Religion* (Albany: State University of New York Press, 1990). Robert Scharlemann's *The Being of God: Theology and the Experience of Truth* (New York: Seabury Press, 1981) represents a major new contribution in a postmodern perspective.

37. The incarnational thrust of Christian thought and sensibility, given a new impetus in the Gothic age, registers in Dante in ways that have been masterfully delineated by Thomas Altizer. In "Dante and the Gothic Revolution," Altizer shows how nothing short of a revolutionary transformation of Western poetry and culture, expressed in a "new Gothic language," was brought about by Dante in the wake of Thomas Aquinas's speculative revolution in discovering "the pure

actuality of existence itself." This entailed the "discovery of a new glory embodied in the very texture of the world ... a glory that here and now is immanent and transcendent at once." *History as Apocalypse* (Albany: State University of New York Press, 1985), pp. 97–136.

Chronology

Ca. 1265	Dante Alighieri is born in Florence, probably May 29.
1266	Guelph victory at Benevento over Ghibellines.
1274	Meets Beatrice, believed to be the daughter of Folco Portinari.
1277	Becomes engaged to Gemma di Manetto Donati.
1283	Dante's father dies. Shortly after his father's death, Dante marries Gemma Donati with whom he has four children (Jacopo, Pietro, Giovanni, and Antonia).
1289	Dante participates in the Battle of Campaldino; The Guelf League (Florence and Lucca) defeats the Ghibellines of Arezzo.
1290	Death of Beatrice. Dante serves in the war between Florence and Pisa.
1292–93	*Vita Nuova*; begins study of philosophy.
1294	Dante meets Charles Martel, King of Hungary and heir to the kingdom of Naples and the country of Provence.
1295	Enrolls in Guild and enters public life.
1300	Becomes prior for bimester (one of the six highest magistrates in Florence)—June 15–August 15.
1301	Opposes extension of troops consignment to Boniface VIII in July. In October he is sent with two other emissaries to the Pope in Rome.
1302	Florence is taken over by the once exiled Black Guelphs. Dante is ordered to appear to answer charges and is banished

	from the city for two years. Later his banishment becomes perpetual and he is sentenced to death.
Ca. 1304–07	Writes *De Vulgari Eloquentia* and the *Convivio*.
Ca. 1306	Probably the year in which Dante begins working on the *Comedy*.
Ca. 1310	Writes *De monarchia*.
1314	*Inferno* completed.
1315	Dante rejects the possibility of a pardon and settles in Verona with Can Grande della Scala. Dante composes the *Questio de acque et terra*.
Ca. 1319	Dante moves to Ravenna with Guido Novella da Plenta. Completes *Purgatorio* and part of *Paradiso*.
1321	Dante dies in Ravenna; September 13–14.

Contributors

HAROLD BLOOM is Sterling Professor of the Humanities at Yale University and Henry W. and Albert A. Berg Professor of English at the New York University Graduate School. He is the author of over 20 books, including *Shelley's Mythmaking* (1959), *The Visionary Company* (1961), *Blake's Apocalypse* (1963), *Yeats* (1970), *A Map of Misreading* (1975), *Kabbalah and Criticism* (1975), *Agon: Toward a Theory of Revisionism* (1982), *The American Religion* (1992), *The Western Canon* (1994), and *Omens of Millennium: The Gnosis of Angels, Dreams, and Resurrection* (1996). *The Anxiety of Influence* (1973) sets forth Professor Bloom's provocative theory of the literary relationships between the great writers and their predecessors. His most recent books include *Shakespeare: The Invention of the Human* (1998), a 1998 National Book Award finalist, *How to Read and Why* (2000), *Genius: A Mosaic of One Hundred Exemplary Creative Minds* (2002), and *Hamlet: Poem Unlimited* (2003). In 1999, Professor Bloom received the prestigious American Academy of Arts and Letters Gold Medal for Criticism, and in 2002 he received the Catalonia International Prize.

CHARLES S. SINGLETON was Professor of Italian Studies at Johns Hopkins University from 1939 to 1985. He also served as director of the Humanities Center. His works include *Essay on the Vita Nuova, Interpretation: Theory and Practice*, and a six-volume translation of the *Divine Comedy*.

ERICH AUERBACH was Sterling Professor of Comparative Literature at Yale University. He is the author of *Mimesis*.

DAVID QUINT is George M. Bodman Professor of English and Comparative Literature at Yale University. Quint is the author of *Origin and Originality in Renaissance Literature, Epic and Empire, Montaigne and the Quality of Mercy*.

309

JOHN FRECCERO is Professor of Italian and Comparative Literature at New York University. His works include *Dante: The Poetics of Conversion* and *Dante: 20th-Century Views*, ed.

TEODOLINDA BAROLINI is Lorenzo Da Ponte Professor of Italian at Columbia University and Chair of the Department of Italian. She is the author of *Dante's Poets: Textuality and Truth in the 'Comedy'* and *The Undivine 'Comedy': Detheologizing Dante*. Barolini is co-editor of *Dante for the New Millennium*.

KENNETH GROSS is Assistant Professor of English at Rochester University. His works include *Spenserian Poetics: Idolatry, Iconoclasm, and Magic The Dream of the Moving Statue* and *Shakespeare's Noise*.

GIUSEPPE MAZZOTTA is the Charles C. and Dorathea S. Dilley Professor of Italian Language and Literature at Yale University. He is the author of *Dante, Poet of the Desert: History and Allegory in the "Divine Comedy,"* and *The World at Play: A Study of Boccaccio's "Decameron."*

JAROSLAV PELIKAN is the Sterling Professor Emeritus of History at Yale University where he served on the faculty from 1962–96. He is the author of more than 30 books, including the five volume *The Christian Tradition: A History of the Development of Doctrine*, *What Has Athens to Do With Jerusalem?*, and *"Timaeus" and "Genesis" in Counterpoint*.

MARÍA ROSA MENOCAL is the R. Selden Rose Professor of Spanish and Portuguese and director of the Whitney Humanities Center at Yale University. She is author of *The Arabic Role in Medieval Literary History: A Forgotten Heritage*, and *Writing in Dante's Cult of Truth From Borges to Boccacio*.

JOHN KLEINER is Assistant Professor of English at Williams College. He is the author of *Mismapping the Underworld: Daring and Error in Dante's 'Comedy.'*

WILLIAM FRANKE is Associate Professor of Italian and Comparative Literature at Vanderbilt University. He has published on poetics and interpretation theory in Dante.

Bibliography

Abrams, M.H. *The Mirror and the Lamp*. Cambridge: Harvard University Press, 1958.

Abrams, Richard. "Inspiration and Gluttony: The Moral Context of Dante's Poetics of the 'Sweet New Style,'" *Modern Language Notes* 91, 1976.

Ahearn, John. "Singing the Book: Orality in the Reception of Dante's *Comedy*," *Annals of Scholarship* 2, 1981.

Altizer, Thomas. *History as Apocalypse*. Albany: State University of New York Press, 1985.

Armour, Peter. "The Theme of Exodus in the First Two Cantos of the *Purgatorio*," *Dante Soundings*, ed. David Nolan. Dublin: Irish Academic Press, 1981.

———. *The Door of Purgatory: A Study of Multiple Symbolism in Dante's "Purgatorio."* Oxford: Clarendon, 1983.

Ascoli, Albert Russell, "The Vowels of Authority (Dante's *Convivio* IV.vi.3–4)," *Discourses of Authority in Medieval and Renaissance Literature*, ed. Kevin Brownlee and Walter Stephens. Hanover: University Press of New England, 1989.

Auerbach, Erich. "Farinata and Cavalcante." *Mimesis: The Representation of Reality in Western Literature*. Translated by Willard Trask. Princeton: Princeton University Press, 1953.

Barolini, Teodolinda. *Dante's Poets: Textuality and Truth in the Comedy*. Princeton: Princeton University Press, 1984.

———. *The Undivine Comedy: Detheologizing Dante*. Princeton: Princeton University Press, 1992.

————. "Dante and the Lyric Past," *Cambridge Companion to Dante*, ed. Rachel Jacoff. Cambridge: Cambridge University Press, 1993.

Bloom, Harold. *Genius*. NY: Warner Books, 2002.

————. *The Western Canon: The Books and School of the Ages*. NY: Riverhead Books, 1994.

Cassell, Anthony K. *"Inferno"* I, *Lectura Dantis Americana*. Philadelphia: University of Pennsylvania Press, 1989.

Copeland, Rita. *Rhetoric, Hermeneutics, and Translation in the Middle Ages: Academic and Vernacular Texts*. Cambridge: Cambridge University Press, 1991.

Davis, R.H.C. and J.M. Wallace-Hadrill. *The Writing of History in the Middle Ages*. Oxford: Clarendon Press, 1991.

Demaray, John G. *Dante and Book of the Cosmos*. Philadelphia: The American Philosophical Society, 1987.

Dronke, Peter. *Dante and Medieval Traditions*. Cambridge: Cambridge University Press, 1986.

Eliot, T.S. *Dante*. London: Faber & Faber, 1929.

Ferrante, Joan M. *The Political Vision of the Divine Comedy*. Princeton: Princeton University Press, 1984.

Franke, William. *Dante's Interpretative Journey*. Chicago: The University of Chicago Press, 1996.

Freccero, John. "Dante's Novel of the Self," *Christian Century* 82, 1965.

————. "Dante's Prologue Scene," *Dante Studies* 84, 1966.

————. "Casella's Song (*Purgatorio* II, 112)," *Dante Studies* 91, 1973.

————. "Dante's Medusa: Allegory and Autobiography," *By Things Seen: Reference and Recognition in Medieval Thought*, ed. David L. Jeffrey. Ottawa: University of Ottawa Press, 1979.

————. "Manfred's Wounds and the Poetics of the *Purgatorio*." *Centre and Labyrinth: Essays in Honour of Northrop Frye*, Cook, Eleanor, et al. eds. Toronto: University of Toronto Press, 1983.

Frye, Northrop. *Anatomy of Criticism*. Princeton: Princeton University Press, 1957.

Gilson, Etienne. *Dante and Philosophy*. Trans. David Moore. repr. Gloucester: Peter Smith, 1968.

Guerriere, David, ed. *Phenomenology and the Truth Proper to Religion*. Albany: State University of New York Press, 1990.

Harrison, Robert. *The Body of Beatrice*. Baltimore: The Johns Hopkins University Press, 1988.

Hart, Thomas Elwood. "The Cristo-Rhymes and Polyvalence," *Dante Studies* 105, 1987.

Hatcher, Anna and Mark Musa. "The Kiss: *Inferno V* and the Old French Prose *Lancelot*," *Comparative Literature* 20, 1968.

Hawkins, Peter S. "Divide and Conquer: Augustine in the *Divine Comedy*," *PMLA* 106, 1991.

Hollander, Robert. "Dante's Use of the Fiftieth Psalm," *Dante Studies* 91, 1973.

———. "*Purgatorio* II: Cato's Rebuke and Dante's *scoglio*," *Italica* 52, 1975.

———. "*Purgatorio* XIX: Dante's Siren/Harpy," in *Dante, Petrarch, Boccaccio: Studies in the Italian Trecento in Honor of Charles S. Singleton*, ed. Aldo S. Bernardo and Anthony L. Pellegrini. Binghamton, NY: Medieval and Renaissance Texts and Studies, 1983.

Holloway, Julia Bolton. *The Pilgrim and the Book*. New York: Peter Lang, 1987.

Kantorowicz, Ernst. *Frederick the Second*, trans. W. Trask. Princeton: Princeton University Press, 1948.

Kleiner, John. *Mismapping the Underworld: Daring and Error in Dante's 'Comedy.'* Stanford: Stanford University Press, 1994.

La Piana, Angelina, *Dante's American Pilgrimage*. New Haven: Yale University Press, 1948.

Le Goff, Jacques. *The Birth of Purgatory*, trans. Arthur Goldhammer. Chicago: Univeristy of Chicago Press, 1984.

Logan, J.L. "The Poet's Central Numbers," *Modern Language Notes* 86, 1971.

Mazzaro, Jerome. *The Figure of Dante: An Essay on the "Vita Nuova."* Princeton: Princeton University Press, 1981.

Mazzeo, Joseph Anthony. "*Convivio IV, xxi* and *Paradisio XIII:* Another of Dante's Self-Corrections," *Philological Quarterly* 38, 1959.

———. *Medieval Cultural Tradition in Dante's Comedy*. Ithaca: Cornell University Press, 1960.

Mazzotta, Giuseppe. *Dante's Vision and the Circle of Knowledge*. Princeton: Princeton University Press, 1993.

McKenzie, Kenneth. "The Symmetrical Structure of Dante's *Vita nuova*," *Publication of the Modern Language Association* 18, 1903.

Menocal, María Rosa. *Writing in Dante's Cult of Truth From Borges to Boccaccio*. Durham: Duke University Press, 1991.

Minnis, A.J. *Medieval Theory of Authorship*. London: Scholar Press, 1984.

Moore, Edward. *Studies in Dante, Third Series: Miscellaneous Essays*, 1903. repr. New York: Greenwood Press, 1968.

Bibliography

Musa, Mark. *Advent at the Gates: Dante's "Comedy."* Bloomington: Indiana University Press, 1974.

Noakes, Susan, "The Double Misreading of Paolo and Francesca," *Philological Quarterly* 62, 1983.

Patterson, Lee. *Negotiating the Past.* Madison: University of Wisconsin Press, 1987.

Pegis, Richard. "Numerology and Probability in Dante," *Medieval Studies* 29, 1967.

Pelikan, Jaroslav. *Eternal Feminines: Three Theological Allegories in Dante's* Paradiso. New Brunswick: Rutgers University Press, 1990.

Perella, Nicolas J. *The Kiss Sacred and Profane.* Berkeley-Los Angeles: University of California Press, 1969.

Poggioli, Renato. "Tragedy or Romance? A Reading of the Paolo and Francesca Episode in Dante's *Inferno,*" *PMLA* 72, 1957. repr. in *Dante: A Collection of Critical Essays,* ed. John Freccero. Englewood Cliffs: Prentice-Hall, 1965.

Popolizio, Stephen, "Literary Reminiscences and the Act of Reading in *Inferno* V," *Dante Studies* 98, 1980.

Quinones, Ricardo J. *The Renaissance Discovery of Time.* Cambridge: Harvard University Press, 1972.

Richards, I.A. *Beyond.* New York: Harcourt Brace Jovanovich, 1974.

Ricoeur, Paul. *Time and Narrative,* trans. Kathleen McLaughlin and David Pellauer. Chicago: University of Chicago Press, 1984. (original 1983)

Robertson, Jr., D.W. trans. *On Christian Doctrine.* Indianapolis: Bobbs-Merrill, 1958.

Scharlemann, Robert. *The Being of God: Theology and the Experience of the Truth.* New York: Seabury Press, 1981.

Schnapp, Jeffrey. *The Transfiguration of History at the Center of Dante's "Paradise."* Princeton: Princeton University Press, 1986.

Scott, John A. "Dante's Sweet New Style and the *Vita Nuova,*" *Italica* 42, 1965.

———. "Dante's Francesca and the Poet's Attitude Towards Courtly Literature," *Reading Medieval Studies* 5, 1979.

Shaw, James E. *The Lady "Philosophy" in the Convivio.* Cambridge: Dante Society, 1938.

Shoaf, R.A. "*Purgatorio* and *Pearl*: Transgression and Transcendence," *Texas Studies in Literature and Language* 32, 1990.

Singleton, Charles S. *Dante's Commedia: Elements of Structure.* Baltimore: Johns Hopkins University Press, 1954.

Spengemann, William C. *The Forms of Autobiography*, New Haven: Yale University Press, 1980.

Sturm-Maddox, "The *Rime Petrose* and the Purgatorial Palinode," *Studies in Philology* 84, 1987.

Taylor, Karla. "A Text and Its Afterlife: Dante and Chaucer," *Comparative Literature* 35, 1983.

Toynbee, Paget. "Dante and the Lancelot Romance," *Dante Studies and Researches*. London: Methuen, 1902.

Tracy, David. *The Analogical Imagination: Christian Theology and the Culture of Pluralism*. New York: Crossroad, 1981.

Vance, Eugene. *Mervelous Signals: Poetics and Sign Theory in the Middle Ages*. Lincoln: University of Nebraska Press, 1986.

Vickers, Nancy J. "Widowed Words: Metaphors of Mourning," *Discourses of Authority in Medieval and Renaissance Literature*, ed. Kevin Brownlee and Walter Stevens. Hanover: University Press of New England, 1989.

Zumthor, Paul. "Autobiography in the Middle Ages?" *Genre* 6, 1973.

Acknowledgments

"Dante Alighieri" by Harold Bloom. From *Genius: A Mosaic of One Hundred Exemplary Creative Minds*: pp. 91–101. © 2002 by Harold Bloom. Reprinted by permission.

"Two Kinds of Allegory" reprinted by permission of the publisher from *Dante Studies I: Commedia ~ Elements of Structure* by Charles S. Singleton, Cambridge, Mass.: Harvard University Press, Copyright © 1954 by the President and Fellows of Harvard College. An earlier version of this essay appeared in *Speculum*, XXV. Reprinted by permission.

"Figural Art in the Middle Ages'" by Erich Auerbach. From *Scenes from the Drama of European Literature*: pp. 60–76. © 1959 by Meridian Books. Reprinted by permission.

"Epic Tradition and 'Inferno' IX" by David Quint. From *Dante Studies*, vol. 93: pp. 201–207. Copyright © 1975 by *Dante Studies*. Reprinted by permission.

"Manfred's Wounds and the Poetics of the 'Purgatorio'" by John Freccero. From *Centre and Labyrinth: Essays in Honour of Northrop Frye*: pp. 69–82. © 1983 by the University of Toronto Press. Reprinted by permission.

"Autocitation and Autobiography" by Teodolinda Barolini. From *Dante's Poets: Textuality and Truth in the Comedy*: pp. 3–84. Copyright © 1984 by Princeton University Press. Reprinted by permission of Princeton University Press.

Gross, Kenneth. "Infernal Metamorphoses: "An Interpretation of Dante's 'Counterpass'." From *Modern Language Notes* 1, vol. 100 (1985): pp. 42–69. © 1985 by the Johns Hopkins University Press. Reprinted with permission of the Johns Hopkins University Press.

"The Light of Venus and the Poetry of Dante: 'Vita Nuova' and 'Inferno' XXVII" by Giuseppe Mazzotta. From *Modern Critical Views: Dante*, ed. Harold Bloom: pp. 189–203. © 1985 by Giuseppe Mazzotta. Reprinted by permission.

Pelikan, Jaroslav. "The Otherworldly World of the *Paradiso*." From *Eternal Feminines: Three Theological Allegories in Dante's Paradiso*: pp. 11–31. © 1990 by Jaroslav Pelikan. Reprinted by permission of Rutgers University Press.

María Rose Menocal, "Synchronicity" in *Writing in Dante's Cult of Truth: from Borges to Boccaccio*: pp. 18–38. Copyright © 1991 by Duke University Press. All rights reserved. Used by permission of the publisher.

"Purgatory as Paradigm: Traveling the New and Never-Before-Traveled Path of this Life/Poem" by Teodolinda Barolini. From *The Undivine Comedy: Detheologizing Dante*: pp. 99–121. Copyright © 1992 by Princeton University Press. Reprinted by permission of Princeton University Press.

Mazzotta, Giuseppe. "Imagination and Knowledge in Purgatorio XVII–XVIII." From *Dante's Vision and the Circle of Knowledge*: pp. 116–134. Copyright © 1993 by Princeton University Press. Reprinted by permission of Princeton University Press.

"The Strangeness of Dante: Ulysses and Beatrice" by Harold Bloom. From *The Western Canon*: pp. 76–104. © 1994 by Harold Bloom. Published by Harcourt. Reprinted by permission.

Kleiner, John. "Finding the Center." From *Mismapping the Underworld, Daring and Error in Dante's 'Comedy'*: pp. 5–22. © 1994 by the Board of Trustees of the Leland Stanford Jr. University. Reprinted by permission.

Franke, William. "Truth Through Interpretation." From *Dante's Interpretive Journey*: pp. 5–23. © 1996 by University of Chicago Press. Reprinted by permission.

Index